ALSO BY TOM CLAVIN

SIR WALTER

Walter Hagen and the Invention of Professional Golf

TOM CLAVIN

SIMON & SCHUSTER
NEW YORK LONDON TORONTO SYDNEY

SIMON & SCHUSTER
Rockefeller Center
1230 Avenue of the Americas
New York, NY 10020

SIMON & SCHUSTER and colophon are registered trademarks of
Simon & Schuster, Inc.

For information about special discounts for bulk purchases,
please contact Simon & Schuster Special Sales at
1-800-456-6798 or business@simonandschuster.com

Designed by Julie Schroeder

Manufactured in the United States of America

10 9 8 7 6 5 4 3 2 1

Library of Congress Cataloging-in-Publication Data

Clavin, Thomas.
Sir Walter: Walter Hagen and the invention of professional golf/ Tom Clavin.
p. cm.
1. Hagen, Walter, 1892–1969. 2. Golfers—United States—Biography. I. Title
GV964.H3C53 2005
796.352'092—dc22   2004056508
ISBN 0-7432-0486-7

To my mother, Gertrude Clavin,
my sister, Nancy Bartolotta,
and my brother, James Clavin.

Acknowledgments

When for a different book I interviewed Gene Sarazen the year before he died, the ninety-six-year-old Squire was at his most emphatic when talking about Walter Hagen. More than once he said, "There ought to be a monument built for that man." I don't know a thing about building monuments, but Mr. Sarazen's comments inspired me to know more about Hagen, and that is how this book began. I am sorry that Mr. Sarazen and others who contributed to this book, among them Paul Runyan, Joe Falls, and Sam Lacy, did not live long enough to see the first full-scale biography of Sir Walter.

During four years of work on this biography, many people gave of their time, recollections, knowledge, and material, or pointed me in the right direction. My thanks go to Rex Aubrey, Karen Bednarik, Pat Brandt, Lillian Burns, Lisa Clark, James Henderson, Ken Janke, Khris Januzik, Rees Jones, Don Kladstrup, Chuck Kocsis, Ruth Matthew, Richard Medinis, Tom Murphy, Byron Nelson, Jack Nicklaus, Arnold Palmer, Jeff Peek, Joe Peck, Gary Player, Carlton and Shelby Plyler, Steve Prothero, Jeff Rude, Anne Schaetzke, Mark Smith, Dick Sorenson, Marjorie Tavoulareas, Mike Turnesa Jr., Victoria Wilson, and Paul Wold.

I am very fortunate that there were a number of books available that provided crucial information. In particular I am grateful to the following authors: Al Barkow, Henry Clune, Henry Cotton, Bernard Darwin, Peter Dobereiner, Mark Frost, Herb Graffis, Salvatore Johnson, Robert T. Jones Jr. and O. B. Keeler, Joe Kirkwood, Stephen R. Lowe, H. B. Martin, Sidney L. Matthew, Charles Price, Grantland

Rice, and Herbert Warren Wind. Thanks also to the U.S. Golf Association Library, Rochester Public Library, John Jermain Library, Tufts Archives, *Rochester Democrat and Chronicle,* the *Times* of London, the *New York Times, Golf* magazine, *Golf Digest,* the *American Golfer,* the *Traverse City Record-Eagle,* the Golf Collectors Society, and the dozens of other sources from which I gleaned hundreds of newspaper and magazine articles. They certainly helped me to separate fact from fiction in Walter Hagen's life.

This book would not exist without the efforts of people who were with me while I was possessed by the Haig. Thanks to Jeff Neuman for giving it a chance, and to Jon Malki and Jack Sallay. Thanks to Nat Sobel at Sobel-Weber Associates and Jennifer Unter at RLR Associates for putting up with me when I hit rough patches. Thanks to David Rosenthal, and especially to Caroline Bruce for allowing me to play through. Sincere thanks for the friendship and support of Fred Baum, Megan Blaney, Kari-Lisa Brangan, Bob Bubka, Heather Buchanan, Bob Drury, Michael Gambino, Kitty Merrill, Amy Patton and David Winter, Danny Peary, Valerie Pillsworth, Rachel Pine, Allen Richardson, Harold Shepherd, and Evan Tiska.

Finally, thanks to my children, Katy and Brendan, for their patience, support, and love. Walter says it's all right to relax at the nineteenth hole now.

Tom Clavin
Sag Harbor, N.Y

SIR WALTER

CHAPTER 1

"JONES MEETS HAGEN TODAY AT WHITFIELD," blared the eight-column headline atop the front sports page of the *Sarasota Herald* on February 28, 1926.

Bobby Jones versus Walter Hagen was the equivalent of a heavyweight world championship bout in boxing. It would take a full week to determine the outcome—36 holes in Sarasota and seven days later an additional 36 holes in St. Petersburg. During that week many of the major daily newspapers and most golf fans around the country were focused on the events in Florida because they believed that the results of the match would determine who indeed was the best golfer on the planet.

For some, though, it was a match made in golf heaven. "The golfing world is not so much interested in the probable winner as it is having the chance to see the greatest professional golfer of the day—if not in the history of American golf—in direct competition with the greatest amateur and the most interesting golfer this country has ever produced," wrote Norman E. Brown, sports editor of the *Sarasota Herald,* four days before the contest.

Two players more different could not have been put into the golf ring together. Jones, from Georgia, was the newly minted challenger on the national and international golf circuits, the upstart who on St. Patrick's Day would turn only twenty-four. He had been born into a family of well-heeled Southern gentlemen and genteel ladies, and from an early age he'd had access to fine golf facilities for year-round play.

He was the boy next door with all-American good looks on a 5'8", 165-pound frame and impeccable manners (if you didn't count the incessant smoking and, offstage, the enjoyment of bourbon and salty talk). In 1923 he had won the U.S. Open, won the U.S. Amateur title in '24, lost the Open in a play-off in '25, then that same summer won a second consecutive Amateur Championship.

A modest and private man, Jones wasn't comfortable with crowds, though he always seemed to find the right thing to say when pressed in front of an audience. He was the poster boy for the honesty and integrity of golf thanks to a recent, well-publicized incident. In the previous year's U.S. Open in Worcester, Massachusetts, he had called a one-stroke penalty on himself. A poor iron shot on the 11th hole left his ball in tall grass. As Jones addressed the ball, it moved slightly. No one but him had seen the ball move, and even though U.S. Golf Association officials protested the penalty, Jones insisted on taking it. The National Championship ended in a tie, and Jones lost by one stroke in a play-off.

In very sharp contrast to Hagen, Jones's mode of dress was understated, his voice soft and even, and he was already married to the woman with whom he would share the rest of his life and raise three children.

Jones was the finest and most famous amateur in the world. Many golf purists hoped he would crush his opponent to demonstrate that playing for love, instead of money, made for a more worthy champion.

But there was more than love of golf to being an amateur at the time. All amateur players of note in the 1920s came from the upper class, were white, were of Anglo-Saxon descent, and belonged to private clubs. At these clubs and at tournaments amateurs were addressed as "Mister" to show the proper respect. Conveniently overlooked in media coverage of the 1926 match was that while, yes, Jones did love the game, he also represented a class of golfer that offered the best opportunity to keep golf the sport of blue-blooded gentlemen.

Hagen hailed from Rochester, New York, but in 1926 wherever he hung his hat was home. He was not only a professional, he also represented the new breed of golfer. He competed for money and was viewed by purists who favored the amateur ranks as being willing to play only if there was coin to be collected. (As will be seen later, this perception ignores the many charity events pros played for free, especially during World Wars I and II.) The upper crust was both fascinated and appalled by Hagen—fascinated because of his dramatic flair, competitive drive, and winning ways, yet appalled because he was a dangerous man: Hagen was at the head of the barbarians approaching the gates of Rome.

The occupation of full-time professional golfer was less than seven years old; Hagen himself had invented it after winning the U.S. Open in 1919. He was the first champion player to emerge from the ranks of the caddies, he was a second-generation German American, and he came from a blue-collar family. He was not called "Mister" Hagen by private-club members and officials.

The Florida match was a classic American clash that this time was being played out in a golf arena: The college-educated Jones had inherited his money and social status; the seventh-grade dropout Hagen had earned his. Aristocracy was being challenged by the expanding working class.

At thirty-three, Hagen was at the peak of his abilities. He stood almost six feet and weighed a robust 180 pounds. He wore silk shirts and a red kerchief, and everything else on him was of the finest quality, down to his $100 custom-made shoes. Because of years of never wearing a hat, his oval face was tanned and weathered. His jet-black hair was slicked back perfectly and when he grinned, which was frequently, sunlight gleamed on his teeth. He smoked cigarettes not with casual or grinding abandon but with sensuous pleasure.

After golf, Hagen loved nothing more than to be out on the town most of the night with one hand on a beautiful woman and the other hand hoisting a full glass of what he liked to call "hypsonica," usually a scotch and water. Women were attracted to this famous, confident man, and he had developed an easy way with them which included calling them all "My dear" or "Sugar" because he had difficulty remembering names. (Men were all called "Junior," "Kid," or "Buddy.")

He could be, however, an awkward or even crude Lothario. Once, at a large party in New York in the 1920s, Hagen was introduced to Ernestine Schumann-Heink, a buxom contralto with the Metropolitan Opera. She wore a low-cut gown; Hagen looked her over and queried, "Madam, do you know what a lovely bunker you would make?"

Hagen was at the top of his game in the late winter of 1926. He had two U.S. Opens to his credit (both won before Jones became a factor) to go with his two British Opens, and he had collected the last two PGA Championships, which were grueling match-play events, to go with a PGA victory back in '21.

The two competitors were opposites, all right, and would never be found traveling in the same circles away from the golf course, but they were united by mutual respect. They had battled each other in several tournaments, including the U.S. and British Opens, and had participated in team exhibition matches, especially in Florida during the winters.

Jones might have appeared to be a stick-in-the-mud compared to his glamorous rival, but he really wasn't dour at all. He liked to laugh with friends, just not on the course, though it seems that being on a course with Hagen did loosen him up a bit in public. One time Jones and Hagen, with partners, were staging an exhibition match. After Hagen's ball landed in a bunker, Jones secretly gave his caddie a twenty-dollar bill and instructed him to crumple it up and toss it into the bunker next to Hagen's ball.

When Sir Walter got ready for the sand shot, he spied the bill and, pretending this was all part of his pre-shot routine, he bent over, scooped up the bill, and smoothly slipped it into his pocket. Then Hagen and his partner lost the hole because of the infraction of removing a loose impediment in a hazard. Flustered for once, Hagen tried to explain, and Jones and the crowd exploded with laughter.

The time had come to pit them—the reigning U.S. Amateur champion and the reigning Professional Golfers Association champion—together just *mano e mano* over 72 holes on two separate days, and beyond that if necessary, to determine who would be left standing as the best in the world. Did the two golf gladiators object to all the hype in the national and especially the Florida press? Not at all. For Hagen, the more attention the better. Even Jones said, "I can't wait to step onto the course with Walter."

Bob Harlow had first suggested the idea of matching up Jones and Hagen. He had started out as a sports reporter and then skirted the line of being a publicist, similar to the role Atlanta sportswriter O. B. Keeler played with Jones. Finally Hagen, once more doing what no golfer had done before, hired Harlow to be his full-time PR rep and manager.

During the 1920s, Harlow had no trouble collecting and feeding good material about the Haig to newspapers and magazines such as the *American Golfer* and the *Saturday Evening Post*. Harlow's efforts, combined with Hagen's dashing appearance and personality, and his winning exploits in golf, which emerged during the decade as a major sport in America, placed Hagen in the upper stratosphere of sports stars, the one which also included Babe Ruth, Jack Dempsey, Red Grange, and Johnny Weissmuller.

Then Harlow had the ultimate brainstorm: With golf writers and fans routinely mentioning Hagen and Jones in the same sentence and debating which one was the better player, why not let the two players settle it and generate a lot of ink and revenue along the way?

It was like Magic Johnson and Michael Jordan playing one-on-one, a Barry Bonds and Sammy Sosa home-run contest, Alydar racing against Affirmed, and Ali versus Frazier all rolled into the same week. Hagen immediately embraced the idea because of the potential for a very bright spotlight, the resentment he felt that Jones was sharing too much of the spotlight that he, Hagen, already had, and the money at stake. Jones was at first reluctant, then found a good reason to pick up the gauntlet.

An exhibition match featuring the two was a brilliant PR coup for golf. Good publicity helped the sport and its major figures carve out attention during a decade in which sports and individuals were followed with unprecedented enthusiasm. The 1920s were called the "Golden Age of Sport," and 1926 was the height of that Golden Age.

Babe Ruth was rewriting the baseball record book and Lou Gehrig was playing his first full season. Red Grange was helping the Chicago Bears dominate football after a brilliant college career. In tennis, Bill Tilden and Helen Wills were taking trophies away from the Europeans. Jack Dempsey was still the king of boxing, in the seventh year of his reign. That August, eighteen-year-old Gertrude Ederle from New York City became the first woman to swim the English Channel, and Johnny Weissmuller was muscling through water like no swimmer had done before. And in golf, it was time for Walter Hagen and Bobby Jones to play the ultimate exhibition match.

At the time, exhibition matches in golf were not unusual. In 1926 there was no official PGA Tour, just a loose affiliation of ten to twelve PGA-sanctioned tourneys with modest purses, not enough for a pro to make a living. While Hagen did not invent exhibition matches as a method of supplementing a pro golfer's income, with his popularity and showmanship he made them a profitable gate attraction. A player could make the same or more participating in an exhibition match as he could winning a tournament—much the way today's players can collect huge fees for less work by doing corporate outings and made-for-TV exhibitions such as "The Skins Game."

The numerous exhibition matches played among the better-known golfers in the 1920s also offered fans in different parts of the United States (and in Hagen's case, the world) opportunities to see top-notch golf being played. Today, of course, there is enough radio, TV, and Internet coverage of golf events that the sport is available almost around the clock. In addition, with the combination of sanctioned events on the PGA, Champions, and LPGA tours and unofficial events, at least one tournament takes place in most of the fifty states.

Eighty years ago, however, there was only print coverage of golf, and the reportage routinely was given less space than baseball, boxing, or college football. For live action, the golfers had to bring the events to the audiences, and exhibition matches—played in the South and West in the winter, the Midwest and East in the spring and fall—were a bit like a traveling theater show.

By the time he hung up his spikes for good, Hagen would play more than two thousand exhibition matches just about everywhere but on the polar caps, at a time of relatively primitive transportation. From approximately 1915 to 1945, for literally millions of people around the world, the only live golf they witnessed featuring a top professional involved Walter Hagen.

Jones, however, played sparingly outside of tournaments, or as golf writer and editor Charles Price put it, "about as much as your average dentist." Unlike Hagen, his life did not revolve around golf, social events, and foreign adventure. He played some exhibition matches to try to keep his game sharp between "regular" events, and even though married with a child in '26, he was still a young man and exhibitions offered some travel. Florida in winter was more accommodating than Jones's Georgia home.

But this matchup was for money, and wasn't Jones an amateur? Was he risking his status? No, Jones thought at the time. In accepting the invitation to play Hagen, Jones stated right away that if he won, he would not accept the prize money, which of course added fuel to the fire of those who viewed Jones as playing purely for the love and glory of the game. Yet Jones was not being completely altruistic here.

In addition to being a brilliant golfer, Jones was a brilliant student who had ambitions that went beyond the fairway. In the fall of 1926 he intended to enter Emory University Law School, and since he wasn't making a penny from golf no matter how high he placed in tournaments, a non-golf source of income to pay tuition and support his family was a good idea.

Jones had been hired by Adair Realty Company in Atlanta as a salesman. One could do a lot worse than being in real estate in the middle of the Roaring Twenties. Adair Realty owned land near the just-built Whitfield Estates Country Club in Sarasota. The course had been designed by Donald Ross, a Scottish transplant who was one of the top two or three golf architects in the country. It was a no-brainer that well-publicized and well-attended golf events at Whitfield would spur the sale of nearby lots and provide plenty of commissions for those on the sales team.

Actually, it was in the interests of both Hagen and Jones to stage this match and make sure it received a great deal of attention. While Hagen had several sources of golf-related income, he was affiliated with the St. Petersburg course and anything good for the course, such as a surge in membership and surrounding development, would be good for Hagen's income. Win or lose, staging half of the match at the Pasadena Golf Club put money in Sir Walter's deep and well-worn pocket.

In more general terms, though, there was a boom in golf in Florida. Given the economic frenzy of the Roaring Twenties, any golf activity attracting attention from other parts of the United States and even Europe meant that more people were visiting and moving to Florida. This created a lively climate for residential and golf-course development, bringing more jobs for golf pros and more venues for high-stakes exhibition matches.

It was a win-win situation for both golfers. But someone had to lose the match, and in the end some fans would exult and some would be disappointed. Even with just the print media available, word spread fast among sports fans, especially pleasing those who were suffering through a winter athletic drought and had yet to receive news on spring training. By the time the Haig and Bobby teed off, millions of sports aficionados would be hanging on the outcome.

Hagen versus Jones would be a great contest, but there could be only one winner. Everyone expected that it would come down to the final putt.

After all the preparation and hype for the match, and with fans in Florida fighting over tickets, Walter Hagen almost didn't make it to the first tee.

He had always taken pride in conducting himself as a professional as an example to others, which included showing up where colleagues, officials, and fans expected him to show up (though not always on time). The Haig couldn't wait to go head-to-head with Jones, for whom he felt both admiration and rivalry. Jones had just recently emerged as an international figure while Sir Walter was in his fourteenth year of competition. And while having won two PGA Championships in '24 and '25 (which Jones, as an amateur, could not enter) was impressive, those feats had been at least equaled by Jones's recent accomplishments in the U.S. Open and U.S. Amateur. A head-to-head win would put the brakes on the threat of Hagen being eclipsed.

But then Hagen's health, usually indefatigable, faltered. A week before the major matchup, Hagen became violently ill and was confined to bed.

A case of nerves? Not Hagen—there wasn't anyone he was afraid to take on, even Jones. He was diagnosed as having ptomaine poisoning, and Hagen was so weakened by it, and with a fever that soared to 102 degrees, that he couldn't stand for several days. (That he had a fever implies a virus or flu rather than poisoning.) There was a real danger that the celebrated match would have to be called off.

Though the ailment was physical, many people wouldn't have blamed Hagen if he had withdrawn for any plausible reason. First of all, a loss to Bobby Jones would be a chink in his armor. Second, Jones was on a hot streak. He had committed to a series of exhibition matches in Florida, partnered with Tommy Armour, the Scottish-born American pro who would establish an equipment and player dynasty. The duo had won six matches in a row, including a 4-and-3 thrashing of Hagen and Gil Nicholls on February 21 on the Haig's home course, the Pasadena Country Club in St. Petersburg.

"It was merciless golf that the amateur champion and his partner hurled at the Pasadena pair this afternoon," reported the *Sarasota Herald*.

To be fair, Hagen played well, but his partner was not even near the level of Jones and Armour, who had played several winters as a team. Still, such a sudden reversal of fortune had to be discouraging to Hagen. Just two days earlier he had played a practice round at Jones's home course, Whitfield Estates. He had come to Sarasota that day already sharp from competition, having just played 36 holes at a course in Jacksonville, several exhibitions at other Florida courses, and a round at a new course he had opened at Brooksville.

At Whitfield, Hagen was greeted by Jones and Armour along with local dignitaries. The weather was wet and windy, and Hagen, playing the course with the club's assistant instructor, shot a 76, not the best harbinger of future success. After the match Hagen and the ever-present Bob Harlow returned to St. Petersburg. From there Harlow issued a statement full of typical hyperbole, that "there has never been such a height of interest attained in any sport event as is being shown in the Hagen–Jones match."

Just as tickets went on sale, Hagen fell ill. His wife joined him in St. Petersburg, though the last role the socialite and party girl Edna Straus Hagen was suited for was nurse. Hagen's temperature shot up. He canceled practice rounds and a couple of minor exhibition matches because he simply was too weak to dress himself, let alone swing a club with any authority. Ever the gentleman, Jones sent a message offering to postpone the match.

But ever the showman, Hagen began to recover. On February 23 Harlow reported: "Walter Hagen got out of bed about 11 o'clock this morning and started to do some Charleston steps in his pajamas. Hagen is good at the Charleston and just got going when Mrs. Hagen called a halt on the dance."

Many years later, in assessing Hagen's career most sportswriters would credit him with being the first and among the best at using psychological ploys on opponents to disarm or intimidate them. One example is the statement the Haig issued through Harlow the following day: "I want the golfing world to know that I appreciate what Jones is doing for me in giving me this opportunity, not only to make some money, but more important, to meet him at match play. I believe that Jones is the toughest golfer in the world today to beat, and that this match is even more important than any open championship I have played in on either side of the Atlantic Ocean."

Though Hagen was being a bit tongue-in-cheek casting himself as quite the lowly underdog, his statement wasn't total exaggeration. As both the local and national golf scribes pointed out in their pre-match commentary, Jones and Hagen had competed six times in the same field in the U.S. Open, which with the PGA Championship and (at the time) Western Open was considered the ultimate test of golf in America. Jones had won once, in 1923, and Hagen not at all (his two National Championships had been in 1914 and 1919). Worse still, in those six U.S. Opens, Jones had finished higher than Hagen five times and in total had played 20 strokes better.

There was some consolation, as Norman E. Brown pointed out: "Jones is without a doubt a great medal player. Hagen is, however, best fitted temperamentally for match play. He is the most superbly confident human being I have ever met."

Despite his match-play track record, which by 1926 included three PGA Championships in total, and the fact that this duel was match play—meaning holes won, not strokes made, are counted—in a few ways Hagen did have the deck stacked against him. He was weakened by a nasty illness; as the veteran professional he may have had more to lose than to gain; he had just lost to Jones and Armour on his own course; the first 36 holes of the confrontation would be played on Jones's course. Also, Jones had some high-pressure match-play experience through U.S. Amateur Championship competition, and there was the distracting irritation that he had rarely finished ahead of the youngster who in some circles had already been placed on a higher pedestal in golf.

It didn't help either that this would be one of the very few events where the majority of the crowd's devotion might be to his opponent. "Jones Passes Up Thousands: Great Golfer Makes Big Monetary Sacrifice as an Amateur," announced the February 26 issue of the *Sarasota Herald.* It went on to offer, "Probably no one figure in the whole realm of sports is sacrificing more in dollars and cents by maintaining his amateur standing than Bobby Jones, national amateur golf champion." There is no mention, obviously, of the sweetheart Adair Realty connection.

The daily went on to emphasize that "the entire gate receipts for the Whitfield Estates play goes to Hagen, or figuring that one match will attract as many as the other, Hagen's total income from both appearances will run something like $10,000," an enormous sum in 1926, looking even larger when your opponent is receiving nothing but applause. The article concluded that Jones "has placed his name among the immortals of American sports as one of the finest, cleanest and most attractive figures that the country ever produced."

Perhaps Hagen realized that a Jones win would be devastating, and even a close loss would be viewed as a moral victory. To truly win, Sir Walter had to win big and prove who was still king of the hill whether amateur or professional, whether playing for love or money. There could be no doubt left as to who was the best in the game.

Two days before the big match Hagen arrived in Sarasota in a speedboat. He began a practice round but quit at noon, heightening concerns that he was not up to the confrontation. A Philadelphia newspaper wired Hagen that they wanted a five-hundred-word story on how he felt. He replied, "Never mind five hundred, I can tell you in two: 'I am okay.'"

The morning of the first 36 holes, Sunday, February 28, below the eight-column *Herald* headline was "Great Golfers Will Begin Their Titanic 72 Hole Engagement," followed by:

"With both actors on the scene, with the stage in readiness and with an audience that gives every indication of surpassing any that ever attended a match on the West Coast, the curtain is about to be raised on the greatest golfing drama of the century." (This made Harlow appear demure by comparison.) "For at 10 o'clock this morning on the Whit-field Estates course," the story continued, "Bobby Jones, American amateur golfer and considered the greatest medalist on the globe, will tee off against Walter Hagen, present holder of the American professional golfers title and looked upon as one of the most brilliant and colorful match players in the game."

On page 2 there was an article about Bobby Cruickshank and Johnny Farrell in a tie for first place in the Florida Open Golf Championship, but the front page was dominated by large photos of Jones and Hagen swinging clubs. Jones was dubbed "The Par Assassin" above his photo and Hagen was awarded the more pedestrian "A Great Match Player."

Writing in his "Sportscope" column in the *Sarasota Herald,* Whitner Cary declared, "Hagen is probably the only golfer in this country that the experts would say has the right to challenge the ability of the Par Assassin. Sir Walter is not the steadiest golfer that wanders over the fairway, but he is one of if not the most spectacular golfer that ever shot out of trouble or rammed home a 20-foot putt from the edge of the green. Whether Walter can be able to bring enough of the spectacular into his game to offset the steady hammering the Par Assassin will unlimber in the 72-hole jaunt, time alone will answer."

The New York papers also were beating the drum. The *New York World,* for example, insisted to its readers that the arrival of Babe Ruth and the World Champion Yankees in St. Petersburg for spring training greatly paled in comparison to this world championship of golf.

As it turned out, after all the reportage, speculation, breathless anticipation, and arguments, the result of the match would turn out to be much different than anyone expected.

Though there were 71 more holes to play, interrupted by a week to recover and reestablish the competitors' focus, the very first hole was a preview of what was to come.

By virtue of winning the coin toss that determined whose home course would host the first 36 holes, Hagen had the honor of teeing off first at Jones's course. He believed that from a psychological point of view, if he could play well or at least break even in Bobby's backyard, he'd be in good shape going to the last 36 holes at his own course. Both players stood at the tee wearing knickers, ties, and pullover sweaters. Hagen's hair was, as usual, slicked straight back and the oil in it glistened in the morning sunlight. Jones's light-brown hair was hidden beneath a fedora.

The Haig addressed the ball and, nothing new for him, his drive hooked into the rough along the left side. And nothing new for him, Jones parked his drive in the middle of the fairway. Advantage the amateur. Perhaps the Haig really wasn't ready for this confrontation.

In a small way he wasn't, and not just because of lingering illness. To celebrate the match in advance, Henry Topping, the father of Dan, who would co-own the New York Yankees, had given Hagen a new set of woods with laminated shafts. Hagen hadn't used them until a practice round the day before, and they still felt strange in his hands. However, Topping was a close friend and Hagen wouldn't risk a report getting back to New York that he had not used the generous gift. In any case, thanks to his extensive world traveling, Hagen was a veteran at getting accustomed to unfamiliar courses and equipment quickly, so he went ahead with the clubs.

Hagen's second shot on the par 4 was okay, not reassuring but not dismal either. He left the ball short of the green. Jones, wanting to get off to a fast start, went for the flag—and overshot, his ball going through the green and down a slope behind it.

Jones's recovery shot rolled 20 feet past the cup. Hagen dropped his ball on the green. Jones's par putt didn't make it to the hole; he managed bogey. Hagen, after beginning by flirting with disaster, sank his putt for par.

Slowly, Hagen compiled a lead, though not an insurmountable one. He and Jones halved the second, third, and fourth holes. On the fifth hole, Jones outdrove Hagen and both were in the fairway. The Haig's second shot landed at the edge of the green, he chipped to within 4 feet of the cup, and sank the putt for par. Jones's second shot landed in a creek, and the lost stroke hurt because he missed a long putt for par. Hagen 2-up.

They matched pars on the sixth hole, then on the seventh Jones rallied. He outdrove Hagen by 10 yards; they both were on the green in two, but Jones sank his 15-footer for birdie while Hagen missed a similar-length putt. Once more, there was only a one-hole difference between the two.

They kept going back and forth, Hagen inching further out front, Jones drawing close. The Haig was still only 1-up after 12 holes. But beginning with 13, the match changed. Hagen birdied the par-3 to go 2-up. After a halve, he birdied the long par-4 15th to go 3-up. On the par-3 16th, Jones found the bunker while Sir Walter birdied; 4-up. Jones recovered to take the par-5 17th, then he and Hagen halved the par-5 18th. The back-nine charge by Hagen had done its damage.

However, being down by three holes wasn't close to disaster for Jones. With 54 holes yet to go and with his recent track record, with his twenty-three years to Hagen's well-trod thirty-three, and Hagen's stamina questionable because of the recent illness, it was easy to believe that Bobby would forge ahead by the finish line.

The rivals had lunch (separately), then in the afternoon round Jones indicated that he had stopped the bleeding by matching Hagen for the first five holes. Then came the sixth hole. Off the tee at the short par-4, Jones hit a perfect drive. Stumbling, Hagen knocked his drive behind a tree. Time for Jones to eat into the lead, and if indeed his opponent was faltering as the afternoon dragged on, this could be an opportunity to stagger Hagen and leave him with somber thoughts for the next 36 holes.

It was not to be. Using a "mashie-niblick"—which would now be akin to a 6-iron or 7-iron—Hagen sliced around the tree with a swift-moving grounder. He had actually mis-hit the ball, yet it sped right through a bunker and up onto the green, coming to rest three feet from the hole. Rattled, Jones left his second shot 10 feet from the cup, missed the putt, and settled for a par. The Haig, of course, sank his 3-footer for birdie and went 4-up.

"Hagen had to play the odd and he hit as wretched a shot as can be imagined—he topped the ball so that it fairly rolled along the turf," wryly reported the *American Golfer*.

It got much, much worse for the amateur. On another par-4, Jones launched a 250-yard drive down the middle of the fairway; Hagen's tee shot wound up stuck in thick brush. Jones hit an iron to the edge of the green; Hagen missed the green completely, with his ball settling in a swamp. Jones chipped to a foot of the cup; Hagen blasted out, and his ball came to rest inside Jones's. Jones had played the hole perfectly, Hagen hadn't been near the fairway, yet they halved.

At the finish of the afternoon's back nine, Hagen had shot 32 and Jones, the wheels coming off, was down 8. On the 36th hole of the day, Hagen sent his drive right into a tree; of course, the ball bounced onto the fairway, and he ended up with a birdie to end the day, leaving a bewildered Jones shaking his head and gritting his teeth.

Adding insult to injury, Jones was a fine putter and had used a respectable 31 putts in the 36-hole first round. Sir Walter, though, needed only 27, meaning that more often than not, once he found the green he was most likely to find the bottom of the cup with his next stroke.

The March 1 issue of the *New York Times* reported that over the 36 holes Hagen had shot 141 to Jones's 151, and in that regard the amateur should be glad this wasn't a stroke-play contest. The last such debacle for Jones, the *Times* offered, was when Jess Sweetser beat him 8 and 7 at Brookline, when Jones was all of twenty.

"Walter Hagen, yesterday over the Whitfield Estates course, partly opened the door of the golfing hall of fame and took one step through the portals of athletic immortality when he finished eight up on Bobby Jones at the conclusion of 36 history-making holes of their scheduled 72-hole engagement," declared the *Sarasota Herald*.

It went on to say that Hagen "convinced a colorful and enthusiastic gallery of some 2,500 golf fans that this appellation [of greatest money player] was well merited; for it is doubtful if any follower of the Ancient and Royal pastime ever flashed a more sensational brand than did Sir Walter."

Being down 8 is surely a pretty tough position to be in, but Jones had a week to regroup. If he could get off to a good start on the Pasadena course and with 36 holes to play, a comeback was possible. He practiced with dedication during the week, and the ever-encouraging *Herald* offered on March 6, "Miracles can happen, and the Par Assassin is still far from a beaten golfer."

What also helped the following day, when Act II began, was that busloads of supporters had made the trip from Sarasota to cheer the "local" on.

Jones parred the first hole, and the second. Hagen managed par on the first, and on the second his ball was on the green but 50 feet from the pin; conceivably, he could three-putt from there and Jones would get a hole back early. Hagen briefly studied the green, stood over the ball, took his putter back, then gave the ball a good whack. It went in for birdie. Jones and his fans stared at the Haig in disbelief.

Alas, this day wasn't going to be any different for the young Georgian. After 5 holes of the afternoon round, he was 12 down. The Haig could do no wrong. On a par-3 hole, Hagen was on the green 20 feet from the cup while Jones was barely on the green, 60 feet away. Jones putted first, and incredibly the ball went in for a birdie. After the crowd quieted, Hagen laughed and said, "What do you think of that? Bob gets a half after all." Without hesitating, Hagen stroked his ball and earned his own birdie.

The rout was irreversible. Jones tried to stem it anyway, chipping in for birdie on the 24th hole of the day to extend the match. But when Hagen won the next hole, it was all over. The final result was a devastating 12-and-11 defeat for Jones and a huge triumph for Hagen.

The *New York Times* reported on March 8 that when the second 18 holes began "it was only a question of minutes before Hagen would vanquish his opponent." The report added: "Hagen put on his fighting mask. He was determined and sure of himself every step of the way. He never faltered and his putter was sure as a rifle."

"That answers any question as to the class of shooting that took place over the home links of Sir Walter," Whitner Cary wrote in the *Saratoga Herald* about how even Jones's best shots weren't good enough.

After the abbreviated match, a frustrated Jones said, "I would rather play a man who is straight down the fairway with his drive, on the green with his second, and down in two putts for his par. I can play a man like that at his own game, which is par golf. If one of us can get close to the pin with his approach, or hole a good putt, all right. He has earned something that I can understand. But when a man misses his drive, and then misses his second shot, and then wins the hole with a birdie—it gets my goat!"

Though his goat was gotten, Jones never made excuses for being dusted by Hagen. In his memoir *Down the Fairway,* published the next year (when he was only twenty-five), Jones referred to the match as "that beautiful lacing in Florida." Elsewhere in the book he wrote, "The biggest golfing year in my life, 1926, began with the most impressive trouncing I ever got—and it was by a professional, Walter Hagen." Jones also conceded, "Walter was simply too good for me." Some consolation was, "I have plenty of distinguished company among the victims of Walter's rampages."

For his part, Hagen for the rest of his life would call his one-on-one demolition of Jones "my greatest thrill in golf."

Dozens of daily newspapers on March 8 reported the outcome of the unofficial "world championship" of golf. Hagen fans were overjoyed; Jones fans were incredulous. One reporter offered about the third round of 18 holes that "Walter had gone around in 69 strokes and Bobby in 69 cigarettes."

The British writer A. C. Croome explained, "[Hagen] makes more bad shots in a single season than Harry Vardon did from 1890 to 1914, but he beats more immaculate golfers because as he has said, 'Three of those and one of them counts four.'"

In its report on the 1926 match, the *American Golfer* magazine stated that one reason why Hagen was almost impossible to beat in match play "is his superb showmanship; his histrionic talent; his gift for 'acting,' and for making of some special shot a ceremony on which the gallery hangs with an hypnotic attention—and which his hapless opponent regards with a distinctly disadvantageous concern, not to say exasperation."

Probably because of the especially satisfying victory, Hagen was extra gracious about the win over Jones. It didn't hurt that he was handed $11,800 in total gate receipts for the two-day competition, the largest paycheck he had ever received and more than the top prize he would ever win in tournament play, including the three majors of the day—British and U.S. Opens and the PGA Championship.

In a brief speech after the match, Hagen thanked Jones, "an amateur, for playing me, a professional, for nothing . . . it's a tribute to golf and American sportsmanship."

The party the Haig threw that night came after he had taken care of two other things to express his appreciation . . . and, no doubt, relief: He took $5,000 of his winnings and donated it to the St. Petersburg

Hospital, and with part of the $6,800 left over he bought and presented Bobby Jones a set of diamond cufflinks, telling Gene Sarazen, "I bought the kid a little something."

After looking the cufflinks over, Jones, recovering his sense of humor, said, "Walter, you have now ruined me twice! First, there was this licking, and now I'll be busted the rest of my life trying to buy shirts to fit this jewelry." (Not to worry—according to several accounts, Jones kept but never wore the cufflinks.)

No matter who won, there would have been calls for a rematch. Especially with the lopsided result, many golf fans and writers exhorted the two to go at it again. Jones, of course, was willing. After such a sinking on the golf course, he could only do better.

But the U.S. Golf Association, which hadn't sanctioned but had allowed the contest, raised an eyebrow about Jones's indirect profit from the event and stated that if he took Hagen on again, his amateur status would be revoked.

Jones sided in favor of remaining an amateur. And he received plenty of consolation during the rest of that year when he won the U.S. Open again and the first of his three British Opens, becoming the first golfer to win both opens in the same year.

This adherence to the amateur "purity" of golf is one reason why to this day Bobby Jones is such a revered figure in the history of U.S. sports. In golf rankings he is always listed with Jack Nicklaus, Ben Hogan, Arnold Palmer, Byron Nelson, Sam Snead, and Walter Hagen as one of the finest competitors who ever walked a fairway.

He was on even his old rival Hagen's best list. When told in 1950 that Jones had been elected the best golfer of the first half of the twentieth century, Hagen responded, "I would've voted for Jones myself. He was marvelous."

So was Sir Walter, and not just because of the forty-four official tournaments won and more than $1 million earned. Hagen was the player most responsible for creating the occupation of professional golfer during the 1920s. Crucial to the explosive growth of golf in America during that decade, from 1923 to 1929 the Haig played in eighteen major professional tournaments, winning seven (he had won four majors between 1914 and 1922). Jones's winning the U.S. and British Opens and U.S. and British Amateur Championships during the same period was a great accomplishment, yet he competed on average in only three to four tournaments a year and could not compete in the PGA Championship.

During the rapid rise of golf in the Roaring Twenties, it was Hagen who carried the golf torch week after week and year after year, especially in the high-profile events.

According to Grantland Rice, the dean of American sportswriters at the time, "Hagen, by his tact, deportment, style, and overall color, did for the professional golfer what Babe Ruth did for the professional ballplayer."

"Hagen was historically important," declared Herbert Warren Wind, dean of American golf writers, in a long essay he wrote for the *New Yorker* sixty-one years after the Florida match. "More than any other individual, he opened the way for young men who wanted to make their living not as golf professionals but as professional golfers.

"He was called 'The Haig' with a respectful chuckle tinged with awe the way Arnold Palmer would be called 'The King' two golf generations later. Hagen was the first great golfer I had ever seen, and both his ability and presence surpassed anything I had expected," Wind wrote in the same 1987 essay. "Not until Arnold Palmer came along did another golfer establish a relationship with his galleries that was as strong and dramatic as Hagen's."

As great as Jones was, without him there would still have been golf. As we'll see in the following pages, without Walter Hagen, there might not be *professional* golf as we know it today.

CHAPTER 2

THOUGH WALTER HAGEN WAS BORN well over a century ago and achieved many firsts in his career, he had nothing to do with introducing golf to the United States. In Europe, golf had been played for centuries. By the time of Hagen's birth Great Britain had been crowning Open champions for thirty-two years. American golf, such as it was in the late nineteenth century, was dominated by British players, a situation viewed by the players and British officials as the natural order of things.

Why? Because the sport had been invented and established in Europe, especially in Great Britain. There and in Holland are references to golf dating back centuries. What is generally considered the first true written reference dates to 1457, when King James II of Scotland issued an edict admonishing soldiers for neglecting their archery practice in favor of playing golf. His son issued a similar edict in 1471, and James IV weighed in with yet another in 1491. He couldn't have been too concerned, however, because James IV is recorded as the first monarch in Great Britain to succumb to the lure of the links.

Golf's origin as an organized sport can be attributed to the formation of the Honourable Company of Edinburgh Golfers in Scotland in 1744. An annual competition was begun by the Edinburgh group, which also created the first thirteen "Rules of Golf." The descendant of this organization can still be found at the legendary Muirfield course, also in Scotland, where it moved to in 1892.

In 1754, the most famous golf organization was founded: Society of St Andrews Golfers. The name we know it by today, the Royal and

Ancient Golf Club of St Andrews, came about in 1834 when King William IV became the society's patron and thus the "Royal" had to be inserted somewhere. While they were at it, they changed the whole title. The Royal and Ancient Golf Club and the United States Golf Association are today the rule-making bodies of international golf.

The first reference to golf in America actually was not related to the British but was from Dutch authorities. On December 10, 1659, the magistrates of Fort Orange (which became Albany, New York) issued an edict: ". . . having heard divers complaints from the burghers of this place against the practice of playing golf along the streets, which causes great damage to the windows of the houses, and also exposes people to the dangers of being injured . . . their honours, wishing to prevent the same, hereby forbid all persons to play golf in the streets, under the penalty of forfeiture of Fl. 25 for each person who shall be found doing so."

In the April 21, 1779, edition of the *Royal Gazette,* a New York City newspaper published by an Englishman, there is an advertisement for the sale of "play clubs and featheries [golf balls] from Scotland." Several accounts suggest that rudimentary courses were laid out in 1786 in Charleston, South Carolina, and in 1795 in Savannah, Georgia. Surviving is an invitation to a New Year's Eve party in 1811 at a golf club in Savannah, though there is no other evidence extant of a course there, and the club did not survive the War of 1812.

Of today's four professional "major" tournaments—the British Open, U.S. Open, PGA Championship, and Masters—the British Open is by far the oldest. The first was held in 1860 at the Prestwick Golf Club on the Ayrshire coast of Scotland, with eight players competing over three rounds of 12 holes each. The top prize was a red Moroccan leather belt with a silver buckle, and it was taken home by Scotsman Willie Park. In second place, two shots behind, was Old Tom Morris.

In America golf really got going in the Northeast—appropriately enough, given that its climate can rival Scotland's, and it was home to a well-populated leisure class. In 1888, John Reid, a transplanted Scottish businessman, asked a friend about to go to England to bring him back some clubs and balls. The friend, Robert Lockhart, went right to the top, buying six golf clubs and two dozen balls from Old Tom Morris at

St Andrews. Wanting to make sure the clubs and balls were okay before giving them to Reid, upon his return Lockhart tested them in Central Park and was arrested for the strange act by perplexed police.

Thus armed, Reid took a patch of land across the street from his house in Yonkers, New York, and created three holes, including fairways and rough greens. February 22, 1888, was an unusually balmy day, and Reid and a few friends, itching to try their "development," went out and played the three holes—no doubt with some people looking on curiously at the players' odd gyrations.

With the exception of the famous blizzard that March, the year 1888 offered many months of good golf weather. Reid and his friends purchased a thirty-acre site not far away from the original three holes and created six holes, organizing as the St. Andrew's Club of Yonkers, with Reid as president (adding the period and apostrophe to distinguish itself). In 1892 the club was moved to an apple orchard, and the members became known as the Apple Tree Gang because, not having a clubhouse, they would hang jugs of their favorite drinks from the trees close to the home hole.

It was not long before actual golf clubs with courses were being created. The first to incorporate was Shinnecock Hills in Southampton, New York, founded in 1891. (It became the site of U.S. Opens in 1896, 1986, 1995, and 2004.) The course was modeled on St Andrews and the other courses in Scotland, England, and Ireland that border the sea and featured tall rough, narrow fairways, few trees, many sand traps, and little protection from the wind. Shinnecock Hills was designed initially as a 12-hole course by Scotsman Willie Davis. Among other distinctions, the Shinnecock Hills Golf Club was the first one to have a clubhouse, built by the firm headed by Stanford White, the premier residential and commercial architect of the day who, among other structures, created the first Madison Square Garden (where, as was described by E. L. Doctorow in *Ragtime,* he was killed by a jealous husband).

One more first—the first 18-hole course in the United States. That honor goes to the Chicago Golf Club course in Wheaton, Illinois, designed by Charles Blair Macdonald and built in 1893. He was to design the National Golf Links next to Shinnecock Hills in 1911. Except for the first Walker Cup in 1922, National has been closed to international play and remains extremely private.

In 1894, six golf clubs—Yonkers, Shinnecock Hills, Newport, The Country Club, Chicago, and St. Andrew's—joined together to create America's own governing body, the United States Golf Association. That September, Newport hosted twenty players in a two-day stroke-play tournament that was supposed to determine the best golfer in the country. However, when the big man from Chicago, thirty-eight-year-old Charles Blair Macdonald (taught golf as a student in Scotland by Old Tom Morris himself), didn't win, he convinced the organizers that it had not been a true championship event.

The members of St. Andrew's agreed to try again the next month, with a match-play event. Macdonald won the first two matches and celebrated until 5 o'clock in the morning with the visiting Stanford White. He caught a couple of hours' sleep, then rushed to the golf course. He won the morning round 2 and 1 despite a horrible hang-over. At lunch, to cure his headache and at White's urging, Macdonald downed a bottle of champagne.

In the afternoon finale, Macdonald weaved from hole to hole, yet amazingly was tied at the end of 18. But in the first play-off hole he ran out of gas and sent his drive into a farm field next door. Incredibly, Macdonald later convinced the powers that be again that the event had not been a legitimate championship.

The following year the six clubs joined forces to create an official United States Open and hold it at Newport. The 36-hole event in 1895 was won by an Englishman, Horace Rawlins, with a 173 total. Rawlins was just nineteen, and only Johnny McDermott won the Open at a younger age (by only a few months). Willie Dunn was runner-up, and Macdonald wasn't anywhere near first place.

With its own National Championship, golf in the United States was off and running. There were plenty of growing pains, though. For example, Englishman Fred Herd won by 7 strokes at the Myopia Hunt Club outside Boston in 1898. His triumph was tainted a bit by the demand by the U.S. Golf Association that he put up a security deposit for the trophy before it would be given to him—based on Herd's reputation, the USGA feared that he would pawn the trophy for drinking money.

By the dawn of the new century, industrious American golf aficionados had built and opened 871 clubs devoted to the sport—715 nine-hole courses, 90 eighteen-hole courses, and 66 six-hole courses. This total was more than the number of golf clubs in the rest of the world combined. Four years later, it was estimated that there were 2,000 golf courses in the States.

The American upper class took to golf, some of the reasons being that they had the most free time and the sport was associated with royalty. However, it remained the case that the rules, the best players, and the best courses belonged to the British. So did the first-place finishes in the early tournaments. The focus was on the U.S. and British Opens as the high-profile events in a still-emerging sport, and without exception British players took home the trophies.

This was understandable because up to this time (and for the foreseeable future) in both Great Britain and the States the golf gods were British. An especially revered figure was Old Tom Morris, who was the head professional at St Andrews when the British Open was born. He was the Leonardo da Vinci of club making and an excellent player to boot. After finishing second in the inaugural British Open in 1860, he won the next year and won it three more times after that before giving way to his son.

He is also credited as being an excellent teacher and, in that role, spawned the generation of British golfers who would dominate the sport into the twentieth century.

His son was called Young Tom Morris. In the British Open, the son took up where his father left off. He won when the first claret jug was presented in 1872, which was the last of his four consecutive British Open victories, a feat never equaled. He could well have become and to this day remained the Open's record holder in wins, but he died at only twenty-four in 1875.

John Henry Taylor was the first English-born professional to win the British Open, though not until thirty-four years after it began, in 1894 at Sandwich, the first time the Open was not held in Scotland. More familiar to golf fans as J. H. Taylor, he would continue to win in Great Britain and compete in the United States until age and the advent of World War I ended his career.

He, James Braid, and Tom Watson share winning the British Open five times (while Taylor was runner-up three times). As a non-playing captain in 1933, Taylor's team defeated the U.S. squad (captained by

Hagen) in the Ryder Cup. He would live thirty more years after this triumph (the last the British would have until the 1957 Ryder Cup), dying at ninety-two in 1963 in the village where he was born.

Braid, a Scotsman, was the first to collect five British Open titles, to go with four British Matchplay Championships. He turned professional in 1893—allowing him to be hired at private clubs, charge for lessons, and accept prize money—yet struggled on the links, not winning his first claret jug until 1901. In 1950, at eighty, he was made an honorary member of the Royal and Ancient Golf Club, and thus installed in the golf equivalent of Valhalla. He died a few months later.

Harry Vardon with the two players above formed what was called the "Great Triumvirate" of British golf. He holds the record of six British Open titles. Of the twenty-one British Opens held between 1894 and 1914, the Great Triumvirate won sixteen.

As impressive as that is, perhaps more of an achievement is his invention of the "Vardon grip," which to this day continues to be the dominant grip of most golfers everywhere. Previous to Vardon's prime years, when his influence was felt throughout Great Britain and the United States, a "normal" golf grip was to hold the club with both hands side by side, similar to the way one would grip a baseball bat. Vardon himself used this grip, but was having a chronic problem with overpowering shots with his right hand.

He experimented with an overlapping grip. "Golf is a two-handed affair," he stated when asked about the change. "The clubhead and the hands, wrists, and arms should be considered as parts of the club, all working together as one piece of machinery." It was a rather simple change, yet it worked for Vardon, and the overlapping grip, sometimes with minor variations, has worked for most players ever since.

With his winning record, technical skills, demeanor, and willingness to travel, no other foreign player had a greater impact on American golf in its infancy than Harry Vardon. When he first journeyed to the United States in 1900 to promote a golf ball called the "Vardon Flyer," the trip changed everything in American golf.

The Morrises and the Great Triumvirate were the first inhabitants of golf's Mount Olympus and, directly and indirectly, helped to establish "golf professional" as an occupation and vocation in Great Britain.

Vardon's 1900 tour was his first visit to the States. Everywhere he went to make an appearance or play an exhibition, thousands of golf-mad Americans turned up. Two thousand people followed Vardon's every move during an exhibition match played in a snowstorm in New Jersey. When a match was scheduled at Van Cortlandt Park in the Bronx, Wall Street activity was suspended for the day so financiers could go watch.

The highlight of Vardon's tour was winning the U.S. Open (with Taylor coming in second). U.S. players had no chance at the time. The Brits appeared to have the sport cornered any way one looked at it. It would seem that an American with dreams of being a successful professional golfer could not have entered a more challenging world.

The golfer who would spend much of his life tanned and grinning, competing in the hot sun, was born on the day winter began, December 21, in 1892 in the Corbett's Glen section of Brighton, New York. Throughout his life he was known as Walter Charles Hagen; however, it was learned at his death that his middle name had been Christian, and no explanation exists as to why he changed it.

At the time, Brighton, with its working-class and immigrant population, was considered on the wrong side of the tracks from Rochester, a city in the northwest corner of the state that sits on Lake Ontario and is subjected to cold, driving winds and snow for half the year. No doubt if Mr. and Mrs. Hagen had listed possible occupations for their only son, golf would never have entered their minds.

Walter's grandfather, Joseph Hagen, had emigrated from Germany in 1855, part of the huge wave of German and Irish immigrants who came to this country in the mid-nineteenth century. It is reasonable to assume that Joseph chose Rochester because the Irish and Germans were then the two largest ethnic groups in that city, and he may have had relatives or friends from Germany already living there. The city was prospering, thanks to its clothing factories and its role as a busy railroad hub for freight trains going to and from the Northeast and upper Midwest. Able-bodied workers like Joseph Hagen were in demand.

In the late 1850s, Hagen married. He and his German-immigrant wife, Mary, had six children—four boys, including William, born in

1860, and two girls. In 1866, the Hagens moved to Brighton, obtaining a few acres of land along Allen's Creek, where they built a house.

In several ways William Hagen represented the new generation of working-class Rochester citizens. In the 1880s he was working with his hands like his father, in William's case as a millwright and blacksmith in the railroad-car shops. He was a second-generation German Presbyterian at a time when Germans had supplanted the Irish as the city's largest ethnic group. He had little formal education but was hardworking and thrifty. Thrift was especially important because during his prime laboring years William earned $18 a week, manageable for a family only if they were careful.

When he was twenty-four, William Hagen purchased land from his parents and built a two-story house next to theirs. He then married Louise Balko, an immigrant from Germany of Dutch and German descent. Their first child, Lottie, wasn't born until 1891, seven years after the marriage, but then four other children arrived in rapid succession: Walter, then three more daughters, Freda, Cora, and Mabel. Reminiscing decades later, Walter Hagen recalled, "We were all healthy and strong. We worked hard and we paid our bills. We had a simple comfortable home and good plain food, but there wasn't much left over for extras."

Despite its harsh, wintry climate for half the year, Rochester at the end of the nineteenth century seems to have been a good place for the working class, aspiring middle class, and expanding upper class. Henry Clune, a friend of Hagen's when they were in their teens and twenties, worked for the *Rochester Democrat and Chronicle* for more than fifty years (and lived long enough to be interviewed by *Sports Illustrated* about Hagen, at age ninety-nine in 1989). He also wrote books, a few of which were memoirs of growing up in Rochester at the turn of the century. Clune wrote in one recollection:

> There were various sections of the city that were villagelike in their singularity, that were neat and cozy, and often exceedingly clannish. Rochester was spoken of as "a city of homes," and this was not a misnomer; a city of homes and trees.
>
> There was only an aspersion of apartment houses, and these for the most part were confined to the downtown sections. Substantial

burghers wanted none of them, and the aspiration of the newly wedded was invariably to own a home on some tree-lined street, of which there were many in both the fashionable and middle-class sections of the city.

Before the motorcar and the movie theater began to lure householders from their homes, the residential districts of Rochester had innumerable neighborhood cliques. The city itself animated a spirit of neighborliness. To be sure, quarrels occasionally developed over the placing of a fence post, a marauding dog, or a boy who batted a baseball through a window pane. But Rochester generally was a genial little city.

On pleasant summer evenings the front porch was the gathering place for the entire family. We were habitual and contented porch sitters. Once the supper dishes were "done," the mother of the family and the daughters of her brood might gather at one end of the verandah, while the paterfamilias, ensconced in his favorite chair at the other end, scanned the evening paper against the failing light and blew smoke from his mellow pipe through the darkling fronds and creepers of the morning-glory vine. Below, on the steps, the small fry would squat, reviewing the day's events and planning for the morrow.

William Hagen had a friend named Sandy, a Scotsman who worked at the Country Club of Rochester, which included among its members success stories like George Eastman, the founder of Eastman Kodak. One day, when Walter was five, Sandy was invited to the Hagen home for dinner and to smoke his pipe on the porch afterward.

He brought with him an old and shortened club as a toy for the youngster, and that evening Walter had a fine old time "knocking a ball around in our living room." Fifty-nine years later, Hagen wrote that his first direct contact with golf was his most vivid early-childhood recollection.

Walter was already inclined toward sports. He had inherited robust good health and energy, and there were plenty of children in Brighton to play with (baseball in the summer, sledding and ice skating in the winter). Perhaps more important for his future in golf, he inherited from each parent an attribute that would be quite useful—from William, large and strong hands, and from Louise, height; she was 5'11", several inches taller than her husband.

During the summer of 1900, the seven-year-old Walter would set off from home in Corbett's Glen, cross Allen's Creek to the top of the hill, and from there look across East Avenue to watch the members of the Country Club of Rochester at play. The golf club, the first one in Rochester, had been founded in 1895 by members of the private Genesee Valley Club of downtown Rochester.

Walter's fascination with golf grew with every viewing, and though still several months from his eighth birthday, he decided to try for a job at the club.

The Country Club of Rochester is not as well known today as its younger neighbor, Oak Hill Country Club, which has hosted a U.S. Open, a Ryder Cup, and a PGA Championship. It is, however, a lush and stately course, very much representative of old Northeast golf courses. What mattered to the young Hagen at the time, though, was that it was nearby and it was focused on a sport that intrigued him. He was also intrigued by the fancy people who played and partied there, and he could earn some money.

Bill Lambert was the caddie master at the club in 1900, and he was also a friend of William Hagen. William made a plea on his son's behalf, and Lambert decided to give the kid a try at ten cents an hour.

Walter's first day at the Country Club came close to being his last. He struggled to carry the bag of Erickson Perkins, a prominent Rochester businessman. At the 10th hole the club member launched his ball toward a tall tree surrounded by thick grass that was in turn surrounded by sand.

A good caddie keeps track of the ball so it can be more easily found. Hagen, on his first day, had lost sight of it, and he and Perkins, even with the help of other golfers and caddies, couldn't find it. Perkins gruffly told his trembling caddie that he would carry his own bag while the search continued for the missing ball. "You'd better find it, too, or don't come back," Perkins pronounced.

The youngster searched and searched, with no luck. Then, with an indication of the improvisational skill he would later bring to golf, he got on the ground and rolled back and forth across the grass, flattening it. Sure enough, after a couple of minutes of such exertions, Walter felt the bump of the buried ball under his back.

He raced after Perkins and returned the ball to him. After the round Perkins ordered him to clean his clubs. "I had them shining like new when he came from the locker room," Hagen remembered. Perkins was pleased enough to give him a nickel tip, and added, "You're a good boy. You'll learn."

Throughout his life Hagen would have a complete carelessness about money, which is odd considering the example of his frugal parents. They certainly attempted to impart their financial style to him: At the end of his first hot and exhausting week as a caddie, Walter tried to give his meager wages to his mother to enhance the family budget. Louise, instead, handed him a small coin bank and insisted that his earnings go into it. When it was filled up, Walter was taken to the East Side Savings Bank of Rochester, where he made a deposit.

Walter did not get the ancestral message, or perhaps rebelled against it. "Like any kid I wasn't above snitching from my penny bank now and then," Hagen recalled. "I'd pry the teeth in the slot apart and shake out enough for ice cream, and eventually for my first suit with long pants, a sort of wild bluish-green in color. In my teens I even saved enough in my account to blow $380 on a piano for a birthday present for Lottie." We can have some doubts about Hagen having the discipline to save up such a large sum, but shedding it to purchase an extravagant gift is quite believable.

As a caddie, Hagen persevered and apparently was good at it. The club kept him on year after year, and he eventually was promoted to assistant head pro. He worked full days in the summer, then hurried to the Country Club of Rochester after school in the spring and fall. Playing golf on Sunday was frowned upon in the upper class, so with members few and far between at the club, Hagen and his friends played baseball that day. Showing entrepreneurial spirit, Walter collected lost golf balls he found in the woods at the club and brought them to La Bourie's Sporting Goods in Rochester where he was given credit toward baseballs and, eventually, a new first baseman's mitt.

Hagen had talent in baseball and enthusiasm for the game. At that time, for someone interested in sports, baseball was a lot more visible in the press than golf, and offered real career possibilities. Hagen was a good first baseman and had power as a batter, but best of all he was not only a strong pitcher but could hurl the ball with either arm. Surely, down the road, an ambidextrous pitcher could be valuable to a ballclub.

On the other hand, golf was a job, with the job site conveniently within walking distance of the Hagen home. As time went on and Walter kept observing the players he caddied for—especially Walter Will, the club's driving champion—he became intrigued enough to want to try it, to go beyond the idle fun he'd had in his house with a golf club gift from Sandy. Because caddies were not yet allowed to play at the Country Club of Rochester, Hagen fashioned a course in a nearby cow pasture.

"I knew nothing about course architecture, so I followed the shape of the pasture, which vaguely resembled the outline of the state of Florida," Hagen recalled years later. "I laid out a four-hole affair. For instance, I teed off at Jacksonville, the first green was on the outskirts of Pensacola, then across to the second hole at Gainesville. From there I went down to the third green at Miami and then back to the fourth green in the Jacksonville area again. I must have had a feeling about Florida even then."

Though no architect, Hagen improvised again. He once told a reporter, "I would herd the cows all in one spot where I had made a hole, so they could eat the grass and make a close putting surface."

His first clubs came from a member, John Palmer, who offered a midiron (a hickory-shafted 2-iron) and a spoon (a 3-wood) he was about to toss out. Gradually, Hagen completed a full set by pointing out to other members how dusty, nicked, or a bit bent their clubs were becoming, and if they were going to get new ones, the helpful caddie would be glad to dispose of the old ones.

In most golf rankings, Walter Hagen is listed as one of the top five putters of all time. This would be startling to those who knew how he developed his style on the green. Hagen would offer various answers and putting tips over time, but the most consistent explanation offered for his unusual style was that in the summer of 1902 polo matches began to be held at the Country Club of Rochester. Caddies made extra money by leading the horses to and from the stables. The youngsters were inspired to create their own polo matches, wielding discarded mallets on their bicycles and using old golf balls. Hagen found that the way he gripped the handle of the mallet with two hands (steering, perhaps, with his knees), with the last two fingers of the left hand controlling the stick, could be used to grip a putter with excellent results.

Yes, this is unconventional. We can speculate that Hagen initially had good results putting with this grip, and with early confidence began to build on that. Many accounts of Hagen in his heyday note that his putting style was atypical yet almost infallible, so it appears that, whatever the inspiration, he found what worked for him, practiced it over and over, and stuck with it, using this same "polo" grip throughout his career.

Even with a growing interest in golf, Hagen was committed to improving as a baseball player and developed a right-handed curveball and a left-handed changeup. There was an intensifying tug-of-war between the two sports in his thoughts and waking hours. There wasn't much room for anything else, like paying attention at the one-room Allen's Creek School. Walter wasn't the best student anyway, and he would later admit that for much of his life the only book he read was the little black one kept in his back pocket.

The day came—it was in late spring—when something had to give. The seventh grader was sitting in the classroom "looking out the window, feeling the nice warm air and the sunshine on my face. I could see the golfers out on the course at the Country Club of Rochester. Suddenly I couldn't take it any longer. When Mrs. Cullen, the teacher, wasn't looking I jumped out the window. I never went back to school regularly again."

According to Rochester newspaper accounts, at a party in 1939 at the Country Club of Rochester, when Hagen was being honored for the twenty-fifth anniversary of his first U.S. Open title, he was reunited with Mrs. Cullen, who was apparently unfamiliar with professional golf and Hagen's success in it. They reminisced about the day thirty-four years before when Walter had jumped out the window.

Finally, Mrs. Cullen asked, "So tell me, Walter, how did you make out?"

"Pretty well, Mrs. Cullen," Hagen replied. "Thanks for asking."

The golf world the adolescent Walter Hagen was jumping into was just beginning to change. British superiority was still pervasive and with the visitors still routinely winning the U.S. Open during the first decade of the twentieth century, the situation didn't appear likely to change in the near future.

Hagen was seven when Harry Vardon made the crossing west for what would turn out to be a very successful exhibition tour that emphasized British golf excellence. Vardon hailed from the island of Jersey, where he was born in 1870. Harry would become a gardener like his father, but one of Harry's first jobs was working for a retired army major who was passionate about golf and gave the impressionable teenager his first set of clubs. Vardon quickly took to the game, and in his early twenties secured a job as a golf pro in Yorkshire, England. At twenty-six he won his first British Open, at Muirfield in Scotland in a 36-hole play-off. He won it again in 1898 and 1899, and thus was the reigning champion when he set off for America in February 1900.

With the exception of a trip back to Great Britain to defend his British Open crown (unsuccessfully), during the next eleven months, at between $200 and $250 per exhibition match, Vardon took on all comers. To emphasize his superiority, Vardon challenged two competitors (most of whom were amateurs) at a time, with the opponents playing their best ball after each shot, and even then some of the results were rather lopsided: In Atlantic City, for example, Vardon defeated H. M. Harriman and Findlay Douglas, transplanted Brits who were the last two U.S. Amateur Champions, 9 and 8, and Willie Dunn twice, 16 and 15 in Virginia and 15 and 14 in Scarsdale, New York. During the tour, Vardon's overall record was 50–13–2.

Part of the tour was a visit to the Jordan Marsh store in Boston, where Vardon effortlessly launched balls into a net and for fun aimed at and hit sprinkler heads and various wall decorations. Though he made the store's managers frantic, Vardon was applauded enthusiastically by a large crowd, many of whom had not played golf before. By the end of the afternoon, all of the store's golf equipment had been sold. (Among the adoring spectators was seven-year-old Francis Ouimet.)

According to Herbert Warren Wind in his memoir *Following Through,* "No one had had any idea that a player could control the golf ball in the masterly fashion that Vardon did."

An exclamation point to the tour was Vardon's victory in the U.S. Open that October at the Chicago Golf Club. It drew the largest crowd yet to attend a National Championship. Vardon held a 1-stroke lead after 36 holes. Despite a cold, swirling wind on the second day, he won by two strokes.

Vardon's U.S. tour ended on December 19 when he boarded the steamship *Majestic* bound for England. He was not about to offer praise for American golf. "I like the country, the golfers, and their links," he told reporters. "But they are not up to the class of the leading players in England and Scotland."

As *Golf* magazine stated when celebrating the hundredth anniversary of the Jerseyman's tour, "By junket's end, Vardon literally had helped change the landscape of the game in America. . . . By the end of 1900, more than 250,000 Americans, many embracing the Vardon grip and the Vardon Flyer alike, vied for space on 1,100 courses, many of them newly built thanks to 'Vardonmania.'"

One other note about Vardon's impact on U.S. golf: No other player would have a greater influence on Walter Hagen, though that influence would not be fully realized for another thirteen years.

After the profitable result of Vardon's U.S. trip—which covered 20,000 miles and, in addition to winnings, netted him a 900-pound endorsement contract from Spalding (compared to the 30 pounds he had received for winning the '99 British Open)—other British golfers made the crossing, to keep winning tournaments and, even better, to try to reap similar monetary rewards in exhibition matches.

If there was any hope that American golfers would emerge via the U.S. Open, it was quickly dispelled during the early years of the so-called National Championship. Horace Rawlins was the first winner, and he was followed by such Scottish and English champions as Willie Anderson, Vardon, and Alex Smith.

By the end of the first decade of the 1900s, there was very little America could call its own in golf. Though the building of courses continued, the high-profile events continued to be captured by the British players. With increasing frustration, American followers of golf looked to see if emerging somewhere, anywhere was an American-born and -bred player who would lead U.S. golf to the promised course.

CHAPTER 3

AS A TEENAGER, HAGEN TOOK ADVANTAGE of his access to the Country Club of Rochester and the kindness of the head pro then, Andrew Christy, to practice when he wasn't caddying. His fascination with golf was growing, yet he was also a bundle of restless energy who enjoyed the keen competition sports offered.

At the club and beyond its boundaries he learned how to ice skate, play tennis and polo, and hunt and fish. Hagen liked the physical exercise and the thrill of competition. "I played to win whether it was pool, marbles, baseball, shooting, or golf," he reported many years later.

Inevitably, he played golf more than other sports simply because he was at the Country Club of Rochester almost every day of the week. Also, as he recalled, "I liked the feel of a golf club in my hand and I was forever swinging a club."

Of course, he did have to put down the golf club—outdoors, at least, if not in the back shop—during the winter, but that time was spent teaching skating at the country club for extra cash. In addition to his in-season caddying, that money was especially important after he jumped out the schoolhouse window, since it was apparent that, unlike his father, he was too restless and infatuated with grass and sunshine for any sort of indoor work. To someone at an impressionable age, it sure seemed that golf offered an earning opportunity with a lot less sweat than the railyards.

According to accounts in addition to Hagen's own, he evolved into a very good caddie and became a favorite of the club members as well as Christy. Presumably, rising through the caddie ranks and looping for the better (and more influential) members gave the teenager a lot of confidence as a person and as an emerging player. At least as important, and another indication of how favored Hagen was, the Country Club of Rochester made an exception for him and allowed him to practice on the course before and after his workday. On long early and midsummer days, Hagen put in fifteen-hour sessions playing, caddying, and playing again. He later boasted, "By the time I was fifteen I had played more golf and practiced more shots than golfers of twenty-one."

Hagen honed his skills through the almost incessant practice at his own impromptu course and then at the Country Club of Rochester. That, and the encouragement of the club members who had taken a shine to the brash but competent boy, sowed the seeds of confidence that years later would yield success in even the tensest moments of championship play.

That brashness was still evident many years later when Hagen recounted that he had "so much confidence in my own ability that I was always thoroughly relaxed in any game. . . . When I was fourteen I thought I was capable of taking on anybody within five years of my age. Of course, I'd never been out of Rochester, but I knew I could beat anybody I'd met so far."

Clearly, he had to be put in his place, and Christy was usually the one to do it. He kept an eye on the young rooster at the club, making sure he didn't get too big for the barn. One day, though, Walter felt cocky enough to say to the head pro, "How about my beating you nine fast holes?"

Christy glared at him, up and down, then locked eyes with him. The young assistant realized he'd gone too far and stood trembling, not knowing what would happen next. Finally, his boss said, "Young man, when I want to play golf, *I'll ask you.*" Then he turned and walked away.

Recalling that incident decades later, Hagen said, "Was my face red! I never forgot the lesson he taught me. Afterward, when I wanted to play with him I was always careful to ask politely, 'Would you play a few holes with me, Mr. Christy, and give me some pointers on the game?'"

His arrogance may have been curbed, but Walter had another reason to feel confident: He was developing into a strong physical athlete. By the time he was seventeen he was close to six feet tall and weighed a solid 175 pounds. What made the most difference, however, was the mental aspect. Though he would never be much of a reader, writer, or public speaker, Hagen was and always would be a keen observer, adopting what suited him and discarding what didn't.

As a teenager, Hagen found the most fertile opportunity for this was observing both what club members did right and what they did wrong. When he'd first begun caddying, it wasn't for the club's better players, because they had their regular and older caddies. Instead, Walter worked for and watched the less talented and polished players and, seeing what they did wrong, experimented with different techniques. (Years later, after Hagen had become a sports star, during his infrequent visits back to the Country Club of Rochester he would entertain his hometown fans "in the grill over a few hoots" by doing imitations of club members' swings, the more outrageous the better.) As he moved up to carrying the bag for more accomplished club members, he filled in the remaining blanks with what worked best. He never had a formal golf lesson but rather observed, recorded, and put into practice what others—mostly the better players—were doing.

This habit would be a big advantage years later in tournaments, especially those involving match play. Hagen carefully but keenly would watch which clubs opponents would use in certain situations, and the results; he examined body language and expressions to determine how nervous an opponent was. And he was a quick study of course layouts, hazards, and reading greens. His powers of observation were more focused during match-play rounds when he could concentrate on a single opponent instead of the field.

Something else that Hagen learned at the Country Club of Rochester during the years 1904 to 1912 that would help him greatly later was how to build and maintain golf clubs. At this time, being a "golf professional" in the United States didn't mean being out on tour and making money. That was a professional golfer, and no one was close to doing this on a regular basis during the century's first decade. Then, being a golf pro meant giving lessons, supervising the pro shop, overseeing the care of the course grounds, and building and repairing golf clubs. He did the bidding of the golf club members, who were from the upper class, and was treated the same way as butlers, chauffeurs, and maids.

Being ambitious as well as skilled, Hagen at fourteen leaped at the offer to become Christy's assistant. There was a new skill to be learned because one of his primary responsibilities was creating and repairing golf clubs.

With the exception of emergency repairs, this work was done during the winter. Walter, finished with formal schooling and hired to work beside the head pro, spent the long Rochester winters in the shop. Christy was a patient teacher, and for Hagen "the next five years gave me invaluable knowledge about clubs, their design and construction. The iron heads were mostly shipped over from England and Scotland, but the woods we made right from the block. I learned how to weight the wood heads. I learned to plane the shafts from hickory, scrape them down, polish them to a fine sheen and attach them to the heads. I could wind a grip with the skill of the old-time club makers."

Another advantage of this sort of craftmanship was that the young Hagen could, with parts from here and there, create a set for himself that suited his developing skills. This he did: a spliced driver known at the time as "Ted Ray's Own," a brassie (a modern-day 2-wood), a spoon (3-wood), a driving iron (1-iron), a midiron (2-iron), a mashie iron (4-iron), a mashie (5-iron), a mashie-niblick (7-iron), a niblick (9-iron), and a gooseneck putter.

It may not be remarkable that an assistant pro constructed his own set of clubs, but it is remarkable that Hagen made them so well that he was able to use them successfully in professional competitions. His "strange weapons," as he nicknamed the motley but well-fashioned assortment, helped Hagen win two U.S. Opens and other tournaments. He retired the set after finishing fifty-third in the British Open in 1920, but it was not forgotten. According to Hagen, he donated the set to the Hall of Fame of the U.S. Golf Association in 1940.

A somewhat less constructive observation that Hagen made during his apprenticeship at the Country Club of Rochester was that some golfers liked or even needed liquid refreshment to bolster themselves during a difficult (or even routine) round. It was not unusual to have members served a cocktail or two during play.

The upside of the relationship between golf and alcohol was a particular incident that ignited in the young Walter a burning interest to be allowed in the clubhouse, where neither he nor his boss, Christy, was welcome. Writing about it decades later, the experience of being inside the clubhouse clearly made a big impression on Hagen.

When still a caddie, he was looping for Harry Strong in a club tournament that ended in a tie between Strong and J. C. Powers (their names symbolizing the Industrial Age robustness that was Rochester). Just before the play-off began, Hagen was instructed to run into the clubhouse and arrange with the bartender to meet the two contestants at the second hole with a full pitcher of "refreshments." Walter followed these instructions, and Strong and Powers shared the pitcher before teeing off.

Strong had more mischief on his mind. He told his caddie to hurry back to the clubhouse for another pitcher, then to lie in wait at the fourth hole. After the adversaries sank their putts, up popped young Walter with the fresh pitcher, and Strong generously insisted that his opponent enjoy the majority of it.

During the match the energetic caddie scurried back and forth, appearing every other hole with a full pitcher. The last two holes were played well over par as both players were spraying shots all over the course. Alas, Strong's strategy was weak: Powers still won the match.

Apparently, the youngster's visits to the inside of the clubhouse took a little bit longer than necessary. He was in an inner sanctum of upper-class life, seeing from the inside what he had watched from the outside, atop the hill near his home. This was *it,* where they drank and smoked, danced and laughed, and exchanged stories of their financial triumphs. The boy from Brighton, the wrong side of the tracks, was dazzled by possibilities no one in his family had ever considered.

"The play-off was most important to me because it gave me the unusual opportunity of seeing the inside of the beautiful and exclusive clubhouse of the Country Club of Rochester. No other caddie had been able to wangle that!" he recalled, probably an exaggeration— other caddies had been told to fetch drinks—but among his peers only Walter had the vision, talent, and drive to see himself as being among the clubhouse swells some day.

As Hagen was developing into a hardworking and hard-playing teenager, golf in the States was experiencing several significant changes.

The pace of course building was increasing, not only to accommodate the recreational pursuits of the upper class but to satisfy an emerging middle-class demand. The country's economy was in generally good shape as the second decade of the century approached, allowing some of the middle class, especially in the Northeast and Midwest, access to both public courses and private clubs with moderate membership fees.

It didn't hurt that portly President William Taft, who was in office from 1909 to 1913, was an avid golfer. Gone was the vigorous exercise and energetic hunting expeditions of his predecessor, Teddy Roosevelt. Taft, far from being an example of fitness—he had the dubious distinction of getting stuck in the White House bathtub—spent his free time on golf courses, beginning a trend up to the present day linking chief executives with the links.

Taft right from the beginning may have nailed what makes golf such a presidential sport. "The beauty of golf," he said, "is that you cannot play if you permit yourself to think of anything else."

If anything changed with Taft's successor, it was that golf's image became more attractive. President Woodrow Wilson played five or six times a week, often rising at 6:00 a.m. to do so. He rarely broke 115 over 18 holes, but he was a confirmed fanatic. During winter evenings, Secret Service agents would paint golf balls red and place them to dry on White House radiators overnight so that the president could play in the snow the next morning.

Another change was that more professionals were leaving their clubhouses to enter tournaments. Of course, there were fewer than a dozen U.S. tournaments at the time, and most pros couldn't be away from their home courses more than a handful of weeks without risking their positions, so there was not a major shift to tournament play. The top prize was the $300 won at the U.S. Open, and the other tournaments paid winners substantially less. With $3,000 a year offering a comfortable, middle-class lifestyle at the time, clearly a living could not be made solely by playing tournament golf.

However, it was true that competition in tournaments was no longer being left to the amateur ranks, most of whom had the time and money to handle not only the length of the tournament itself but the travel to and from it. The better head pros, leaving their assistants in charge of their shops, were giving tournament play a shot as best they could because they could earn extra money and by doing well increase their stature (and salary) back home as teachers.

Those who ran the private golf clubs had mixed feelings about this development. On one hand, a pro representing a club who won a tournament or at least finished high up brought credit to the club, which if nothing else stroked egos. On the other hand, though, when a pro did very well, especially on a consistent basis, he could expect a job offer from a bigger golf club, and the one he represented had to approve a higher salary or hang a "Help Wanted" sign on the clubhouse.

The third change was perhaps the most significant: On the bigger stage of tournament play, especially the major events—at this time the four "official" majors were the U.S. and British Opens and the U.S. and British Amateur Championships—the American players were starting to chip away at the Brits' domination.

The Western Open offered some clues. It was viewed by playing professionals as a tournament only a fraction below the British and U.S. Opens because it attracted the strongest field of mostly American pros and alternated among the best courses, many of which also hosted U.S. Opens and later PGA Championships. Indeed, at the time, winning the Western Open was counted as a major (later replaced by the Masters).

To this day, the Western Open, first played in 1899, is the second-oldest tournament still played in North America, after the U.S. Open and predating the Canadian Open. In the Western Open, Americans were winning more than visitors during the century's first decade. Chick Evans, from Chicago, who would be one of golf's greatest amateurs (later overshadowed by the brilliance of Bobby Jones), took the title in 1910.

The British Open was still closed to American ambitions. In the British Amateur, though, there was a chink in the armor—well, more than a chink, it was the golf equivalent of Lexington and Concord, and worse for the Crown, it happened on British soil.

Walter J. Travis had been born in 1862 in Australia. While he was in his early twenties, his employer sent him to New York City to open a new office. Travis had no interest in golf until he was thirty-four. Then living on Long Island, New York, with his family, he took it up at the urging of a few neighbors. His progress was astonishing and in 1900, four years after he started out, Travis won the U.S. Amateur Championship. He would win the U.S. Amateur a total of three times and place third in a U.S. Open before he was finished.

That in itself was a great feat, but taking his talent to the home of golf was a different and much more difficult story. He wasn't the most gracious visitor in 1904 when he entered the British Amateur for the first time. He was a stern man with a thick black beard, who spoke rarely, preferring to puff continuously on a cigar. His dour personality could be attributed to frequent bouts of bad health.

However, he worked hard on developing better golf skills, and he was the first "American" to be hailed as an excellent putter. Many people today use the grip on the putter that he originated, the "reverse overlapping grip," which allowed the index finger of his left hand to override the little finger of his right hand; when putting, he kept his body still, head down, and only his arms and wrists moved.

Grantland Rice recalled asking the taciturn Travis what the secret was to his competitiveness. "'I never hit a careless shot in my life,' he replied. 'I bet only a quarter, but I play each shot as if it was for the title. I concentrate as hard for a quarter as I do for a championship.' He was hard boiled, grouchy, and tough, but I liked Walter Travis immensely."

At forty-three, Travis traveled to Great Britain to practice for the British Amateur Championship, which no foreigner had ever won. Three weeks later he played St Andrews and North Berwick. His practice rounds were unsatisfying. He tossed out his clubs and tried a new set, including a friend's "Schenectady" putter, so named because it had been created by A. W. Knight, who lived in the upstate New York city.

However, his problems continued, then he ran out of time and, as if he were heading for his fate in the Tower of London, he returned to England, to the course at Sandwich.

He was not treated warmly there, but as an interloper who was soiling holy ground by walking on it. Not being a friendly person to begin with, Travis didn't try to curry favor and instead had a few sharp words for his hosts. They countered by assigning him a caddie who was cross-eyed. Travis also believed that the caddie was mentally defective, but his request for a different caddie was denied. Travis was also refused a locker in the dressing room and lodgings in the hotel where the other players stayed.

The mistreatment of Travis backfired. He became even more dour and determined, vowing to win no matter what. The slights were not going to affect his game. "A reasonable number of fleas is good for a dog," he said. "It keeps the dog from forgetting that he is a dog."

Travis won his first match in a heavy rainstorm. He asked for a delay of the second match that afternoon, so he could go back to his hotel to dry off and change. Request refused. Instead, Travis toweled off on the first tee and faced an opponent who had won by forfeit in the first round and thus was warm and dry.

Still, Travis squeezed out a 1-up win, despite the fact that on the 11th hole, his cross-eyed caddie had picked Travis's ball up off the green. Travis's opponent had shouted for the flagstick to be pulled out, and the confused caddie, closest to the hole, went for Travis's ball instead.

More gracious than the rest of the hosts at Sandwich, Travis's opponent, James Robb, refused to call a penalty. Still, Travis immediately made another request for a change of caddie; it was denied. After the match, Travis's opponent offered his caddie, but the caddie master of the tournament would not allow the switch. Resigned, Travis told his caddie he could follow along, doing nothing more than carrying the clubs, and to stay well clear of him.

Showing true grit, Travis won his next four matches, including two over Harold Hilton and Horace Hutchinson, who had for many years traded the British Amateur Championship between them (and Travis had sternly studied the latter's instructional books). In the final match Travis faced Ted Blackwell, who counted among his accomplishments being the long-drive king of Great Britain.

Routinely, the American was outdriven by a hundred yards or more, but his putting was impeccable—except when he missed a 5-footer, and the partisan spectators broke into applause. However, when Travis's putt slid into the cup at the 33rd hole, the match was over. An American had indeed won. His victory was greeted with complete silence on the course.

"Where a match has been won by default or by some obscure official ruling, then there is some modicum of excuse for the gallery's lack of enthusiasm," offered the great British golf player and writer Henry Cotton, "but I think that the crowd's brutality at this stage in Travis's triumph demonstrated an enormous lapse in British manners."

In a less-than-gracious speech at the trophy presentation ceremony, Lord Northbourne credited everyone except Travis and expressed the hope that such a travesty as an American winning the British Amateur would never happen again.

"His lordship in making the presentation speech gave me quite an earful of unfelicitous remarks," Travis recounted afterward. "One passage is indelibly engraved upon my memory: 'Never since the days of Caesar has the British nation been subjected to such humiliation'—which might charitably be construed as conveying an indirect compliment were it not for the general tenor of his speech, coupled with the fervent hope that 'history might not repeat itself.' "

Being a better sport about it, the "Old Man," as Travis would come to be known because of his relatively advanced years in amateur tournaments (he won his last tournament, the Metropolitan Amateur, in 1915 at fifty-four, then retired), accepted the trophy with a nod and simple thanks.

Travis was responsible for one more sign of the ascendancy of U.S. golf in the first decade of the century. In 1908 he founded the *American Golfer,* a magazine that he edited until 1920, when the reins were turned over to Grantland Rice. It was not the first publication devoted exclusively to golf. In 1890 in Great Britain, *Golf* was founded; nine years later the name was changed to *Golf Illustrated.* During the first decade of the new century in the States, *Golf and Lawn Tennis,* the *Golfer,* the *Golfers' Magazine,* and *Golfing* began publishing. But until its demise during the Depression, the *American Golfer*—subtitled "The magazine that put the 'go' in American golf"—was the most popular and authoritative magazine, and it featured the written work of both the better golf journalists and players.

In the U.S. Open, it was business as usual for the British. They came, they saw, they swung and putted, they conquered. During the first decade of the century, nothing fundamentally changed, though Travis's victory had been a tug on the British moustache. Then in 1911, the Brits received another shock.

That year started out auspiciously with Harold Hilton sailing back to England after capturing the U.S. Amateur trophy. (When he won the British Amateur, Hilton became the first player to hold both titles in the same year; Bobby Jones duplicated the feat in 1930.) Buoyed by

Hilton's success in the amateur ranks, a contingent of British professionals sailed west to pluck another national championship, another U.S. Open trophy. The previous year Alex Smith had won in a play-off (after missing a 3-foot putt on the 72nd hole) against his brother, Macdonald Smith, and an American, Johnny McDermott. At only eighteen (just a few months older than Hagen), McDermott, the son of a Philadelphia mailman who had caddied as a youngster, had made a surprising run at the title.

The latter's close finish was viewed as an aberration, even by the U.S. press, which up to that point paid little attention to professional golf anyway. After all, in the 1909 Open a player from Boston, Tommy McNamara, had finished a round with a 69, becoming the first man to break 70 in a major competition in America, but that didn't turn out to mean much of anything as once again, a Brit, George Sargent, had won, by four strokes.

But according to H. B. Martin, there was a shift under way. "The year 1909 was the beginning of a new era in professional golf, as it was this year that the American 'homebred' began to make his presence felt," he wrote. "Heretofore he was hardly to be considered a match for the foreign-born professional." Martin cited McNamara, Travis, Mike Brady, and "J. J. McDermott" as worthy challengers to British rule.

"The word 'homebred' as applied to golf meant everything in those hectic days when the American-born was fighting for recognition among the foreign-born invasion," Martin continued. "The young man to bring about the change in conditions and to lead us to a realization that our own brand of golf was quite as important as, if not yet the equal of, the British, was John J. McDermott."

The feisty McDermott, less than six feet tall and all of 125 pounds, not only tied again for first in the 1911 National Championship at the Chicago Golf Club (the course designed by Charles Blair Macdonald) by mounting a final-round charge, but he won the playoff against Mike Brady by two strokes to become the first homebred American to capture the U.S. Open.

This was a watershed moment in American golf, but a quiet one. Sports fans around the country received their news only via newspapers, and in most of the major dailies at the time golf was relegated to the back pages. Also, the field McDermott bested was not filled with household names. Yes, it was nice that a homebred American had won the National Championship, but the achievement did not directly propel golf higher in the U.S. sports hierarchy.

Those connected to golf were impressed, however. In August 1912, 125 golfers arrived at the Country Club of Buffalo to try to qualify for the U.S. Open, the first time there had been more than a hundred players. This was also an indication that professional golf was being given more attention, though it still couldn't compete with the stature of amateur golf. For example, to qualify for the U.S. Amateur Championship in 1910, 217 players had presented themselves.

McDermott won again in Buffalo, besting Brady and Tom McNamara, in the process becoming the first player to break par (twice) to win a U.S. Open. Back-to-back wins in the National Championship was a big accomplishment, but the twenty-year-old pro had become a big fish in what was still a small pond. Without defeating one or more of Great Britain's best, the U.S. Open and with it American golf would not attain front-page stature. It didn't help that McDermott traveled to Great Britain in a bid to capture the Open there, then shot a 96 to not even qualify for the event.

According to Wind in *The Story of American Golf*: "McDermott had not beaten any 'real foreigners,' just the Scottish- and English-born professionals who had become as permanent a part of the American scene as Swedish masseurs and Chinese laundrymen. . . . From its unofficial inception in 1894, the [U.S.] Open had been a gathering of the clans . . . and topped off their annual convention with seventy-two holes of medal play to see which one of the old familiar faces was playing the best golf that week."

The dramatic spark that would fire a nation was yet to be struck.

Walter Hagen didn't see himself as being part of, let alone leading, a new generation of American golfers. In fact, despite the perks he enjoyed and the skills he was gaining at the Country Club of Rochester, he had serious doubts about choosing golf as an occupation at all. A sport was his top priority, especially with inadequate schooling not opening any doors. In the early twentieth century baseball offered much more opportunity for glory and money.

It wasn't just opportunity Hagen was looking at. The fact was, he was a very good baseball player and this was *the* major sport in the U.S. During the first fifteen years of the century the big stars included Ty Cobb, Honus Wagner, Christy Mathewson, Bill Terry, and Walter Johnson. Their exploits inspired tens of thousands of teenagers to grow up to be just like them. If you wanted to be on the front of the sports pages and get paid for doing what you loved, baseball was the way to go, if you had the talent.

Hagen had the talent. There were many pickup games with other kids in his neighborhood, and on Sundays and the few in-season hours he wasn't at the country club, Walter showed up and wanted to play every position. His top preference, though, was pitching, left-handed or right-handed. As he ascended the local ranks, so did his value to teams because he could start, play other positions, and then come in to relieve, throwing from one side or the other depending on the batter who had to be erased.

A close friend of Hagen's was George Christ, who was also a pitcher. At fifteen, both tried out for a semipro team, the Rochester Ramblers, and both made it, which at the very least brought in additional income, $1.50 a game per player. Typically, Hagen started, then went to play another position when Christ relieved. There was a city championship in Rochester, and after Walter and his friend joined the team, the Ramblers won it three years in a row.

What also held Hagen back from devoting himself exclusively to golf while a teenager was that he was curious enough about other occupations to try them. Actually, only part of this was curiosity; the rest was, as the only male child, an attempt to help the family gain more financial breathing room.

William Hagen had continued to work steadily in the railroad yards, and his son would always credit him with being a good provider. However, there were five children, and as they grew older, expenses increased, particularly for parents looking at marrying off four daughters. His parents were being practical when they urged Walter to try out jobs that could lead to a dependable income. William had been able to earn a steady income working with his hands as a tradesman, and had seen his father, Joseph, do the same.

Walter gave a sincere effort thanks to a combination of fidelity and curiosity. He tried an apprenticeship to a car mechanic, a job that certainly had promise with more and more cars rolling off the assembly lines. But this was a rather grimy job, and the work caused injuries to Hagen's hands, jeopardizing his baseball and golf dreams. Adding to his woes was having to pay $27 a month to Harry's Garage for the privilege of working on cars.

Another occupation he attempted was as a mandolin maker, which was more delicate and hand-friendly work. Walter enjoyed this job, but the long-term potential was as limited as the number of mandolins in Rochester. Another try was as a taxidermist, which had much more potential because of the bountiful hunting in upstate New York. Walter studied the techniques but balked when it came time to actually apply them to the bloody carcasses. One more attempt was working as a wood finisher at a piano company, but the fumes made him ill.

Even if he had made some headway in any of these crafts, it doesn't seem likely that the athletic and restless Walter would have stuck to one indefinitely, especially during the warmer time of year. "These were cold-weather occupations," recalled his friend Henry Clune. "Walter had to be out in the sun with grass under his feet."

The fact was that Hagen's primary talent was in sports, and just maybe he did have the talent, stamina, and intelligence to make a living at it. William Hagen in particular thought this was rubbish—he would be seventy before he ever went to see his son play in a major tournament. True, William had introduced his son to golf via the visiting Sandy and by getting him a job at the Country Club of Rochester, but it was quite another thing for his son to actually consider an occupation in the sport. Work with your hands and work hard at a traditional job was William's view. However, Walter was an independent sort and determined to find his own way.

As he had improved as a caddie, Hagen had not only looped for better golfers but for higher-profile members of the Country Club of Rochester. Among those for whom he carried the bag were George Eastman, whose financial and artistic influences are still felt today in Rochester; Walter and John Powers, hotel owners; Harry Strong of Stromberg Carburetor Company; Beekman Little, a prominent businessman who fortuitously was head of the greens committee; and others who were turning Rochester into an important city on the North-east-Midwest border.

These high-powered people took a shine to the energetic and skill-ful caddie, and there was no objection to Walter using the course for frequent practice rounds. Because he was allowed to practice more than his peers, and because of his talent, Walter emerged as the best player in the caddie ranks at the club. Strong came up with the idea of sending Hagen, as player-captain, with five other caddies to a nearby course to challenge a team of caddies there in a three-match tourna-ment. The Country Club of Rochester team won two out of three, and Strong rewarded the players with trophies.

What he observed of country club life turned out to be almost as important for Hagen as improving his golf skills. He was fascinated with how club members and their wives acted and dressed. Young Walter looked, listened, and remembered. And as he recalled many years later, "I was tremendously impressed by the conversations and discussions of these men regarding their vacations in Florida and other famous resort spots both here and abroad [and] about big-game hunting in Africa and India. I admired the ease with which they spoke of huge money deals, and I certainly eyed wishfully their fancy golfing outfits—tweed jackets, colorful argyles, and knickers."

On off-duty weekend nights during the season, Hagen sat atop the hill and gazed toward the Country Club of Rochester. He took in the orchestra playing, couples dancing, the finery of their clothing and jewelry, their waiting cars and chauffeurs, the colorful drinks and drift-ing cigarette smoke (though he neither drank nor smoked until after he moved away from Rochester), and the men wheeling and dealing on the verandah. Walter aspired to be a gentleman, preferably one with deep financial resources.

After Walter Hagen's death, reflecting on this experience his father had, Walter Hagen Jr. said, "It set Dad's standards. He always wanted a look of success all up and down the line."

To Hagen, the appearance of success was as important if not more so than success itself. One of his two most famous sayings would be, "I never wanted to be a millionaire, I just wanted to live like one."

As an aside, Walter Hagen has a rival in being the most famous person associated with golf to come from Rochester: Robert Trent Jones Sr., the top golf course architect and designer in post–World War II America. They did not know each other in Rochester—Jones was sixteen years Hagen's junior—but their paths crossed in later years in some remarkably coincidental ways, especially at the 1951 U.S. Open at Oakland Hills in Michigan.

Hagen had dreams of entering the U.S. Open in 1912, not only because he wanted to take a shot at the country's best-known golf contest (along with the U.S. Amateur) but also because it was to be held in Buffalo, an easy trip. He asked Andy Christy if he could go for it.

"Not a chance," the head pro said. "I don't mind giving you three days off to go up there and maybe learn something, but I'm not letting a nineteen-year-old kid make a fool of himself in that fast Open crowd."

Though Christy didn't think Hagen was ready to qualify, let alone compete in the U.S. Open, he did want the young man to be introduced to the National Championship experience. He invited Hagen to accompany him and Alf Campbell, the head pro at a nearby course, to Buffalo. The two pros had arranged for themselves and Hagen to play a practice round preceding the Open. Walter shot a 73, bettering his elders.

Hagen couldn't stay for the Open itself, however, because the shop and members of the Country Club of Rochester had to be attended to. As the boss, Christy got to stay in Buffalo, so his assistant was sent back to work.

Though glad that McDermott had successfully defended, Hagen told Christy when the pro returned, "They're not the players I expected." Part of this is arrogance, as Hagen had up to this point not been involved in competitions outside the Rochester area and couldn't knowledgeably evaluate the level of talent. However, except for McDermott and a handful of others, the lineup of professional golfers in the U.S. was neither long nor deep. Perhaps, especially after shooting the 73 in Buffalo, there was not a large gap between Hagen and the American players competing in professional tournaments. Offering more support than he had the week before, Christy suggested that Hagen sign up for the Canadian Open, to be held a few weeks later in Toronto.

Hagen might not have been awed by the caliber of play in Buffalo, but something else he saw there made a lifelong impression: how a professional golfer should dress, especially if he wants to be the center of attention.

Tom Anderson Jr., the brother of four-time Open champion Willie Anderson, was in the 1912 field. He wore a pure white silk shirt with bright red, yellow, blue, and black stripes; his white flannel pants had cuffs turned up just once; around his neck was a red bandanna and on his head was a plaid cap; and his white buckskin shoes had thick red rubber soles and wide white laces.

"His outfit just about knocked my eyes out," Hagen recalled forty-four years later. "Tom had class! In my small-town life he was the most tremendous personality I'd ever seen. I decided right then to copy that outfit from white buckskins to bandanna."

However, he was still a lowly assistant pro, so when the Canadian Open began, all Hagen could afford was the red bandanna.

A friend of Christy's, George Cummings, a former winner of the Canadian Championship whom Hagen had caddied for in Rochester years earlier, entered the brash nineteen-year-old in the tournament. With his clubs over one shoulder, Hagen got on a boat, only the second time he'd been on one (the other being a tourist boat under Niagara Falls), and crossed Lake Ontario to Toronto. No one there had expectations for the unknown player participating in his first professional tournament.

Hagen recalled being excited about being in Toronto and in a "foreign" country for the first time. He didn't get to experience much of the city, though. Other than a dinner arranged by Cummings to meet some of the other players , Hagen spent his time on golf.

He didn't generate headlines, but he didn't do badly either. George Sargent won the Canadian Open, transplanted American Jim Barnes was second, and Hagen finished tied for eleventh. With over a hundred entrants, Hagen had made a solid pro debut, but he hadn't met his own expectations—maybe professional golf was a tougher business than he thought, after all. He had never threatened the top of the leaderboard, but he was consoled by the fact that he finished a stroke ahead of one of his golf heroes, Alex Smith, the Scot who had won the U.S. Open in 1906 (his 295 breaking 300 for the first time in the event) and 1910.

There was no fuss about Hagen's finish back in Rochester. Indeed, few club members noticed he was gone for a week. After this one fling with tournament golf, it was back to work. He was asked to fill the role of head pro temporarily at the Owesco Country Club in Auburn, New York. With Christy's permission, Hagen went, bringing with him one hundred clubs the two had made the previous winter.

He was at Owesco for two weeks, and they ran him ragged. Hagen was not only the head pro but the club manager, bartender, greens keeper, instructor, and manager of the pro shop. He began his day at 4:00 a.m. and turned off the lights at 11:00 p.m. Helping him stay awake was selling ninety-nine of the clubs for $2.75 each, for a very tidy sum. The one hundredth club Hagen presented to a young lady who danced with him his last night there. With this experience coming on the heels of the one in Toronto, Hagen had surely tasted what life was like beyond Rochester's borders.

He had been such a hit at Owesco that the club members asked him to stay on as the permanent head pro. Hagen promised to consider the offer on the trip home. When he arrived back at the Country Club of Rochester his consideration became more complicated. Christy was leaving to take the head pro job at the Equinox Club in Manchester, Vermont. Did Walter want to take over here?

He was flattered by the offer. After all, he was still a few months shy of his twentieth birthday. He would be paid the solid sum of $1,200 a year plus $2 an hour for lessons. Swelling the pot was the $1.50 a month per set for keeping two hundred sets of clubs clean during the eight-month off-season. He could also spend the off-season making clubs to sell the rest of the year. With his father getting older while still working a backbreaking job to feed a family of seven, Walter knew that being the head pro of Rochester would make life a lot easier for all of them. And as a sideline, he could keep making money from the Rochester Ramblers.

At the same time, he had just gotten several whiffs of the world beyond Rochester and specifically how exciting real tournament competition could be. Being head pro meant he would have very little time for traveling, and as an instructor he would have to pay a lot more attention to the games of others than to his own. For the most part, any dreams he had of being a championship-level golfer would be dashed, or at least put on hold indefinitely.

The job offer placed him at a crossroads, with dozens of questions to be answered: Did he want to dedicate his life to golf, which meant, among other things, that he could not pursue professional baseball? Was he really talented and tough enough to make a career as a club professional, a job which in America didn't have much of a track record yet? Could his ego stand it? After all, at that time being a head pro at a private golf club, though a position of some respect in the immediate golf community, still meant that you were hired help.

What if he turned down the job? (The Owesco one was already out because the compensation was much less.) He could go after tournament golf, but it could turn out that golf was just a fad here. Was there really much of a future in it? What if Americans never quite caught on to the game and were always second place, or worse, to the British? Was this where he wanted to go?

For the last time in his life, Hagen took the conservative approach by accepting the job. He hired his baseball buddy, George Christ, as his assistant. Then he got his father out of the railroad car sweatbox by hiring him as the club's greens keeper.

Good sense had won out. Better to be on the safe side, because with the British still essentially owning golf—McDermott's wins had to be an aberration, and the early word was that Harry Vardon and Ted Ray were coming over next year to recapture the U.S. Open—the future of the sport as a profession was just too dicey as far as Americans were concerned.

It might not be so bad to stay and work in Rochester, whatever the job, just like his father and grandfather had done.

CHAPTER 4

THE REPORTS WERE TRUE: The British were coming. They were sending their most powerful ships across the Atlantic to fire broadsides at the upstart American golfers and bring the U.S. Open trophy back to Great Britain. Enough with this McDermott fellow, who clearly had conquered because of thin and inferior competition. And what better place for Harry Vardon and Ted Ray (who had won the 1912 British Open, dethroning Vardon) to spank the Yanks than The Country Club outside Boston, not far from where other upstart Americans began to think better of themselves.

For American golf, 1912 had been a good year. A "homebred," McDermott, had successfully defended the U.S. Open Championship. And the sport continued to grow in popularity, though editors still wouldn't let it share the front page of sports sections with baseball. Unknown at the time was another reason that 1912 was a very good year: It produced Byron Nelson, Sam Snead, and Ben Hogan, all born within a few months of each other. This trio would grab the torch passed on by Walter Hagen, Bobby Jones, and Gene Sarazen.

The year was good to Hagen personally. He had gotten his first taste of professional tournament golf at the Canadian Open, then landed a good job at the club he had been connected to for over half his life. Conceivably, given his golf skills, energy, and charm, he could remain a club pro indefinitely, becoming more of a favorite among the well-heeled members and playing in the occasional tournament for the prestige and extra income. This would be the safe and secure direction to take.

For a time, Hagen followed this path. He spent the winter again in the shop making and repairing clubs, this time as the head man (though he was just turning twenty) with George Christ at his side. During spring Hagen was in charge of the pro shop, he gave lessons, he dealt with the club's officers, and he carried out all the other duties of head professional that had previously been the responsibility of Christy.

However, as summer progressed Hagen increasingly felt the urge to compete—not just in the Country Club of Rochester events but the real thing, like he had experienced in the Canadian Open. On his home course it had become routine to shoot 70 or lower. No one else affiliated with the club came close to matching his scores. For a young man with dreams of sports glory, who had observed some of the National Championship and acquitted himself well enough in a pro tourney the year before, it made sense to think big and, given his gumption, act upon it.

In 1913, the U.S. Open was being held in Massachusetts, and the great Harry Vardon was expected in the field. This was an opportunity Hagen couldn't resist. And this year, he didn't need anyone's permission to send off an entry form.

Still, having the head pro of the Country Club of Rochester make the short trip to Buffalo to watch a U.S. Open was one thing; letting him have enough time off to travel to Boston to participate in the National Championship was another. Once Hagen had made up his mind to take the plunge and play in the 1913 Open, he had to beg the officers of the Rochester club to grant him four days to let him go to it.

Aside from Vardon's and Ray's presence in the event and the flowing of competitive juices, Hagen had another reason to give the National Championship a shot. As he recalled years later, "I figured if I were ever going to make a name for myself, I'd better be getting started. After all, I was twenty years old."

Club officials gave their permission. Hagen packed his "strange weapons" and some clothes and took the overnight train to Boston. On September 15, he checked into the Copley Square Hotel, where most of the other top players were staying. He would gladly blow a week's salary, or more, to be with the big boys and add to the attitude that he belonged at the Open. According to Hagen's account, he asked the desk clerk, "Where's the National Open being played?"

"At The Country Club," the clerk replied.

"Which country club?" Hagen insisted, thinking that in the Boston area there might be quite a few.

"*The* Country Club," said the clerk to one who was obviously a Rochester rube.

An hour later Hagen was at The Country Club. According to the golf writer Charles Price, he "showed up at Brookline dressed like a minstrel minus the banjo and announced to the other pros in a squeaky voice that he had come to help them 'stop the British.' Even Johnny McDermott laughed."

At the time, in the middle of the course was a racetrack and next to it was a polo field. Parked all around the clubhouse were long red and yellow touring cars, and emerging from them were well-dressed men and women. An impressed Hagen recognized that this was indeed the big time, and he liked the excitement rippling through the air.

Perhaps it was his self-confidence from dominating the Rochester course, or feeling that he really didn't have anything to lose—Hagen had no intention of being just a bit of set decoration during the drama. As Price mentioned, and as Ouimet later reported to Grant-land Rice, upon arrival in the locker room Hagen announced, "The name is Hagen. I've come down from Rochester to help you fellows stop Vardon and Ray." While McDermott laughed, a few others snickered and others within earshot stared at the brash unknown dressed like a dandy and then went about their business.

The 1913 U.S. Open, held twenty-five years after John Reid and his friends played their first round in Yonkers, is truly a David versus Goliath story, even more so because in this contest David had to face two Goliaths at once. Harry Vardon and Ted Ray not only brought to The Country Club their experience and skills but also an aura of in-vincibility. With the exception of Johnny McDermott and the cocky kid from Rochester, many of the players believed that at best they were competing for third place.

Vardon and Ray were anxious to win not only for God and country but also to stick it to McDermott. It would be especially sweet to topple the defending champion because of what had happened at the Shawnee Open a few weeks before.

Played in Pennsylvania on a course overlooking the Delaware River, the Shawnee Open had been the first official tournament the English duo had entered upon their arrival in the States. It gave them a chance to size up the American competition before they embarked on an event-packed exhibition tour. Also in the field was McDermott, who had just won the Western Open and was practically hyperventilating at the prospect of sending the Brits a strong message. Up to this point, the Brits had won every exhibition match, including one that included McDermott.

As it turned out, the mercurial McDermott did win, and win big, by 12 strokes, 13 strokes over Vardon, and 15 strokes over Ray. At the Shawnee Open award ceremony, the victor made a gracious speech, complimenting Vardon and Ray and expressing the wish that their stay in the States would be a pleasant and profitable one. Then he suddenly held aloft the 1912 U.S. Open trophy and shouted, "But you are not going to take back our cup!"

The officials and some of the spectators were embarrassed at the discourtesy. It was clear that the two vaunted visitors were insulted. The tournament committee asked McDermott to apologize. He did, emphasizing that he hadn't meant to damage any feelings. Then, glaring at Vardon and Ray, he insisted, "But you are *still* not going to take back our cup!"

They were a formidable twosome. Harry Vardon was familiar to some Americans from having won in the U.S. in 1900, his exhibition tours, and the Vardon Flyer golf balls (which were no longer in use). His collection of claret jugs made a strong impression too. At forty-three, he was a serious, disciplined golfer who wore serious clothes, including a jacket no matter what the temperature.

Ted Ray's reputation, while not that of Vardon's, had been growing stronger in the States. He was thirty-six, a big, husky man who could hit the ball farther than most competitors. He wore a white snap-brimmed hat in competition and swung with a pipe protruding from his mouth. He and his compatriot were determined to reassert the British way of golf—that way including domination of the U.S.

Open, which had been the case until McDermott defeated second-rate fields.

The British duo finished their summer exhibition swing in time for the Open, which had been moved to September to accommodate them. They had amassed a record of 40–1 in exhibition matches against American and expatriate British challengers.

While perhaps allowing himself to dream of winning the National Championship, and despite his confidence in his abilities, Hagen realized that at the very least if he could compete with the two British pros he could learn a lot from them, not only golf skills but how champions carried themselves. He was quite in awe of Vardon and Ray when introduced to them, especially Vardon, who had won both the U.S. and British Opens, the latter five times. (Vardon would win the British Open for the sixth and last time in 1914.)

"I stood around and gawked at him like any other greenhorn from the pastures," Hagen recalled. The gawking was only partly awe, though: To improve his own game, he vowed to observe and adapt everything the great Vardon did. Indeed, before the end of the Open, Hagen would abandon his own swing and use the copy he made of Vardon's, which he would keep for the rest of his competitive career.

Herbert Warren Wind later explained that during the '13 Open, "Hagen carefully studied Vardon's uncomplicated, classic swing, paying particular attention to Vardon's stance and rhythm. Hagen's awareness that his own method of hitting the ball could be improved had earlier helped him make his swing more technically sound, and the adjustments he made after watching Vardon were also steps in the right direction."

He never became as smooth a technician as Vardon. "Hagen, however, was never able to eradicate a tendency to sway on his backswing," Wind continued. "This was probably due to the unusual wide stance he took when addressing the ball and to his penchant for turning his hips excessively on the backswing. He understood the importance of hitting through the ball, and in his concern for getting his right side into his hitting action he developed a distinctive follow-through, in which his right shoulder was the part of his body nearest the hole at the finish of his swing."

It might seem odd and unwise that Hagen would alter his swing or any part of his game during the National Championship. But he was only twenty, his game still evolving, and he was observing firsthand the finest player on the planet. It was, actually, a smart move on his part to use his observational skills to absorb what Vardon had to display and improve his own game accordingly.

Other than the two big Brits and the defending champion, there were other indications that the 1913 Open would be the biggest event in the history of golf in America. Mike Brady, Tommy McNamara, Jerry Travers, Macdonald Smith, and Jim Barnes, the cream of the emerging American crop, had entered. Overall, there were more entrants—162— than any previous National Championship. The great French golfer Louis Tellier had made the crossing and so had Wilfrid Reid, an Englishman (and Tellier's brother-in-law), who was starting to challenge the top level of players in Great Britain. Thanks to Vardon and Ray there was heightened press interest. And the setting couldn't be better—one of the first golf clubs in the States, in Massachusetts in September.

Unofficially presiding over the event was William Howard Taft, who only ten months before had unsuccessfully run for a second term as president, turning the office and the White House golf facilities over to Woodrow Wilson. Taft represented the closest that the U.S. Open would come to matching the British Open in hosting royalty and further raised the stature of the 1913 National Championship.

Completely overlooked by competitors was a fragile-looking twenty-year-old named Francis Ouimet, an American whose only distinction to that point was having won the Massachusetts State Amateur title. Friends had talked him into entering the U.S. Open just to gain some experience.

According to Charles Price, in his *The World of Golf,* "Into this ultra-sophisticated picture stepped Francis, pure of heart and innocent of mind, with the look about him of someone who doesn't quite know what it's all about. He didn't smoke, drink, swear. He honored his mother and respected his father. He believed in honesty, politeness, and hard work. Were it not for the fact that he was brought up next to a golf course, his favorite games probably would have been baseball or football and his heroes would have been Christy Mathewson or Pudge Heffelfinger. He somehow wasn't real, this Francis. He was Tom Swift with a golf club in his hand."

Because there was an unprecedented number of entrants, there were two days of qualifying. It became clear during the 36-hole rounds that in this tournament there would be an elite group and then everyone else. Also at this time, Ouimet made his first impression. Over 36 holes Vardon led the qualifiers with a 151, but the young amateur was just one stroke back.

The second day, the second-seeded Ray shot a 148 to top the qualifiers. Smith, McDermott, Brady, and a few others posted good scores, as did a no-name from New York State, W. C. Hagin—as he was referred to in the Boston papers and even the young Grantland Rice's reports back to New York City—with a 157 on the second day, alone in third place. Whatever happened after this, both Ouimet and Hagen had made their friends proud by qualifying.

It was time for golf history to be made.

The U.S. Open itself was 72 holes on the par-74 course with 36 holes on one day and 36 the next. At the end of the first day the only surprise was that the Englishman tied with Vardon for first place, at 147, was not Ted Ray but Wilfrid Reid. Ray was in good shape, though, just 2 strokes back, and at 150 were Smith and Barnes.

The new kids on the block, Ouimet and Hagen, had pleasantly surprised the Bostonians and other American spectators by shooting 151s, just 4 strokes from Vardon. Not exhibiting any Open rookie jitters, Hagen had shot a 73 in the morning round. According to one account, "When Hagen teed off on Thursday morning, he stuck his drive in the middle of the first fairway, acknowledged the polite applause he received, and walked off the tee whistling like a man on his way to the barbershop."

On Thursday's second 18, he went out in 38, but suffered some reversals, including a double-bogey, and finished the back nine at four over par for a 78. Hagen was not out of it by any means, though, finishing the day only 4 strokes back.

Perhaps the British visitors were a tad tense at not having run away with the Open on the first day, or what happened that night was due to the postplay nerves of those involved in the biggest golf event America had ever seen. Ray and Reid were also staying at the Copley Square

Hotel, and at dinner they had a discussion about the British tax system that escalated to an argument and then to volleys of personal insults. The burly Ray reached across the table and punched Reid in the nose. Reid recovered and went after Ray; the two went at it in the middle of the dining room until staff pulled them apart. As it turned out, the fight energized Ray and effectively (if not literally) knocked Reid out of contention.

At the end of the first 18 holes of the second day, Ray caught up to Vardon and they were tied at 225. But what had the crowd abuzz was that Ouimet had caught the two Brits for a three-way tie atop the leaderboard. Who *was* this kid?

The Ouimet family had moved into a house across the street from The Country Club when Francis was six. His father was a laborer with no interest in golf. Francis became intrigued, however, when he watched members play while he was cutting through the grounds of The Country Club on his way to school. Along the way he discovered and picked up gutta-perchas (made from a rubberlike substance obtained from a species of Malaysian tree), including Vardon Flyers, the golf ball in use in 1900.

Wilfred Ouimet became a caddie at The Country Club, and when he was done with them he passed on to his younger brother the golf clubs members had discarded. Francis looked through the fence at players on the course. Back at home he imitated the swings of the ones who made the best shots. Eventually, he and Wilfred built a small and rudimentary 3-hole course behind their house. Ironically, because Francis was too young to caddie, he got to use the family course more than his brother, and the daily practice made him a better player.

Francis acquired a caddie's job at The Country Club when he was eleven. There he watched players such as Jerry Travers, Walter Travis, Alex Smith, Willie Anderson, and others compete in various events. He kept watching and practicing, and after finishing eighth grade he entered his first tournament, the Greater Boston Interscholastic Championship, which was only for high schoolers, but an exception was made for Ouimet. He was eliminated in the first round by J. H. Sullivan. During the tournament he met Sullivan's sister and later married her.

He tried again the following year, and the year after that. Finally, at fifteen, Ouimet won the championship, crushing his opponent in the final of the match-play event 10 and 9.

Conveniently enough, the U.S. Amateur in 1910 was to be played at The Country Club. Ouimet borrowed $25 from his mother for the entry fee (paying her back by working in a dry-goods store after school) but failed to qualify by one stroke. Next year, same story. In 1912, same story again.

However, in 1913 he won the Massachusetts State Amateur (the first of six times he won this tournament) and thus qualified for the U.S. Amateur. He lost in the semifinal on the 34th hole to Jerry Travers, but withstanding the pressure of one of the country's two National Championships would be an invaluable experience later that year.

With all the top-notch talent in town for the U.S. Open, the more experienced caddies were taken. Agreeing to loop for Ouimet was Eddie Lowery, a local ten-year-old, the second of seven children in a fatherless family whose mother worked two jobs. Thanks to his older brother, Eddie had just started doing some caddying at The Country Club for 25 cents a round.

A problem with being on the bag for Ouimet during the U.S. Open was that was it was mid-September and school had started up again, so when the qualifying rounds were held and then the Open itself, Eddie had to play hooky from school. The first day he and his brother Jack were caught and returned to school. Eddie escaped again, though, and made it to the club where he hid out behind the caddie shack until the qualifying round was about to start; he then grabbed Ouimet's bag and headed out on the course, where there were no truant officers.

"W. C. Hagin" could easily have been overlooked in all the excitement over the duel between Vardon and Ray and the surprising challenge of Ouimet. And it's true that very little mention is made of Hagen's play during the first two rounds. However, though his day was a subdued one, he was making a good impression on the crowd.

By the end of the first 36 holes that Thursday, Vardon and Reid led at 147. But the big news for the hometown crowd and press was that Ouimet was only 4 strokes behind. Another local favorite, Tom McNamara, whose brother was the caddie master at The Country Club and had been Ouimet's boss, was still in the running at 158.

It was on the second day, despite cold nor'easter conditions, that Hagen threatened to win. His early holes were almost disastrous, with a double-bogey 7 on the 3rd. But then he eagled the sixth, evening things up. As most of the other players fell back in the horrendous weather, Hagen stayed steady, shooting a 76 to put him alone in second place, two shots back of Ouimet, Vardon, and Ray in his first National Championship and only his second professional tournament.

According to Wind, Hagen "showed at The Country Club he was already a talented shot maker. He excelled on pitch shots to the green . . . and on the greens he was something to behold. He had a lovely natural putting stroke, an ability to read the contours and the speed of the greens, and the confidence to hole the different putts when it counted."

It was almost comical by the start of the final 18 holes: Standing between the two best golfers in the world and the U.S. Open trophy were a pale, twenty-year-old stringbean who had only just won a state amateur championship, a caddie who was supposed to be sitting in a sixth-grade classroom, and a kid from Rochester who couldn't get his name spelled right by anyone. (The *New York Times* was one of the worst offenders, referring to him as Willie Hagin.)

As startled as the competitors, spectators, and media were, no one expected Ouimet and Eddie to survive the last 18 holes under National Championship pressure. It was time for Vardon and Ray to take Ouimet to school and capture the trophy. There was a crucial ingredient overlooked, though: During both days of the Open there had been some off-and-on rain that became a downpour Friday afternoon, creating soggy conditions, and Ouimet's local knowledge of the course gave him an advantage. And as it also turned out, the young man also had steel guts.

Ted Ray finished the final round first, struggling to a 79 and a 304 total. Vardon was also slipping and sliding and notched a 79 to match his countryman. Barnes rallied, then quickly faded. Hagen mounted a genuine challenge, and for a while it seemed like another twenty-year-old unknown would stand up to the great British veterans.

During the first nine of the last round, Hagen had an eagle and two birdies, which allowed him to actually tie the leaders. He stayed even with them through 10, 11, 12, and 13. If he could just keep this up and look for an opportunity to jump ahead . . .

He couldn't. The par-5 14th was a Waterloo for Hagen. He knew that Vardon and Ray had birdied this hole and he endeavored to do the same. But on his second shot he played a brassie out of a close, wet lie and topped the ball into more trouble. He wound up with a double-bogey that ended his chances. He finished at 307.

Smith and McDermott, who had begun the round 5 strokes back, couldn't get enough going. If U.S. hopes had to be pinned on the skinny kid and his barely-out-of-diapers caddie . . . well, bring the Open trophy to the dock for the trip across the Atlantic.

On the front nine Ouimet shot a 43, which left his chances on life support. The only excitement remaining was whether Vardon's or Ray's name would go on the trophy after the next day's play-off. The local newspapers could report that the kid played hard and lasted longer than anyone expected. He could go back home with his head high and one day tell his grandchildren how he almost beat a member of the Great Triumvirate.

Apparently, everyone thought this way except Francis Ouimet. Creating a "darkest before the dawn" situation, Ouimet took a five on the short par-4 10th hole, and fell further back. A par on 11 stopped the bleeding, but only temporarily because he then bogeyed the 12th. To gain a tie he had to play the remaining six holes at 2 under par, a seemingly impossible feat considering that the great Vardon and Ray had each played his round 8 over par, and the weather hadn't improved.

Ouimet birdied the 13th, holing a chip from the edge of the green. He parred the par-5 14th hole. After a nice drive from the 15th tee, his second shot went into deep rough. He dug the ball out and it landed 3 feet from the hole. Par. He needed to play the last three holes at 1 under.

At 16, he was in trouble, needing a 9-footer just to save par. He got it. His drive on 17 landed in the fairway, his second shot wound up 20 feet from the cup, much of it downhill. It was time for what Herbert Warren Wind would call the most crucial of "the golf shots heard 'round the world."

Because of the drama of the moment, not only was the green surrounded by thousands of hushed spectators, but traffic on the road that ran past the 17th hole had come to a standstill, and a few impatient and disinterested drivers were beeping their horns. Ouimet wasted no time. He gave the putt a good ride. The ball hit the back of the cup, popped straight up into the air, then dropped in. Birdie.

It would remain the most dramatic putt on this hole for eighty-six years, until Justin Leonard's 45-footer on the same 17th won the Ryder Cup for the U.S. Writing about the U.S. Open in anticipation of the 1914 event at Midlothian outside Chicago, the columnist Will Grimsley declared that Ouimet's putt on 17 in Brookline in the final round "was responsible for the great awakening of golf in America."

The crowd let loose its pent-up tension, shouting and jumping and pounding each other on the back. They calmed, though, both out of courtesy and the realization that Ouimet still had to handle the long par-4 18th to be part of the play-off.

His drive was straight. His second shot was at the flag, though it landed short of the green. He chipped to 5 feet from the cup. Ignoring the tension and significance of the moment, Ouimet took the putter from Eddie, stood over the ball, and sent it toward the hole. When it fell in, the crowd was convulsed with cheering and crying. Ouimet was hoisted up and carried by the crowd.

Once Ouimet finally made his way to the locker room—where the pros could meet him, since they were not allowed in the clubhouse— the other American players greeted him warmly. When all had seemed lost, young Francis had come through to give the United States the chance to keep the Open cup. Hagen took Ouimet aside to say good-bye; he had to get back to the Country Club of Rochester and resume his everyday duties. "You did it, kiddo," Hagen said. "And you'll do it again tomorrow." (Hagen pocketed $77.50 for finishing tied for fourth with Barnes, Smith, and Tellier.)

Hard to imagine this happening today, but after Ouimet finished the 72nd hole of the U.S. Open, was tied with the two best players in the world, had been carried by a tumultuous crowd, and faced a play-off the next day for the National Championship, he walked across the street to have supper with his parents and siblings at home.

He took a bath and was in bed in the same old room by 9:30. A tossing and turning night? Nope. He slept until 8 o'clock the next morning, Saturday, September 20, 1913, the day that would change golf forever in America.

· · ·

Francis Ouimet ate a simple breakfast and walked back across the street to The Country Club where Eddie, wearing a white shirt and tie like Francis, was waiting. So was Frank Hoyt, a good friend of Francis's. On the practice range Hoyt pointed out the obvious: Ouimet was going into the most important round of golf in his life with a caddie who was ten, had only a few weeks' experience, and during the past two days had struggled to keep pace with Ouimet's long strides. Hoyt offered to carry the bag.

Ouimet was unable to make a decision, not wanting to insult his friend and not wanting to spurn the adolescent loyalty of Eddie. Finally, Hoyt offered Eddie money to give up the bag. Eddie said no. Hoyt made another appeal to Francis. He looked at Eddie. Seeing the tears in the boy's eyes, Ouimet gently thanked his friend and said he already had a caddie.

Eddie ran out on the range and tossed back every practice drive. As he was about to go to the first tee, Ouimet felt a hand on his shoulder. He turned to find McDermott standing next to him, about to pass the torch. "You're hitting the ball well, kid," the two-time champion said. "Now go out there and pay no attention to Vardon and Ray. Play your own game."

The three play-off participants drew straws, and Ouimet drew the first position. He hit a good drive, but so did his competitors. The rain persisted, and during the round it turned the course into something like a swamp. Undaunted, a crowd of thirty-five hundred to four thousand followed the trio from hole to hole. (Several accounts state that by the end of the play-off there were close to ten thousand people in the gallery.)

On the 5th hole Ouimet sent his second shot skipping out of bounds. He managed to bogey the par-4. But Vardon and Ray missed taking advantage of the opportunity by carding bogeys themselves. The three remained even, and Ouimet realized that the two older professionals were not levels above him—everyone's nerves were frayed. At least Francis was playing in front of a hometown crowd.

Incredibly, at the end of the first nine holes and in such soggy conditions, the three contestants were tied at 38.

Ouimet parred the par-3 10th; both Vardon and Ray bogeyed. For the first time, the local boy led in the play-off. All three made par on 11. On 12, Ouimet, gaining in confidence, outdrove both rivals. They bogeyed, Ouimet got par, and he was up by 2 strokes with six holes to go.

Vardon made birdie on 13, while Ray and Ouimet secured pars, so the lead was cut to 1. It was time for the experienced campaigner to move in for the kill, and his steely gaze was meant to melt young Francis. But perhaps with McDermott's words in his mind, Ouimet focused on his own game. All three got pars on 14.

Ray had a disaster on 15 and put himself out of the running. He was the first one of the three on the day to find a bunker, on this hole with his second shot. (His drive had been poor too, but had hit a spectator standing on the right in the head and bounced onto the fairway.) It took two swings to get the ball out of the bunker, and the second one had been so furious that the ball went through the green to the fringe. Two putts from there and the enraged Ray had a double-bogey 6. Ouimet and Vardon each earned pars.

It was between the British legend and the kid who lived across the street and looked as though the stiff wind should knock him down. Ouimet and Eddie carefully went about their routine. Vardon, allowing a sign of nerves, lit up a cigarette. The two in the duel parred 16. Vardon had two holes to catch the pup.

On the 17th, a 360-yard dogleg left, Vardon teed off first. Running out of holes, he decided to gamble by cutting the corner and going for the green. The ball hooked and was short, coming to rest in a bunker. His next shot had to be conservative, just get the ball back into the fairway. He was on the green in 4 but missed the putt, meaning bogey.

With his opponent in trouble from the tee, Ouimet had the luxury (and sense) not to take any risks. His drive was in the fairway, and the shot from his mashie landed 18 feet from the cup. All he needed was par to gain a stroke. With steady hands he gripped his putter and stroked. The ball dropped in for a birdie. With one hole to play, Ouimet had a 3-stroke lead.

He and Lowery were all business. Ouimet's tee shot on the 18th was down the middle. His second shot landed on the green. His putt left him with 4 feet to go. That's when his nerves faltered. It finally became clear to Francis that he was going to win the U.S. Open. He hesitated, his hands quivering, stepped back, took a deep breath, exchanged looks with Eddie, and stood over the ball. He holed the putt for par and the National Championship.

Ray had birdied the hole but was already too far back. Vardon had double-bogeyed. Ouimet had won the U.S. Open play-off by 5 shots.

The British golf writer Bernard Darwin had been with the trio of players every step of the way, carrying Ouimet's scorecard (two American reporters had carried the Brits' cards), and he too was astonished by the outcome. "I felt like a war correspondent on some stricken field, sending home news of the annihilation of the British Army," he wrote. "But the victory had been so glorious that no grudging of it was possible."

At the trophy presentation, with a sheepish grin Ouimet said, "I am as much surprised and pleased as anyone here. Naturally, it always was my hope to win out. I simply tried my best to keep this cup from going to our friends across the water. I am very glad to have been the agency for keeping the cup in America."

The twenty-year-old celebrated by drinking Horse's Neck, a blend of ginger ale and lemon juice.

Ouimet's astonishing victory was a hot news story that spread like fire across the country. More important, it put golf on the front pages of the major dailies, brushing aside even the baseball pennant races that September. American children everywhere put down their bats and picked up mashies and niblicks.

Gene Saraceni, eleven at the time and before he changed his name to Sarazen, was one of those who tossed the bat aside for a golf club. In his final interview, published in *Golf Digest* in August 1999, the ninety-seven-year-old Squire recalled hearing that an ex-caddie had defeated the great Vardon and Ray: "So from then on, I became very interested in golf, and I copied everything that Francis Ouimet did, even the way he gripped the club."

"Ouimet World's Golf Champion," blared the headline on page one of the *New York Times,* the first time the outcome of a professional golf tournament in the country had been put on the *Times'* front page. The subheads went on to proclaim "Twenty-Year-Old Amateur Defeats Famous British Professionals for Open Title," "Remarkable Golf Feat," and "Splendid Display of Nerve."

The article reported, "When Ouimet holed his final stroke on the home green of the Country Club this afternoon the 4,000 persons who had tramped through the heavy mist and dripping grass behind the trio of players for almost three hours realized what the victory meant to American golf, and the scenes of elation which followed were pardonable under the circumstances."

The piece jumped to the front page of the sports section, under an eight-column headline, and was accompanied by photographs and two sidebar stories. The newspaper had far exceeded any previous golf coverage.

On its front page the *Boston Traveler and Evening Standard*'s headline declared that the contest between the local lad and the visiting British pros had been the "Greatest Battle in the History of American Golf."

Darwin, reporting on the scene for the *Daily Mail,* wrote, "I did not believe in the possibility of an actual defeat . . . And if I had no real fears, I think that the Americans had no real hopes. That their boy hero, after a night to sleep on it, should go out in cold blood and beat, not one, but two champions, was too much to hope for."

Defeating the British at their own game on American soil and in Boston to boot caused great excitement and curiosity among sports fans. Golf began to soar as a recreational (and spectator) sport. At the end of 1912, just before Ouimet's win, there were 350,000 Americans playing golf; ten years later, by the end of 1922, with the accomplishments that year of Hagen and Sarazen, close to 2 million Yanks were having at it on golf courses.

After the Open, Vardon and Ray finished up their exhibition tour. (One eager spectator when they played in Atlanta was eleven-year-old Bobby Jones.) They then sailed for home. Upon arrival in England, they were unhappy to discover that their representatives had booked them in three consecutive tournaments. By the end of the third, the physically exhausted (the big, lumbering Ray struggled to complete the last two holes) and mentally punished duo (from all the queries about the U.S. Open) had had enough.

After a reporter asked Ray what he was going to do next, the fed-up golfer shouted, "Do? I'm going back home tonight and have a bloody good sitdown!" And Ray returned to his home club, sat in his favorite chair, and remained in it brooding for two weeks.

Ouimet turned out to be far from a flash in the pan and ended up being one of the most revered and respected figures in golf. He won the U.S. Amateur Championship in 1914, again turning back Britain's best in that field, and won a second amateur title seventeen years later. As a player or captain he was on every Walker Cup team from the international amateur event's official inception in 1922 to 1949 (being a friend and mentor to Bobby Jones along the way). For many years Ouimet served on the Executive Committee of the U.S. Golf Association, was an executive in the baseball Boston Braves organization, and served as president of the NHL's Boston Bruins franchise.

A measure of the respect he was accorded on both sides of the Atlantic is that in 1951 he was the first American nominated to be a captain in the Royal and Ancient Golf Club at St Andrews. There is an entire room dedicated to him at the U.S. Golf Association Museum in Far Hills, New Jersey. When Ouimet died in September 1967, he was second only to Jones as the most admired figure in amateur American golf.

The cherub caddie Eddie Lowery was literally embraced by the crowd to the point that he almost had to seek shelter under the presentation platform. He had worn a red, white, and blue ribbon during the play-off, and the cheering crowd, flush with patriotism, passed the hat and presented the ten-year-old with over $100. This was $100 more than his amateur boss earned by winning the U.S. Open.

Like Ouimet, Lowery had a longtime connection to golf. He too won the Massachusetts Amateur, in 1927, he too served on the USGA's Executive Committee, and he was president of the Northern California Golf Association. He was part of the inaugural Crosby Pro-Am in 1937 (Bing Crosby, Bob Hope, and Lowery became good friends), and he became a close friend of golf legend Byron Nelson and later U.S. Open winner and golf commentator Ken Venturi.

In 1963, Lowery and Ouimet, who had kept in touch for half a century, were honored in Boston on the fiftieth anniversary of their Open victory. They remain united in two other ways: In the medal minted to celebrate the USGA's centennial in 1995, the image used was Ouimet and Lowery walking down a fairway in the 1913 event, and the Eddie Lowery Scholarship and the Francis Ouimet Scholarship are awarded each year to club pros and caddies in Massachusetts.

There is a much sadder story to tell about Johnny McDermott, the first one to take the National Championship away from the British. After the 1913 Open his skills and behavior became more erratic, and he was also subjected to some bad luck. The first homebred U.S. Open winner entered to play the British Open in 1914, but because of travel delays he arrived too late to tee off in the championship, which was won by Vardon. McDermott turned around and steamed back to the States; en route, his ship, the *Kaiser Wilhelm II,* collided with an English ship and sank. The golfer and other survivors drifted in a lifeboat in the middle of the Atlantic for over twenty-four hours before being rescued.

He returned to discover that he had been wiped out financially thanks to Wall Street investments that had gone sharply south. He took a job as a pro at the Atlantic City Country Club and retired from tournament play at twenty-three. According to Wind's *The Story of American Golf,* "Four scant years after Johnny McDermott had won at Chicago, golfers had to pause a moment and ponder before they could remember the name of the little firecracker who was the first American to win the United States Open."

Soon after, he suffered a mental breakdown, and despite several attempts by friends and family to turn things around, he was declared a lunatic and committed to the Norristown Hospital in Pennsylvania, where he remained for the rest of his life.

Some years later the hospital administration allowed McDermott to design and build a short 6-hole practice course on the grounds, and he played an occasional round on it. And one time, under supervision, he was allowed out of the mental hospital to play a full round of golf. He was brought to a course on Staten Island in New York. Over 18 holes, McDermott shot a 70. He was brought back to the institution and never played golf again.

There is a poignant epilogue to McDermott's story. In 1971, McDermott, with attendants, attended the U.S. Open at the Merion Golf Club just north of Philadelphia, where he had grown up and learned to become a champion. He was dressed so poorly that he was ordered out of the golf shop and then wasn't allowed near the clubhouse, where he had hoped to visit the players.

As McDermott slowly walked away he was recognized by Arnold

Palmer, who was on his way to the first tee. Palmer put his arm around the elderly two-time National Championship winner; they had a conversation about putting, and McDermott remained to watch the day's events as Palmer's guest. Two months later, a few days short of his eightieth birthday, McDermott died in his sleep.

On that day in 1913, Ouimet eclipsed everything McDermott did for golf. According to a retrospective that *Golfweek* published in 1999 on the most significant golf accomplishments of the twentieth century, "With his stunning upset victory in the 1913 U.S. Open, twenty-year-old Francis Ouimet singlehandedly accelerated the pace of golf's growth in America."

Though completely overlooked by the subsequent news reports, Hagen had acquitted himself well in the National Championship, far better than just about anyone back in Rochester could have expected. He had been in contention through 67 holes. And it was important to his future as a competitor that after the 14th-hole disaster on Friday the twenty-year-old Hagen didn't give up. He matched Vardon and Ray the remainder of the round. His 307 in difficult weather conditions, only 3 shots back at the end of the fourth round, was a fine U.S. Open debut.

He returned to Rochester as required, but served notice that the club should plan on giving him a few days off during the high season next year too. Upon his return from Boston, the brash head pro declared, "I'm going back next year and win that tournament." As was becoming very clear, Hagen was able to back up even the boldest statements.

As Al Barkow points out in the retrospective *Golf's Golden Grind: The History of the Tour*, ". . . something, or someone, happened at The Country Club in September 1913 that received only scant notice at the time but was to augur the rise, the ascendance of American professional golf and the tour. That someone was Walter Hagen."

CHAPTER 5

DESPITE HIS BOAST OF GOING BACK to the U.S. Open to "beat those guys," during the following fall, winter, and spring Hagen weighed other possibilities. Yes, there had been his strong showing in the 1913 U.S. Open and the thrill of being part of such a headline-making event. But Hagen discovered during the long Rochester winter that he still wasn't ready to make a commitment to competitive golf, or perhaps to golf at all.

He didn't want to jeopardize his job by adding tournaments to his schedule. His parents persisted in their belief that golf was not a way to make a steady living, though they acknowledged that as head pro he was earning good money for a twenty-year-old. The position also kept him close to home, and William Hagen was presumably better off in his middle age not having to work a steamy, backbreaking job thanks to his son having the authority to hire him at the Country Club of Rochester.

Another factor was that Hagen was still strongly attracted to baseball. His dedication to the sport and being an important member of the city championship team three years running made him think he could indeed carve out a career on the baseball diamond. Golf could be a sideline or a supplement to his baseball income during the off-season should he get a club pro position in Florida.

In December 1913, Hagen turned twenty-one. He didn't smoke or drink, was well regarded by the club members and their families, and though he had an eye for pretty girls he wasn't distracted by skirt chasing. Twenty-one seemed pretty old to him, though, and he decided it was now or never to reach for the Major Leagues.

No one cared at the time about Hagen's wavering between golf and baseball, so no account other than Hagen's own discusses his being torn between the two sports. However, in an interview with O.B. Keeler in the June 1925 issue of the *American Golfer,* Hagen talks at length about his infatuation with baseball and compares the sport to golf.

"I started out with the idea I'd like to be a professional ballplayer," he told Keeler. "As between baseball and golf, I fancy I was a more promising ballplayer than golfer."

Hagen went on to point out that what eventually began to sway him toward golf is that baseball is a team game, and players face a team of opponents. This was not as appealing as the solitary endeavors of a golfer, who for the most part is challenged only by the characteristics of the course and himself. There's also the indication in his remarks to Keeler that he could feel like more of a pioneer in golf than in the more established national pastime.

"There are such a lot of baseball players, and so many teams and leagues and stars," he said. "And I never could get away from that staring fact that in baseball my own game, however hard I might be trying, or however well I might be playing, was mixed up with and dependent on the game of a dozen or more other fellows, some with me and some against me, but all affecting me and my performance.

"That was the sticker, and it decided me against baseball," Hagen continued. "To be perfectly frank, I wanted to play my own game, in my own way, and take my drubbings or win my victories all by myself . . . I believe I am safe in saying I took [golf] up definitely while I was a better ballplayer than I was a golfer. It was individualism got me, I suppose."

At twenty-one, the choice was still to be made. There was no problem getting time off from the Rochester club in February. Hagen bought a train ticket and set off for Florida, his first journey to the South. After arriving, he made his way to the training site of the Philadelphia Nationals (soon to become the Phillies), a National League club, in Tarpon Springs.

The players worked out in the morning, then some of them played golf in the afternoon. Hagen arranged to show up a few afternoons in a row to help round out a foursome. He also just happened to mention to his new friends that he was a heck of a pitcher for a team that had won the Rochester City Championship three years in a row.

The ballplayers went back to Pat Moran, who agreed to invite the supposedly talented man for a tryout at the camp. (In his autobiography, Hagen cites Moran as the manager; however, Moran was a coach at the time and would later become manager of the Phillies. He was manager of the Cincinnati Reds when he died in 1924.) After a couple of days of observing that Hagen was a very good athlete with a powerful swing in batting practice, Moran arranged a tryout to see how good a pitcher Hagen was away from Rochester glory.

Being able to throw from both sides sure was an advantage, and Hagen did display a strong arm, but otherwise the tryout was not successful. Perhaps it was being so far from home for the first time or facing professional hitters, but Hagen suffered from wildness. When the control problems persisted, Moran announced that he'd seen enough.

He didn't drop the prospect hard, though. He liked that Hagen could hit from both sides of the plate and that he could throw the ball a mile. Moran suggested that Hagen work on all the aspects of his game and try again next year, for an outfield or first-base position.

Hagen took the train north feeling somewhat encouraged that he'd made a decent impression and a solid contact in Moran. Maybe 1914 wasn't going to be his year, but he could lay the foundation for a successful 1915 as an outfielder for the Philadelphia team.

But 1914 did turn out to be his year, in a way he didn't anticipate.

Hagen spent the rest of the winter and then the spring of 1914 doing what he usually did at the Country Club of Rochester: making and repairing clubs, giving lessons in ice skating and then tennis in addition to golf, and planning on playing more baseball so he could make the Philadelphia squad next time out.

As far as he was concerned, he had a real shot at making the team, and with baseball having been his first love, he was willing to put the sport ahead of golf. Apparently forgotten was the boast to go back and win the U.S. Open next time.

The Open that year was to be held at the Midlothian Golf Club just outside Chicago in August. Because of the distance and the expense involved and the fact that he had rated baseball as his priority sport, during the summer Hagen didn't make plans to participate in the National Championship. He rationalized too that during the summer he wouldn't be given permission to be gone a week.

"W. C. Hagin" might well have ended up being no more than a footnote to the amazing Francis Ouimet story of 1913 if not for the intervention of Ernest L. Willard.

One day in July, Hagen and a friend, Dutch Leonard, were sitting in the pro shop of the Country Club of Rochester talking about baseball. Actually, "talking" isn't quite accurate—Hagen was boasting of how he felt ready to make a big impression on the Nationals as a hitter when he got his next crack at a tryout.

At that moment Willard, who in 1910 had stepped down as the editor of the *Rochester Democrat and Chronicle* and was now chairman of the Rochester chapter of the Red Cross, entered the shop to pick up his clubs for a vacation at Loon Lake. As Hagen got up to get the clubs, Leonard asked his friend, "Aren't you going to enter the National Open in Chicago?"

"I'm not thinking of it," Hagen replied. "I'm going to work harder in baseball and let up on golf."

In addition to Willard having the reputation of being a kindly gentleman, he had started his career in the early 1870s as a sportswriter in Buffalo and had a special interest in the emergence of golf. He became upset that the young Rochester pro might be giving up a golf dream. "Haven't you plenty of time for the Open and baseball?" he asked. "You did so well at Brookline last year, I think you should try again this year."

Hagen was flattered but responded that he'd been discouraged by his golf playing lately and now believed that baseball was his game. Willard then pointed out that Hagen was the first pro from the Country Club of Rochester to qualify for the Open, let alone finish fourth. The next step was to go to Chicago and win it.

When Hagen still hesitated, Willard said, "If you go, I'll pay all your expenses." Then to Leonard he added, "If you can make the trip with Walter, I'll pay your expenses too."

It was an offer the young men couldn't refuse. And having it come from an influential club member like Willard meant Hagen wouldn't have any trouble being allowed to take time off. He immediately sent in his Open application, just making the deadline.

The bad news was he had focused most of his free time on base-ball, and now Hagen had only a few weeks to be ready to compete in the National Championship of golf. "I worked harder than I'd ever worked in my life during the time which was left me, trying to perfect my game for another shot at the big boys," Hagen recalled many years later.

His preparation included more than practicing on the course: "I got my fancy golf outfit cleaned and ready with only one change, the white buckskin shoes with the red rubber soles. I'd slid all over the course at Brookline in the wet weather. . . . Now I bought a pair of hobnailed shoes for the 1914 Open, and I played in hobnailed shoes from that time on."

When the time came, he and Leonard took the train to Chicago. For someone who had never been "out west" before, the journey to the U.S. Open was quite an adventure. The train curved around the southern rim of the Great Lakes and the young men, too excited to doze off, stared out the windows at the changing landscape. Upon arrival, they were presented with more tall buildings than they had ever seen. They checked into the rather elegant Great Northern Hotel, happy to spend Mr. Willard's money.

Initially, Hagen wasn't as jaunty as he'd been the year before when he arrived at Brookline. This time, the Open was far from a lark where he had nothing to lose—it was serious business this year, and he felt the burden of not wanting to disappoint Mr. Willard with a poor showing. Except for the outfit he'd brought to wear, there were no grand entrances to the locker room; a friendly but serious one seemed more appropriate.

Most of the competitors remembered him, and they greeted the young man from Rochester warmly. Though he hadn't done anything else in tournament play in the past year, finishing fourth in the previous U.S. Open was enough for Hagen to be accepted by the upper ranks of American players.

There is a legend about Hagen connected to the 1914 Open that, like many legends, contains facts and embellishments. The U.S. Golf Association had imposed a rule that divided amateurs and profession-als at the Open. Amateurs had the run of the Midlothian clubhouse while the professionals were relegated to a building which had too few hooks—not even lockers—to hang their clothes on, and as an added insult, the "lavatory conditions were poor," according to the *American Golfer*, which spared readers additional details.

What apparently happened is that Hagen, not aware of the rules at Midlothian or naively thinking that they didn't apply during the pre-Open events, walked into the clubhouse locker room the morning of the qualifying round and used it to change his clothes along with the amateurs (including Chick Evans, who later reported that Hagen was immediately followed by other pros upset by their building's conditions). Faced with an unintended but apparent revolt, USGA officials backed off and the rule became moot. Because of Hagen's proactive stance concerning professional golfers having access to clubhouse facilities in later years, he is credited with having begun the campaign in 1914, but his presence in the "inner sanctum" was probably accidental, and it was an event Hagen didn't even mention in his autobiography.

To entertain the crowd arriving for the qualifying rounds, get in some practice, and to try to calm their nerves, the volatile Johnny McDermott linked arms with Hagen and challenged the defending champion and Tommy McNamara to an 18-hole exhibition match. Out they went on August 17, and the following day the *Rochester Union and Advertiser* reported:

"Walter Hagen, of this city, distinguished himself in an exhibition match with J. J. McDermott, of Atlantic City, at Midlothian yesterday. He and his partner played Francis Ouimet and Tom McNamara in a foursome. Ouimet had 75 and McNamara 76, while McDermott did 80. Hagen's score was the best of the lot, 74."

Despite the 151–154 defeat, Hagen had more than held his own with the big boys. Most important, he had learned the par-72 Midlothian course, which at 6,355 yards was considered long at the time. Though during the rest of his career Hagen was known for playing well on unfamiliar courses, at this point he needed all the help and knowledge he could get.

Exhibitions were fun, but the bottom line was Hagen had to qualify or the trip to Chicago (and Mr. Willard's money) would have been wasted. Under today's USGA rules, Hagen's fourth-place finish in Brookline the year before would have automatically earned him a berth in the National Championship. However, in 1914 the Open was still truly open, meaning that all challengers—and there were close to 130 that year—had to earn their way in.

Hagen did qualify on that Wednesday, shooting a 152 for 36 holes—not spectacular, but not bad either considering he was playing the unfamiliar course for only the second time and under National Championship pressure. His score was fifth lowest. Jim Barnes had come in first with 146, followed 2 strokes back by Ouimet, who seemed intent on successfully defending, and Macdonald Smith and then Mike Brady at 150. (Smith would later withdraw from the Open due to illness.)

Hagen was in an enviable position in the Open. Ouimet was there to defend, but Vardon and Ray had stayed home in England, offering an opportunity to the Rochester head pro. Now that he was a bit more comfortable with the course, Hagen knew it was crucial that he get off to a good start the next day and establish himself as a contender.

He did more than establish himself during Thursday morning's 18 holes—he broke the Midlothian course record by 3 strokes and posted a 68. More astonishing, he had done it while having felt deathly ill only hours earlier.

Feeling like true *bon vivants* in a new and strange, even exotic city and with Mr. Willard's money burning in their pockets, the night before the first round of the U.S. Open Hagen and Leonard went out on the town. They didn't cruise saloons or seek women but instead wanted a big, fancy meal.

They wandered around a section of Chicago with plenty of restaurants, and finally entered one that had a huge red lobster in the display window. Hagen had never tasted lobster, and he decided it was time to become more sophisticated.

The men about town ordered lobsters and oysters, and plenty of both. Filled to bursting, they waddled out of the restaurant and went to a picture show. Before it was over, Hagen began to feel pains in his stomach. The young men headed right back to the hotel.

By midnight, Hagen was in agony. Leonard called the hotel physician, who diagnosed food poisoning and gave Hagen some pills and the advice to "ride it out." Many years later Hagen would report that he'd had ptomaine poisoning, and most other accounts go along with his version. However, without denying that he suffered for many hours, it is more likely that instead of food poisoning he had eaten to excess food that was totally unfamiliar to his digestive system. He went overboard, and paid the price for it (one of the few times this could be said about him).

All through the night Hagen alternated between holding his throbbing head and rubbing his turbulent stomach, moaning the whole time when he wasn't retching. Leonard called the doctor again, who arrived bearing more pills, then left.

By dawn, Hagen could stand only with his friend's help. The prospect of playing golf at all that week appeared too daunting, let alone that morning, and 36 holes by the end of the day to boot. Actually *win* the National Championship? Beyond imagining.

Though it was a lot easier for Leonard to say it than for Hagen to do it, Hagen agreed to his roommate's suggestion that they at least ride out to Midlothian and see how he felt by starting time. Also neither one of them wanted to return to Rochester having spent Mr. Willard's money with nothing but a mysterious intestinal attack to show for it. Hagen painfully got dressed. The doctor reappeared with milk toast and aspirin. The duo left for the South Shore Railroad station, Leonard carrying the strange weapons.

Adding to the misery was that the day was stifling hot, as Illinois can be in mid-August, and to make matters worse the wind carried from the city's factories and railroad yards clouds of coal soot and cinders. Still, Hagen persevered, steered by Leonard out to the practice field. Every swing of the club was agony, though when Hagen was finished practicing the headache had gone away.

Encouraged, Leonard said that Hagen could at least give the first round a try. "I can start," Hagen replied, "but I'm so sore I can scarcely swing a club."

The career-long characterization of Hagen not being accurate off the tee justifiably got its start in the 1914 Open. His physical condition exacerbated an unorthodox driving style and, in front of the sports press and the top competitors of the day as well as a large audience, his shots were sprayed all over the place. Recalling the first round at Midlothian more than forty years later, Hagen described that after every drive he was "in the rough. Yet on the recovery shots I was deadlier than the ptomaine from which I was suffering."

The first hole set the tone. He had to drive his ball over a lake and didn't think he had the strength to do it. The ball did get over, but veered off into thick rough. His second shot was a beauty, landing the ball on the edge of the green. He two-putted for par.

Hole after hole his drives flew off in new directions, endangering spectators and small wildlife, but each recovery shot, like his physical recovery, was spectacular. Just as amazing, Hagen rarely needed more than one putt to finish off the hole.

To earn the 68 he'd sunk three putts that were between 25 and 40 feet, and apparently gaining strength as his ailment subsided, he racked up four 3s on the last five holes. Setting a new course record energized the crowd, whose excitement didn't include the knowledge that the young man from Rochester thought the night before that death would have been a blessing.

Hearing that he had established a new course record, Hagen, feeling much better, said, "Then I must be ahead." He was, but not by much: Joe Mitchell from Upper Montclair, New Jersey, had turned in a 69, as had Francis Ouimet. After the first round of the 1913 Open, Hagen had led Ouimet too.

When this was pointed out to him, the twenty-one-year-old Hagen responded, "Yeah, but back then I was just a kid."

How remarkable, really, was a round of 68 in the U.S. Open in 1914? On the seventy-fifth anniversary of that Open, *Sports Illustrated* tried to put it in perspective: "Those were the days of hickory shafts, carelessly mowed fairways, and infrequently watered greens, so a 68 then would be more like a 62 now." The lowest-round score in U.S. Open history is a 63.

The afternoon's 18 wasn't as successful, but still a good round for Hagen. He shot a 74, and the 36-hole total of 142 was good enough to put him in first place halfway through the U.S. Open. His lead was far from insurmountable, however: Tom McNamara, playing with solid consistency, was just a stroke back; Ouimet had slipped to three strokes behind.

The third round wasn't better, wasn't even, but was a stroke worse, a 75. However, with everyone else wilting in the continuing heat, Hagen finished the morning at 217, ahead of Chick Evans, whose 70 had put him only 3 strokes back after two 75s on the first day. Evans, from the Chicago area, was playing in front of a very supportive home crowd.

In the final round Evans refused to fold. "Evans's spurt made him the biggest attraction of the afternoon, and he was followed by a gallery of nearly 1,000," reported the *American Golfer*. After 9 holes of the final round he had pulled to within a stroke of Hagen, who had shot a pedestrian 38 while Evans had notched a strong 35, including missing a 3-footer on the 9th green.

Perhaps gasping in the heat of the air and the pressure, Hagen couldn't widen his lead during the back nine, though he managed to maintain it by making clutch pars, including sinking a tricky 12-foot putt on 13 (after hooking his second shot).

He parred 14 and 15. He didn't know what Evans, three holes back, was shooting, but the shouts from the partisan crowd informed him that at the very least the challenger hadn't faltered. "Hagen had a rather small and undemonstrative following," according to the account in the *American Golfer*. "Not far behind was the big gallery following Evans. Cheers and the noise of hand clapping coming over the course occasionally told Hagen that the amateur was on his track. It was a good test of nerve for the former Rochester caddy."

The only way Hagen could ensure victory was to play solid, play his golf, and not give anything away to Evans. This was a lot to ask of a youngster in only his second National Championship, far from home, and trying to deny the charge of a confident challenger encouraged by a hometown audience.

In all likelihood, this was the moment that, like Ouimet's experience the year before, made the difference between greatness and golf obscurity. The twenty-one-year-old Hagen seized it.

Showing the first evidence of what would become a patented "stretch run" throughout his career, on the par-5 15 Hagen's second shot found a deep bunker, his third shot got him out but barely on the green, his long putt stopped 12 feet short of the hole, but he sank it for par. He parred the 490-yard par-4 16th. On 17, he bogeyed, then his drive on 18 went into the rough.

This could have been the wheels coming off in the midst of too much pressure. But in a remarkable shot under the circumstances, Hagen dug the ball out and landed it within 8 feet of the cup. With the crowd not necessarily supportive but impressed, the coolheaded youngster sank the putt to finish at 290, tying George Sargent's U.S. Open record of five years earlier. (Hagen remains one of only three players, along with Joe Lloyd in 1897 and Bobby Jones in 1926, in U.S. Open history to birdie the 72nd hole to win the championship by 1 stroke.) He had played the last nine in 35 after the 38.

If we are to accept two accounts other than Hagen's, both written many years later, another indication of keeping cool under pressure was that on the 15th hole he had noticed a blond woman in the gallery, then stunned spectators by walking over and asking her for a date. The nineteen-year-old, whose name was Mabel, said yes and Hagen said he would collect her at eight that evening, win or lose. (Still another account claims that when Hagen was told after his round that Evans was closing in, he replied, "So what? I've got my score for the day." This is most likely apocryphal, thanks to Hagen's later, well-deserved reputation as a ladies' man. However, it's unlikely he would have spoken this way, especially at twenty-one, because throughout his life he was circumspect about women.)

Like Hagen, Evans was playing for the American ranks, but he was also representing the amateur class, who were within range to win back-to-back U.S. Opens. Perhaps more of a motivation was that Evans was looking to win the championship in front of the partisan crowd, who cheered his every stroke. As Evans played 16, 17, and 18, in the locker room Hagen could hear the cheers approaching.

However, Evans, for all his talent and determination, had an Achilles' heel: putting. On the 9th hole he could have tied Hagen, but Evans missed a 3-footer for birdie. He missed from inside 10 feet on the 11th, three-putted the 12th, and missed another crucial putt on the 16th. Then, a burst of sunlight: Evans sank a 25-foot putt on 17 to pull back to within 2 shots.

The 1914 National Championship came down to the final hole. Evans had a 30-footer for an eagle and a tie with Hagen, who emerged from the locker room to watch his fate. With the crowd holding its collective breath, Evans stroked the ball and it went right at the hole . . . and stopped less than a foot short. The courageous amateur, playing on an ankle he had twisted in the morning round, had shot a 140 on the day, 7 shots better than Hagen, yet it wasn't enough.

"If Mr. Evans could have putted as well as Hagen, he would have won the tournament," lamented "Lochinvar" (who may have been Walter Travis himself) in the *American Golfer*.

Late Friday afternoon, after a thoroughly exhausting two days, Walter C. Hagen was the new National Open champion. After Evans came Britishers George Sargent (the '09 winner) and Freddie McLeod (the '08 winner). A few more strokes back were Ouimet, Mike Brady, Louis Tellier, McDermott, and Jim Barnes.

In the national press Hagen's victory made headlines, but they weren't as big as the ones that had followed Ouimet's win the year before. Hagen hadn't defeated Vardon and Ray in a play-off, and a twenty-one-year-old professional winning was not as awe-inspiring as the triumph of a twenty-year-old amateur. And with Americans having now captured the U.S. Open four years in a row, it was becoming routine. Let an American win the British Open. Now *that* would deserve international headlines.

Still, the achievement was an enormous one for Hagen, and he was pretty excited about it. The next morning, having breakfast with Dutch, his stomach felt queasy again. This time, though, he knew it wasn't illness but nerves finally catching up with him.

Startling his friend, Hagen jumped up and shouted, "Good *night*! I'm champion of the whole goddamn country!" Then he finished breakfast.

For winning the U.S. Open, Hagen earned $300. This looks like a ridiculous amount now with the first-place National Championship check over $1 million, but in 1914 dollars this was a pretty good piece of change for a twenty-one-year-old.

What about the fanfare when the champion returned home? Certainly there was some. The August 22 issue of the *Rochester Union and Advertiser*, albeit on page 13, blared, "Rochester Boasts Open Golf Champion in Walter C. Hagen." The 150-word story was accompanied by a photo of the local hero headlined "Our Newest Champion."

In the same issue, the column "Looking 'Em Over" by Art Ray offered that Hagen "is really a Rochester product. He is a true home bred, and he showed the way to all sorts of players over the Midlothian course, showing nerve and stamina in the three days of play, including the qualifying round and two days of nerve-wracking competition. . . . When Hagen comes home, which should be in a day or two, he will be king of the county. And he deserves to be. He has done much to advertise Rochester throughout the country. The only fear is that some club will come along and take him away from Rochester."

The *Rochester Herald* offered, "Walter C. Hagen of this city, now the holder of international fame, won on the links, is a twenty-one-year-old lad, a good-natured, easy-going chap, one who has earned his honors modestly, but by no end of hard work." The *Herald* piece was accompanied by four photos, one of them showing Hagen standing among the caddies at the Country Club of Rochester who had covered the caddie house with American flags and other decorations. Once again, as with Francis Ouimet, an American had stepped from the caddie ranks to become the best in the nation.

The praise in print was nice but far from overwhelming. After a couple of days, the city went on with its usual concerns. In his memoirs, Henry Clune wrote that Hagen "returned to Rochester with little more panache than a factory hand punching a time clock in the morning. His brief vacation was over; he went back promptly to instructing club members in the niceties of the game in which he had won supreme honors."

Clune continued: "There was no dancing in the streets and streamers were not festooned between the lampposts with huge stenciled letters, 'Welcome Home, Champ.' The Country Club members were conservative souls; they liked their pro, they were pleased with his victory, but golf was a pastime with them, not a passion. Hagen had grown up around the course and learned his game there and overnight they couldn't canonize him merely because he had played a winning round in 290."

What wasn't stated directly is that the club members could be proud of Hagen and having the National Championship trophy in Rochester, but being head pro meant Walter was still an employee like the groundskeeper and food service manager. It was assumed that he would accept the thanks and get back to work. Hagen couldn't do anything about this condescending view at the time, but he took note of it for the future when change might be possible.

In his comprehensive essay on Hagen in the *New Yorker,* Herbert Warren Wind pointed out, "Among other things, [the win] completely altered the way he looked at the world, and the way the world looked at him. As the Open champion, Hagen found himself flooded with offers to give exhibitions for the kind of money he had never dreamed existed for a golfer, whatever his achievements. On top of this, a number of highly regarded companies offered him substantial sums if he would endorse their products.

"It came home to him with a thump that a professional golfer could make a good deal of money if he could win important championships on a fairly regular basis. Hagen became a more astute person in every way. . . . His belief in himself became surer, and he was realistic enough to know that his expanding horizon would fade away unless he retained a major-tournament title that counted."

The dramatic way Hagen won was perhaps more important to the future of American golf than that he had won the Open. As Al Barkow pointed out, "Straightaway Hagen exhibited a personal flair that matched his golfing talent, a combination that in all the past history of golf had never been so totally fused. It would take an upstart American to break the crusty mold of Scottish stoicism at golf . . . Hagen was a flamboyant dandy next to Ouimet's gentle knight, and for that reason, and also because he decided to make golf his profession, he became an instrumental figure in the rise of American golf."

Even with this awakening, Hagen resumed his routine tasks at the Country Club of Rochester, not fully aware that changes he couldn't imagine, personal as well as professional, were on their way.

CHAPTER 6

WALTER HAGEN'S U.S. OPEN WIN and sports in general were soon overshadowed by the escalating conflict in Europe. The headlines of battles, reports of troop movements, hawkish pronouncements by some government and business leaders, the increasing number of casualties, and Americans' pleas to either keep out of the war or to jump in pushed sports well back in the editions of major newspapers.

In Great Britain and the rest of Europe, golf was virtually suspended because people and resources were needed for the war effort. The British Open was held in 1914 but would not be held again until 1920. The suspension of the tournament robbed Hagen of the chance to participate as the reigning U.S. Open champion.

The outbreak of war had an impact on the game within U.S. borders too because the crowd-pleasing top British players were unavailable. Harry Vardon and several others had planned to sail to America on May 15 on the *Lusitania* for an exhibition tour and the U.S. Open. But on May 7, 1915, the ship was sunk by the Germans with 1,201 killed (including 128 Americans). The British players canceled their plans entirely, and thus fans of the game on both sides of the Atlantic had to do without the top foreign golfers for several years.

Though the situation didn't allow Hagen to explore all the opportunities available to a U.S. Open champion, there were some he could tap. He was asked to endorse a few products, including a contract from A. G. Spalding & Bros. to exclusively play its golf ball, dubbed the

"Red Hot." However, Hagen turned down cigarettes and alcohol because he still didn't partake of either.

It may seem odd to us today that the winner of the U.S. Open would simply return to the family household in Rochester and resume his routine duties as head professional. But consider how drastically the golf landscape has changed. Today the members of the PGA Tour are full-time players and are not affiliated with specific courses as club professionals. When one wins the U.S. Open—or any tournament, for that matter—he deposits a seven-figure check and then goes on to the next tournament, relaxes for a few weeks, or has his agent/manager arrange several endorsement endeavors or corporate outings worth as much or more than the winner's check.

After Hagen and Leonard returned from Midlothian, the members of the Country Club of Rochester held a dinner in Hagen's honor and presented him with a gold watch. This had to have been a very satisfying event and a warm welcome home.

In 1914, nothing remotely like today's PGA Tour existed, especially a schedule of tournaments stretching into early November (with a lucrative "silly season" of made-for-TV exhibitions to follow) and the major money. While the $300 U.S. Open winner's check was a good amount in golf, it would only stretch so far. In all probability at this point in his life, Hagen was glad to be back in upstate New York where he had a steady job and family and friends. The head pro's regular existence of giving lessons, repairing clubs, and keeping the pro shop stocked wasn't a comedown at all because then, and for decades to come, there was not a very different life awaiting the U.S. Open winner.

However, for the national champion there were ways to pick up extra income not available to the typical head pro. When he could spare time from his job, Hagen gave talks about his Open victory to the members of golf clubs in the northwest portion of the state and conducted clinics at those clubs and his home course that attracted crowds considerably much more interested in him after his Midlothian triumph.

These endeavors didn't bring in much money, but every little bit helped. Hagen also accepted the contracts and invitations because they made him feel like a celebrity. In only a few years he would go from being the boy on the hill watching the elegant couples dancing at the country club to being someone other people came there to watch.

What about that other sport, the one where the Hall of Fame was a cinch? According to Hagen's autobiography, "I notified Pat Moran of the Phillies that I would not be in Florida for a tryout with the team. After all, I'd hit the big time in golf, so why bother with baseball?" This should be taken with a big grain of salt, as it's unlikely that Moran, in the midst of trying to win a pennant, remembered or cared that Hagen might show up for spring training in 1915.

Devoting himself full-time to golf and envisioning a future in it, Hagen worked hard on his game and on learning every syllable of the rules of golf. He had, of course, knowledge of the rules handed down by the U.S. Golf Association, enough to perform his duties as head professional. But being the U.S. Open champion, everything was changed. He had to be thinking of competing in future tournaments, and winning like he had at Midlothian; in addition, perhaps he felt some responsibility as the national champion to have a more thorough knowledge of the rules that guided his sport.

"I learned the rules forward and backward," he recalled in his auto-biography. "Through the years that knowledge has rewarded me many times over. I also began to improve my form. I believed the public had a right to expect the best I could give. In those early exhibitions I was more nervous than a wagering spectator."

As the reigning U.S. Open champion, Hagen was paid hand-somely for exhibitions, usually $100. This extra income allowed him to make things more comfortable for his family—he was still living at home in Corbett's Glen—and to expand his wardrobe, especially golf attire, because he wanted to make a good impression on his audience.

That audience was not found at tournaments, since in 1914 there were only a half dozen or so on the schedule. Plus, his unexpected, sudden Open win meant that Hagen and the officials of the Country Club of Rochester had not had time to work out a plan for when he could do the time-consuming travel necessary to participate in the other tournaments.

But there were exhibitions within a reasonable radius of Rochester, and thanks to them Hagen was getting his first sustained taste of being the center of attention and interacting with an adoring crowd.

"My ability to put on a good performance increased through time and experience," Hagen reported. "I loved the excitement of the tournaments, the admiration of the gallery, the words—complimentary or otherwise—tossed my way by the sports writers."

He also had his first taste of having money burning a hole in his pocket: "The amounts of cash dribbling in from endorsements and exhibitions were sauce for my first big thick steaks. I was twenty-one and the world was my oyster."

One might assume that Hagen's family was delighted by his success and their improved circumstances. We don't know what his mother and sisters thought, but what Hagen chose to include in his autobiography over forty years later implies a wound that hadn't healed: "Only my dad could see no future ahead for me. He considered knocking the little white ball around a pasture a silly way to make a living. Although I always thought the British tough people to convince—you had to win their Open more than once before they acknowledged your game was championship caliber—my dad was tougher." (While we have only Hagen's account that his father did not approve of golf as a profession, it's telling that it would be many years before William Hagen watched his son play in a tournament.)

Eventually, Hagen and the directors of the Country Club of Rochester worked out arrangements that allowed the ambitious and hungry young professional to fulfill his head pro duties and pursue the revenue available to him. The club officials really didn't have a precedent upon which to draw for how to accommodate Hagen. With one exception, the previous winners of the U.S. Open had been visiting and transplanted Brits and an American amateur. How do you treat a young man who is both the national champion and an employee? The fact that Hagen remained as head pro at Rochester for four more years indicates that the arrangements worked out were mutually agreeable.

During the winter and then early spring of 1915, instead of making and repairing clubs in the back shop, Hagen took on exhibitions that offered a shot at more extensive travel and money. As the Open winner he was center stage. This was several levels above the previous winter when, while in Florida to audition for the Philadelphia ballclub, he had tried "syndicate golf."

There are rules against this sort of golf in any form involving pros today, but it was quite commonplace in Hagen's era. Four to eight players would go on tour together to play exhibitions, and the winnings would be shared evenly so that the entire group could make expenses and turn a profit. Of course, if one of the players is winning the majority of the events, he's carrying the others yet making not a penny more, but an advantage remained in that the hot golfer was developing a good reputation.

Due to Hagen's competitive nature, he didn't take a shine to syndicate golf. He preferred walking the tightrope without a net and letting his play determine if he stayed aloft or fell financially. The previous year he and Tommy Kerrigan had hooked up with Mike Brady, Gil Nicholls, Tommy McNamara, Johnny McDermott, and Jim Barnes, who treated the two rookies like runts trying to squeeze in to the dinner dish. After several attempts to get a fair share of the pie, Hagen and Kerrigan gave up.

The early part of 1915 was a different story. Barnes invited Hagen on a tour of the Northwest. Hagen agreed, but with one stipulation: what each earned, he'd keep. The arrangements with the Country Club of Rochester allowed Hagen to do what he pleased during the snowbound months, so off he went on his first trip further west than Chicago.

They made the rounds of golf clubs in Washington and Oregon. Members were delighted to host the national champion, and Barnes was already popular there for having once been a club pro in Tacoma. By early spring, the duo had worked their way down to Northern California. Barnes was glad to be making a nice piece of change on the tour, yet he also found himself living with a younger and looser man feeling (and sowing) his oats.

"I was content to let Jim rest his more mature bones in bed, but being only twenty-two at the time, I preferred to fill my evenings with the theater, dancing, and romancing until the wee hours of the morning," Hagen related a half century later.

At the conclusion of the tour Hagen won an official event, the Panama-Pacific Exposition Tournament, held at the Ingleside Club in San Francisco. On 36 holes the first day he broke the course record with a 140 (including a 30 on the front nine of the first round). He coasted the second day with a 146, and still won by 8 strokes. With

Barnes, Chick Evans, and the cream of the West Coast crop participating, this margin of victory was impressive.

The winner's check was $1,000, the first time that money mark was reached in a professional tournament in the U.S. The victory also confirmed that Hagen's U.S. Open win the year before was not a fluke, and gave him some momentum going into the U.S. Open a month later, in May, at the Baltusrol Golf Club in New Jersey. A successful defense of his title would really dispel any doubts about his abilities. All of twenty-two, Hagen was ready to head back east and take on the best—on the American side of the Atlantic—once again.

First, he had to make sure he got there. The notorious activities of the Barbary Coast were in full swing and they must have made Hagen feel quite the adventurer being part of the nightlife. If we are to believe his account, the activities in San Francisco could be more adventurous than he cared for.

Enjoying his winnings, Hagen and a friend were touring the sights of the city and stopping in at a few nightclubs to catch some of the entertainment.

As they were leaving one club, a man rushed up the stairs past Hagen and reached for the door to the street. A bullet whizzed past Hagen, almost skimming his neck, and the man at the door fell just as the door opened. Not looking back, Hagen and his friend hurtled the body and raced through the streets until exhausted. In the next day's newspaper, Hagen learned it was the twenty-eighth murder in the city that month.

Life was a lot safer in New Jersey, but Hagen didn't even come close to keeping the U.S. Open title, finishing 9 shots back of the winner, Jerry Travers. Travers's victory meant that Americans had taken their National Championship five years in a row, but with a world war in progress and the better British players sidelined, this was not that impressive an accomplishment.

The runner-up at the Open was Tommy McNamara, who was somewhat consoled by the $300 first-place check which couldn't be accepted by the amateur Travers. Several familiar names were on the upper part of the leaderboard, including Mike Brady and Jim Barnes, then came Walter C. Hagen at 306. His 151 on the first day had set him back, then the 155 the second day blew him out of the water, and this was without ptomaine poisoning. By tying for eighth place, he received $6.25.

Why did Hagen end up this far back? A poor start, then a poor finish. His 78 in the first round put him an imposing 7 strokes back of the pace set by Jim Barnes and Chick Evans. The defending champion made up some ground with 73 in the second round, but a 76 in the third hurt him. A 79 in the final round finished him off.

It was after this galling loss that Hagen called upon his confidence. Instead of going back to Rochester where he would still be viewed as a golf hero (albeit a slightly tarnished one), two weeks later he was back in competition, this time at the Massachusetts Open Golf Championship at Brookline. His 298 total was 5 strokes better than Mike Brady, and Francis Ouimet and Jim Barnes were left in the dust. Poor Tommy McNamara of Boston carded an embarrassing 320.

Maybe Hagen just needed more adversity—during the last 36 holes he played and pulled away from the pack during a torrential downpour. He'd learned from the 1913 Open experience how to play The Country Club in wet weather, and he now had the footwear that provided better traction on wet grass and mud. His first-place check from the Massachusetts Open was $150.

In August, Hagen, in his first Western Open, tied with Mike Brady 5 strokes behind a revived McNamara, then exhibition play kept him occupied well into autumn. Because of his victory at Brookline and the dramatic way he closed out exhibitions, Hagen was beginning to get the reputation of being a "money player." The October 31, 1915, issue of the *New York Times* reported, "Spurred on by the fact that some real money was at stake, Walter Hagen, Massachusetts 'open' golf champion, paired with Tom McNamara, Western 'open' champion, decisively won from Gilbert Nicholls, metropolitan 'open' champion, and Alex Smith, former national 'open' champion, by the margin of 6 and 5 over the Wykagyl course yesterday. The match was played among sprinkles of rain, flurries of snow, and a gale of wind."

With this exhibition victory under his belt, Hagen returned to Rochester to stay at least through the holidays. The previous months had been hectic because of his juggling a moneymaking exhibition schedule with being at the Country Club of Rochester often enough to keep members happy. Because of the war, there might not be a

Florida exhibition schedule, so Hagen probably planned to content himself with the comfort of the heated back room of the pro shop.

However, his winter was interrupted by a request for help to form what would become the world's largest golf organization.

The beginning of 1916 saw a shift in golf in the U.S. There was no lack of amateur players, but there was an increasing number of professionals. Many of those professionals resented that they were viewed as second-class citizens by country club members who employed them and by tournament officials who displayed respect for amateur competitors but at best tolerance toward the pros because the latter had to work for a living in golf. It was not uncommon for some club members to refer to a pro as "boy" and to view pros as indistinguishable from caddies. In addition, as tournaments were created, the fact that there were restrictions like not being able to use locker rooms put professionals at a competitive disadvantage.

Some professionals were calling for an organization that would represent their interests, challenge restrictions, and coordinate a schedule of sanctioned tournaments. This reflected the growing desire of American golfers to compete against British professionals once the war was over as well as to coordinate the efforts of sectional professional associations. Also, some club pros thought that organizing would result in more respectful treatment and eventually the leverage to get wages raised.

The effort to create what would become the Professional Golfers Association had begun.

On January 17, 1916, a lunch was hosted at the Taplow Club in New York City by the department store magnate Rodman Wanamaker of Philadelphia. This initial meeting included amateurs, such as Francis Ouimet. It was at first believed that amateurs could have a role in the proposed organization. The U.S. Golf Association soon quashed this odd idea, and from 1916 on the two organizations traveled different paths.

The infant organization may also have hoped to persuade Ouimet, the hero of 1913 and with Hagen and Barnes one of the most popular players in America, to turn professional. After unsuccessfully defending his U.S. Amateur title in 1915, Ouimet was told that his amateur status was being revoked because with a boyhood friend he had opened his own sporting-goods store in Boston and thus was profiting from golf. Though angry and deeply hurt, Ouimet refused to turn pro.

After Ouimet had enlisted in the army when America entered World War I, the USGA quietly reinstated his amateur status. (Ouimet graciously recovered from the USGA's insult. In 1955, he was given the inaugural Bob Jones Award, the USGA's highest honor, for "distinguished sportsmanship in golf.") Even if Ouimet wouldn't turn pro, perhaps he would compete in several PGA-sponsored events, giving them credibility and attracting larger crowds.

What were Wanamaker's motives in forming the Professional Golfers Association and through it raising the popularity of golf? Surely, he wasn't terribly concerned with pros' feelings of inferiority, and he may well have shared the perspective of wealthy club members who disdained men who had to try to earn a living from golf as opposed to playing for the pure sport of it.

Wanamaker had some sound ideas involving the professional ranks, so there was that. But in addition, speeding up the pace at which people were becoming interested in golf, especially playing golf, meant more consumers for the products sold in the stores that bore his name. As had been demonstrated by Vardon in 1900, golf products could be a profitable part of the retail industry, and Wanamaker already had plenty of stores and equipment in place, awaiting increased demand. Why not help it along?

It was clear that his call for an organization to preserve and promote professional golf had struck a chord. At the lunch were seventy-five people, and one of the most prominent was Walter Hagen. It was important that he be there as the most recent professional winner of the National Championship. Also among the pros at the luncheon was Jack Hagan, a journeyman player. Because of the older man's existence in American golf, in his first few years as a pro Hagen entered tournaments as Walter C. Hagen or W. C. Hagen to separate himself, yet some newspaper reports still referred to him as Jack Hagan or Walter Hagan. The last time he used W. C. was on his first trip to England in 1920, when over there he suffered the embarrassment of fans calling him "Water Closet Hagen."

Wanamaker advocated that the proposed organization have more say in the selection of courses for tournaments, including the U.S. Open; in finding jobs by being a clearinghouse for pros looking for clubs and clubs looking for pros; in establishing standards of ability and conduct to be certified as a teaching golf professional; and to create a tournament for professional golfers exclusively.

To give the new tournament an immediate and attractive boost, Wanamaker offered a $2,850 total purse (more than double the U.S. Open purse) and to pay for a trophy to give to the winner of what would be called the PGA Championship. (The trophy awarded to the winner of what is now the golf year's fourth major is called the Wanamaker Cup.)

A follow-up meeting of a committee of seven professionals was held on February 7 in New York City. One member of the committee, James Hepburn, had been secretary of the Professional Golf Association of Great Britain for many years, and he had provided that organization's bylaws and constitution. It was agreed to use these documents as a model for the formation of the new PGA of America.

Before the end of the month, rules for and classifications of membership had been decided. In March, the committee sent out a letter to club professionals around the country outlining the rules and classifications and purpose of the PGA of America, and requesting that the pros submit applications to join the new organization.

There were 114 pros (including Hagen, who lobbied for the new venture in upstate New York) who signed up as members of the PGA, a total that appears paltry now but was encouraging to the organizers, who went ahead with plans to hold the first PGA Championship. The U.S. Golf Association turned over to the PGA its data on employment of pros and greens keepers, ceding this aspect to the emerging group so that the USGA could focus on amateurs and no longer be connected to employees of golf clubs.

With pros signed up, a new tournament planned, a reasonable understanding with the USGA about the purview of each organization, and Wanamaker and others underwriting the efforts, the Professional Golfers Association of America became official on April 10, 1916. There were thirty-five original charter members of the PGA, with Hagen being one of them.

It was determined that the first PGA Championship would be held at the Siwanoy Country Club in Bronxville, New York, in October. Hagen immediately announced that he would participate, which helped to entice other players to the event. Hagen's record and reputation were already strong enough that even at only twenty-three what he said and did among golf professionals was influential.

It was also decided that the PGA Championship would have a match-play format—perhaps to create a tournament for pros that was the same in format as the U.S. and British Amateur Championships, or to distinguish itself from the stroke-play British and U.S. Opens. (The PGA Championship converted to stroke play in 1958.)

Hagen did not win the inaugural PGA Championship that October, but fortunately for the fledgling organization, his main rival among golf fans, Long Jim Barnes, did, 1-up over Jock Hutchison, who had defeated Hagen 2-up in the semifinal.

It was a stirring victory for Barnes, as he was down a hole with only two to play. On the 35th hole, Hutchison put his approach shot in a trap while Barnes was safely on the green. He sank his next shot, Hutchison didn't. It was all square going to the last hole. The sturdy Scot again faltered, missing a 4-foot putt and having to watch Barnes sink his from the same length to snatch the championship.

"Evidently, Jim Barnes has no nerves," the sports writer of the New York Times offered. Barnes won $500, a medal, and the silver cup underwritten by Wanamaker.

Despite the enthusiasm with which the inaugural PGA Championship was promoted and conducted, it was in real danger of becoming a one-shot wonder. The New York–area press covered it with some fanfare, but the rest of the country was not awfully interested, with the Western Open being a closer, bigger, and more established event. And as America's entry into the war became a reality, the PGA Championship was suspended indefinitely.

It was a different story for Walter Hagen. The peak World War I years took him in an especially busy and productive direction, personally as well as professionally.

As the war in Europe escalated in 1916, the golf writer H. B. Martin suggested a way for players to help the Red Cross. His plan was a series of exhibition matches with spectators paying admission and in other ways contributing money, with the proceeds going to the charitable organization. Hagen and his colleagues immediately embraced the plan, and soon after the PGA of America officially sponsored the matches with the Western Golf Association—which sponsored the Western Open and state and regional amateur events in the Midwest—jumping aboard.

At the clubs where the matches were held, most of them in the Northeast and Mid-Atlantic sections, members would bid at auction to caddie for their favorite pros, and at the end of every match the golf balls used would be auctioned off too. The exhibitions were very successful. From mid-1916 through the end of World War I more than $1.25 million was turned over to the Red Cross. In most cases, players were not paid for the exhibitions, but their travel and other expenses were covered.

No one was more consistently involved than Hagen and the amateur Charles "Chick" Evans. It was estimated that the matches just the two of them participated in were worth close to a quarter of the total funds raised. Evans deserves special mention because with Hagen or others as partners, by war's end he had played exhibitions in forty-one different cities and traveled 26,000 miles.

The matches had an advantage other than war relief. With most tournaments suspended (the U.S. Open was not played in 1917 and 1918) and wide-ranging exhibition tours on hold until after the war, there were fewer opportunities for the top players to compete. While the Red Cross matches were generally relaxed and friendly affairs, they did allow the better players to keep an eye on each other and to further hone their skills in semicompetitive settings. And with prominent pros selflessly raising money to help our boys "over there," American attitudes began to change about professionals. Perhaps they deserved some of the dignity and respect accorded to amateurs.

Chick Evans wasn't the only well-known amateur raising funds. Even the "Old Man," Walter Travis, who had stopped playing competitive golf to devote himself to publishing the *American Golfer* and designing courses, gave it a go for the war effort. He and Findlay Douglas, who had been rivals at the turn of the century, put on an exciting match which Travis eventually won 1-up. Afterward, Travis offered for auction the putter that had won him the British Amateur in 1904. It sold for $1,700, with all of that going to war relief charities.

An indirect advantage of exhibition matches had a significant benefit for Hagen. During the war, golf fans became accustomed to paying admission to see exhibition matches, whereas previously players had either passed a hat around or the sponsoring club offered a pot to be shared. Admission, though, meant there was a "gate"; this went to charity during the war, but afterward it (or a good portion of it) went to the participating pros. The collecting of admission money to increase the purse of a tournament further distinguished the PGA of America from the USGA in the postwar years (though the latter eventually did charge admission to the U.S. Open).

The audience that knew of Hagen expanded, thanks to the charitable exhibitions, so much so that with his professional record that year, the December 20, 1916, edition of the *Rochester Herald* announced, "Walter Hagen Picked as World's Premier Golfer." The article went on to report what had recently been published by several New York City sports writers, that based on Hagen's overall play in exhibitions and his having won five official tournaments, these writers believed that he would beat the top six international amateurs and professionals. (Of course, this couldn't be proven in actual competition because the best British players were unavailable.)

"Hagen would be considered first on his wonderful ability to play best when the opposition was keenest," the hometown *Herald* piece continued. "Any golfer above the average knows how to play his shots well, but it is the man who can perform best under trying conditions that enters the championship ranks. Such a man is Walter Hagen, whose fighting spirit is the equal of any player in the country."

The more popular pros attracted the larger crowds and the heftier gates. Based on what he had raked in for the war effort, after the war Hagen stood close to being the most popular American pro. "The publicity accorded the Red Cross matches made it much easier for me to ask, and to get, an even higher fee after the war [than before it]," he recounted. "I raised my charge to $200 and then to $300."

Given that he was a durable road warrior who would do exhibitions anywhere and everywhere, Hagen was on his way to becoming golf's first million-dollar player.

Real earnings in golf, whether it be a dollar or a million bucks, meant doing it in official tournaments. Professionally in 1916, Hagen collected the majority of the cash available, and with one exception it was a very good year.

The disappointment in 1916 had been once again not making a strong run at the U.S. Open title. The event, held in Minneapolis at the Minikahda Club, was the last National Championship until 1919 because of the war. Going to Minnesota was a long and expensive trip for most of the players, even those raking in exhibition cash. Members of the Country Club of Rochester passed the hat and collected $100 to defray their pro's expenses. Certainly after this gesture, Hagen hoped to come home with another National Championship.

It was not to be. Chick Evans finally broke through. Taking full advantage of the excellent weather the first two rounds, Evans earned a 70 and 69 to take a large lead. A 74 and 73 in the final 36 holes slowed his momentum. Hutchison gave his best, scoring a 68 in the last round, but it still wasn't enough as he finished 2 strokes back and 2 ahead of Barnes.

Though Hagen's 295 was only 5 strokes above his winning total at Midlothian two years earlier, it was good only for seventh place in Minneapolis. For the second year in a row and third time in four years, the winner of the U.S. Open was an amateur and a homebred player. Evans's 286 would stand as the lowest total in a U.S. Open for the next twenty years.

Evans would be a rival of three generations of golf professionals. From 1907 to 1962, he played in every U.S. Amateur Championship and quite a few other tournaments too. His last win of a match in the U.S. Amateur came in 1958, when he was sixty-eight years old.

He was born in Indiana, but spent almost all of his life in Chicago. He began caddying at eight, and by his late teens was competing in amateur and other tournaments. In 1916 he won the U.S. Amateur Championship in addition to the U.S. Open, becoming the first golfer to hold both titles at the same time. (Bobby Jones would do the same in 1930.) Evans received many offers that would require him to turn professional, such as endorsing products and going on an exhibition tour, but he declined them because he was very proud of his amateur status, and perhaps because of the view held by many amateur players, club owners, and those in the press about the "purity" of being an amateur.

Failing for the second year in a row to repeat as winner of the National Championship had to be a bitter disappointment for Hagen. However, there soon came an opportunity to redeem himself. Another high-profile tournament was the Metropolitan Open; the winner would emerge with a lot of positive press from the tri-state area.

In an 18-hole play-off with Jim Barnes and Charles Hoffner, Hagen trailed by 2 strokes after the front nine, but shot a 35 on the back nine to just clip Barnes by one. (Hoffner was 3 strokes back.) "When Walter Hagen of Rochester pitched a shot over the pond on the eighteenth hole at Garden City yesterday, and ran his putt down for a three, he monopolized all the glory which goes with the winning of the Metropolitan Open Championship," cheered the *New York Times* on the front page of its July 16, 1916, sports section. He received $150 in gold and a medal.

In August, Hagen's 298 beat Barnes and Gil Nicholls to win the Shawnee Open, the event in eastern Pennsylvania at which Johnny McDermott had thrown down the gauntlet to Vardon and Ray three years earlier. Then it was on to the tournament that before the birth of the PGA Championship would have been the season's final contest.

The Western Open, held in Milwaukee in '16 at the Blue Mound Country Club, remains the second-oldest continuously held tournament in North America, first contested in 1899. (Today it is played in Illinois.) In 1916, it was not equal to the British and U.S. Opens in stature but was regarded by many of the players, sports reporters, and much of the golf public as a major because of its founding in the nineteenth century and because it attracted a field as strong as the U.S. Open.

Though Jack Nicklaus himself might not consider the Western a major, on the bronze plaque dedicated to Hagen at Muirfield Village, Ohio, site of Nicklaus's annual Memorial Tournament, is this: "He also won the Western Open five times between 1916–1932, during which period it was generally regarded as a major championship."

Hagen set out to win it and complete a sort of professional trifecta on the year. The scorching heat made the course hard and fast. This was apparently to the players' liking because scores in all four rounds were low. Hagen began with a 70, then he shot rounds of 74 and 72. Meanwhile, Jock Hutchison and Chick Evans were doing well, and by the end of the final round they each turned in a 69. Hagen fought to stay ahead, during one stretch of five holes using only 13 strokes. At the 17th hole, leading by a stroke, Hagen had to par the last two holes, both par-4s, to win.

He did, and in dramatic fashion, sinking tough putts on both greens. Hagen's 286 overall score equaled what Evans had carded at the U.S. Open.

This win meant Hagen had collected trophies in six official tourneys in three years, including a true major. Today, of course, winning the Open and five PGA Tour events in three seasons would be viewed as a very good but not a great stretch. Since 1916 we have seen Byron Nelson win eleven tourneys in a row in 1945, Ben Hogan win five out of the six events he entered in 1953, Jack Nicklaus winning seventy times on Tour in his career, and Tiger Woods win ten times in 2000 and, with the 2001 Masters, win four consecutive majors.

But when you consider that there were only a half dozen tournaments per year available to professionals in the 1910s, winning a third of them in a three-year period—head to head with the likes of Barnes, Hutchison, and Evans—and still being only twenty-three years old, put Hagen at the pinnacle of the game. When the *American Golfer* dubbed Hagen the leading professional of the year in its September issue, that was high and deserved praise from the taciturn Travis.

Somehow, during the summer of 1916 Hagen managed to keep up with his responsibilities at the Country Club of Rochester. It was at that time he met nineteen-year-old Margaret Johnson, and they became smitten with each other.

According to what he later told on-course rival and longtime friend Gene Sarazen, Hagen first met Johnson "when he went crazy over a handsome hunting dog he saw at a country club [which had to be the CC of Rochester]. He asked the woman who owned the dog if he could buy it and she yielded to his persistence," Sarazen recalled in his autobiography, *Thirty Years of Championship Golf.*

"The ex-owner wanted to make sure that her pet was receiving the proper attention, and made frequent trips to Hagen's house to check," Sarazen related. "After a while she found that, while she wasn't exactly bored with the dog's adjustment, she was more interested in its owner."

Except to Sarazen, apparently, Hagen never mentioned anything about a dog playing Cupid. His succinct account was that "life wasn't all golf for me. For some months in 1916 I had been seeing quite a lot of Margaret Johnson, the attractive daughter of George Johnson, owner of the Clinton Hotel in Rochester (and a prominent club member).

"Some of my pals humorously insisted I called for her with a golf club in one hand and an assortment of hard candies in the other . . . and that I spent time waiting for her to appear by chipping the candy into cuspidors spaced around the lobby. Nevertheless, I was in love."

A photograph of Margaret Beatrice Johnson taken in 1919 shows a very pretty woman, pale and delicate-featured with an abundance of light-enhanced dark hair. Her smile is both shy and generous. It's easy to see why Hagen or any male would be attracted to Margaret.

Toward the end of 1916, Hagen returned to Rochester for the holidays and, as it turned out, to be married. He was twenty-four when on January 29, 1917, he and Margaret were married in the rectory of St. Mary's Church by the Reverend Simon FitzSimmons.

The marriage was pretty big news in Rochester. According to Henry Clune, he told his editor at the *Rochester Democrat and Chronicle*, Morris Adams, who was "a golf enthusiast," about the impending marriage:

"Walter had long been a friend of mine, and his wife-to-be, too. . . . Mr. Adams was enthused about the story. When it appeared next day it was illustrated by a double column picture spread showing the golfer in full swing with a driver and an insert of Miss Johnson. This was a radical departure from the more sober *Democrat and Chronicle* of those days, and to add to the decor of the ordinarily unillustrated local page, a border of white golf balls was strung down one side of the cut."

Where to live as newlyweds had been a bit of a dilemma. There was no room for them in the Hagen household, which had continued to house him when he wasn't on the road, and in any case Margaret was not about to live in Brighton, on the other side of the tracks. Neither were they going to live in the Clinton Hotel, under her father's watch. Conceivably, the Johnsons were less than enthusiastic that their daughter, previously available for much better matches, had married the club's head pro.

The problem was solved when Erickson Perkins offered his bungalow on the grounds of the Country Club of Rochester. The couple moved in and life was good. Walter could literally roll out of bed and go to work. He had a good job that had become even more secure by marrying a powerful club member's daughter. His wife was beautiful and offered further entrée into country club life and Rochester high society. A National Championship was on his résumé, which meant he could always go out on exhibition tours and earn extra money and the crowd's applause.

Clune was a frequent visitor to the bungalow "near the first hole of the Country Club course on the south side of Elmwood Avenue, where Mrs. Hagen used a can opener to prepare the meals and in which some of us had more fun than a monkey on a grapevine."

Despite his top-echelon perch among pros, with his wife and steady job back in Rochester, Hagen couldn't go too far from home nor stay away very long, though he tried. It was true that he helped the war effort through Red Cross exhibitions, but it was also true that Hagen enjoyed travel, meeting new people, playing new courses, and learning new ways to beat opponents.

During 1917, as much as war restrictions allowed, his trips to Florida, the Midwest, and elsewhere (such as visiting the bright lights of New York City to see hit shows) were of longer duration. Florida, where in one 18-hole exhibition match he carded a 58, was especially fertile ground for Hagen because real estate magnates like Henry Flagler and Carl Fisher were building hotels and golf courses as fast as they could to take advantage of the $50 million Americans were now spending annually on the sport.

The war-relief exhibition matches in '17 didn't feature only Hagen, Evans, and others but also allowed parts of the country other than Georgia to see in action a precocious amateur named Bobby Jones (who in person preferred to be called Bob). To help raise funds, he and two young women and another young man—Alexa Stirling, Elaine Rosenthal, and Perry Adair—all teenagers, had teamed up to become the Dixie Kids, who took on older amateurs and even well-known pros.

Rosenthal was the best woman golfer in the Midwest, Stirling had been the winner of the U.S. Women's Championship in 1916, and Adair was no slouch on the links but was part of the quartet because of being Jones's friend, and during matches the two wore Swiss Guard berets. As the group made the rounds in 1917, it became very clear that the fifteen-year-old Jones had enormous talent (though not yet poise, illustrated by his angry outbursts after poor shots) and wasn't far from holding his own with the top professionals.

For Hagen, no matter how interesting travel and exhibitions and the occasional tournament—his defense of the Western Open in 1917 was unsuccessful, though he finished second (there was no U.S. Open that year)—could be, time spent in Rochester was not drudgery. He could visit with his parents and sisters, socialize with his longtime friends, practice golf, and be with his young, pretty wife.

"Margaret Johnson Hagen was a lively, witty, stylishly dressed young woman," was how Clune described her. "Brought up in a hotel, where her meals had been prepared by the hotel's chef, Margaret had cultivated no culinary talents, and to make matters worse, Walter complained, she was a damn poor can opener."

While her lack of skills in the kitchen didn't persuade Hagen to take up cooking, in other ways Margaret had a strong influence on her husband. "She aspired to high life," recalled Clune when he was in his eighties. "She wanted to swing, to join what today would be known as the jet set. The time would come when Hagen's flamboyance, his imperiousness, and his command presence on a golf course would cause admiring sports writers to knight him—to dub him Sir Walter. In Rochester he was an abstemious and ingenuous young man, rather provincial in his attitudes and tastes."

This would seem to contradict Clune's comment about having as much fun as "monkeys on a grapevine," but it appears that over time Margaret got her husband to loosen up, to accept the increasing advantages and fun coming their way through his golf and her connections.

According to Clune, it was Margaret Hagen's "scornful dictum that while you could take the boy out of the country, you couldn't take the country out of the boy. She taunted him; he had been champion of the nation. Why didn't he act the part? She got him to wear fancy pants and fancy shirts and jackets. He himself got a gaudy automobile with a hood that seemed half the length of a city block and a motor the size of a shoe box. Margaret was a talented dancer (she and her brother had finished third in a dance contest sponsored by Irene and Vernon Castle when the Castles stopped in Rochester on a transcontinental tour), and she instructed Hagen in the art."

According to Herbert Warren Wind, Hagen "learned to dress better both on and off the golf course. His shining black hair and his deeply tanned face became his trademark. For golf, he wore well-tailored knickers, and he put together ensembles—shirts, ties, knickers, golf socks, and shoes—that were made up of shades of brown, blue, or gray, with a little white or black added for contrast. He began to meet people of high social standing and big wheels of the business world, and he could see that it meant something to them to be in the company of the national champion."

On Saturday nights the Hagens rounded up a group of friends and went dancing to the music of a live orchestra in the Pompeian Room of the Hotel Seneca or some other favorite location. Clune observed that Margaret was "witty, ambitious, and at first more ambitious" than her husband.

"I remember one night being with the Hagens and another couple at the old Windsor Hotel, which stood near the lake at Summerville. . . . Margaret left the table. Later, I was called away for some purpose. As I passed the bar, Mrs. Hagen was downing her second Tom Collins. When she returned, her husband looked up questioningly.

"'Why, where you been, dearie?'

"'I just went out to get a drink of water.'

"'Why, there's water right here on the table,' and he indicated a filled tumbler at her place."

Despite being naïve in some ways, Hagen was on his way it seemed to becoming a familiar figure in Rochester high society, a dream fulfilled. He had to accept, though, that he was a club pro and thus had to earn money; he would never be a full-fledged member of the upper class, and as an employee of the Country Club of Rochester, he could never be the equal of its members.

Some doors were opened to him because of his wife and his Open title, not for his occupation. Indeed, what had to be frustrating for Margaret was that because of her husband's occupation, she was excluded from some club activities—such as members-only dinners and certain social committees—in which as the unmarried daughter of a prominent club member she would have been allowed to participate. Still, Hagen had come a long way from being one of five children whose father had brought home $18 a week from the railroad yards.

During the latter part of 1917, Margaret had to cut back on her dancing and other socializing because she was in the later stages of pregnancy. On January 11, 1918, almost a year to the day when she married Walter, Margaret gave birth to Walter Hagen Jr. Hagen would later say that "that event made the year a most important one in my life." (An indication of how Hagen viewed family life was that he did not regard the year of his only child's birth as *the* most important year of his life.)

The arrival of Walter Jr. pretty much resolved what had to be a dilemma for Hagen. America had entered World War I nine months earlier, and at twenty-five and in excellent physical condition, Hagen would seem a prime candidate for service. However, he was also the best or at least one of the three best in his sport, so, professionally, it was not a good time to go into the military. Also, being of German descent, Hagen may have had mixed feelings about taking up arms against that country. On the other hand, for a top sports figure, not serving one's country during war could have serious consequences. For example, Jack Dempsey would be crucified by some boxing fans and the media for not having enlisted during the war, and was actually brought to trial for the offense.

The timing of Walter Jr.'s appearance did make a difference. When Hagen was called to the local draft board in Rochester in the early spring of 1918, he was classified in the B category because he was married with a son.

According to his own account, which may be nothing more than an alibi concocted years later, Hagen then tried to enlist in the air force, though the only time he'd been off the ground was when sleeping on the upper floor of a hotel. "In fact," Hagen contended, "the draft board suggested that the money I helped raise through golf had more value than my entry into armed services."

When spring arrived and with military service not a factor, it was time to hit the road again. Leaving Margaret and Walter Jr. in Rochester, Hagen played in a string of fund-raising matches and then headed to the already famed Pinehurst course in North Carolina for the North and South Open. Before the final round, a man named Al Wallace from Detroit bet heavily on Hagen to win.

"Al Wallace followed me around worrying like mad about his bet, for I was joking and clowning around with Tommy [Kerrigan] and the gallery, really having fun," Hagen recalled about the final round of the stroke-play tournament. "However, I won. He made me a present of $500 from his winnings and asked if I'd ever heard of the Oakland Hills Club near Detroit. I had not." (Hagen's 293 bested Jim Barnes and Emmett French by 2 strokes.)

Oakland Hills, now one of the most famous courses in the U.S. and site of U.S. Opens and Ryder Cups, was being constructed in 1918 with financing from people connected in various manufacturing ways to the Ford Motor Company (which means they were all getting rich and richer). Wallace was a charter member. He told Hagen that the two men running the club, Norval Hawkins and Joseph Mack, were looking for a head pro. The job description and compensation sounded attractive to Hagen.

By this time Hagen had his own car to get around in and a few days later he headed for Detroit. Arriving, he "slammed on the brakes at the entrance to the Detroit Athletic Club. I leaped over the side of the car and entered the building that was to become more familiar to me than any other building in the world."

Hawkins and Mack liked Hagen right away, and with Wallace's description of Hagen's performance at Pinehurst fresh in their ears, they made the prospective pro an offer well above what he was receiving in Rochester. Shrewdly, Hagen said he would think about it on his way home. Before he left, the salary offer had been increased.

Hagen described the offer to Clune on a Saturday night after the newsman had dropped into the Pompeian Room. Margaret, recovered from giving birth to the healthy Walter Jr., and Hagen, taking a break from road work, had resumed their Saturday night socializing at the hotel.

According to Clune, he assumed his friend would leap at the opportunity. "That's what I keep saying," Margaret jumped in. "The dope, he won't make up his mind."

"I don't know," Hagen said. "I've always been around here. When I walk down Main Street, everyone knows me."

Though it meant Hagen moving away and possibly the end of their friendship, Clune argued that Hagen should head for Detroit. (As it turned out, Clune would go there himself when he accepted a reporting job, and the friendship with Hagen would be renewed.) He pointed out that Oakland Hills wanted Hagen more as a playing representative, and you couldn't do better than a U.S. Open winner.

Time off for tournaments had not been a big issue at the Country Club of Rochester. If anything, Hagen's participation in the U.S. Open, Western Open, and other official events was good PR for the club, especially if he won them. But Hagen liked making money and the noncharity exhibitions were the way to do that. The officials at Rochester expected him at least to go through the motions of being head pro, which included giving some lessons and supervising the pro shop, both of which required being on site for some of the year.

Hawkins and Mack weren't looking to have an Open winner giving lessons, and Oakland Hills didn't even have a pro shop yet. They liked the idea of him representing their club in both tourneys and exhibitions as though he played while wearing an Oakland Hills sandwich board. Combine this free rein with a bigger salary, and Hagen and his young family would be rolling in clover.

"You're a national figure now," Clune reminded him. "You've won the American championship. You'll win it again. You're known to a lot of people beyond our Main Street."

"Well, I want to think it over," Hagen said. "No hurry."

Margaret said firmly, "We're going."

It took a week for Hagen to agree with his wife. Then he called Clune, asked him to stop by the Pompeian Room that Saturday night, and told him of the decision. The reporter had an exclusive for the *Democrat and Chronicle,* but he wrote it with mixed emotions.

Walter and Margaret packed up their belongings, said farewell to family and friends in Corbett's Glen and at the Country Club of Rochester, and with their son set off around the curve of the Great Lakes to Detroit.

As the crow flies, it's not a great distance from western New York to southern Michigan. However, it would turn out that by leaving Rochester and the first twenty-five years of his life behind, Walter Hagen was beginning an unprecedented adventure as a professional golf champion.

CHAPTER 7

THE HAGENS SETTLED IN DETROIT and were impressed by their new surroundings. "Detroit was booming when I hit town in 1918," Hagen recalled. "The atmosphere was entirely different from Rochester. The few families with established social position were put into the background by the power and money of the automobile men and their wives. The city was rugged, vibrant, and growing."

He enjoyed being told about the millions being made by the Ford family and such other Detroit business barons as Tom Webber, Walter Chrysler, Fred Zeder, and Larry Fisher. "They took me in as one of their own," Hagen wrote. "I was a golf champion and a good fellow, and that was enough for them."

The environment and energy of the developing city made Detroit a good fit for a young man with working-class roots and grand ambitions. However, it turned out that Hagen didn't spend a lot of time there in 1918. There were plenty of exhibitions—paying gigs along with charity events—to go to. The Fords and other backers of Oakland Hills were smart enough to realize that having Hagen on the road representing the club was much more to their benefit than keeping him in the back shop building clubs or giving lessons to members' wives. In any case, the Oakland Hills facility and buildings had not yet been completed and Hagen was not the type to wait around.

When he was in town, Hagen's duties included telling visitors to the club how terrific Oakland Hills was going to be when fully finished (this was certainly true about the Donald Ross–designed course) and that they should sign up right away to become members—and while they were at it, buy a piece of property near the club. He was also expected to be present at some social functions hosted by club officials at local hotels, which was fine for both Walter and Margaret.

Hagen was given plenty of attention, enabling him to continue to become comfortable in the spotlight. He was surrounded by wealthy, sophisticated, and ambitious people who saw him not so much as a golf professional employed by Oakland Hills but as a headline-grabbing sports champion with a U.S. Open notched on his belt. Hagen knew he was this, but also could not ignore that he was head pro there and was being treated with respect because of his victories, not his occupation.

As interesting as Detroit was, there was still a short period of adjustment. "I was very homesick for Rochester those first few months," remembered Hagen. "Detroit was a big, rushing, bustling city. I missed the quiet slow-moving traffic in the streets of Rochester. I missed the countryside where Margaret and I had lived in our little cottage. I missed the huge trees and the meadows and the little brook that ran through Corbett's Glen. I even missed the telephone poles on the road to the Country Club of Rochester."

But there was no turning back. Life had changed irrevocably: "Detroit was a long jump for me, and it took me a while to get over the homesick feeling. But when I did get over it, life in my new home city hit me big!"

Margaret was the wife of the center of attention and thus basked in the same spotlight. This allowed her to get a fresh start at Oakland Hills. No more non-invitations or occasional pitying glances for her as there had been back at the Country Club of Rochester for marrying a social inferior.

It appears that Margaret was welcomed by her husband's new friends and business acquaintances in Detroit, and that she could enjoy the high life there as much as the responsibilities of being a mother to Walter Jr. allowed. It was certainly possible that the Hagens could now afford child care, but Margaret's responsibilities were lightened because when he was in town Walter Sr. doted on the baby.

When he was in town, though, became less and less frequent. Hagen's suitcase had not been unpacked for long when it was time to hit the road again, to the Midwest and up and down the East Coast so he could take advantage of all the events on his golf dance card.

In one of a series of exhibitions, Hagen (with the best score on the day) and a local pro, John Anderson, teamed up to defeat Jerry Travers and Jim Barnes in a four-ball exhibition that raised funds for the Red Cross. A month later, Hagen and Barnes were a team and they downed Travers and Chick Evans in another Red Cross four-ball event, this one at Siwanoy, despite Evans sinking a 35-foot putt on the 18th hole to tie and prolong the match. The very next day in Philadelphia, Evans and local Max Marston beat Barnes and Hagen even though the latter had the day's low score.

Hagen had a sincere commitment to raising funds for the war effort, but he also loved making money over and above what Oakland Hills was paying him. He accepted invitations for paying exhibitions, and when he was in or near major cities, especially New York, he was happy to play golf with the members of wealthy families and corporate big shots. His top-shelf résumé and gregariousness made him a desirable partner or foe. Hagen's get-togethers with corporate executives and magnates presaged the tradition of the high-paying corporate golf outing that is commonplace among moonlighting pros today.

Inevitably, as Hagen traveled and accepted more and more invitations, especially those in the big cities, he became at ease with a "fast" crowd that partied as much as they could stand (prompting, the following year, the Prohibition Act). According to several accounts, including Hagen's own, it was at this time that he took up smoking and drinking.

Clearly, living somewhere other than Rochester meant his childhood and young adulthood, and everything that went with them, were over. Out of sight and out of mind were parents, acquaintances since birth, and the clean living that now paled next to the parties in Detroit and on the road. Hagen embraced the smoking and drinking habits enthusiastically, and took full advantage of them for the next fifty-one years.

At the same time, the twenty-five-year-old Hagen had become a popular figure to men because of his golf success and to women because of his appearance and success. "In Detroit Walter came fully into his own," wrote Henry Clune in a newspaper reminiscence published twenty-five years later, referring to the image of the freewheeling Hagen that had by then become familiar to the public. "He was a big fine-looking fellow, his broad, good-natured face browned by the sun and wind to the hue of a well-stained meerschaum bowl. He wore giddy golf hose and sweaters and blazers, and his dark hair was slicked down to a patent-leather shine. He was as gay and carefree as a Spanish caballero, and the dollies on the golf club verandas would suck in their breath when he passed, nearly swallow their gum and exclaim, ecstatically, 'Oh, isn't he won-der-ful!'"

When Hagen was in Detroit, the family home was often the center of social activities, though he still wasn't as interested in such things as Margaret was. He wanted to be the best in golf. The period after World War I finally ended offered that opportunity.

He took full advantage of it.

The end of World War I and the return to peacetime routines allowed for a revival of golf competition in the States and in Europe, and especially in America there was a surge of interest in playing the sport.

A subtle but effective part of the boom in golf was the creation of Daylight Savings Time in 1918. This added another hour to afternoon and early-evening activities, such as golf after work. With more than two thousand courses in the States by the end of that year, providing more time to play was as important as space to play.

As 1919 dawned, Hagen was viewed as one of the four best players in American golf, with the others being the professionals Long Jim Barnes and Jock Hutchison and the amateur Chick Evans. Of the pros, Hagen was the only homebred, with Barnes born in England and Hutchison in Scotland. But such a perception by golf fans and the press was pretty much meaningless given that there had been no majors in '17 and '18 and the competition pool was rather shallow because of the war.

Fortunately for everyone concerned, for the first time in three years there would be a U.S. Open Golf Championship, which was set for the Brae Burn Country Club in West Newton, Massachusetts. Also in 1919, other tournaments were being revived or initiated, meaning that the "tour," such as it was, would return to a prewar schedule and possibly exceed it. With the backing of the officials at Oakland Hills, and having been chomping at the bit to further prove himself as a professional, Hagen was ready.

He wasn't the only one. With the war over, the entire sports scene in America was undergoing a sea change. In his classic *The Story of American Golf,* Herbert Warren Wind describes how the war's end and the new year "found Americans in a furious hurry to enjoy themselves. . . . The nation played sports and watched sports with a wild-eyed seriousness it has never abandoned and modified only slightly in times of depression and war. The nation asked for champions, and got them aplenty . . ."

In baseball, Babe Ruth was creating a stir as a pitcher in Boston. In boxing, all eyes were on Jack Dempsey as the main challenger to the giant Jess Willard. In tennis, Bill Tilden was becoming a star. There had already been glimpses of the enormous talent and fire of Bobby Jones. In upstate New York seventeen-year-old Eugene Saraceni was getting ready to try his hand as a professional golfer.

"Golf rode forward on the crest of the wave," Wind wrote. "Golf courses cut their grainfields and resurrected the plans for enlargement that the war years had postponed. The men newly rich from the war became the most ardent of the ardent recruits, the country-clubbers made architecture a paying profession, the golf ball manufacturers started their search once again for golf balls that would go ten yards farther and possibly develop an allergy to sand traps and rough."

More golf courses meant more golf professionals, and the scale started to tip. There were still plenty of amateurs and indeed the success of Jones in the 1920s would be the high-water mark of amateur golf. But as an occupation, being a golf pro was starting to become as good as a growth stock because as the demand intensified, and with a good economy, weekly wages and perks for pros rose (they were now getting as much as $3.50 per lesson). They might still be regarded as hired help not allowed in the clubhouse or to share other facilities with members, but the better ones were being treated more like the professionals they were.

Hagen represented the new golf pro. He collected a salary for representing the Oakland Hills Golf Club. Presumably, once the facilities were complete, he would give lessons to club members and be in charge of the pro shop. He took time off to play in tournaments, albeit a lot more time off than the average professional. He gave exhibitions, though it was certainly true that more people came to see Hagen than the average pro. He was sought out for advice on playing and equipment and viewed as an expert on golf. It's hard to say if he would have been allowed in the clubhouse, because Oakland Hills was still a few months shy of having one, but it would not be surprising for the club to adhere to the general policy of the time.

What was different and would become more of a prominent factor in the public's view of Hagen is that he was starting to form the mold of the professional tournament golfer, something like a minstrel who traveled from town to town to put on a show. Increasingly, he performed this role with flair and charisma as well as skill.

Describing him in *The Golden Era of Golf,* Al Barkow wrote, "Hagen was a character. . . . He had a flair for the grand gesture. Because of his wildness with the driver, he had many opportunities to play tough shots, and it was his shtick to make them seem even tougher. He would take a lot of time considering all the problems, checking angles like a pool shooter, grimacing as if in psychic pain, then play a brilliant recovery at which the crowd raved. Many didn't know much about golf and didn't realize they were getting a bit of a con job; but even those who were in on it enjoyed the act."

"Above all, Hagen was interesting to watch," according to Herbert Warren Wind. "A born showman, he could feel the grip he gained on galleries. He discovered that they liked him best when he gave full rein to his developing personality—his unruffled poise in the face of disaster, an unmalicious condescension toward his opponents and toward the galleries themselves, a touch of bravura at those very moments when he could have been forgiven for quailing. But he built his performance on good golf."

In addition to the influence on the public of Hagen and other top golfers, a constructive impact on the sport was that the Professional Golfers Association had survived the war and was poised to create, co-ordinate, and schedule tournaments with higher than ever purses. While it was still impossible for someone to make a living just playing tournament golf—even if you won every event, there weren't enough of them yet, and the postwar purses were still too paltry—an affiliation of tournaments was being formed through the PGA and thus for pros there was a "tour" on which money could be earned. It was a beginning, and at the very least doing well on the still-forming tour opened doors to better club pro positions.

In the ensuing years, as more events were added to the PGA schedule and club pros earned more, it made less sense for an ambitious player to remain an amateur. Crucial to the rise of professional golf in America was the emerging view that it was okay to appreciate and even become fans of tournament pros in the same manner as following the exploits of baseball stars. During much of 1919, when people opened up their newspapers, the sports sections regularly reported on the victories, travels, and exploits of Walter Hagen and his top rivals who were playing the biggest role in reviving postwar golf.

Because the war had been fought in Europe, golf was slower to make a comeback there. Perhaps for this reason and the need to earn money, the best players were preparing to invade America again when travel across the Atlantic resumed. Incredibly, Harry Vardon, almost fifty, was still playing good golf and was a formidable competitor. Ted Ray was in his forties and fading a bit, though as it turned out he had one last hurrah left in him. The new British players flexing their muscles were Abe Mitchell, George Duncan, Arthur Havers, the three Whitcombe brothers, Tommy Armour (who had been wounded in the war), and Cyril Tolley (who had spent thirteen months in a German prison camp). They believed they would usher in a new era of British domination in golf.

The first war-free year was a pivotal one for Hagen: more travel to more exhibitions, more tournaments with winnings for the taking, another crack at the U.S. Open, the potential for more of the fame he craved as a youngster—and the end of his marriage. However much Walter and Margaret may have loved each other, the arrival of Walter Jr. after only a year of marriage had to have changed the relationship. Yet the biggest toll had to be the more frequent and lengthy separations. Hagen doted on his son when he was in Detroit, but aside from that he didn't want to be weighed down with responsibilities when there was an entire golf and social world to enjoy. Perhaps Margaret recognized the irony that the socialite she had developed was now more interested in traveling and partying than being a husband.

Whatever Hagen thought about the growing crisis in his marriage, it seems that resolving it was not his top priority. He took off for Florida to play exhibitions for all of January, February, and March 1919. From a professional golfer's perspective (as well as that of a restless husband), this made perfect sense. What could you do in Detroit in the depth of winter to keep your game sharp? Florida was where one could play every day, make some money, and avoid personal confrontations.

The construction of golf courses in Florida had been slowed a bit in 1918 because of America's full participation in the war, but things were starting to come back the following year. It was not unusual to find a pro from the Northeast featured as the playing professional at a Florida club. Hagen had a casual affiliation with the Palma Ceia Golf Club in Tampa, meaning he had a place to stay and could call it his home course.

One of the most popular shows for Florida residents and tourists and a way for players to pick up some easy winter cash was engaging in challenge matches with pros representing other Florida clubs. For example, on February 9 Hagen (still often referred to in print as "Hagan," confused with the other player) and another winter itinerant, Charles Lorms from Toledo, challenged Alex and George Smith, who back home were affiliated with the Wykagyl Club in New York and in Florida represented Belleair Heights. In the match-play event, the Smith brothers won 2-up.

In March, also at Belleair Heights, another special event was staged. As the *New York Times* reported: "Sensational golf was played here today in the professional tournament in which six noted players took part. Walter Hagen of Detroit won with a score of 71, one stroke above par, but he was pressed closely all the way by Jim Barnes of Sunset Hill, who ended with 74. Alex Smith, the Wykagyl star, who has charge of the course here, was right at Barnes's heels. Jock Hutchison of Glenview did not get his long game working and had too much left to do around the greens."

In the spring Hagen was back and forth between Detroit and the events he had committed to. This schedule suited him fine as a way to fulfill his few obligations at Oakland Hills and to participate in tournaments and exhibitions, but it intensified tensions between the Hagens.

"I saw little of Hagen during the summer of 1919 that I lived in Detroit," reported Henry Clune. "He was continually on the road playing tournaments and exhibition matches. Mrs. Hagen did not accompany him on these travels. I met her occasionally in shopping marts and we'd lunch together.

"She had achieved at Oakland Hills a status that had been denied her at the Country Club of Rochester, but she was losing her hold on her husband. Walter had become the darling of the golf courses, gushed over by fashionable women, a bon vivant who had far transcended the compass of Margaret's own high-life imaginings. 'Walter goes away,' she lamented, 'and writes me pages and pages of golf. I want romance.'"

One day when Clune and Margaret met on the street, she told him that her husband was in town for a couple of days and invited their old friend to their home for dinner. Clune arrived at 6:30; Hagen didn't get home until 7:30, and he brought with him that day's caddie. This wasn't the good-old-days dinner party Margaret had in mind.

She brought out a couple of side dishes and as the main course a ham "that I must say looked a little worse for wear," Clune commented in his memoirs.

"'We got that old hacked ham again?' Walter remarked querulously.

"'Shut up, you,' Margaret answered testily. 'I can remember, you had ham on the table, you thought it was your birthday.'

"Matters were obviously not well in the household," Clune concluded tactfully. "I'm afraid Walter was as ill suited for the restraints and ordinances of the conjugal state as a pirate."

A victory in the North and South Open at Pinehurst for the second time had to be satisfying, even though the ranks of top players had been depleted by the war. But what really mattered to Hagen and to American golf in general was the resumption of the U.S. Open, at the Brae Burn course.

Hagen arrived in Boston several days before the National Championship began and got some practice in, but not too much because he preferred "to be keen, fresh, and eager when play actually started." Total prize money for the 1919 National Championship had been raised to $1,745, and another change was the Open would be played over three days instead of two, with 36 holes on the third day.

Most of Hagen's play took place off the course. In his travels during the past year or so, which included seeing the shows on Broadway, Hagen had been introduced at a postperformance party to the entertainer Al Jolson. Hagen may not have cared all that much about singing and dancing, but he had to be impressed by getting to know a well-established stage star; on his part, Jolson was an occasional golfer, and befriending one of the best in the sport couldn't hurt. At this time in his life for Hagen, a spotlight-loving performer and a nocturnal carouser like Jolson, who had racked up plenty of mileage, had to engender some camaraderie.

The good news for Hagen in Boston was that Jolson was there too, appearing in the musical *Sinbad.* The bad news for Hagen was the Jolson experience meant that "most of my time was taken up with meeting pals and having parties each night." This was not very good preparation for the U.S. Open.

A memorable record was set in the first round, though one never boasted about. Jim Barnes was partnered with Willie Chisholm, who had calmed his nerves with several shots of scotch before teeing off. He avoided disaster until the 8th hole, a 185-yard par-3. The tee shot had to carry a rock-strewn ravine.

Chisholm was still feeling the effects of conferring with Johnny Walker. His tee shot was well short, landing in the ravine, behind a boulder. Determined to get it out without a penalty stroke, he swung at the ball with his niblick, striking the boulder and unleashing a shower of sparks. Impressed by the display, he did it again.

Standing on the wooden footbridge over the ravine, Barnes offered to keep count. On the 14th swing of the hole, after the ball had ricocheted around the ravine several times, it popped up and landed on the green. A sweaty and shaking Chisholm staggered out of the ravine and lined up his putt. He missed. He missed the comeback. When he finally tapped in, Barnes grinned—he was, after all, a witness to history—and told his partner to write *18* on his card. This tournament record would not be broken until 1938.

Hagen was faring much better despite his nighttime rituals. After 54 holes he had a decent score of 226. However, what would have done the trick in Brookline in 1913 wasn't enough at the par-71 Brae

Burn in 1919. Mike Brady of Boston had jumped ahead, shooting a relatively glistening 221. Make up 5 strokes in 18 holes in an opponent's hometown? Not very likely.

In his recollection *Unplayable Lies,* Fred Corcoran, who grew up in Boston and, among other accomplishments, was tournament director for the PGA of America, wrote about the 1919 Open: "I was working the scoreboard for the USGA, my first assignment of that kind. Hagen was already a sports page celebrity and well on his way to becoming the legend he is now, a bronzed fine specimen of a man who strode down the fairway with his head high. Hagen always walked with his head in the air as if, subconsciously, looking over the heads of ordinary mortals."

But as would be a hallmark of Hagen's career, he did what he had to do to win, whether it be a dramatic charge or just keeping himself in contention and letting the pressure or bad luck undo the competition. In the final round of the National Championship, witnessed by more than ten thousand spectators, it was the latter strategy that worked. It couldn't have hurt that Brady remembered Hagen overtaking him to win the Massachusetts Open four years earlier at Brookline.

Hagen shot a 75, which meant he didn't fall any further back as the wheels came off of Brady's round. Though older and more experienced than his competitor as well as playing in front of cheering fans, Brady stumbled around the course to earn no more than an 80 (with a humiliating 41 on the back nine). After 72 holes, Hagen and Brady were tied.

Hagen had actually come within a whisker of winning the Open on the 72nd hole. His drive on the par 4 was adequate, which for Hagen was the equivalent of putting it in the middle of the fairway 300 yards away. The second shot, however, would be a challenge: a long carry to a small, slick, two-tiered green with a stone wall close enough that if he was off line the ball could ricochet out of bounds, ensuring only second place, at best.

"Most golfers would have played for a safe 4, aimed for the middle of the green and allowed themselves two putts to get down for a tie," according to Herbert Warren Wind. "Hagen wasn't built that way."

The club he drew from his bag was comparable to today's 2-iron. Hagen set himself—he was going for the win; second place or anything else didn't matter—then lashed at the ball. It went a bit right but held the line, then landed and climbed the first tier to stop 8 feet from the cup. Slumped in the locker room, Brady heard the cheers of the energized crowd.

Hagen arrived at the 18th green and fully took in how close he was to another U.S. Open trophy. After acknowledging the seething crowd that had just witnessed a courageous shot that rivaled Ouimet's on the 17th at The Country Club, Hagen gestured toward the locker room, beckoning Brady to come out.

Out he came, plodding as though heading for the guillotine. As Brady and the crowd watched, Hagen lined up the putt and stroked it. It caught the lip and spun out. He had to settle for par and a tie. The play-off would be tomorrow.

According to a couple of accounts, there was some consolation for not winning the Open in regulation. Hagen had spotted an attractive woman among the spectators around the 16th tee. He struck up a conversation with her, continued it on the 17th, and by the time he arrived at the last tee he had arranged a date with her for that evening.

To help prepare for the 18-hole play-off, Brady had his own bed and home cooking. Hagen participated in the biggest party of a week of parties. Jolson and his troupe were finishing up *Sinbad* in Boston, and a farewell bash was arranged for that night.

"The party lasted all night . . . champagne, pretty girls, jokes and laughter . . . no sleep," Hagen recollected. The woman he had met on the Brae Burn course was with him; however, since he couldn't remember her name, to be on the safe side Hagen kept calling her "my dear" all night.

"In the small hours of the morning I recalled that I had an important date within a few hours. I dashed back to my hotel for a quick shower, a bit of breakfast, and fresh clothing. Then I wheeled my big Pierce–Arrow out to Brae Burn for the play-off. I found Mike out there. He'd been hitting practice shots for more than an hour."

Still, even without having slept (assuming we fully accept his account), Hagen had dressed well, wearing knickers and a snazzy bow tie. He also knew that he had Brady beaten before they teed off. The night before the local hero had not gone anywhere but home, yet he looked hungover—his eyes were red, his cheeks shook, his hands trembled, and his mouth was dry. "While [Mike] was still taking practice swings," Hagen recalled, "I jogged into the grill to bend a quick elbow," no doubt toasting Brady as he did so.

Hagen waited until the second tee (they parred the first hole) to get his dig in. As Brady was about to address the ball, Hagen said, "Mike, if I were you, I'd roll down my shirt sleeves." Brady straightened and asked, "Why?" After lighting a cigarette, Hagen replied, "The way they are now, everyone can see your forearms quivering."

Brady tried to ignore his rival but hooked his shot deep into the woods and double-bogeyed the hole. Hagen parred and held that 2-stroke lead through the 10th hole. Surveying his long putt, Hagen absentmindedly picked a discarded match off the green. He made the putt and moved on.

On the next hole, though, a U.S. Golf Association official approached Hagen and told him that he had removed loose debris from within 20 yards of the hole. Hagen disagreed that he had violated a rule and argued against the 2-stroke penalty. A fan stepped forward and said that Brady had removed a stone from near the hole at the 9th, which Brady, demonstrating that nervous or not he was a man of honor, admitted was true. When he accepted the 2-stroke penalty, Hagen dropped his protest and accepted his penalty.

"I was trying to be as unconcerned as possible about the entire deal," Hagen recalled. "But I certainly did not want to win the National Open Championship on penalties." Actually, if Brady had not admitted his infraction, Hagen faced *losing* the Open on penalties.

There was another incident in the 1919 U.S. Open play-off that has become one of the most famous in the event's history. By the par-3 17th hole, according to Hagen, "playing was not my only problem. I was having a darned difficult time just staying awake." His tee shot, not surprisingly, went awry and the ball landed in a muddy bank.

"Landed" is being too generous—it became embedded in the mud. Ironically, it might have been determined lost except that after some searching by both competitors, the upstanding Brady spotted it and alerted his opponent. When Hagen arrived at the scene of the crime, he could barely see a patch of white.

This was a fix all right, with the 2-shot lead he had nursed as deeply endangered as his ball was in the mud. His first thought was to contend that the ball was in so deep that a spectator must have stepped on it. Alas, the USGA officials he approached with this possibility had not seen anyone near that spot, so that appeal was dismissed.

Thinking fast, Hagen's next request was that he be allowed to identify his ball. But he and Brady were the only two players on the course, everyone knew where Brady's shot had landed, and the spectators had seen where Hagen's ball landed. What was to identify?

One might think that Hagen was either trying to bend a rule or was not adhering to the spirit of fair play with this second argument. And one might be right. Hacking away at a ball embedded in mud could have resulted in a fate similar to that of Willie Chisholm, and farewell National Championship. It is rare today to see a pro golfer protest a penalty, especially while still on the course. (Think of poor Ian Woosnam in the 2001 British Open, penalized for having fifteen clubs in his bag while he was only a shot off the lead in the final round—he soldiered on and still almost won.) But we can't overlook that Hagen's argument had some validity because of rules in place at the time.

Given that the play-off was the fifth round played on this course in four days, it is conceivable that the embedded ball could have been lost anytime by anyone in the previous few days. If Hagen hit it out and then discovered he'd played the wrong ball, the 2-stroke penalty coupled with the trouble he was already in at 17 could cost him the National Championship.

The USGA officials on the scene had to agree. They couldn't possibly take the chance of costing a player the Open by not following the rules. Permission was given to lift and identify the ball. (In 1954, the USGA changed the rule so that a player can remove any covering material to see the top of the ball, and there would be no penalty for playing the wrong ball from a hazard.) Using his thumb and forefinger, Hagen carefully raised the ball out of the muck.

It was indeed his. As he examined it, the socket in the mud filled in so that when Hagen put the ball back down in the same spot (which the rules in 1919 called for), it was no longer sunk. He struck his second shot with a niblick from there, putting the ball in a greenside bunker. He ended up with a double bogey, but again Brady did his part, getting only a 4 on the hole. Hagen held a 1-stroke lead as the competitors faced their 90th hole of the National Championship.

Brady put his drive right down the fairway. Hagen half-topped his and was immediately in trouble. Using a brassie, he walloped the ball, and it carried to just off the green. Brady's second shot came up well short. The crowd roared when Brady chipped and almost holed his third shot. Unfazed, Hagen landed his ball 3 feet from the hole. He putted in from there, and Brady's shorter putt became moot. The final result: Hagen 77, Brady 78. The first-prize check was $500.

The twenty-six-year-old from Detroit had captured his second National Championship, near where it had all started for him in this event. Compared to today's scores, those of Hagen and Brady are not impressive (especially after Tiger Woods's destruction of Pebble Beach in 2000), but they were acceptable for the time, and most important for Hagen was establishing in front of a U.S. Open crowd that he could do what he had to do to win.

The reaction to Hagen's victory was much more boisterous than at his 1914 U.S. Open. First of all, whoever won the 1919 Open would get a good deal of attention because the sports press was pleased that the National Championship had resumed, and specifically in this case, it had featured a taut 18-hole play-off. Second, now the Detroit press was as wild about Walter as the press in Rochester, and the press in New York City for that matter because since '14 Hagen had become a familiar figure there.

Hagen returned to Detroit as a triumphant adopted son. No one was more pleased than officials at the Oakland Hills Golf Club. A celebratory dinner was arranged for the conquering hero. When Hagen arrived back home, how gracious, it seemed, that he had brought Mike Brady with him.

It was indeed gracious, but he had another motive: With two U.S. Open wins under his belt, he didn't want to return to being a simple club pro, however nice and easy his situation with Oakland Hills was.

During the dinner there was one speech after another boozily praising the conquering hero, then the time finally came for Hagen to stand and deliver his own speech. Though he would never be fully comfortable with public speaking, he had his act down pat for this occasion: After only a year, he was resigning.

Even the most inebriated member of the audience gasped at that one. Casually, Hagen elaborated that he was going to devote himself to being a full-time golfer—not a club maker or teacher or real-estate shill, but a tournament player, living on his skill and his wits and not aligned with any club. At that moment, Walter Hagen was inventing an occupation.

What was the Oakland Hills Golf Club to do, suddenly losing its prestigious pro? Hagen had that figured out—hire the next best thing. With complete confidence in the members, he offered Mike Brady as the new head pro.

Accepting what seemed to be the inevitable, the club members agreed. (They would go even further two years later when they voted Hagen, no longer an employee, in as a lifetime member.) Then after a fine party that lasted well into the night, Hagen packed his bags and left Detroit, and with it, Margaret. He would return to the city, and eventually live there off and on for the rest of his life, but in more than one way he had hoisted anchor and it was time to travel America and the world as a professional tournament golfer.

CHAPTER 8

BECAUSE OF JOHNNY McDERMOTT'S back-to-back wins in 1911 and 1912, Hagen was not the first American to win the U.S. Open twice. However, poor Johnny was no longer part of the golf scene, plus his victories came at a time (pre-Brookline) when less attention was paid to golf by the U.S. press and the public. This left Hagen and Francis Ouimet as the most well-known representatives of the National Championship, with Hagen being the only professional to have won it since 1914.

There was another milestone for pros at the 1919 Open in addition to Hagen's victory. As A. Linde Fowler noted in the *American Golfer,* "Eight professionals finished better than any amateur in the championship at Brae Burn, which is the first time the amateurs have finished worse than second since 1913."

After the win at Brae Burn, once more endorsements and other opportunities came Hagen's way. This time, he was able to take advantage of more of them, such as for alcohol, cigarettes, and cars. A somewhat unusual offer, though one that was made available to top baseball players and boxers (such as Dempsey), was to be part of a vaudeville show that would tour the country. The tour would last for forty weeks, and Hagen claimed that an especially lucrative offer was dangled before him: "In those days with no popular radio or television, sponsors with fantastic bankrolls didn't exist, and $1,500 a week was big dough," he recalled.

But he turned down the offer. As great as the money was, forty weeks meant giving up competing against his peers on a regular basis.

No doubt, too, he considered that he would be part of a show with other performers, many of them more well-known than he was to stage audiences, and it had to be hard to give up being the center of attention in his own world. There may have also been the concern that by going into vaudeville he would become a trick-shot artist, which pleased crowds but wasn't the way to be a winner.

With vaudeville spurned, his second National Championship offered Hagen chances to have a strong impact on golf that would be witnessed by club officials, organizations, the press, fans, and anyone else connected to the sport. His career was going to be that of the touring golf professional, and he would support himself by playing golf year-round. He wanted to win more tournaments, especially the U.S. Open again, and maybe take a stab at the British Open in '20, an attempt which had been denied him as a reigning U.S. Open champion in the spring of 1915.

In professional golfer terms, Hagen was going to show that the world wasn't flat, that there was undiscovered country waiting for those who had enough talent, ambition, desire, nerve, and opportunity.

Hagen embarked on a coast-to-coast barnstorming tour. At both big and backwater courses spectators flocked to see the two-time National Champion who had a reputation for dramatic flair and colorful attire.

Charles Price, in his memoir *Golfer-at-Large,* wrote that Hagen "made countless one-day stands in the outlands of golfing America playing matches against any and all comers, charging spectators a dollar a head and making in the process more money than Babe Ruth [who, actually, was not yet making big money]—and eventually spending more than the entire Yankee outfield. . . . You could say that is how the Tour began—a combination of matinee comedy and golfing fireworks."

Any concern that Hagen was wasting too much of his time and talent on touring was dismissed by his winning the Metropolitan Open for the second time a few weeks after the Brae Burn victory. Perhaps his first win in this event in 1916 could be considered tainted by a mid-war dearth of talent and press scrutiny. A win in 1919, though, and so soon after the ordeal of a U.S. Open play-off win, was the real thing.

The field at the Metropolitan Open at the North Shore Country

Club on Long Island was a strong one. Jim Barnes was in it, as was Louis Tellier of France (who had become head pro at Brae Burn) along with Mike Brady and most of the top professionals and amateurs of the time. On the second day of the tournament, Hagen began six strokes down to leader Charlie Hoffner, but he clawed back into contention. Over 36 holes on the second day he shot a 72 and a 71, the best of the tourney; this included sinking a 15-foot bogey putt on the final hole. The result was a 294 and a 3-stroke victory over Tellier.

The year had been so successful (with the North and South win, too) that what was being written about him could be compared to some of the early commentary on Tiger Woods:

"No longer is there any reason for an argument as to where the premier honors belong among American golfers," a column in the *New York Times* intoned in July 1919. "Walter Hagen has settled that question so decisively that the only arguments in the case center around the identity of the player who is best qualified to give [Hagen] the best fight for top honors. . . .

"In Hagen golf enthusiasts have a homebred golfer with every promise of reaching as great heights as were ever reached by any devotee of the sport. He stands today alone at the head of his field, with every prospect of holding the position for a very long time."

Not everyone was convinced. Another columnist weighed in that Barnes, who had won the well-regarded Western Open that year (by 9 strokes) and had come close in the U.S. and Metropolitan Opens, was "several strokes better than Hagen" overall. The column concluded, "The rivalry between the two men is extremely friendly and the game gains much by the fact that they are so closely matched. Real competition is the life of sport, just as it is the life of trade."

It was disappointing, then, that an opportunity for "real competition" between Hagen and Barnes was missed that summer. According to the September 4, 1919, issue of the *New York Times,* "One of the biggest surprises of the golfing season was sprung yesterday when Alec Pirie, Secretary of the Professional Golfers' Association, announced that Walter Hagen, national open champion, had failed to qualify and therefore is not eligible to compete in the association's tournament. . . .

"To a marked degree the failure of Hagen to qualify robs the event of much of its luster, for there had been a great deal of rivalry manifested among the professional golfers, and more than one has openly expressed the desire to meet Hagen on the links in tournament play before the season skids off the sporting calendar."

The implication here is that Hagen had tried and failed to qualify. But that wasn't what happened. He hadn't made the effort to qualify, and for this he was, it seems rightly, subjected to some criticism. He had been busy on the road doing exhibitions, then instead of going to the PGA qualifier the last week in August, he participated in a 36-hole exhibition match with Mike Brady (taking the $500 purse with an 8-and-7 knockout). This was a blow to the PGA Championship, which wanted to resume with a bang after the war.

Hagen may have been lining up one gig after another because his personal life was in turmoil—he and Margaret kept attempting to reconcile, but each attempt went awry, probably because he was unable to resist the romance (and romances available) of the road and the size of the paychecks there. He couldn't have had any idea that he would be one of the most visible players in the Golden Age of Sport, but he may have had an inkling that he was on to something by keeping his focus on exhibitions and tournaments as the decade came to a close.

Much has been written about the Golden Age of Sport of the 1920s in the United States, so all that can be offered here is some (brief) perspective. Compared to almost a century ago, sports today are much more "golden," in that at any given moment year-round we can witness a wide range of superior athletes engaged in high-level competition for sums of money that would make Midas envious. Even so-called sports junkies can become a bit queasy.

So why were the 1920s regarded as a Golden Age? One explanation is that in several sports, dominating athletes and personalities emerged and titillated the public imagination. A few examples involve just the decade's first year. In baseball, Babe Ruth, who had abandoned pitching after the previous season, in 1920 played outfield full-time for the Yankees and swatted an unimaginable fifty-four homers. (Two years earlier, Wally Pipp had led the league with nine, and Ruth's total in '20 was more than that of any Major League team.)

Jack Dempsey was in his first full year as heavyweight champion in boxing. In tennis, Bill Tilden won both the U.S. Amateur and Wimbledon championships. Red Grange was tearing up the football fields as a college player (and later would be the centerpiece of the great Chicago Bears teams coached by George Halas). In golf there was Walter Hagen, with Bobby Jones getting notice as a potential rival and Chick Evans winning his second (and last) U.S. Amateur Championship, defeating Francis Ouimet. Then there was the colt Man o'War, which started and won eleven races in '20. Collectively, they were raising the bar for future generations.

Another explanation is that as the decade progressed, more people could participate in their heroes' exploits. The postwar economy made the newspaper business profitable, and across the country new dailies in medium-sized and small cities were blooming like flowers in spring, all with expanding sports sections. Also important was the initiation of broadcasting. No longer would sports events be staged in a national vacuum—first regionally, then nationally, radio would report the results of sports events as they finished and by mid-decade would begin to broadcast events live to a spellbound audience.

Radio didn't lend itself to the play-by-play of golf contests as it did to baseball, boxing, and college football. Print remained the best way to get the message across and newspapers did their part. Making a significant contribution was the *American Golfer.* The monthly magazine had turned out to be a survivor. Walter J. Travis had remained its sole editor, still obsessed by golf and more than willing to put into words— thousands of words—what the taciturn man could not say on the course. He wrote about the game with an unprecedented knowledge and passion. Travis once wrote seven thousand words about the Versailles Conference that ended World War I, comparing the negotiations to a golf match.

When Travis stepped down, in his late fifties and on the eve of the 1920s, he had one last brilliant shot in his bag: He appointed Grantland Rice as his successor. Along with Ring Lardner and Paul Gallico, "Granny" was the best American sportswriter of the decade (and beyond). While he did not exclusively focus on golf, when he wrote about it people were informed and inspired. He wasn't about to write exclusively for the *American Golfer*, but his attachment to the publication during the 1920s helped it and made it more reputable and necessary to followers of golf.

The influence of the *American Golfer* was pervasive. Of course, there was not the distribution of it that there is today of *Golf Digest*, *Golfweek*, and *Golf* magazine, but at the time more and more people interested in golf were being offered a well-written magazine that catered to their interests. Some articles viewed golf as a science and/or an art form, possibilities few newspapers had the time, space, or inclination to explore. Combine this with the thrilling exploits of Hagen and Jones and eventually the broadcasting of results nationwide, and no wonder golf hit its stride in the Golden Age.

Walter Hagen was the poster boy of a new era in golf with his slicked-back black hair, colorful clothes, tanned skin, cigarette protruding jauntily from his lips, and winning ways. As 1920 got into gear, his first full year as a full-time professional player, his goals were to win, make money, and have fun.

The dawn of the new decade found Hagen back in Florida for exhibition matches with club pros needing to collect some cash. Until the spring took hold up north, the pros played both coasts of Florida with the occasional side trip to Georgia and Louisiana.

Hagen was a top draw as the reigning national champion, and with each event he was learning more how to play to a crowd. It would seem that the best attraction for the fans—and the best way to make money—was to match him against Jim Barnes, who had won the 1919 PGA Championship that Hagen neglected. It was more common, however, in exhibition matches at the time for teams of two to play each other, which meant that the two top players didn't go head to head. One example was that on February 29 in New Orleans, Hagen and Alex Smith took on Barnes and David Robertson.

Hagen's team won, and he shot a 70 to Barnes's 73. A newspaper report of the match offered, "Today's meeting provided the first inkling of the comparative strength of Hagen and Barnes for the new golfing season," a statement that implies the reporter was fishing for a way to handicap the 1920 competitions.

But this event did produce an opportunity to put the two friends and rivals in the arena together. The fans in New Orleans took up a collection and $1,500 was offered for a 36-hole match between Hagen and Barnes a few days later—an offer impossible to refuse.

The contest was held on March 7 and witnessed by fifteen hundred people. "Today's match will not be a good-natured love feast," commented the *New York Times*. "It appears that Hagen has been thoroughly angered by Barnes's backers, and the champion is going after this match with the same eagerness he showed last year at Brae Burn."

It took 37 holes to decide the match. Barnes was ahead most of the day, as much as 4-up, but Hagen rallied again and again, never giving an inch. "Circumstances called on Hagen to display his powers of recovery on more occasions than they did Barnes, because Hagen got into more trouble, either through misjudgment or misfortune," the *Times* reported.

He finally caught Barnes on the 35th hole when he birdied the par-4 17th, thanks to making a 12-foot putt. They halved the last hole, then began sudden death. Barnes hooked his tee shot and never recovered, and Hagen made an easy par. Drinks were on him as he pocketed the $1,000 winner's check.

Two weeks later the two rivals were in the same tournament, an unofficial one (such as those not sanctioned by the PGA Tour held today in November and December) called the West Coast Open Golf Championship, held at Belleaire. Hagen again was victorious, winning by 12 strokes over Leo Diegel and 14 strokes over Barnes.

Once the southern swing was completed, it was time to enter the few official tournaments available, and for Hagen as the Open champion, participate in easy, moneymaking outings with business executives. The money flowed in. And it flowed out. Hagen was twenty-seven and technically unattached, people in the expanding high society sought him out, and long gone were the Rochester days when one had to make do with a fixed, meager salary.

When not on the road, Hagen continued to spend a lot of time in New York. He saw Broadway shows, went to nightclubs, hobnobbed with other sports luminaries like Jack Dempsey and Babe Ruth (after being traded by the Red Sox to the Yankees for the '20 season), partied in spacious Park Avenue apartments, and used his keen powers of observation to learn more about how gentlemen dressed and behaved.

By being the best in golf and acquiring such social skills while continuing to win, he was establishing the image of the professional tournament golfer in the eyes of New York society, which in the 1920s had the most powerful influence on American culture. Then in his travels, Hagen was presenting this image to other parts of the country.

And when Hagen did something on the golf course, others wanted to do it too. Of the many firsts credited to Hagen, one is use of the tee. George Grant, an African-American dentist in Boston, first created a tee in 1899. However, Dr. Grant did little more than hand samples of his invention to friends at their local golf course, and when he died in 1910 no one outside of Boston had ever heard of such a device.

Then in 1920, William Lowell, a dental surgeon in South Orange, New Jersey, created a wooden peg so he could raise the ball off the teeing ground to compensate for the lack of loft on his driver. Up to that point as well as in Dr. Grant's day, players would hit their ball off a tiny mound of sand or mud that had to be created at every hole, resulting in a lack of consistency in the mounds. It was also more convenient for players to have a pocketful of tees with them than to find out the group ahead had used the last of the sand or water the course provided.

After trying out the device, friends thought that Dr. Lowell was on to something. He patented it under the name "The Reddy Tee." At first, golfers were dubious, then Dr. Lowell had the bright idea of offering Hagen and Joe Kirkwood $2,500 to use the tee, at least during practice rounds. They did, and they liked the tee so much they began to use it during exhibitions and tournaments. Seeing this, and the way Hagen stuck the tee behind his ear like a pencil after every drive, influenced fans and fellow competitors, and tees became a hit.

Dr. Lowell gave up dentistry and formed the Reddy Tee Company. By the mid-'20s the company was grossing over $300,000 annually. The F. W. Woolworth Company alone ordered a billion tees. Alas, there were problems with Dr. Lowell's patent. He spent the '20s distracted by expensive legal battles, trying unsuccessfully to keep an exclusive on the tee. The company didn't survive the Depression, and the former dentist died close to being broke in 1954 at the age of ninety-one.

• • •

Walter Hagen's 1919 U.S. Open victory was the seventh win in a row for an American in the event, so it was clear that Americans had taken hold of their own National Championship. The series of wins by McDermott (twice), Hagen (twice), Ouimet, Travers, and Evans implied that the Americans had shifted this event's balance of power away from the British indefinitely. (Indeed, the next British-born player to win the U.S. Open would be Tony Jacklin in 1970.)

But what about that other Open? Winning or at least contending in the oldest tournament in golf would be an achievement equal to if not better than capturing the much younger U.S. Open. To go across the Atlantic and win the claret jug was incentive enough, but U.S.-born players of Hagen's generation were well aware that beginning in 1895 British players had steamed west to routinely take *their* National Championship, so by the 1920s it was time to get something back. That no American had won the British Open in the sixty years of its existence had to make the prospect of victory even more enticing.

Winning a British Open had to be attractive for Hagen specifically. The outbreak of World War I had denied him the opportunity to compete the last time he was the reigning U.S. Open champion. Having won two National Championships by 1920, he had to view the British Open as the next significant challenge on his drive to be the top professional golfer. And by being a more experienced person, player, and traveler than he was as a twenty-one-year-old U.S. Open winner in 1914, Hagen had to feel more ready for the experience of going overseas to seek golf glory.

No doubt there was one more consideration. According to the *New York Times* in February 1920, "Prize money offered in open tournaments in this country to golf professionals seems small compared to the British purses, which go up into the thousands." How appealing it was to challenge the British in their own land and have the potential to win bigger purses at the same time.

The article went on to offer that because of several big-money events scheduled in Great Britain "it would not be surprising to find Hagen, Barnes, Hutchison, and other invaders packing their duds earlier than expected for the trip to the other side."

Who would the top competitors be? The article's commentary continued, "The leading golfer of the world is, obviously, impossible to name. On this side Hagen or Barnes would receive the consensus. England would nominate Abe Mitchell on a first ballot. But in Australia they have in J. H. Kirkwood a player whom they choose to describe as the 'superman' of the game. If Kirkwood isn't the greatest linksman on this planet, then the Antipodeans want to know who is."

Perhaps the "Antipodeans" had been sampling some native ale when drawing this conclusion about Kirkwood. Although Kirkwood had made a good impression the last couple of years in tournaments in the U.S. and Great Britain, trophy-wise he was not the equal of Hagen, Mitchell, Barnes, Hutchison, and a half dozen other players. However, Kirkwood would have an enjoyable and profitable career, a large part of it due to his association with the man whom he would always call the Haig.

With comparatively more green to be harvested across the Pond, it made sense that in the spring of 1920 Hagen planned a trip to England that would include exhibition matches, tours to play some of the country's better-known courses, and an attempt to win the British Open. He was, in some ways, going to emulate what Harry Vardon did in America in 1900, only Hagen was bringing a bunch of friends with him.

The trip to Great Britain in May 1920 was expensive, especially so for Hagen because he had no intention of having anything other than first-class accommodations in transit and when he arrived. Fortunately for him, as had happened in 1914 for the trip to Chicago and the U.S. Open, a benefactor appeared to underwrite Hagen's first attempt to capture the British crown jewel of golf. Al Wallace of Oakland Hills offered to pay the expenses and Hagen accepted. Wallace had to know what his wallet was in for, but he must have believed in Hagen enough to underwrite an assault on the Open (and was probably planning to wager six ways from Sunday on the event, which was and is legal in England).

When Hagen left New York he was accompanied by Wallace and someone who had become a good friend, H. B. Martin, a reporter for the *New York Globe*. He had first tried to persuade his old friend Henry Clune to go along. Clune said yes, although nervously because he'd never been very far from Rochester or Detroit before. Also, despite his friendship with Hagen that had begun when they were teenagers, Clune didn't play golf and knew little about the sport.

"Heck, what's the difference," Hagen said. "You can fake it." But Wallace vetoed the idea and Martin signed on.

Martin's official job was to report on the Americans' exploits in Great Britain to golf fans back home. Unofficially, he ghostwrote a column for Hagen that was syndicated to fifty U.S. newspapers.

Sailing on the *Mauretania,* Hagen was introduced to the actress Constance Talmadge, and the two hit it off. When the ship arrived in England, and learning that Hagen and Martin had overlooked making hotel reservations, Talmadge offered her suite at the Carlton Hotel. Years later, Hagen would comment laconically, "Having a glamorous screen star offer me her reservations at one of London's best hotels seemed like a lucky omen for my trip abroad."

As it turned out, the appearance of the U.S. players and the level of play they brought with them—which prompted the great British golf writer Bernard Darwin to echo the *Times* reporter by labeling it an "invasion"—was a bad omen for British superiority and would completely reshape the course of international golf.

They went across the Atlantic in late May, with the ship's hold containing four trunks' worth of Hagen clothing. The Americans were eagerly awaited by British golf fans because their presence helped intensify the golf revival after World War I and professional visitors had never before come by the dozen or so to take on the home boys. By defeating this perceived flotilla of fairway phonies, Britain would reestablish who was the best in a sport they invented.

There were several relaxed exhibition matches with mixed results, with the top priorities being gentlemanly competition and gracious socializing. Hagen and the other Americans were offered the best hospitality, including plenty of food and drink—much the same way that cows are fattened up for slaughter.

As the British Open of 1920 drew closer, things became more serious. A match was arranged between Hagen and Barnes and Mitchell and George Duncan, who had emerged as the best of a new generation of British professional players. At the Addington course in England, on June 10, the Americans won the best-ball match 3 and 2. A British reporter in the *Chronicle* sniffed, "Both Hagen and Barnes played strong and stable golf, but there was no evidence of that genius which British champions have shown."

Not given much notice by the press at the time was that Barnes and Hagen displayed what appeared to be a new technique, that of hitting past the flag and then spinning the ball back toward the cup. Actually, it was a technique born out of an advance in equipment technology. American players had begun to use "ribbed" clubs—the mid and short irons had deep, wide grooves in their faces, which helped to put backspin on the ball. This was a special advantage on the flatter British courses because the ribbed clubs allowed players to fire at the flags, and if the ball went long, it simply spun back toward the cup.

Apparently, British hospitality had its limits, especially with the Open only a few days away. Hagen recalled that "they didn't invite us to their tournaments to get acquainted with the British links before the Open was played." Apparently, while the Americans could try to make whatever practice arrangements they wanted, with the Open right around the corner their British competitors were becoming less generous with invitations to play exhibitions at courses that were similar to the one at Deal in Sandwich, site of the '20 Open. It may not have helped that the man viewed as the leader of the American contingent, the U.S. Open champion, became involved in a publicity nightmare.

During the exhibition stage of the Americans' visit, Hagen was approached by Bob Howard, a reporter for the *Daily Mail* in London. During the ensuing interview, Hagen discussed how he would attempt to play the course at Deal, trying to adapt the strengths of his game to a course he was unfamiliar with. He expressed confidence that he could play well on any course, even one he'd never played in a country he'd never been to before. He expected to qualify for the Open and be contending for the lead during the last round.

According to Hagen and H. B. Martin, the quotes in the story that appeared in the newspaper the next day, under the headline "Cockle-Doodle-Doo," were much different from what Hagen had given to Howard. "Walter Hagen, boastful American champion, is boyishly confident of winning the British Cup which only once in its history has ever left British shores," the article began. "Hagen says that anyone who cannot play this Deal course in 72 is no golfer. . . . He intends to show us how to play the game. He will pitch the ball dead to the cup, but if he should miss in his calculations and overrun the mark he will take out his famous goose-neck putter and putt the ball into the hole from any angle."

(Another London paper printed that Hagen had picked up the claret jug and caressed it, exclaiming "Oh, you little baby! Come to papa's arms! I'm going to take you back home with me." This was a blatant fabrication, as neither Hagen nor any of the other pros were allowed into the clubhouse where the jug was kept.)

"Howard's article the next morning was anything but flattering inasmuch as it contained little truth and appeared designed to give Hagen a black eye at the very beginning," wrote Martin.

"First I was hurt," Hagen remembered. "Then I was mad. Boiling mad! My words had been twisted and misquoted into a story which made me appear an ignorant, smart-aleck young fool."

Hagen remembered Lord Northcliffe, owner of the *Daily Mail,* who in 1913 had attended the U.S. Open and played golf with Hagen at the Country Club of Rochester while on a tour of American manufacturing cities to buy supplies for the anticipated British war effort. Hagen had apparently had one of his better rounds because afterward Lord Northcliffe said to him, "I wouldn't be surprised to hear of you winning the American championship someday. And when you do, come over to England and have a try at our Open."

Hagen was finally here, and he got on the horn to Lord Northcliffe, who remembered the young pro, was well aware of his two U.S. Open victories, and invited him and Jim Barnes to his estate, North Forelands, which included a private golf course.

After a round of golf and during drinks Hagen showed the article to his host and contended that his words had been twisted. At first, Lord Northcliffe tried to defuse the situation. "You must not feel hurt about anything the English might write about American golfers," he counseled. "Our British Cup is the most treasured sports trophy, and feeling runs high at the time of the Open. British readers won't take it the way you have."

"American people wouldn't care much for [Howard's] wording," Hagen countered. "And I sure don't."

Hoping he had planted a seed, Hagen with Barnes returned to London. Arriving at their hotel, they found Bob Howard waiting, and clearly nervous, ordered by the owner to be there and settle the matter.

"I never came so close to socking a man in my life," Hagen remembered. "I told him I wanted that article retracted in the next issue, and to put the retraction on the front page where the original article had appeared."

There it was, in the next morning's edition.

Perhaps to escape the controversy, Hagen made a trip that would pay dividends the following year. He and Barnes headed north to watch the final 37-hole match of the British Amateur, played at Muirfield between Cyril Tolley and American Robert Gardner. Tolley emerged with the hard-fought win.

The two pros then headed to St Andrews and played a practice round there. But there was no time to linger at "the home of golf": it was time for the qualifying rounds of the Open. Hagen and Barnes drove down to Deal, got out of the car in front of the clubhouse, and strolled inside. At first not finding anyone around, they decided to change and go out to play a practice round.

Suddenly, a man in a white jacket, the head locker steward, rushed to them and said urgently, "You're in the wrong place!"

"This is Deal, isn't it?" Hagen asked.

"Oh yes, indeed. But you gentlemen are professionals. You'll be using Mr. Hunter's golf shop for dressing."

Hagen was not keen on this at all, especially as he and Barnes watched the amateur players walk past them with complete access. With Long Jim in tow he left the clubhouse. They changed their shoes in the car and went out to play. Hagen insisted that they would certainly not use the back of a shop to dress for the Open.

It's interesting to speculate why Hagen was offended and acted accordingly. The Open at Deal occurred before the U.S. Open of 1920 at Inverness when there was the breakthrough in the U.S. concerning professionals. Hagen could not have expected, especially never having been there before, that the treatment of professionals—no access to the clubhouse, if necessary coming in via the servants' entrance only, and being on a social par with butlers and gardeners—would be any different in the U.K. Perhaps it was being the reigning U.S. Open champion and expecting better hospitality, or a moment of pique, but according to numerous accounts Hagen was genuinely put off by his greeting at Deal and decided to do something about it.

First order of business, however—qualify. It would be rather embarrassing after all their initial expectations if many of the American contingent didn't even make the qualifying cut. Hagen did okay with a 76, but Barnes was in danger with an 81 after the first try. Mitchell led all the aspirants with a brilliant 68.

It's possible that Hagen felt special pressure in the first qualifying round, or at the end of it. On the 18th hole at Deal Hagen looked up to see Harry Vardon, James Braid, and J. H. Taylor observing him. For the young American it was like trying to finish before the gods of golf's Mount Olympus, the Great Triumvirate.

Braid and Taylor commented to the press afterward that they were a little disappointed in Hagen's swing—a criticism which wasn't really off base because of the American's lunging style. But Vardon was not only more generous but prophetic: "Hagen seems to have all that is necessary for championship golf, since he does the right thing at the right time. I predict he'll win our Championship, not once, but several times."

Hagen's 71 in the next day's qualifying round got him in, tied for fourth. Barnes recovered with a 74 for forty-first place, which was enough to qualify because everyone from seventy-second place on was invited in. Noticed at least as much as Hagen's score was his outfit: black-and-white shoes, white knickers, and a white shirt under a sleeveless black jersey.

Whatever the primary motive was, while practicing on the course he discussed with players from both sides of the Pond the barriers facing professionals and that maybe it was time they came down. But the host players would have none of it. The class system was deeply ingrained in the British professionals, and the American pros were not inclined to insult their hosts.

Hagen wasn't looking to insult anyone either—he just came up with a different way to make his view of professional players known to the powers that be.

For his arrival on the first day of the 1920 British Open, Hagen hired a car, a long Daimler, and a well-dressed driver-butler. (Al Wallace may not have counted on these expenses at all.) Hagen's appearance made quite an impression, yet there was no invitation to the clubhouse waiting for him.

When it was time for dinner, the amateurs were allowed into the club's dining room but the professionals were pointed to a tent behind the clubhouse. In response, Hagen had delivered to him pheasant under glass and assorted delicacies and ate his dinner in the backseat of the luxurious car. The secretary of the Deal Golf Club was furious and tried to get Hagen to move. The American pro dismissed him with a wave.

The next day, the *Times* of London reported on a smiling, indefatigable Yank who had "outswelled the swells."

Even better for Hagen was to have outplayed the British to capture the claret jug and really drive home his point. He didn't. Still, what happened at Deal made him a much smarter golfer.

Because he had played exclusively in the United States up to this point (except for the Canadian Open in 1912) and was strong, if erratic, off the tee, Hagen had never had much difficulty with wind, or at least consistent difficulty. Blustery conditions on the golf courses he played in the North in summer and the South in winter were the exception, perhaps just a day's interruption. When harsh weather affected the U.S. Open, it was usually intense heat or rain, and the latter was not likely to last more than a few hours or a day. When Hagen did have a poor round thanks to stormy weather, there was always tomorrow, or at least every U.S. player had to contend with the same conditions.

Deal was a very different matter: Not only was wind the norm, it was often shifting and unpredictable. The Brits knew and respected the wind, and over the decades had learned shots that blunted some of its harmful effects, such as hitting low off the tee. The American contingent wasn't yet acquainted with these tactics.

It was windy every day at Deal for the '20 British Open, and Hagen was even more vulnerable to it because of his cockiness. "There are no bunkers in the air," he declared before the first round, meaning he would hit over fairway sand traps and at the stick.

Thanks to the notoriety gained from the *Daily Mail* flap, and being the U.S. Open champion, Hagen had a larger spectator presence than most of the competitors when he teed off in his first British Open. What the onlookers saw left them scratching their heads: "*This* fellow is what all the hullabaloo is about?" was likely going through their minds. Hagen shot an 83.

Much of the bloated score was attributed to tee shots that the wind sent astray or stopped in flight. He was unable to adjust during the round and frequently his first shot had left him in such a bad spot that even his amazing skills at recovery shots weren't enough.

"I've never in my life seen such wind," Hagen recalled. "Women were holding umbrellas over them when they passed sand traps to be protected from the grit, sand, and pebbles that blew across the fairway. On one tee shot the ball stayed up in the wind so long I turned my back on it to keep from being smacked in the face—I needed a catcher's mask. That shot didn't even carry the rough in front of the tee. The whipping, blustering wind was a new and puzzling experience for me."

And the bad spots his tee shots wound up in were worse than what he was accustomed to because Deal, like St Andrews and some other British courses at the time, used sheep as mowers and thus the different areas of grass and rough were at best uneven.

He may have already shot himself out of a chance to win the British Open and was humiliated. But he still had the big, beautiful car and chauffeur waiting and a point to make. For lunch, before the start of the second round, Hagen returned to the Daimler and enjoyed an order of smoked salmon, caviar, and champagne. Then he changed his shirt and emerged ready to play. He still refused to use the golf shop as a locker room.

When the Open, which was won by George Duncan, was over, Hagen ended in fifty-third place. That sounds bad enough, but worse was the fact that fifty-fourth was last place. He had never finished so far down in a tournament.

His powers of observation and being a quick study weren't beaten out of him, though. Before heading back home, Hagen participated in a few exhibition matches and in them he practiced low-trajectory shots, imitating the native players who had done the best job at Deal.

The *London Observer* reported that "Hagen, the American champion, was a complete failure. His long game in the wind was the feeblest thing imaginable." The other dailies were not much kinder.

But the finish at the Open didn't knock the self-confidence and showmanship out of him. Toward the end of the tournament, when some players with better scores but who were well out of contention had slunk away, Hagen marched off the 18th green with his head high. He stood before the board as his fifty-third-place cumulative score was posted, then he turned to the crowd. "There it is!" he announced, pointing at the board. "But I'll be back."

The Deal secretary couldn't pass up the opportunity to get a last dig in. "I'm sorry you didn't do better, 'Eye-gen,'" the man chortled. "But golf over here is very difficult. I hope you'll come back some future year and try again."

"Don't worry about me," Hagen replied. "You'll see my name on that cup." Then he got into the Daimler (which had met him at the 18th hole the day before too) and was driven to his hotel.

He wasn't ready to head home, though. Hagen had sailed east to win the British Open and if that couldn't be then he was going to win *something* of value. He wanted to visit other parts of Europe anyway, since this was his first international experience. When he arrived in France, with George Duncan and Abe Mitchell, he saw an opportunity.

He entered the French Open, being played at La Boulie near Versailles. Duncan and Mitchell signed up too. The event had never had such a star-studded field. If Hagen thought the treatment of professionals was bad in England, France was an eye-opener.

The players were directed to an old and still active stable to use as a locker room. "The vile odor and the hundreds of flies swarming about added to the disgust I felt," Hagen remembered. "Duncan and Mitchell were long accustomed to acceptance of the rigid ruling which barred pros from using, or even entering, the clubhouses of the famed old British golf courses. But we had a meeting and they agreed with me that it was an impossible situation."

The trio marched to the office of Pierre Deschamps, president of La Boulie. He was told that the professional players get to eat and change in the clubhouse "or else," clearly implying that they would withdraw from the tournament. Deschamps couldn't risk such an embarrassment and caved in. For the first time a French golf club opened its inner sanctum to professionals.

According to Hagen, "The shock of winning our point was so great for Mitchell and Duncan that I had to half-push them into the sanctified area of the members and the amateurs. For those two British golfers, this was a major revolution we had staged."

By the end of the final round in the French Open, Hagen and Eugene Lafitte of Biarritz were tied at 298. A 36-hole play-off was planned for the next day. In the morning round, Lafitte's 76 left him 1 stroke behind the American. That was as close as he got. In the after-noon round Hagen shot another 75, but Lafitte crawled in with a 78, losing the play-off by 4 strokes. True, it wasn't the claret jug, but Hagen did have a trophy to bring back to the States.

According to Hagen's account, the evening after the victory he dressed in white tie and tails and hosted a party in the banquet hall of his Paris hotel to celebrate. Even Deschamps was there, "astonished," Hagen recalled, at how a professional golfer could also look and act like a cultured gentleman.

Over the years other American players would enter the French Open, but Hagen would be the last American in the winner's circle until Byron Nelson thirty-five years later.

Back in the States after the unhappy experience at Deal, Hagen focused on what had earned him fame and money at home—winning golf tour-naments and exhibitions. He didn't win every one, but he won enough to keep him in high regard among golf fans. They, in turn, were looking forward to a Dempsey–Willard sort of Hagen–Barnes matchup, in a bout that really mattered.

That opportunity came about at the thirteenth Metropolitan Open, which in 1920 was played before the U.S. Open. It was held in July at the Greenwich Country Club in Connecticut, and fans couldn't have been happier when after 72 holes Hagen and Barnes were tied for first. Hagen had again made up ground with a 69 in the 3rd round to catch Long Jim, and the two had played even in the 4th round. An 18-hole play-off would be held the next day.

If Barnes was going to show that he could keep up with Hagen, this was the time and place to do it, in a high-profile event covered by the New York press and witnessed by fans from at least five states.

But it was not to be. Hagen was 4 strokes ahead after the first nine and just coasted after that, scoring 70 to Barnes's 74. The bottom line was that Barnes had not demonstrated that he could outduel the gen-tleman golfer who was starting to be referred to as "the Haig," who had won the Metropolitan Open three times in four years, now twice in a row, and had two U.S. Opens to Barnes's none.

The *New York Times* summarized, the day after the play-off, "Loser misses many putts, while Hagen displays admirable form throughout the match." Sticking in the needle a bit, the report continued that the fans saw Hagen "play pluperfect golf and give his never-tiring but generally losing rival, Jim Barnes, a thorough, old-fashioned trimming."

If Barnes had any, there was no time for sore feelings. He and Hagen had to hustle from Greenwich to the Hollywood Golf Club in Deal, New Jersey, the next day to take on, in an exhibition match, a familiar duo making their first appearance in the States since 1913: Harry Vardon and Ted Ray. Yes, they were back—the British and unfinished business from before the war—to suppress the American insurrection in golf.

Vardon, twenty years after his first triumphant tour of America, was well past his prime at fifty. His British Open win six years earlier had been his last capture of golf glory. Too old for military service during World War I, he had given exhibition matches to raise money for the war effort. It was unlikely that he had anything left for a run at the U.S. Open trophy.

Ray was getting a bit long in the tooth too. During the war years he had gone from being in his prime to trying to hold on in competitive war-related events. He had won the British Open in 1912, then the old lions J. H. Taylor and Vardon had won, and there had not been an Open until that spring.

Among American golf fans, the names Vardon and Ray were still uttered with some awe, and Vardon especially was treated with enormous respect. On their part, the British duo (Ray, like Vardon, was born on the channel island of Jersey) were generous with their time and treated American fans with somber courtesy.

During the summer of 1920, Vardon and Ray were on an exhibition tour. In Boston they had defeated Jesse Guilford and Francis Ouimet (some revenge for 1913, anyway, but way too late). Next up was the New Jersey site where they would take on America's best professionals, in a match that would raise money for the Benevolent Fund of the PGA of America. The largest crowd of their tour, seven thousand people, was expected, and train and boat service from Manhattan and New Jersey was stepped up.

The first 18 holes were played in the morning. Hagen and Barnes—who were rivals in official tourneys but were also friends and experienced teammates in exhibitions—meshed well together in the best-ball match and ended the morning 4-up. There was a long break for lunch, then the second 18 began. The British duo, instead of being fatigued, bounced back, trimming the lead to 2-up. But the Hagen–Barnes team held fast, increasing the lead again, and the final result was 4 and 2. Hagen's 70 for the first 18 holes during the day had broken the course record.

"They can stack up against America's amateurs and get away with it," sniffed the New York Times, referring to the British pair's previous exhibition match with Ouimet and Guilford, "but when facing the greatest pair of shotmakers on this side of the ocean it is a different story altogether."

This is an especially interesting remark by the Times because it seems to take the view that defeating amateurs is tolerable, but it would have been quite another thing for Vardon and Ray to have beaten the American pros. Only a few years earlier, the opposite would have been true in the press and among many golf fans. To the Times in 1920 at least, being professional was equated with being a better golfer in competitions.

Coming off the win in Greenwich and the defeat of the Brits in New Jersey, expectations were high that Hagen would successfully defend his National Championship in August 1920. The best professional and amateur golfers from two continents headed to Toledo, Ohio, to compete in the U.S. Open at the Inverness Golf Club. History would surely be made here. It was—as much off the course as on it.

In his book Following Through, Herbert Warren Wind writes that the 1920 National Championship "was in many respects a watershed Open. To start with, it marked a changing of the guard; it was the last big championship in which Vardon and Ray, who had come to the fore in Britain in the distant days of the gutta-percha ball, played a prominent part, and it was the first appearance in our Open of a clutch of young men, among them Bobby Jones, Gene Sarazen, Johnny Farrell,

Tommy Armour, and Leo Diegel, who went on to become outstanding golfers."

It was an historic Open before the first ball was struck. There were an unprecedented 265 entrants, which forced the U.S. Golf Association to again have two days' worth of 36-hole qualifiers. The Inverness Open saw the debut of Bobby Jones, listed as "Mr." Robert T. Jones II, a sign of respect for an eighteen-year-old amateur not afforded the defending champion. (He would be paired with Vardon the first two rounds.) Another professional not called "Mr." was an Open rookie too, Gene Sarazen.

Sarazen was awestruck in the company of U.S. Open competitors, because they were the best and he was only eighteen. "I shall never forget the locker room at Inverness," the Squire wrote more than thirty years later. "I sat there for hours, first trying to identify the stars from the pictures I had seen in the newspapers, then trying to catch as much of their conversation as I could.

"There was an unusual spirit and a camaraderie at Inverness that August. Our 'homebreds' were smarting under the inferiority complex that the transplanted British pros like Barnes and Jock Hutchison gave them, but they felt so intensely about the challenge of Vardon and Ray that they were willing to stretch a point for this championship and to consider Jim and Hutch and their colleagues as comrades in arms. They weren't American as Hagen, for example, but at least they had developed their games in our country."

As intrigued as Sarazen was by the company of golfers around him, there was just one player who was king as far as the eighteen-year-old was concerned, "the golfer I idolized above all others." Because of other commitments, Hagen arrived in Toledo only the day before the qualifying rounds got under way.

"When he arrived, though, you were aware of it," Sarazen wrote. "Word spread through the locker room that Walter's Rolls–Royce had just been moored near the first tee. A hush and then a nervous murmur spread through the locker room. 'Here he comes!' someone shouted with a tremor in his voice. The door opened and a man in livery staggered in under a load of expensive luggage and Hagen's ponderous golf bag. Then Hagen entered, gleaming with that big, expansive, confident smile.

"Everyone rose from the benches to shake his hand. 'Hi, boy,' Hagen greeted one after another in his high-pitched voice, 'Hi, boy.' He slapped some of his well-wishers on the back and followed his footman imperially to his locker. He was dressed just like the millionaires I had caddied for at Apawamis, and he looked like he had been born to wealth. As he strode past the bench I was sitting on, he waved and shot me a casual 'Hi, kid,' as if he had known me all my life."

Unfortunately, Francis Ouimet was not in the field because he had accepted an offer to cover the Open as a newspaper reporter, so an opportunity to try for another Brookline was lost. Play began, and incredibly, after three rounds the leader was Vardon, 1 stroke better than Jock Hutchison and Leo Diegel, and 2 more than Ray.

The great champion, going for an unprecedented eighth major, was still leading after the front nine of the last round. He parred the 10th hole, birdied the 11th. Then as he stood on the tee of the par-5 12th hole, the sky grew dark and a brutal storm blew off Lake Erie and swept Inverness.

Bombarded by blustery wind and rain and soon feeling all of his fifty years, Vardon faltered. Bogey followed bogey. "The acres and acres which compose the Inverness course were overrun by frenzied mobs of spectators," reported the *New York Times*. "They would follow Vardon for a couple of holes, see him lose a stroke, then transfer their allegiance to Ray or to Diegel. The young Chicagoan, the last of the homebreds, then became the gallery's favorite. Golfers actually approached hysterics as they watched every shot Diegel made, held their breath while he putted, cheered when he drove straight down the fairway, and prayed."

Vardon crawled in with a 78—amazingly, still tied for first, with Jack Burke Sr. Diegel and Hutchison also staggered through the storm. Despite the crowd's urgings and with the help of Chick Evans (the national champion in '16; having played Inverness many times, he took over the bag as caddie during the final round to guide the homebred youngster home), Diegel, like Hutchison, could do no better than tie Vardon and Burke.

Hagen was paired with Hutchison in the final round, and was about to complete his second consecutive 77 for 11th place. On the last green, with Hutchison badly needing a birdie to tie, the two friends were met by Bobby Jones. "Walter, from the edge of the green, sank a long one [a 30-footer] for a birdie 3," Jones wrote six years later in *Down the Fairway.* "He threw back his black head and laughed as the gallery of ten thousand roared. 'I wish you had it, Jock,' he said. Then Jock, his face twisted with the strain, putted and missed his chance at glory."

Ray was also affected by the storm, but he had shot a 35 on the front nine thanks to making putts ranging from 15 to 40 feet. His 40 on the back nine was more an exhibition of veteran endurance than skill, and the 75 total was enough to win the U.S. Open by a single stroke over Vardon, Burke, Diegel, and Hutchison. At forty-three, he was the oldest player at the time to win the Open.

Ray's victory and Vardon's close call were most satisfying to golf's old guard and gave a big lift to fans and the resurrection of golf in postwar Britain. At the same time, there had to be worries among the American players and golf fans. The U.S. competitors had not done as well as hoped in the British Open, and here were the seemingly ageless British stars avenging 1913, taking the Open trophy across the Atlantic for the first time in a decade, and the U.K. was raising a new crop of strong players. Perhaps the postwar American surge had run out of gas, or was an aberration, and domination of the sport would revert to its ancestral home.

The outcome of the '20 Open had to be particularly galling for Hagen. A year that had begun with such high expectations fueled by being the reigning Open champion and the endeavor of being a full-time player had seen the widely reported failure at Deal and then a modest, at best, defense of the National Championship, with a sixth-place finish. What if he too had run out of gas as America's top professional golfer?

But there was a silver lining for Hagen and American professional golf at Inverness. Why was Sarazen's recollection about the locker room? Because for the first time ever at a major golf tournament, professional players were allowed into the clubhouse to use the locker-room facilities. And Walter Hagen led the way.

Before the tournament began, the powers that be at Inverness had been in a quandary: Hagen was the defending champion, and he had let the U.S. Golf Association know that he had every intention of using the locker room; if banned, as at Deal he would make other arrangements for changing his clothes, which would likely embarrass the USGA and Inverness officials, or perhaps refuse to defend his title. Even if officials were considering making an exception for the country's most popular professional and the reigning national champion, with all the other top-flight players expected in Toledo too, including the best Great Britain had to offer, it could get ugly if an exception was made for Hagen and not others.

Displaying wonderful wisdom and changing the course of professional golf, when Hagen and his colleagues arrived, the officials pointed them to the clubhouse's locker-room facilities.

The pros recognized the significance of this. When the U.S. Open was over, they took up a collection and bought an eight-foot-high cathedral-chime clock and, with Hagen in the lead, marched into the clubhouse and placed it in the foyer. Hagen read aloud the words that had been inscribed on a brass plaque on the clock:

God measures men by what they are
Not what in wealth possess.
This vibrant message chimes afar
The voice of Inverness.

CHAPTER 9

DURING THE REST OF 1920 Hagen was making money on golf courses in the Northeast, Midwest, and Florida. But it was hard to forget turning down that vaudeville offer of $1,500 a week, or forget the disappointing outcomes at Deal and Inverness. Glancing around, it seemed that everyone was making money on Wall Street or as entrepreneurs in an escalating economy. If golf's most high-profile player could turn into an astute businessman, maybe he could cut himself a piece of the pie. An opportunity presented itself in early 1921.

Hagen had become friends with Fred Pulsifer, who was the head of the Clark–Childs brokerage firm. Pulsifer became convinced—perhaps after the two had bent a couple of elbows at a party—that Hagen would be a good stock and bond salesman. He offered Hagen $2 million of backing on Wall Street as soon as the golfer would buy a seat on the New York Stock Exchange, for $96,000.

"To me, the country boy from Rochester, this talk of $96,000 and $2 million was completely staggering," Hagen remembered. "Where would I get that kind of dough?"

Hagen said thanks and went on his way. But a few days later, he was playing a round of golf on Long Island with Gabriel Salant, a manufacturer and Wall Street tycoon. After hearing of the offer made to Hagen, Salant offered $10,000 to Hagen to set up a company and to use the profits from it to buy himself a seat on the New York Stock Exchange, which in turn meant Hagen could take advantage of Pulsifer's largesse.

Hagen rented an office on Broad Street in Manhattan. It had a cashier's cage and bookkeeping ledgers. He hired a cashier and a book-keeper. On the door was a sign that read, "Walter Hagen, Brokerage Sales, Inc." He inquired about a seat on the Stock Exchange. The price had gone up to $100,000. Assuming that the figure went up and down like stocks, Hagen decided to wait a few days for the price to go down. It rose to $106,000. Meanwhile, his cashier had put nothing in the cash drawer and his bookkeeper had written nothing in the books. Apparently, few knew that Hagen was dabbling in another line of work, and those who did were not going to chance their cash with a Wall Street rookie, however famous he was on a golf course.

Pulsifer called to see how he was doing. When Hagen told him he had no customers, no income, and no seat on the Stock Exchange and couldn't possibly approach Salant with such a situation, Pulsifer told him to shut down the office. The stock market was in a slump; this wasn't a good time to get in, Pulsifer concluded.

Hagen didn't have to be told twice. He closed the office, returned the unused money to Salant, let go his cashier and bookkeeper, and returned to the much greener fairways. The market indeed was slumping for Pulsifer—some time later he committed suicide in his Fifth Avenue apartment.

At this time Margaret Hagen finally and sadly accepted that the marriage was over. Her husband just wasn't going to be around much, and for him the road offered too many enticements. As Hagen summed it up, a schedule that included "following the winter circuit, going any place and every place the sun was shining and the fairways green was not conducive to a satisfactory family life." In the spring of 1921 "our marriage was dissolved."

That May, Margaret had gone to court in Detroit, and before a judge she and her mother contended that Walter had abandoned his wife. Hagen was in New York during the proceedings, which lent more credence to the allegation. The judge granted the divorce, with custody of Walter Jr. to Margaret. Soon after, she and her son returned to live in Rochester.

For Hagen, it was a good time to get away. And he wanted another crack at capturing the claret jug.

For the British, it was an unhappy event that Jock Hutchison won the Open in 1921, but the news could have been worse. Hutchison played in America and had a home there, but he had been born in Scotland, and of all places, in St Andrews itself. To win the '21 title, at St Andrews, he'd narrowly defeated Roger Wethered, who at twenty-two was a year removed from being captain of the golf team at Oxford University. Frenchman Arnaud Massy had won in 1907, the first foreigner to take the Open, and as disturbing as that was, at least he wasn't an American, nor was Hutchison really.

For the most part, the "real" U.S. players again failed to make much of an impression in Great Britain. Previous to the Open the first U.S. professional team in international competition—consisting of Hutchison, Hagen, Bill Mehlhorn, Tommy Kerrigan, Barnes, and others—had been defeated by a British squad 6–3 at the Gleneagles course, an event that is considered one of the precursors of the Ryder Cup, which did not officially debut until 1927. Hagen was a modest bright spot, halving his singles and foursome matches.

It had to grate on the pros that a month before a team of American amateurs that included Bobby Jones, Chick Evans, and Frances Ouimet had won nine of twelve matches against their British hosts at Hoylake. This event was a precursor of what would become the Walker Cup, founded by George Herbert Walker and played for the first time officially in 1922. (Walker's grandson, George H. W. Bush, became the forty-first president of the United States, and his great-grandson, George W. Bush, became the forty-third.) Among other attractions in the Hoylake contest, the event gave British fans an opportunity to be introduced to the nineteen-year-old Jones, who would win three British Opens.

The American squad was unable to follow up its exhibition success in the British Amateur. One by one they fell, Jones being defeated in the 4th round. The last American fell in the 6th round, dispatched by none other than the writer Bernard Darwin.

The '21 Open was a disappointment for Jones, but it was a turning point for him too. He didn't play well in the first two rounds, then on the front nine of the third round the wheels fell off completely. By the 11th hole, after recording several double-bogeys, Jones picked his ball up off the green, retiring from the competition. In years afterward, he considered quitting in the middle of the British Open his most embarrassing moment on a golf course. His own shame at his anger coupled with the criticism he received in the British and American press made a deep impression on the nineteen-year-old, and it turned out to be a maturing experience.

It also stung the American pros a bit that they had not completely upheld the "Oath of Inverness." After the 1920 U.S. Open was taken by Ted Ray, the American players had vowed to capture the claret jug. Hutchison's win was welcomed by his American peers, but it didn't inspire a feeling of triumph as much as a British Open win by a native-born American would have. The Americans also noted that after he won the North and South Open at Pinehurst on April 2 (his 291 beat by 2 strokes the record Hagen had established there in 1918), Hutchison had essentially moved back home to St Andrews and spent almost two solid months practicing on the Old Course for the major he wanted most.

Whatever the Yanks' feelings, the spectators in 1921 had seen an Open that was one of the most exciting in the event's history. Playing skillfully and with remarkable composure at "the home of golf," Wethered was ahead until a huge gaffe in the third round. Playing the 14th, he had walked forward from his ball to survey the direction and distance to the hole. Walking back, and keeping his eyes focused on the green, Wethered kicked his ball, incurring a penalty stroke.

Still, he finished the round with a 72, a stroke in the lead. A fourth-round 71 made his position even stronger. However, Hutchison shot a scintillating 70 and tied the younger man at 296. The following day featured a 36-hole play-off, and Hutchison's preparation and competitive experience paid off, because when the day was done, he had won by nine strokes.

Despite the fans' appreciation of the competition and dramatics, the fact was that the claret jug was going across the Atlantic. This had never happened before. It was some consolation that it was in the hands of a Scotsman, and given the Brits' record in their own National Championship, most likely the jug would have no more than a one-year exile in America.

The members of the Royal and Ancient Golf Club were not good sports at all about Hutchison's victory, especially one right under their noses at St Andrews. After the '21 Open, the R&A outlawed ribbed clubs, insisting they had given Hutchison an unfair advantage. (To his credit, Hutchison returned the following year with smooth-faced clubs only and ended the Open just two shots back.)

Unlike the previous year, Hagen had been a bit overlooked during the 1921 British Open. Smarting still from the attention he had attracted in England, in Scotland Hagen kept a low profile, with no grand entrances or interviews. Also, he was no longer the reigning U.S. Open champion; it was the much more popular Ted Ray who was. And the duel between Hutchison and Wethered overshadowed everything else.

Few people made much about Hagen's showing, a sixth-place finish and a score of 302. Since the Deal fiasco, he had learned a lot about how to play in erratic and swirling winds. Hagen had gone from fifty-third to sixth in one year, and left Scotland realizing that it was a much smaller leap to land in the winner's circle.

Long Jim Barnes had finished well, but another homebred American had given a good account of himself: Hagen's old friend Tommy Kerrigan, who had finished 72–72 to end just 2 strokes behind Hutchison. As the U.S. contingent set sail back to the Colonies, its members had to believe that Hutchison's accomplishment had opened the door halfway, and perhaps as soon as next year it would be knocked down completely.

Hagen had gone without a major championship in 1920 and, as it turned out, half of 1921. He had watched Jim Barnes capture the U.S. Open in Chevy Chase, Maryland, and it looked like the rest of the year would be somewhat of a washout too (though he had won the Michigan Open).

Hagen had also watched nineteen-year-old Bobby Jones in the Open that year and told the sportswriter O. B. Keeler, "He's got everything he needs to win any championship except experience, and maybe philosophy. He's still a bit impetuous. But I'll tip you off to something: Bobby will win the Open before he wins the Amateur."

This is a curious comment in that as an amateur, up to this point Jones had played in more U.S. Amateurs, which were match play, than U.S. Opens, which were medal or stroke play. However, Hagen was proved right when Jones won the National Championship in 1923, before he won his first U.S. Amateur.

Hagen was a distant second at the '21 Open, but an incident there added to his growing legend. Attending the event was President Warren G. Harding, who had requested a pretournament practice round with Hagen. That morning Harding showed up on time at the first tee. Hagen, however, ever deliberate in his preparations, remained in the locker room until he was finished shaving. This was reported in the national press the next day, that the Haig had achieved such a status that he could keep the president of the United States waiting. (Harding was one of the more enthusiastic golfers to occupy the White House and served on the governing board of the USGA until his death in 1923.)

After being bested by Barnes by 9 strokes, Hagen was especially determined going into the PGA Championship at Inwood, New York. Another reason why he was determined is that it would be his first PGA Championship since 1916. In a mercenary way, he had chosen the exhibition with Brady over qualifying in '19, and as a result, in '20 the PGA of America disinvited him to qualify, using as an excuse that Hagen was not affiliated with a golf club since quitting the head pro position at Oakland Hills.

At Inwood, he drove and putted his way through the first match-play rounds, though not without controversy. In every match on the 13th hole, Hagen sent his tee shot onto the 18th fairway, then hit his second shot back to the green on 13. This ploy meant he could avoid a lagoon on the 13th that had to be carried on the second shot. On the night before the final match, a work crew showed up and planted a big willow tree in the direction that Hagen had been sending his tee shot.

"I wasn't aware of this conspiracy until I got to the 10th tee," Hagen told others years later in one of his favorite stories (though he remembered which hole it was incorrectly, according to contemporaneous accounts). "The members roared when I saw that the tree completely blocked the shot I'd been using. I had to join them in laughing, but not until Jim and I had stopped in at the club grill for a cup." This account is highly suspect as it's unlikely that the serious Barnes would have joined Hagen in a drink with the PGA Championship on the line, and stopping in at the "club grill for a cup" would have required quite a hike from the 13th tee.

"A terrific wind sprang up," Hagen continued in his reminiscence. "I stalled as long as I could, joshing with the members, and then what happened? The gale blew the tree down." Once again, his second shot landed on the 13th green.

To the delight of fans and most of the other competitors, in the final match Hagen was indeed facing Long Jim Barnes. This was it for sure, the two best in the U.S. (Hutchison, the reigning British Open champion, was nowhere to be found—in the second round he had been destroyed 8 and 7 by a nineteen-year-old making his PGA Championship debut, Gene Sarazen.)

As if Hagen needed any more motivation, Barnes had already won two PGA Championships of the three played; with Jock Hutchison having won in '20, a homebred American had yet to win the event. And if he didn't win the PGA, Hagen would go two years in a row without a victory in a major tournament.

The final match was not as close as the score indicated. Barnes played well, shooting the equivalent of a 71 in the morning's 18 holes. But Hagen carded a 69. Seeking to finish Barnes off, Hagen went out in 33, 4 under par. Long Jim never recovered, though thanks to a late rally, he lost by only 3 and 2.

Hagen had finally earned title to the tournament run by the organization he had played an important part in founding five years earlier but had had a rocky relationship with since.

Hagen's victory in the PGA gave him a ledge to land on in what had become a slippery slope. Further evidence that he was back in the thick of things competitively was winning his second Western Open that summer, needing to overcome 3rd-round leader Bobby Jones to win by 5 strokes, and capturing the Michigan State Open.

With at least a dozen official victories (or fifteen, depending on the spotty record keeping then) in ten seasons which included World War I when almost all official tournaments were suspended, and with three majors and two Western Opens among them, Hagen was clearly the top American homebred player.

• • •

Much was at stake in the British Open of 1922. The Yanks were coming back in force again. As had become the postwar custom, another American assault would be made on the Open, with a win by a homebred viewed as finally shattering that door. For the British players, they had to repair the '21 crack in their national armor and pride, gang up, shove the door closed, and take back their National Championship. The showdown would take place at the Royal St. George's course.

In addition to having played much better in the previous Open, Hagen headed to England with some momentum. In number of victories and accomplishments, 1921 had ended up being one of his best years and had gotten his career back on track. He had won two big events on the schedule, the PGA Championship and the Western Open, in addition to the Michigan Open; he'd shot a 62 during the West Coast Open at Belleair in Florida (at the time the lowest round recorded by a professional in an official tournament); and he had finished second to Barnes (albeit a distant second) in the 1921 U.S. Open.

The rest of the year had been spent profitably, with an increasing number of exhibitions and corporate outings. Word had gotten around that Hagen had some good stories to tell about the golf life and tourneys, that he was becoming quite polished in entertaining crowds, and that he was a delightful and enduring party guest. Socially and professionally, Hagen was in demand, a situation he relished.

The first few months of 1922 found him in Florida again. With the Roaring Twenties getting into full gear, golf courses were being built in the state with unprecedented speed. More professionals from the Northeast and Midwest clubs were heading south. Not only were fans being treated to more top-flight exhibition matches, but well-heeled businessmen with vacation homes in Florida were paying players to compete on private courses. A pro with name recognition and willingness to take on all comers could see frequent and lucrative paydays.

No American player had more name recognition than Walter Hagen, and whoever was paying the freight, he gave the audience their money's worth.

Several accounts of the time by reporters and players tell of a favorite Hagen ploy: If a shot looked in any way difficult, he would take extra time to size it up, choose the right club, and even glance skyward for help. The tension among spectators intensified, though in fact the shot, for Hagen, wasn't all that tough and he may have successfully played the exact same shot in a private practice round. And when he made the shot in front of the fans work, it was like he'd pulled a rabbit out of a hat—the fans had witnessed a miracle!

The year thus far included more than showy exhibition matches. In March, Hagen won the West Coast Open in Florida for the second time and the Deland Open. The following month he cashed a first-place check by winning the White Sulphur Springs Open in West Virginia. In May, he spent some time in New York, then packed up his trunks with plenty of finely cut clothing. It was time to set sail east.

"Barnes and Hagen Off For England," blared the *New York Times* in its May 30, 1922, issue. "American Golf Champions Sail Today to Take Part in British Open Tourney," on the *Berengaria.* An item on the same page reported that Jess Willard was in training to retake the heavyweight title from Jack Dempsey and on the following page was a story on how a "clout" by Babe Ruth had allowed the Yankees to break even in a doubleheader.

Upon arrival, Hagen was open to interviews, having grown more sophisticated and careful with the press since the experience in London two years earlier. At Royal St. George's, in Sandwich, Hagen was asked why American players were winning more tournaments and British domination of the majors had become endangered.

This was his chance to stick up for pros and he took it. "There are two reasons," Hagen replied. "First, we have more tournaments at home. There's no substitute for competition. Secondly, and perhaps more important, in America the golf professional—in fact, the professional athlete—is respected far more than he is over here. He is encouraged to rise in the social as well as in the financial scale, and this gives him greater confidence in himself and in his work. We American professionals are proud of our calling."

Hagen may have been speaking about golf professionals in general, but it is clear that he was speaking about himself and his own career.

A sidebar to the '22 Open: Barnes, Hutchison, and Hagen went to the Prince's Golf Club to practice one day and encountered six-year-old Laddie Lucas, son of the club's head professional. After the practice round, with the boy having followed them the entire way, the kindly Barnes offered twenty-four of his own golf balls and told the boy to fetch his clubs—the boy could keep every ball he hit that landed in the fairway from the first tee. Long Jim didn't know that Laddie had been playing since diaper days and knew how to work the wind off Pegwell Bay.

With Hagen and Hutchison barely suppressing laughter at Barnes's predicament, Laddie put every one of the twenty-four balls in the fairway off the tee. Triumphantly, the boy ran out to collect his winnings as the three visiting pros drove away.

Lucas became one of Great Britain's best amateur golfers and captained a Walker Cup team. When World War II broke out, he joined the Royal Air Force and flew numerous combat missions. One time, returning from France, his Spitfire was attacked by a German plane and severely damaged. Lucas managed to make it across the English Channel and then spotted familiar Prince's Golf Club down below. He landed the Spitfire in the rough of the ninth hole. After climbing out of the smoking cockpit, Laddie reportedly groused, "I never could hit that fairway."

Bernard Darwin could see a change in Hagen as he observed him in the practice rounds and exhibitions that led up to the Open. This was not the brash British Open rookie of 1920 but a seasoned professional exuding more confidence as he prepared to compete.

"That Hagen had an overpowering effect on some of his opponents was clear enough," Darwin wrote. "His demeanour towards them, though entirely correct, had yet a certain suppressed truculence; he exhibited so supreme a confidence that they could not get it out of their minds and could not live against it. They felt him to be a killer and could not resist being killed."

Darwin also saw this Open as a pivotal one, that its outcome could very well demonstrate if British golf would be the standard by which other countries judged their game: "This Championship, far more than any other I have ever seen, is regarded as a match between Britain and the World, with the betting on the World."

During the qualifying rounds, Hagen and Joe Kirkwood tied for first at 147. But Hagen certainly didn't start the Open itself like gangbusters, though he looked smashing in a light brown jersey, gray knickers, and black-and-white shoes. His first-round score was a pedestrian 76, in relatively calm conditions, leaving him three strokes behind Ted Ray and J. H. Taylor.

Maybe it was from being up too late the night before and having an early-morning tee time. He and a few other visiting Yanks had been involved in a high-stakes putting competition on the carpet of the hotel lounge until 2:00 a.m. When someone reminded Hagen that most of his opponents had been in bed for hours, he responded, "Maybe they're in bed, but they're not sleeping." Being with friends and practicing his putting was Hagen's way to relax, and he needed that more than sleep. Let the others toss and turn.

During the second round, the wind picked up and many of the players faltered. Hagen, however, shot a 73. He successfully dealt with the wind, and with the weather conditions causing havoc for many of the competitors, Hagen's 36-hole total of 149 was actually good enough for him to be in first by 2 strokes over Taylor, Jim Barnes, and George Duncan.

"Golf Championship In Danger" was the warning headline in the June 23 *Times* of London. The local press didn't mention that Hagen was mounting his challenge without the banned ribbed clubs.

The next day, Hagen's bloated 79 in the 3rd round would normally have spelled doom for anyone in a major championship. (He had avoided 80 or more thanks to several stunning recovery shots.) But the golf gods were with Hagen because again conditions were so difficult, with a relentless rain, that few of the other players were able to gain ground or run away with the championship.

The gutsy Jock Hutchison, with a 73, had worked himself into first at 226. Barnes had ballooned to a 77 and was 2 strokes back of Hutch. Britisher Charles Whitcombe, perhaps having more experience in such conditions, had notched a 72 and was at 228, tied with Hagen and Barnes. Duncan had seemingly shot himself out of the tournament with an 81, 6 strokes behind.

The British fans received an extra treat during the Open thanks to J. H. Taylor. Turning back the clock, Taylor had shot a 151 on the first day. "All hearts were evidently with him, and it was equally evident that

Taylor was in his old fighting mood," Darwin reported in the next day's *Times* of London.

"There were all the old gestures we know and love—the pushing back of the cap from the heated brow, the holding up of the hand to check the applause, the loud and formidable encouragement of his partner's ball," Darwin continued. "It was all perfectly delightful, and withal to the sentimental onlooker almost too moving to be bearable."

Taylor's 76 in the 3rd round put him a stroke ahead of Hagen but, more important, only a stroke behind Hutchison. Then fatigue and the weather conspired to weigh down the older man, and his 77 in the final round cost him a last, miraculous British Open (he lost by only 4 strokes).

That final round, with the blustery and damp conditions still a factor, was more a matter of endurance than brilliant shotmaking. Hutchison, with a 76, and Whitcombe, with a 75, fell short. Barnes went out to shoot a seemingly impossible 73, which included a 6 on the 247-yard 3rd hole. Given the tough scoring, his 301 total looked pretty good.

Hagen's 72 was grittily earned. During the round he collected the variety pack of bogeys, pars, and birdies. It was survival of the fittest out there, and as he watched the rest of the field fade away (he'd paid a runner to give him updated news on Hutchison's round), Hagen realized that persevering and avoiding disaster might be enough.

For him too weather and fatigue were factors over the final holes. On the par-3 16th, from off the tee, typically one of his danger spots, Hagen launched a laserlike drive that came to rest 6 feet from the pin. He missed the birdie putt and tapped in for par. With all the other competitors that he was aware of going the wrong way because of the rotten weather and the pressure, a string of pars coming home was a big accomplishment and could prove to be enough. Hagen took care of the par-4 17th hole, then there was one more par-4, the home hole, into the teeth of the wind. Hagen bogeyed, which left him a stroke ahead of Barnes.

Hagen's score, which would turn out to be the second-lowest in the 4th round, and 300 total looked pretty solid. Knowing how Hagen had finished prompted George Duncan, the '20 Open winner who had teed off an hour later, to play without caution. Gamely ignoring the 81 of the morning round and the fact that he needed a nearly impossible 68 to tie, Duncan played fearlessly.

"Trudging across the course, I picked up Duncan and his partner by the twelfth green and then I had my reward in six holes of delicious agony," reported Darwin. "He had but a handful of spectators with him [presumably, because of the 81] and these were divided between joy and despair."

No one had ever broken 70 in a British Open at Royal St. George's, but Duncan was intent on not just breaking 70 but doing it by 3 strokes for the victory. A birdie at 16 and he was even with Hagen. He made par at the 17th. A birdie on the home hole and once again the claret jug would reside in Great Britain.

Hagen paced and smoked on the sidelines. He was facing his greatest triumph. On the other hand, he was facing his most crushing defeat. For someone who had embraced taking charge in pressure situations, the worst role for Hagen at the conclusion of the Open was spectator. Standing with Harry Vardon, J. H. Taylor, and Arnaud Massy, Hagen watched Duncan play the 18th hole.

"He [Hagen] was clearly anxious for the first time since he set out to win the championship," reported *Golf Illustrated*'s R. Endersby Howard. "Hagen did his best to conceal his emotions . . . he sat down in front of the crowd, then he stood up, then he sat down again. Evidently, it was as much as he could do to contain himself."

Duncan's second shot on the par-4 18th landed left of the green. Hagen said to the people next to him, "Well, I'm going to miss the boat tomorrow. George and I will have to play off."

Then Duncan faltered. His chip fell well short of the hole. His 15-foot putt for par hit the hole and spun away. He had bogeyed, and lost. The English reporter Fred Pignon noted that Hagen's hands were trembling as he walked out to commiserate with Duncan.

A native-born American had won the British Open, and the golf world tilted. Darwin lamented that from this point on "the Open trophy made the journey across the Atlantic with monotonous regularity. Walter Hagen was the winner on four occasions, 'Emperor' Bobby Jones on three, but it was Hagen who started the landslide."

Howard gave the valiant runner-up his just due: "How very close he was to accomplishing it will be remembered forever by those who had the good fortune to see his finish. Duncan's golfing genius never rose to such a higher pitch of brilliancy."

Hagen made a gracious-enough speech upon accepting the claret jug, thanking his hosts, praising Duncan, and paying special tribute to Taylor. No doubt he recalled the painful experience at Deal two years earlier, and more importantly, how he hadn't quit.

"Walter was overjoyed at his success, but this did not prevent him from expressing his thanks to all in the most modest speech that I was ever privileged to hear," according to Taylor.

With aplomb, Hagen took the first-place check, worth about $500, not bad for the time, and handed it over to his caddie.

"Walter Hagen won to-day at Sandwich, and thoroughly deserved to," Darwin wrote for the next day's *Times* of London. "He is a great golfer, and a great fighter. His last round was a wonderful effort of skill, concentration, and courage."

During the brief victory speech Hagen picked out the astonished face of an eight-year-old boy and gave him a wink and a smile. The evening before, Hagen had gone out to the practice green to get some more putting work in, and he found the boy there.

"What are you doing?" Hagen asked. "Practicing golf," the boy replied. Hagen wondered, "What's golf?" As the boy explained it to him, he gave the man several lessons.

Standing in front of the crowd after winning the British Open, Hagen beckoned to the boy and hoisted him on his shoulders. The new British Open champion nodded as the boy told everyone how he had taught the man how to play golf just the night before and now look where it got him.

"This time there was no escape from the facts for the British," according to Herbert Warren Wind, "as there had been the year before in Hutchison's dual nationality. Hagen was a homebred, as American as apple pie. Walter's breakthrough at Sandwich, in the minds of both the American and British publics, signalized success-at-last for the American invasions of the island where golf was born."

In the June 24 issue of the *Times* of London, Bernard Darwin related that he had seen more than just a win for Hagen in the outcome of the

Open: "It becomes tolerably obvious that, unless our younger professionals do some hard thinking and learn to hit the ball truly on the green, America will win it again and again," he wrote prophetically. "It used to be good enough to play wonderful shots up to the green and then waste a gentlemanly number of putts. Against a player of Hagen's class it is not good enough. The ball must be hit on the greens, and we do not hit it. There is the matter in a nutshell, and we should be grateful to Hagen for teaching us this lesson."

Apparently, the lesson wasn't taken to heart by the new generation of British players. As Darwin wrote many years later in his book *Golf Between Two Wars,* "The true beginning of American triumphs was Walter Hagen's great win at Sandwich in 1922."

CHAPTER 10

WITH THE CLARET JUG GRIPPED TIGHT in his hands, Hagen boarded ship at Southampton and sailed for home. It was a voyage of celebration. For the second year in a row the jug was going to America, and Hagen knew that in the States his win of the world's oldest tournament would be greeted with more widespread enthusiasm thanks to him having been born in Rochester, New York, rather than Hutchison's native Scotland.

As would be a standard practice on future such journeys, Hagen picked up the tab for most of the shipboard celebrants, which included Jim Barnes (who had tied for second), Hutchison (fourth), and Joe Kirkwood. Thanks to tournament wins and especially exhibitions the past two years, gone were the days when Hagen needed an Al Wallace to underwrite a transatlantic trip, though as would also be a standard practice, having or not having a full pocket didn't prevent Hagen from treating his pals.

Cables traveled a lot faster than a boat crossing the Atlantic, so while Hagen and Co. sunbathed and partied, the U.S. press weighed in on the significance of the British Open win. "There has never been a parcel of news that caused as much rejoicing among golfers on this side of the water as the announcement of Walter Hagen's victory in the British Open at Sandwich, England last week," commented the *New York Times*.

"With Hagen, however, there is no chance for argument in the matter," the *Times* continued. "Hagen was not only born in this country, but his game has been learned in this country, and here alone.

Hagen has long held a distinct place in American golf as one of the most picturesque and colorful players in the game, and not only the greatest player in America, but one of the greatest in the entire world."

Though aware immediately that he had achieved a personal dream, Hagen had avoided boasting after the win. In an interview with journalists before he had boarded the *Aquitania* in Southampton, Hagen again lauded the play of J. H. Taylor and George Duncan in particular. He also praised the British fans. "I've played three times in this country," he said, "and always found the best of feeling existed."

When this interview was published in the American sports pages on June 25, the same pages carried a much shorter article that offered a glimpse of the future: Twenty-year-old Bobby Jones had won the Southern Amateur Golf Championship with a dominating 8 and 7. It would turn out that because of the ascendancy of Jones and Gene Sarazen—who proved to be more formidable challengers than Barnes, Hutchison, and the rest of Hagen's immediate generation—June 1922 was the last time Walter Hagen had the center stage of golf completely to himself.

Preparations were made in New York City to welcome the conquering hero and his court. The June 29, 1922, edition of the *New York Times* reported, "In recognition of his achievement in being the first American homebred golfer to win the British Open championship, Walter Hagen will be presented with an automobile at the welcome home dinner . . . at the Westchester–Biltmore Country Club on Saturday night."

Before this took place, a contingent of fellow golfers and several hundred fans accompanied by the Seventh Regiment Band met the boat at the pier after the Cunard liner docked.

"Barnes, tall and gaunt and bronzed, was the first of the quartet to rush down the gangplank, his first words being: 'Gee, I'm glad to get back,'" reported the *Times*. "Immediately following came the always smiling Hutchison, and both were engulfed by their admirers. But when Hagen made his appearance it was the signal for an outburst that drowned out the band, which was doing its best to render 'Hail, the Conquering Hero.' Hagen, brown as a berry, his face wreathed in smiles of boyish happiness, was swept away in the midst of a flag-waving, cheering crowd."

Sir Walter and his large entourage marched down Broadway to City

Hall. Along the way, people stuck their heads out of office windows to cheer the British Open champion. In the midst of all the distractions, Hagen didn't forget two of his priorities—playing a practical joke and ensuring there would be some good "hyposonica" available.

One of the greeters at the pier was industrialist L. A. Young. He was regarded as an upstanding man and was a teetotaler adhering to Prohibition. But Hagen had a magnum of champagne he wanted to get off the boat to the party planned in his honor. The answer? Stick the magnum in the same case as the claret jug, close and lock it, and have Mr. Young carry it off the dock, through Customs, and to the party.

This was accomplished, though Young had to work for it. Without a key to open the mysterious case, he was questioned by U.S. Customs inspectors and threatened with detainment. Young had to call in a few favors from New York City and Washington, D.C., friends, and finally with that help and enough righteous bluster he was sent on his way.

When he arrived at the Manhattan hotel hosting the victory party, he handed Hagen the case and shouted, "There's your double-be-damned trophy!"

"L.A., old boy, now the party can start," responded a happy Hagen. He pulled out the key and opened the case, then before a sputtering Young he popped the cork and poured champagne.

The welcome-home dinner was held on Saturday, July 1. The event had been coordinated by the club's reception committee, headed by Grantland Rice. The Westchester–Biltmore Country Club, on 650 acres with two Walter Travis–designed courses, was packed. The only person missing was President Warren Harding, who had been invited but was unable to attend. He sent a personal letter praising "Mr. Hagen and his associates on their triumphal return from England."

There was accolade after accolade by many a well-oiled partici-pant. Hagen was made an honorary member of the club and was given the keys to a new Cadillac (so new, in fact, it was not there at the club). Finally, it was Hagen's turn to speak. He stepped forward and was admired by all.

"It was the Jazz Age," wrote Charles Price, one of the best American golf writers, trying to put in perspective the impression Hagen made at this point in his life. "Into this gaudy period stepped the Haig, with the sang-froid of Valentino, his black hair pomaded to an iridescence, his handsome features browned by the sun and wind until they had the hue of brierwood.

"At the time when most pros were still dressing in sack coats and brogues, Hagen wore silk shirts, florid cravats, alpaca sweaters, screaming argyles, and black-and-white shoes which he had custom-made by Oliver Moore, at a hundred dollars a pair. When he strolled past the verandahs, he was enough to make the flappers choke on their gum."

There were probably few flappers at the Westchester–Biltmore dinner, and in any case Hagen was not the most practiced or comfortable public speaker. He had a somewhat high-pitched voice that only decades of smoking eventually gruffed up, and with what seemed to be an instinctive showmanship he knew when to exit the stage. His remarks to the crowd at the victory dinner were brief, echoing what he had said before to the press in England, but they spoke volumes about how far American professional golf had come.

In the estimation of the golf press, fans, and fellow players, Hagen was the top player in the world. No one else had on his résumé wins in the U.S. Open (twice), British Open, and PGA Championship, along with two Western Open titles. And while winning, he had created and given serious credence to the occupation of touring professional golfer, and had done it with flair.

He had won national championships in the United States, Great Britain, and France, the only American who could make that claim. He was considered to have won more professional tournaments than any active player and perhaps any player to date, though with the PGA tour—such as it was, with anywhere from six to ten "official" tournaments a year—still in its infancy, record keeping was unreliable, and comparing Hagen to anyone who had come before was like apples and oranges. What would become the PGA Tour was in the 1920s being constructed around Hagen, and what he accomplished, especially if done with flamboyance and sartorial splendor, gave the tour step-by-step boosts.

With the growth of the popularity of golf in America and with more people having the means and time to play the game, good golf facilities were in demand. Players at the higher levels, in both skills and finances, not only required more courses, they wanted better, more challenging courses. The 1920s, then, saw the last great burst in the building of what are now labeled the "classical" courses in America, before the Depression and World War II took their toll. Pine Valley and Baltusrol in New Jersey were both opened in 1922. Winged Foot in New York opened in 1923. The Olympic Club in San Francisco followed the next year, and the year after that the Oak Hill Country Club in Rochester opened its gates.

Finding themselves with commission after commission were architects and designers such as Donald Ross, Alister MacKenzie, Seth Raynor, H. S. Colt, A. W. Tillinghast, and Charles Blair Macdonald. Soon to follow the early '20s courses at the midpoint of the decade were Riviera Country Club in Los Angeles, Medinah in Illinois, the Seminole Golf Club in North Palm Beach, Florida, and the first stirrings of what would become the Links at Pebble Beach.

During the decade Hagen played many of these courses—along with dozens if not hundreds of others that don't make any "best" lists—in tournaments and during his various exhibition tours. His fame and showmanship brought spectators to the courses in unprecedented numbers. It is not too much of a stretch to think that the popularity and accessibility of Hagen inspired golf course construction so that one day Hagen or at least another top professional would come for a visit and play an exhibition, or if the course was good enough, it could host a pro tournament as the tour grew.

The proliferation of courses, and particularly more sophisticated courses, was a boon to golf professionals. There were more jobs to fill. The better pros had opportunities to work at the expanding number of top courses, and the demand meant that these pros could command higher pay. So while Hagen was trying to improve the way professional golfers were treated, golf professionals were slowly rising in compensation and stature at golf clubs. They were still employees who labored and tended shop and weren't invited to attend clubhouse parties, but it was the equivalent of them going from being regarded as cooks to chefs and being viewed more as *professionals*.

This was an especially opportune moment for Hagen to hit the road on his most ambitious tour yet. During the voyage back from Great Britain, he and Kirkwood had discussed a barnstorming tour of the States that would capitalize on Hagen's increased fame. Combined with Kirkwood's trick-shot performances, the two could make a lot of money playing exhibitions. As a by-product, they could bring golf to areas that had never hosted a player of Hagen's renown and thus make the game more popular.

First, though, was the U.S. Open in July, played at the Skokie Country Club in Glencoe, Illinois. It would surely be an achievement for an American to win the British and U.S. Opens back to back. Hagen started auspiciously by leading all qualifiers, then shot a 68 to hold the lead after the 1st round.

But a 77 in the 2nd round deposed Sir Walter. Still, he was in third, tied with Gene Sarazen and a stroke ahead of another twenty-year-old, Bobby Jones, who had played with the Haig that first day. "Walter found all the bunkers and I caught up with him," Jones recalled. Jones was the co-leader, with Bill Mehlhorn, after the third round by shooting an even-par 70. Sarazen stayed in contention, four shots back (birdieing three of the last five holes to salvage a 75), but Hagen, with a 74, could not gain ground.

Gene Sarazen was a prodigy. Like Hagen, he came out of "upstate" New York (though Harrison was only a half hour north of New York City) and learned golf while being a caddie. He also came from a working-class background and was a descendant of immigrants. After first meeting Hagen at the U.S. Open at Inverness two years earlier, Sarazen had finished in thirtieth place.

It was clear, though, that Sarazen had promise and Hagen, who towered over the 5'5" man almost ten years his junior, encouraged him to keep at it. Sarazen qualified for the U.S. Open in 1921 but didn't set the course on fire. "I don't remember a single photographer pleading with me to show the public the swing that had carved out successive rounds of 83–74–77–77," Sarazen wrote in his autobiography, *Thirty Years of Championship Golf.*

His breakthrough event was the U.S. Open at Skokie. Maybe Sarazen felt something special. The night before the Open began, he told Jones and Johnny Farrell, "I've got a hunch I'm going to win this one. I am going to be pretty close in the running the first two rounds. My bad round will be my third [75], but on the last round I'll burn up the course."

Despite the prediction, Jones seemed ready to win when the final round began, which would prove Hagen's prophecy about him. But Sarazen, who had played sure and steady golf to stay near the top of the leaderboard, dashed everyone's hopes. He started the 4th and final round 4 strokes back, yet was brimming with confidence.

He bogeyed the second hole to drop another shot back, but birdies on 3 and 4 turned things around. Sarazen's drives flew longer and straighter, and his putting was crisp. When the first nine was completed, he had shot a two-under 33. Meanwhile, Mehlhorn had finished the day with a 74 and was the leader in the clubhouse at 290.

But Sarazen bogeyed the 10th. Had he used up his fuel? A birdie on the 12th earned the stroke back, then he cruised with 5 straight pars. A par on the par-5 18th would give him a 289 and replace Mehlhorn as the leader. A tall order, though, given the 485-yard distance and the wind in Sarazen's face.

His drive landed in the middle of the fairway. Then, determined to reach the green in two and with a good lie, Sarazen used the driver again. The ball landed on the green, 15 feet from the stick. He two-putted for birdie, and a 68 and 288.

"With everything riding on that tense, final round, I cut loose with the finest eighteen holes I had ever played in competition," Sarazen wrote in his autobiography.

The end of the effort did not mean the end of pressure. "All I had to do then was to sit back and sweat out the three players still on the course who had a chance to tie or beat my mark—Walter Hagen, old John Black, and a youngster from Atlanta one month younger than myself named Bob Jones," Sarazen reported.

Hagen, with a 72, ended up offering only token resistance. Journeyman John Black, a grizzled fifty-one years old and a grandfather, from Oakland, surprised everyone by finishing with a 289 total, just one shot shy of Sarazen. It was up to Jones, who was paired with George Duncan, to catch up to the clubhouse leader.

He put himself in a good position, needing just a 36 on the last nine to tie Sarazen. When told of Jones and others chasing him, Sarazen announced, "I've got mine [the 68]. Let them get theirs."

For Jones, it was close but no cigar. He missed a tying putt on 18, and the young man from Harrison was the U.S. Open champion.

Jones had the consolation that for the first time since 1916 someone other than Chick Evans was low amateur in the Open. The runner-up finish for Jones began a string that may be impossible to ever duplicate—in nine consecutive Opens, he finished first or second eight times.

"Inside the clubhouse I treated myself to a long warm shower," Sarazen remembered. "Hagen, who finished about that time, with 291, complimented me on my final round of 68 and bought me a drink. I sipped my drink slowly and puffed happily on a big cigar."

Another distinction of the '22 Open at the Skokie Golf Club near Chicago was that it was the first time that spectators were charged admission—one dollar per round, or five dollars for the entire week. More than ten thousand spectators were on hand for the final day's dramatics.

The '22 Open was also the first time that the celebrated sports and theater writer Damon Runyon (*Guys and Dolls*) saw Hagen play. In the copy he filed, he called Hagen "The Big Fellow."

"It was easy to see where Mr. Runyon got the idea," wrote O. B. Keeler in the *American Golfer*. "Hagen is not a 'big fellow,' in the sense that Dempsey and [Luis] Firpo and Ted Ray are 'big fellows.' Hagen is a well-proportioned man of about five feet ten, weighing, I should guess, around 175; not a 'big fellow' at all.

"But watching him tear into a golf ball for a full shot, with the tremendous drive of his right side carrying all his weight far forward onto his left foot, it is impossible to escape an impression of bulk; the vast power of the man seems to dilate him; the action is expansive, in a way. I do not wonder that Runyon called him 'The Big Fellow.'"

Hagen played one more tournament before a rendezvous with Kirkwood and the start of their national exhibition tour. He headed east and won the New York State Open. Then it was time to put the official tournaments aside and reap the fruits of golf fame and his partner's crowd-pleasing trick shots, which included hitting the ball off a prone volunteer's nose and sending balls skipping and soaring in various sharp-angled directions.

With the tour with Kirkwood set to begin, Hagen had an idea:

What better way to keep his name out there in a positive light and increase his fame even further than to hire a press agent? Hagen became the first player to have such a person working for him when he hired Bob Harlow.

Robert E. Harlow, the son of a New England minister, was a veteran sportswriter from Boston with extensive knowledge of golf. He and Hagen respected each other's talents, and it made sense to have Harlow fill the role that H. B. Martin had filled temporarily on the first trip to Great Britain in 1920. Harlow, who quit his job with the Associated Press to partner with Hagen, would ghostwrite columns and feed short items about the pro golfer to the press.

But Harlow soon became more than a press agent. His role expanded to that of manager. He coordinated the many exhibitions Hagen played each year. According to Charles Price, "Harlow booked Hagen, who had the constitution of a rhinoceros, in exhibitions everywhere he could find a golf course that a title-holding pro hadn't played yet, and Hagen would accommodate him by winning a title of some sort every year. There were weeks when Hagen would play nine of those exhibitions."

The 1922 exhibition tour followed the sun. During the summer, Hagen, Kirkwood, and Harlow concentrated on the Mid-Atlantic states and the Northeast. Some of the matches were high-profile ones, such as when Hagen returned to the Westchester–Biltmore in August so he and Kirkwood could take on Tommy Armour and Sarazen, with the latter duo winning. As the fall progressed, the tour headed south and then west.

The money flowed in. Typically, spectators would pay a dollar to see the show on weekdays, two dollars on weekends and holidays, and five hundred people was considered a small crowd. When other famous players participated, such as with the Armour–Sarazen match, the crowd was as large as three thousand and a two-dollar ticket was reasonable whatever day it was. A conservative estimate is that after Harlow's cut and expenses were taken care of, during any given week Hagen and Kirkwood were splitting between $4,000 and $6,000 (in addition to their earnings from side bets), which had to place them near or at the top of the pay scale for professionals in any sport in 1922–23.

Harlow served as companion and sounding board to Hagen on

their various trips. He also helped Hagen negotiate endorsement contracts, and during the decade Hagen appeared in ads for cigarettes, golf products, and clothing.

"Aside from his golf, that to me was why he was so famous in the 1920s," said Sam Lacy, who caddied for Jim Barnes when he defeated Hagen in the '21 U.S. Open at Congressional outside Washington, D.C. Lacy became a baseball player in the Negro League, then a journalist, and when interviewed at ninety-six he still wrote a weekly column for the *Afro-American* in Baltimore. "Seems like you couldn't turn around or read a newspaper without seeing Hagen on a billboard or on a page promoting some product."

Another service Harlow provided Hagen, the golfer would only fully come to appreciate years later. The manager was flabbergasted by how quickly Hagen's income evaporated, or worse, that it went out faster than it came in no matter how skillful or prolific Harlow was in arranging high-paying golf outings. Without Hagen's knowledge, Harlow began to take a little bit here, a little bit there and put it aside, in bank accounts and solid investments.

A benefit of sports fame was that the major politicians of the day, from President Harding on down, wanted to play golf with Hagen, and it sure didn't hurt to be in the company of a famous sports star in newsreel footage and newspaper photographs. Hagen was usually the most handsome and well-dressed man in the picture, thanks to his constant tan and the care he took in dressing.

During a Florida exhibition swing that year, Hagen wore two pairs of white flannel slacks a day, and it cost him six dollars a day for each pair to be cleaned. Then he found a store selling the same pants for five dollars each. From that point on, Hagen wore a pair of white flannels once, then gave them as tips to hotel bellhops, thus saving two dollars a day on two pairs of pants and countless dollars on tips.

Harding had gotten a big kick when Hagen was finishing up the '21 U.S. Open. With a 15-footer left, Hagen pointed to the president sitting behind the green, then at the ball, then at the hole, then proceeded to sink the putt. Until the hard-living Harding's death in 1923, there were frequent invitations to the White House, if we are to believe Hagen's account.

"Dining with the Harding family, my regular place at the table was next to the President with his dog Laddie Boy sitting on the floor between us," Hagen recalled in an autobiography that includes numerous exaggerations (in other words, a typical sports biography of the '50s).

Hagen contended that not only would he play golf with the president but with members of Congress and the Cabinet who were invited along by Harding. In addition to the president's mistresses—a practice that may have further endeared him to Hagen—during the height of Prohibition, Harding had a standing order when he played golf that an underling was to bring him a full glass of bootleg whiskey every fourth hole when he played at his regular course, which was in Chevy Chase, Maryland.

Adding some credence to Hagen's account is a reminiscence of Sarazen, who attracted presidential notice after his first U.S. Open victory. Sarazen recalled being invited to the White House and spending an afternoon with Harding, concluding, "Harding made me feel at home."

One more benefit of fame at that time for Hagen was manufacturing and selling golf clubs bearing his name, a big step forward from Harry Vardon and the golf ball named after him. What is common practice today was first explored in 1922.

In 1915, while still the reigning U.S. Open champion, Hagen had begun a contract with the A. G. Spalding Company and used some of its equipment (eventually replacing all his "strange weapons"). After winning the British Open, it was time for a raise: He wanted $20,000 a year to continue representing the company. It offered $12,000 a year. Hagen took a hike.

With two former Major League baseball players, John Ganzel and Joe Tinker (of "Tinker to Evers to Chance" fame), Hagen formed the Walter Hagen Golf Products Corporation in Longwood, Florida. The city donated the property and constructed the manufacturing plant, anticipating a booming business that would benefit everyone in the area. But the enterprise got off to a rocky start.

"Those early clubs were beautifully designed, but the humid climate caused the hickory [shafts] to swell," Hagen ruefully observed. "While the heads fitted perfectly, once they arrived in drier temperate zones, like Arizona and states with a similar climate, the iron heads almost rattled off the shafts. When the hickory shafts dried out they gave off slivers of thin wood like porcupine quills which got into a player's hands."

As the company tried to rectify the problems, Hagen had to pour more and more money in to keep it going. Soon his partners bailed out. From tournaments and other ventures Hagen had to come up with $5,000 every Friday to make payroll at the factory. He persuaded his sister Freda, a teacher in Rockport, New York, to move to Longwood and be the company's bookkeeper so at least he would have a good idea of where the money was going, arrange credit for the venture, and to employ some of that old frugality the rest of the Hagen family had practiced in Rochester.

After three years Hagen owed more than $200,000 to various creditors, a big debt in any decade. To the rescue came Al Wallace back in Detroit, who suggested that L. A. Young of Michigan, who owned the company that manufactured the most automobile springs in the U.S., buy Walter Hagen Golf Products. Apparently not holding the claret jug practical joke against Hagen, Young did so. Hagen was not only bailed out of debt but also was given a contract to keep his name on the golf equipment. Despite the company being sold to Wilson Sporting Goods Company in 1944, Hagen's contract lasted the rest of his life.

Cashing in on his fame was more crucial than ever for Hagen, and with the success of the tour thus far, it seems he and Kirkwood grew more ambitious. "Golf Stars Plan World-Wide Tour . . . Hagen and Kirkwood Arrange for First Trip of Kind Ever Attempted," reported the *New York Times*. It went on to offer, "Bitten by the wanderlust bug, which is causing so much restlessness among athletes of the present day, Walter Hagen, America's most notable homebred golfer, and Joe Kirkwood, the Australian trick shot specialist, have formed a team to make a world's tour."

What would turn out to be a long and strong friendship between Hagen and Kirkwood took hold even though they were quite different people. Hagen was very social and turned down few party invitations. Kirkwood was reserved and didn't drink. Hagen was American, Kirkwood Australian. Hagen spent money as fast as he made it (sometimes faster), while Kirkwood was a penny-pincher.

Kirkwood, though he had come close to winning the British Open at St Andrews in 1921, would never win a major. One can speculate that the years he spent on tour performing trick-shot routines instead of a steady diet of tournament competition curbed his career as a championship player. Still, his record does include victories in the Australian Open, Canadian Open (twice), Texas Open, and the California Open.

As a competitor on the pro tour as well as exhibitions, if there was anything Kirkwood had over Hagen it was in the hole-in-one department. Incredibly, in his career Kirkwood had twenty-nine aces. One of them came in an exhibition in Cedar Rapids, Iowa, when an errant shot caromed off a spectator's watch onto the green and into the cup. Perhaps more incredible, in his entire career Hagen, who always preferred to fire at the flag, had only one hole in one.

There were other differences, but the fact is that Hagen and Kirkwood, who was five years younger, bonded as friends. Something they did have in common was a powerful desire to make money. They had spent a lot of time together at that year's North and South Championship at Pinehurst (which Kirkwood won) before the British Open, and realized that in the desire to travel, make money, and perform for a crowd they were kindred spirits. Hagen was also impressed by a trick-shot exhibition Kirkwood gave after the North and South that earned the Aussie close to $800 for a couple of hours' work.

The plan they pursued was to combine the winters-in-Florida routine with the time-honored touring of pros from city to city (such as what Vardon and Ray had done in 1913 and 1920) and do it over a larger expanse of territory, including other parts of the world. During the fall, however, reality set in. Perhaps thanks to the much more practical Harlow, the players grasped that with so much of North America waiting to be explored, a worldwide golf tour was too much. So instead, Hagen and Kirkwood continued to introduce golf to the golf-starved fans in America's hinterlands, and got paid handsomely for it. Hagen supplied the fame, Kirkwood the tricks, Harlow the itinerary.

Though not worldwide, their tour would be long and wide enough, not concluding until the fall of 1923. The duo was a big hit, even in some of the more remote parts of the country.

Playing exhibitions was for Hagen's "own welfare, of course, but by not limiting his exhibitions to already established golf centers, he spread the story of the game," according to Al Barkow in *The Golden Era of Golf*. "[Hagen] appeared in such out-of-the-way places as the Dakotas, Wyoming, and Utah, striding regally along dusty fairways and putting on sand greens, but always giving the crowds a show. Many of the spectators may not have known a thing about golf and were just there to catch a glimpse of a celebrity, but because Hagen didn't seem to take golf too seriously, he made the game all the more appealing.

"How many new golfers were enticed to the game after a Hagen visit is impossible to say, but even if it was just a few at each stop, this interest was what golf needed in its American infancy. Hagen was the Johnny Appleseed of American golf, a big planter of the game in the soil of the nation."

Hagen and Kirkwood were like golf gunslingers coming into town, ready to challenge the local talent. They rode in Hagen's long touring car, with its driver and occupants undeterred by the dustiest roads or incomplete directions. The match that had been arranged would be against whoever the nearest pros or amateurs were, or Hagen and Kirkwood would play against each other in a well-rehearsed round full of banter. In a way, years after the opportunity had first been offered, Hagen had become part of a traveling vaudeville act.

According to several accounts, Hagen greeted even the roughest backwoods courses with a smile and the same saying: "Sporty little course you've got here." Then it was time to encourage various side bets.

What may be amusing now, but may not have been the best thing to happen then to impressionable minds, is that the people Hagen was exposing to professional golf were not seeing the game's best technician despite what he had copied from Vardon. Though he was Jones's right-hand man, O. B. Keeler liked and admired Hagen, and he was, when not wearing his Jones PR hat, a good and observant golf reporter. In an essay titled "The Style of Walter Hagen" published in the *American Golfer* in 1923, Keeler gave this description:

"At the top of the swing, Hagen's right leg is rigidly braced and his weight seems to have moved back on to it, but the left foot is gripping the ground firmly; the foundation is solid all through the stroke. But once the downswing is underway, Hagen does not hesitate to shoot the left hip into a leading position, and at impact his right heel is well off the ground—his weight is coming through with a rush as his right side goes driving on. But his head remains still until the ball has gone; the rush of his right side fairly yanks it from its position.

"I have never seen Walter play in a hat or cap, but I firmly believe that that terrific snap would flip his head from under its covering. He finishes the stroke with his right shoulder the nearest portion of his anatomy to the objective, and his weight so far forward that a photograph of his finish looks as if he were running after the ball."

During the tour Hagen played all day and at night enjoyed what there was of the local nightlife. Kirkwood stayed in and counted and tucked away much of the money, yet his more conservative nature did not prevent him from participating in some wild schemes. During one leg of the tour, in Southern California, accompanied by the silent film comedian Harold Lloyd, Hagen and Kirkwood went across the border to play a match in Caliente, Mexico. After it was done and the crowd had dispersed, Hagen suggested a new match: from the clubhouse to the toilet bowl back in their hotel room.

A $50 bet was made, with Lloyd serving as banker and referee. (Not surprisingly, in his next movie, released in 1923, Lloyd included a comedic golf sequence.) Hagen and Kirkwood teed off from the front of the clubhouse, then kept hitting their balls, down Caliente's Main Street, through traffic, across lawns, out of flower beds, and over any obstacles like fences.

As they neared their hotel, the duo had attracted a large following of excited spectators who were making their own bets. The players hit into the lobby of the hotel, then through the corridors, and finally to their room. On his first try, Kirkwood's pitching wedge got the ball up nicely off the tile floor of the bathroom, and his shot splashed in the center of the bowl.

More fun was to be had during a stay in Chicago. After a busy Saturday and a late night for Hagen, the two were lounging on Sunday morning in their hotel room, which overlooked Lincoln Park. Hagen glanced out the window and, according to Kirkwood, "noticed a bunch of bums stretched out in the sunshine on the grass. A sly grin came over his face, and with a casual wave in the direction of the open window, he said, 'Bet you couldn't land one by those rummies, Kirkie!'" The excitement of the challenge clearly outweighed any concern for the safety of the poor fellows below.

Kirkwood was up to the challenge. He grabbed balls and his 7-iron, opened the window, and made the first try. The ball flew through the window, over the traffic-filled road, toward a man sleeping on a park bench. The ball was two feet off. The thud as it landed woke the man, who stood up to look around, spotted the ball, stooped, and pocketed it.

Another one was already on its way. This one landed a foot from the nonplussed man. Hagen had gathered his own balls and had chosen a 9-iron. The man bent down to pick up the second ball and the third landed at his feet. He turned one way then another, seeking the source of the bombardment. He took his catch to another man sleeping nearby and woke him. Together they searched the sky. Meanwhile, Hagen's artillery had joined in and the two men in the park were being showered by golf balls. Finally, the "rummies" turned and ran away.

Another time, in Maine as the sun was setting and the air was turning cold, Hagen and Kirkwood were motoring down a road and they came upon a driving range lit by floodlights. Intrigued by the lit-up, remote setting, Kirkwood wanted to stop and watch the hitters. They did for a few minutes, then Hagen offered out the window to one particular player some advice about his swing.

The man resented the intrusion. "What do you know?" he shouted. "You can't hit the ball any farther than I can."

Hagen got out of the car. He asked to borrow the man's club and, without taking off his thick coat, he swung and sent the ball deep into the night. He handed the club back, returned to the car, and off they went, observing the stunned man in the rearview mirror.

In Massachusetts, at a course in Springfield, Hagen and Kirkwood were matched up against local pros who didn't stand a chance. As if to emphasize that, Hagen broke the course record by 6 strokes.

In New Orleans, Hagen and Kirkwood were to play an exhibition with two local pros, and the gate money was all set, but the Haig couldn't get a side bet going because the two pros and everyone else within earshot were intimidated. Determined, Hagen asked what the course record was, and when told it was 69, he announced, "I'll bet $1,000 that I break it."

A portrait of Hagen taken when he was fifteen and working at the
Country Club of Rochester. *(Corbis)*

Twenty-one-year-old Walter Hagen after winning the U.S. Open in 1914. This is one of the very few times Hagen can be seen wearing a hat. *(USGA)*

A large gallery watches Mike Brady and Walter Hagen at the 1919 U.S. Open playoff in West Newton, Massachusetts. *(Corbis)*

Walter Hagen (left) and the rest of the American team at Gleneagles in Scotland, where a pre–Ryder Cup match was played against British golfers in 1921. *(USGA)*

Walter Hagen and the decade-younger Gene Sarazen remained friends from 1920 despite their strong on-course rivalry. *(USGA)*

Hagen once said, "I never wanted to be a millionaire, I just wanted to live like one." He succeeded, as this photo taken in 1923 attests. *(USGA)*

Edna and Walter Hagen, along with American amateur Fred Wright, walk
the Hoylake course during the 1924 British Open. *(USGA)*

Bobby Jones and Walter Hagen flank an official before the start of their
February 1926 exhibition match in Florida. *(AP)*

In England in 1926, Abe Mitchell and Hagen played for what was at that time the largest exhibition purse ever: $500. *(USGA)*

Host Walter Hagen greets the British captain, Ted Ray, before play begins at the inaugural Ryder Cup Match in Massachusetts in 1927. *(USGA)*

Hagen and one of his closest friends, Joe Kirkwood, at the 1927 PGA Championship in Dallas, where a young Byron Nelson played a role. *(Corbis)*

The Prince of Wales presents the claret jug to Walter Hagen after Sir Walter wins the 1928 British Open. *(USGA)*

M. H. Hoffman and John M. Stahl, executives at the Tiffany-Stahl studio in Hollywood, welcome Hagen as he reports to begin filming *Green Grass Widows* in 1928. *(Corbis)*

Good news: Hagen on the ship heading home after he won his fourth British Open in 1929, accompanied by (left to right) Horton Smith, Ed Dudley, Johnny Farrell, and Joe Turnesa. Bad news: the Ryder Cup stayed in Great Britain. *(Corbis)*

Three generations of Hagens: Walter Jr., Walter, and William. This photo was taken at the U.S. Open in 1931, the only time the elder Hagen saw his son play professional golf. *(Corbis)*

Walter Hagen, Francis Ouimet, Jess Sweetser, and Gene Sarazen at a charity exhibition match in 1932. *(USGA)*

Old pal Babe Ruth acts as referee at the International Four-Ball Tournament in Miami in 1936, featuring (left to right) Hagen, Johnny Farrell, Willie MacFarlane, and Willie Kline. *(AP)*

"Eddie" holds the flag while (left to right) Bobby Jones, Gene Sarazen, and Tommy Armour watch Hagen putt during a charity match in Bermuda in 1940. *(USGA)*

At the 1942 PGA Championship, Hagen gets a laugh out of the unusual putting style of longtime friend Leo Diegel. *(USGA)*

An ill Hagen was honored at the Traverse City Golf and Country Club in August 1967. Sitting closest to him at his left is Arnold Palmer, who flew his own plane to Michigan for the occasion. *(AP)*

This was something different. Officials and some spectators gathered and tossed the thousand bucks in the pot. Thus motivated, Hagen's round was brilliant, and on the par-4 18th hole, he needed birdie for a 68. His second shot landed 12 feet from the pin. His betting opponents, including the man holding the collected $1,000, rimmed the green. Hagen called to them, "Miss this putt for a thousand dollars? Not a chance."

He studied the green, stood over the ball, and stroked it. He turned away while the ball was still rolling and put his hand out to the man with the money, not even bothering to watch the ball drop into the cup.

So it went, from state to state, region to region, one course after another. Many of the courses were rough sites that the most famous golfer in the world would reasonably reject as unsuitable to play on. Hagen, however, not only wanted to entertain wherever he was but wisely realized that playing in varied conditions offered knowledge and experience that could prove valuable later (as it did). And, if nothing else, after showing up, whatever greeted him he wanted to complete the commitment so he and "Kirkie" would get paid.

The demands of the tour combined with the need and/or lust for money cost Hagen the opportunity to defend his '21 PGA Championship and Western Open titles. The 1922 PGA Championship was at the Oakmont Country Club in Pennsylvania, and Hagen was way up in the Northeast. Once more displaying a lack of loyalty to the organization he helped to found, Hagen decided to pass on the PGA Championship and instead keep pursuing exhibition money. There was little the PGA could do other than grumble because at this point Hagen was bigger than the organization.

Sarazen won the event, becoming the first player to win the National Championship and PGA in the same year. H. B. Martin refers to "the sudden rise of Gene Sarazen" in 1922 in combination with Hagen's victory in the British Open that year as giving golf a huge boost in the national golf arena. "Gene immediately set himself up as a rival to Walter Hagen and issued a general challenge to professional golf by taking a place among the leading stars," Martin wrote. "The cocky little bantam had developed his own game and he had plenty of competitive nerve."

But the absence of the defending champion and the game's most famous player took some luster off Sarazen's victory, and the PGA wasn't pleased at all that Hagen had put commerce above competition.

Sarazen did not miss out on going head-to-head with Hagen, though. As the winner of the year's other major, Hagen was invited to take on Sarazen at Oakmont (for 36 holes) then at the Westchester–Biltmore (second 36 holes) in an "international championship match" for a $3,000 pot, which the *New York Times* declared was "the highest amount ever played for by two professionals in the history of golf."

At the end of the day at Oakmont, Hagen was 2-up, and he and some friends traveled to Rye, New York. In the hotel that night Hagen and Sarazen shot dice, and after winning the Haig said, "Kid, I can beat you at anything," which had Sarazen gritting his teeth through a sleepless night plagued by stomach pains.

As Sarazen slept, or tried to (the Squire recalled finally falling asleep at 4:00 a.m.), Hagen was in his room with other friends displaying ties he'd purchased in England. One crony held up an especially loud number and suggested it be given to Sarazen with a note from a female admirer.

A bellhop was sent to deliver the tie to Sarazen's room in the morning with a note that read: "Dear Gene, You probably don't remember me but I'm the blonde from the Follies you met. Don't look for me in the gallery. I don't want you to take your mind off Hagen. I want you to wear this tie for good luck."

Sure enough, when Hagen arrived at the first tee that morning, Sarazen wore a new golfing outfit and the blaring tie. "I'm all ready," he told Hagen with a big smile. "Let's get going."

Hagen couldn't help asking, "Where did you get that funny tie?"

"Never mind," Sarazen replied. "You think you've got all the dames on your side, but you haven't. This is my mascot. Just you wait and see." The mascot got a bit messed because some rain fell on the competitors during the day and the orange in the tie washed out onto Sarazen's shirt.

It was all Hagen could do not to laugh at how successful his ruse was. But Sarazen caught fire, and his opponent felt less like laughing. The Squire won the day 4 and 2 and the overall match 2-up. When informed of the joke, Sarazen got a big laugh out of it and returned the tie.

Sarazen didn't laugh long, though, because as they were walking toward the clubhouse, he collapsed with a sudden attack of appendicitis. He was rushed by ambulance to the nearest hospital, where he survived an emergency appendectomy. Meanwhile, Hagen pocketed $1,350 of the $3,000 purse, so second place still had its merits.

The win "established Sarazen even more than his other victories, as anyone who was good enough to take over 'The Haig' at that time was deserving of all the praise that could be bestowed upon him," declared Martin.

The Western Open was to be held, of all places, at Oakland Hills, and officials there assumed that Hagen would drop everything to be there. He probably should have, as the folks at Oakland Hills had been good to him, and the Western Open was one of the anchor events on the emerging PGA tour. Hagen had every intention to put Detroit in his touring schedule, but then ran into a financial catch-22.

When Harlow tried to arrange for exhibition matches in and around the city to coincide with the Western Open, club owners refused, believing that people wouldn't pay to see Hagen if they could see him perform at Oakland Hills in the Western. Harlow crunched the numbers and realized that by giving up a week to be in Detroit for just the one event with a relatively paltry $500 first-place check, Hagen and Kirkwood would be passing up ten times that much. Harlow insisted on following the money, and Hagen went along with his manager's decision.

During the fall, nothing else mattered but the tour. Although beginning to feel fatigued, their pockets were bulging, and the pair played their way through Texas and then to the West Coast. Hagen spent the holidays in California. Afterward, he and Kirkwood teamed up again to make some more "green stuff" on the coast before making their way back to Florida. While doing this, Hagen wanted to prepare for his first important goal of the year, to repeat as British Open champion.

For him, 1923 got off to a very good start with he and Kirkwood dusting Sarazen and Hutchison 8 and 7 in a San Francisco exhibition. Late in January, Hagen and his partner entered the Texas Open. This was the second year of the event in San Antonio, and it featured the highest first-place check of any official tournament, $1,500. After 36 holes Hagen was 6 shots back, but he made them up in the next 36 holes and beat Bill Mehlhorn in a play-off.

February was spent putting on exhibitions in the deep South, and it wasn't until mid-March that Hagen and Kirkwood arrived in Florida. They entered the West Coast Open in St. Petersburg. For the second straight year, Hagen won it, shooting a 62 in the 3rd round and totaling 276. A week later, Hagen won the Asheville–Biltmore Open in North Carolina, then finished second in the St. Augustine Open back in Florida, and finally he set a tournament record of 289 while winning the North and South Open at Pinehurst.

The exhibition results were rather impressive too, if we accept Bob Harlow's record keeping. His tally showed that from the time the tour began the previous July through the first week of April 1923, Hagen and Kirkwood had managed a 97–14–4 record in exhibition matches.

Both were ready for the British Open, and an extra incentive was for the defending champion to show that the '22 victory hadn't been a fluke. He arrived in New York City to make travel arrangements, then picked up the Cadillac he had been given the keys to at the West-chester–Biltmore Club the previous year and drove it to Rochester. He visited his family, ex-wife, and especially Walter Jr. A photograph taken at the Country Club of Rochester shows Hagen giving his five-year-old son what may have been his first golf lesson.

It is likely that another reason Hagen went to Rochester was to in-form his family and ex-wife that he was about to be married again. Edna Straus had first been introduced to Hagen in New York City in 1920. In the intervening years he saw her with some frequency when he was in New York and Florida enjoying the social whirl, though the rest of the time he was on the road.

Edna Crosby was from a Jewish family in Philadelphia. She had married a man named Straus, a leather manufacturer, who died in 1919. The dark-haired, attractive woman was twenty-nine to Hagen's twenty-seven when they met.

Apparently, despite Hagen's industrious travel schedule, the relationship became increasingly serious. When the couple announced plans to marry in April 1923, it was reported in the New York society pages. The ceremony was held on April 30 at the Westchester–Biltmore Country Club, with Al Wallace as the best man and Kirkwood and H. B. Martin as witnesses.

It isn't quite clear why Walter took another trip down the aisle, given his enjoyment of the social life available during his travels. Presumably, he was in love with Edna, and she also liked to travel. They both liked good times and the social circles that provided much of them. And as with Margaret, Walter may have derived some satisfaction by marrying above himself socially.

Though Edna was no novice in relationships, she may not have fully appreciated what she was getting into. A week before the marriage, Hagen was in Albany where he had played an exhibition match after being in Rochester to see his family and son. He called Henry Clune, who had returned to the old hometown to work for the *Rochester Democrat and Chronicle*. Flush with cash and with the new Cadillac, Hagen told Clune, "Get me a pretty girl, get your wife, and we'll have a party tomorrow night at the Sagamore."

According to Clune, "I telephoned one of the prettiest girls in town, whom I scarcely knew. When I asked if she would care to be the dinner companion of the great golfer Walter Hagen, she was delighted." When they all met at the hotel, Hagen of course was resplendent in the finest clothes Rochester had seen in many a day. "Don't say anything to the young lady," he whispered to Clune, "but I'm getting married next week."

After dinner, with Hagen and the girl "getting on famously," the foursome went on a drive into the country in the Cadillac "with an array of glittering gadgets," Clune recalled. "To my recollection, Walter never called his companion by name, which I fancy he had already forgotten. It was always 'my dear,' or 'sweets,' or 'honey.' He drove with one hand, his other arm lightly embracing 'my dear.' They were cuddling a little in transit."

Clune and his wife knew when they were no longer welcome. He suggested that Hagen take the "old married couple" home. "He couldn't turn the car fast enough," Clune wrote years later. "In ten minutes, he dropped us at our doorstep."

A headline in the Sunday paper announced that Hagen was to be married, and Clune lamented, "The pretty girl I had gotten for Walter never spoke to me again."

Perhaps Edna thought she could tame Hagen, and he was discreet enough that she continued to think so for some time.

The newlyweds set sail on the *Aquitania* in May. The Open was at Troon in Scotland, and more than one reluctant British reporter pegged Hagen as the favorite because of how well he had been playing in the States. He very much wanted to prove them right.

Hagen was in contention throughout the tournament, and striding to the 72nd tee in a cold, windswept rain he was several strokes better than his 1922 total of 300. But Arthur Havers, an Englishman, had posted a 295, the lowest since Ted Ray had posted the same score in 1912. Hagen needed a birdie on the par-4 final hole to tie and force a play-off.

His drive was fine, a good sign, but his second shot went into a greenside bunker. He did not notch a birdie from the sand, and had to settle for a par and second place. The gracious Scottish fans cheered as Hagen walked off for what the press the next day would call "a gallant effort."

Havers had his only moment of golf glory. "When once he had won he raised high patriotic hopes and everyone looked on him as a future rock of strength against invasion," wrote Bernard Darwin in *Golf Between Two Wars*. "And yet in fact he never won again and never but once looked likely to."

Hagen was invited into the clubhouse in Troon for the trophy presentation. As police held back the large crowd, Hagen walked to the clubhouse entrance, then he turned around. "At no time have we Americans been admitted to the clubhouse, not even to pick up our mail," he told the crowd. "At this particular time, I'd like to thank you all for the many courtesies you've extended to us. And I'd like to invite all of you to come over to the pub where we've been so welcome, so that all the boys can meet you and thank you personally."

Then like the Pied Piper, Hagen headed to the pub with the large crowd following. The committee was furious, and poor Havers was rather lonely as he was handed the claret jug. Hagen had nothing at all against Havers and had congratulated him effusively earlier, but the young man was caught in the middle of a point that Hagen wanted to make.

Though disappointed, Hagen could console himself as he headed back to America that he had played very well in the Open, continuing the '23 hot streak. He liked his chances in the U.S. Open, being held at the Inwood Country Club on Long Island, New York. Harlow had arranged several weeks' worth of exhibitions in the Northeast and Mid-Atlantic regions, which Hagen expected would further fine-tune his game.

But there was more disappointment, as his prophecy about Bobby Jones proved true and came back to haunt him.

Hagen and Jones both finished 6 strokes behind Macdonald Smith in the qualifying rounds. The two were also paired during the first 36 holes. Their games were quite different, however. Hagen struggled, carding a 77 and 75. Jones's 71 and 73 put him at 144, 8 strokes ahead of his playing partner and 2 behind the halfway leader, Jock Hutchison.

Hagen rebounded with a strong third round to be in fourth place, but then he suffered a complete meltdown. His 86 in the final round would always be viewed as one of his most embarrassing moments in major competition. After 72 holes, Jones was tied with Bobby Cruickshank of Scotland, who had sunk a birdie putt on 18. "I didn't finish like a champion," Jones said, referring to how he had let Cruickshank catch him on the final hole. "I finished like a yellow dog."

They were still tied after 17 holes of the next day's play-off, but when Cruickshank double-bogeyed on the 90th hole of the week and Jones made par, it was the first National Championship for the twenty-one-year-old from Georgia.

Having been shut out at the two highest-profile golf events of the year, Hagen was especially keen on entering and winning the PGA Championship. He and Harlow made sure that the ongoing tour with Kirkwood would not interfere with Hagen being in the New York City area for the PGA. By doing so, Hagen became a participant in a battle that still stands as one of the finest in golf history.

In a look back at the PGA Championship in the October 27, 1980, issue, *Sports Illustrated* offered that "The Haig vs. Eugene Saraceni was a golf match that was made in heaven. . . . The finest individual match [of the 1920s] probably was the 1923 PGA final at Pelham, N.Y.—the first time Hagen, thirty, and Sarazen, twenty-one, met with a major championship at stake. These two were the best match-play golfers of their time."

"I'll never see a tougher match than this one," wrote Grantland Rice after it was over.

The two were primed and ready for the 1923 PGA Championship. Neither had won the Opens that year, and it was Hagen's turn to grit his teeth over the challenge the younger, arrogant man presented. As if the golf gods ordained it, both men successfully navigated their way through the match-play rounds to face off in the 36-hole finale.

"The final of the PGA between Walter and myself might not have taken on the proportions of a grudge match, which it did, if our supporters hadn't been clawing at each other," Sarazen remembered. "Hagen's camp followers were an arrogant bunch. They made it very clear they thought it an indignity for their hero to have to put up with a roughneck like Sarazen who had never dined with royalty and who had been seen fumbling for the correct fork and the right words. The chill of expressed animosity was in the air that October when Walter and I went out to see which of us would be champion."

It was tight all the way. On the 6th hole they argued over Sarazen moving leaves around where his ball landed. On the green an upset Sarazen missed his putt. "I'm glad I missed that," he said, "so when I beat your brains out today there will be no alibi." Hagen had a putt of only a foot, and he expected Sarazen to concede it. "Hole it," Sarazen said. "I'm giving you nothing but hell today." Hagen did, and the two didn't speak from that point on.

After the morning's 18 holes neither player had managed more than a 1-hole lead, and they were even.

From spending some time with Hagen the last couple of years in tournaments and Florida exhibitions, and being an especially observant man, Sarazen had gotten wise to the Haig's tricks and looked forward to the chance to turn the tables on him. According to Sarazen, such an opportunity came in that final match of the PGA.

On a par-5, Hagen's drive wound up a few feet short of Sarazen's. Preparing his shot, Sarazen drew the equivalent of a modern 2-iron from his bag. Hagen discreetly observed this and chose the same club.

He struck the ball . . . and it came to rest 20 yards short of the green. With a grin and a wink at his opponent, Sarazen exchanged the mid-iron for a brassie and his shot reached the green.

They halved the first four afternoon holes, then Sarazen birdied from 30 feet on 5 and 12 feet on 6, then on 7 Hagen three-putted to fall 3 holes behind.

Time for a stretch run. Hagen won the 11th hole. The next four holes were halved, with two of Hagen's putts rimming the cup. Hagen won the 16th hole; he was only 1 down. After sending his drive out of bounds on the 17th and seemingly losing the match, Hagen launched a gargantuan third shot and the ball came to rest 20 feet from the stick. He sank the putt; Sarazen missed his shorter one. All tied. Both parred the 18th, and it was sudden death.

After two birdies on the first play-off hole, the especially tense match between the two friends and rivals came down to the 38th hole of the day. Hagen's tee shot landed in the fairway; Sarazen hooked his to what surely had to be out of bounds. However, it apparently bounced off the greens keeper's cottage back into bounds.

Hagen found the ball and told Sarazen that it had to be his ball because "it's got spaghetti sauce on it," referring to the red "Wilson" lettering and Saraceni's heritage. (Perhaps with this in the back of his mind, Sarazen far outdid Hagen in their affiliation with Wilson Sporting Goods—shortly before his ninety-seventh birthday in 1999, the Squire signed a new contract to continue his relationship with the company, which had begun in 1923, for two more years.) Sarazen, understandably, was insulted by Hagen's remark.

Using the insult as fuel, an angry Sarazen struck. As Rice reported, "He blazed it out with a niblick, two feet from the flag! For once the Haig flubbed one in the clutch, right into the little bunker. He nearly holed his recovery."

Hagen parred, which wasn't good enough because Sarazen birdied and won the match 1-up. From the $500 first-place prize the former caddie gave his caddie, Harry Mellon, a hundred-dollar bill.

A disappointed Hagen played a few more scattered exhibitions with Kirkwood, but he had run out of gas. Though $7,000 was raised for charity, an exhibition match at Winged Foot in New York turned out to be another blow, as Jones and Jess Sweetser downed Hagen and

Sarazen. A second place in the Western Open, his last chance to score an important victory in the year, was just salt in the wound.

Except for financially and personally, thanks to his marriage to Edna, 1923 had been a disappointing year. He badly needed some R&R, so he called off any further touring with Kirkwood and headed with his wife to New York City. For the second time in four years, Hagen was without a major title to his credit. With the ascendancy of Sarazen and Jones, ten years younger, Walter may well have wondered if he'd had his day as the top player in the world.

CHAPTER 11

THE WAY FOR HAGEN TO RELAX AND REFRESH was not to lie in bed with a good book but to lift glasses at parties instead of lifting clubs out of a bag. The remainder of 1923 was spent living the high life. He was arrested in New Rochelle for speeding—going 33 miles per hour on Pelham Road—and pleading nonexistent golf commitments, he managed to have his day in court postponed six times. Finally, in November he pled guilty and was fined ten dollars.

When 1924 began, Hagen thought that maybe a change in the equipment in his bag would help. He began carrying (or, rather, his caddie did) in the early-year exhibitions and tournaments a "trunk bag," which is similar to the golf bag used today. As he became more experienced in shot selection and course management, Sir Walter wanted more weapons at his disposal. This was a big step forward in the effort toward the now-commonplace practice of having available certain clubs for certain shots. (This effort would take a great leap forward eight years later when Sarazen first used his invention, the sand wedge.)

Hagen wanted in his bag, in addition to the usual clubs, an extra driver, a shallow-faced spoon for tight lies, an all-purpose jigger (a narrow-bladed iron used for chipping and recovering from bad lies), a spoon with a big pear-shaped head for especially good lies, a left-handed club, and a second putter. Most professional golfers embraced the availability of more clubs (making being a caddie more backbreaking), but eventually this practice went out of control when in 1934 Lawson Little had his poor caddie carry around a trunk bag stuffed with thirty clubs. Now, the USGA and R&A limit is fourteen clubs, established in 1938 and 1939, respectively.

Feeling revitalized by not being involved in an exhibition tour and having spent the first months of 1924 playing a much more relaxed (yet still lucrative) schedule in Florida, Hagen set his sights on the most important priority of the year, winning the British Open.

The future of the world's oldest golf championship was balanced on a precipice: In the last three years it had been won by a Scottish ex-pat in Hutchison, a homebred American in Hagen, and then by an Englishman in Havers. Unless there was a surprise winner from a different country, the winner of the '24 Open could well indicate if the event was going to go America's way or would still be held fast by the British and British-born players.

That spring Edna and Hagen and his entourage (which included newlyweds Gene and Mary Sarazen) sailed first-class east on the *Mauretania* and arrived at the Royal Liverpool links in Hoylake. However, it looked like the trip would be wasted because of the 83 Hagen shot in the first qualifying round. But he recovered with a 73, and just barely qualified.

The Hagens and Sarazens stayed in adjoining rooms at the Adelphi Hotel in Liverpool. One day, the two players left the hotel together. A crowd was gathered outside, waiting to see the Lord Mayor in his robes of office. Seeing the figures emerge, the crowd began cheering. Hagen, believing the adulation was for them, mounted the small platform outside the hotel entrance and waved and smiled to the crowd.

A true honor was bestowed on Hagen the first day of the Open. At age sixty-three, John Ball was playing in his last British Open; his first had been in 1876, at fifteen. He won the Open in 1890, and he had won the British Amateur title an astonishing eight times. Ball was a very respected and popular player in England. The honor was that he requested to be paired with Hagen on the first day, surely an act of great generosity as well as respect on Ball's part.

Hagen, wearing a lavender sweater and knickers with black-and-white shoes, carded a 77 and 73 in the first two rounds and was 3 shots behind Ernie Whitcombe and 1 behind the seemingly ageless J. H. Taylor, once more making a run at the title and hoping to draw even with Harry Vardon by winning his sixth Open. (Taylor would also have become the only player to win the Open in four different decades.)

Hagen, a bit more subdued in a gray-and-white outfit, shot 74 and was in a tie with Whitcombe at the end of the third round. Taylor had a bloated 79, and worse for local fans was the 80 the defending champion, Havers, posted. It was a two-man fight to the finish.

Whitcombe wound up with a 302 for the tournament, and Hagen, even with a bumbling 41 on the front nine, was the only player within range of him, but he needed a 36. Putting the embarrassing front nine behind him, Hagen got stronger on the back nine. He sank a 20-foot putt for par on the 10th. On 11, he got out of a bunker and sank another long putt for par. On 12, out of a bunker again, then an 11-foot par putt. The par-3 13th: tee shot in the bunker, he got out, par putt.

By the time he teed off at 17, Hagen was holding on to a 1-stroke advantage. The 17th hole had been disastrous for many that day, and in the late afternoon Hagen was facing a stiffening wind. His tee shot was fine, but his second shot was extraordinary, carrying the traps in front of the green yet holding on the small, fast green. His long putt laid up well, and he sank the next putt for par. He had maintained the slim lead over Whitcombe.

Sarazen, cheering Hagen on, later observed, "Walter was the finest short-iron player the game has ever known. He was a magnificent putter. He had courage, and unquestioning faith in himself. Hagen is the only golfer I know who would have passed up the safe route to the green and risked the championship by going straight for the flag."

It came down to 18, a long par-4, but the wind was at Hagen's back. His tee shot measured almost 300 yards. His second shot went long, through the green. He chipped from there but wasn't as close as he wanted to be, 9 feet from the cup. If he sank it, he won; if he missed, he had a bogey putt to force a play-off.

Hagen's putter moved, the ball rolled, and it fell in. He threw his putter in the air and ten thousand paying customers (the first time there had been admission to the British Open) cheered. Hagen had not only collected another major, but the American had won the world's oldest championship twice in three years. The crowd lifted him on its shoulders and brought him to the clubhouse, past R&A officials who could stop neither the flow of people nor of history.

Inside, Hagen was presented with the claret jug and the crowd sang "For He's a Jolly Good Fellow." Perhaps the generous British crowd wouldn't have been so cheerful if they had known that Hagen's victory slammed the door on British golfers in their own Open—none of them would win it for another decade as Hagen and Bobby Jones dominated the event.

The British press was far from joyful but gave Hagen full credit for his fortitude on a windy back nine that had derailed other competitors. And as Bernard Darwin succinctly summarized, "The difference between Hagen and the other players is that he just wins and they just don't."

There was another rousing welcome expected for Hagen when he returned to the States with his second claret jug. Not that he was in a rush to receive it: A side trip with Edna to the Continent followed by collecting some British cash seemed like good ideas.

The *Times* of London reported in its June 30, 1924, issue that with the claret jug in hand, "W. Hagen, the Open Champion, left on Saturday night for Paris. He will take part in the French Open Championship at La Boulie." He was unable to duplicate his success of 1920. However, while he was on the Continent he entered and won the Belgian Open; he had now won four national championships, the first golfer to do so.

Then it was back to England to put on exhibitions, and during that July large crowds turned out to see the homebred Yank who had taken their Open twice. On July 10, Hagen and Macdonald Smith took on Abe Mitchell and George Duncan in the so-called International Four-Ball Match, played over two consecutive days, at St. George's Hill and then at the course at Oxhey.

"It was a lovely sunshiny day, with a cooling breeze; the course was in admirable order and made for good scoring," according to Bernard Darwin's report in the *Times* of London about the first half of the match. He noted that some very fine shots were made, especially a seemingly impossible putt on 14 by Hagen. The day ended with the British pair 1-up.

The home duo won the overall match 2-up. One wonders if Hagen had partied too much the night before or the long stay in Europe had tired him, because of Darwin's observation in his July 12 report:

"Hagen, though he was steady from the tee and through the green, did not seem happy and was not at his best."

Finally, it was time for a leisurely steam west. According to Hagen, in a typical understatement about events that included mention of his ex-wives, "After several weeks of fun at the famous resorts and attendance at the Olympic Games, Mrs. Hagen and I headed for home."

There were celebration dinners in New York City when he and Edna disembarked. American golf officials, players, and fans believed that Hagen's second win in Great Britain meant that the British Open wins by Hutchison and then the homebred Hagen were not aberrations but a true change of direction in that event.

"Friends of Hagen Welcome Him Back," stated the July 23 issue of the *New York Times*. There were sixty golfers present, and Hagen, holding the claret jug, made a modest speech, according to the *Times*: "Hagen reiterated the remarks that he had made when he landed, again claiming that he was 'lucky to turn the trick.' 'It was just luck that enabled me to win the title,' he said. 'I didn't play championship golf, but I got away with it,'" referring to winning by just one stroke and his 301 being a stroke higher than his winning total in 1922.

"'I want to pay my respects to British sportsmanship. They might well have claimed that it was a lucky win, but they didn't, and the ovation that I got from them was something worth remembering the remainder of my life.'"

History would show that Hagen's British Open title in 1924 was indeed a turning point in American domination of that tournament. As Darwin would state in his excellent *Golf Between Two Wars*, "From 1924 to 1930, except in one single year, the Open Championship was won by Walter Hagen or Bobby Jones." That one exception was Jim Barnes in 1925, and beyond that three American citizens—Tommy Armour, homebred Gene Sarazen, and Densmore Shute—would win the Open in 1931, '32, and '33.

For Hagen personally, his second British Open win seemed to give his career renewed momentum and proof that at thirty-one he had not peaked at all. In fact, he had begun a strong run that can only be compared to the success of Bobby Jones in the 1920s, who won seven professional majors (and six amateur ones) in eight years; Jack Nicklaus in the 1960s and '70s; and Tiger Woods from the 1999 Masters to the 2002 Masters.

Hagen's success in majors from 1924 on does not include two Western Open wins during the same period and the fact that he did not have the Masters available to him. One might argue that during this run his main rival, Jones, could not play in the PGA Championship and thus Hagen's success in that event was more than it might have been. However, Hagen could not play in the U.S. Amateur, and being that he was an excellent match-play golfer, if Hagen had been able to compete, would Jones have won five U.S. Amateurs during the same period of time? (Sarazen remained a rival of Hagen's, but after his PGA Championship victory in 1923, he did not win another major until 1932.)

Hagen apparently did have the "constitution of a rhinoceros" (as Charles Price had commented) because he played golf all the time; there was no off-season for him thanks to Florida in the winter, tournaments in the spring and summer, and exhibition tours that took him west in the fall. His dance card was much more full than other established champions of the early to mid-'20s. Jack Dempsey's handlers' philosophy was if Dempsey didn't fight he couldn't be dethroned, so at most he defended his heavyweight belt once a year. Babe Ruth didn't play baseball from mid-October to mid-February. Because of his family and going to school, Jones played in no more than a half dozen tournaments and just a handful of exhibitions a year.

While baseball and boxing were indeed more high-profile sports at home, Hagen's work on the hustings in exhibitions and his string of victories in important tournaments in the States and Great Britain through the end of the decade complemented Jones's achievements, and between the two of them golf became more firmly established as one of the top three or four sports in America. Newspaper editors were no longer going to relegate golf to the business pages.

Along the way, maybe as much as Michael Jordan and Tiger Woods today, Hagen was a popular pitchman in the emerging advertising industry for golf products, cigarettes, men's clothing, and warm-weather resorts. "If you picked up a newspaper in any major city in the '20s, you couldn't miss him," said Sam Lacy, Barnes's caddie. "Walter Hagen was a powerful sight for products because of his accomplishments and the way he dressed. Everyone else was ordinary . . . Walter was special."

And he knew it. He enjoyed being a sports celebrity, and marriage did not slow down his wanton ways. "I met beautiful and charming women all over the world," Hagen recalled in his autobiography, and there is little reason to doubt this statement. "A roving eye was my Geiger counter. My claim was staked with a devoted appreciation of their potentials and ability to make my travels and my leisure moments more enjoyable."

The paths of Babe Ruth and Walter Hagen crossed, more than once, and they enjoyed playing golf together, in the New York area during the baseball season and in Florida during spring training. (Ruth had taken up golf to strengthen his legs.) They also enjoyed the 19th hole, which at times lasted until the wee hours of the morning and could include chorus girls, waitresses, debutantes, and socialites— whoever the Haig and the Babe encountered as the two sports titans cut a swath through the local nightlife.

The two had a genuine appreciation for each other that went beyond their physical capacities to party and show up for a contest the next day. Both were larger-than-life figures to their fans, and they enjoyed cheering crowds and performing under pressure. Hagen still loved baseball and recognized in Ruth the most accomplished and exciting player of his day.

The Babe saw in Hagen a man of great skill and poise who was in the process of breaking whatever world golf records had been tallied and establishing new ones. Hagen admired Ruth's raw power, and Ruth admired Hagen's charm and panache. Both were robust, broad-shouldered men who were all-round better athletes than many might expect.

Two psychologists affiliated with Columbia University had the bright idea of conducting a battery of tests on Ruth and Hagen at the university to try to discern why they were the best in their respective fields. The results, titled "A Duel Between Champions," surprised the researchers and mainly served to show how much more different than alike golf and baseball were.

Among the results for the Babe: His bat speed was 110 feet per second; he could complete an electrical circuit by inserting his left hand into successive holes 132 times a minute, when the average was 82 times; his eyes responded to briefly flashing lights in a darkened chamber two-hundredths of a second quicker then the average person; he could count 12 black dots of a group exposed on a card for 1/50,000th of a second and the average was 8; and he could react to a sound 1/100th of a second faster than anyone else.

The conclusion of the psychologists stated that Ruth's "eyes, ears, brain and nerves worked more quickly and accurately than those of the average person, and the coordination of all was much nearer perfection than that of the average man."

Then it was Hagen's turn. His results were not equal to Ruth's when it came to speed but were much higher when it came to deliberation and accuracy. This makes sense when you consider that a baseball player must react almost instantly to a thrown baseball, while a golfer has to decide the best way to hit a stationary ball. Other tests showed that Hagen exhibited greater and more consistent concentration than Ruth. This also makes sense because a baseball game lasts two hours (in those days, anyway) with maybe five hours total for a doubleheader, but an average 18-hole round of golf takes four hours, with some tournaments at the time (such as the Opens) having 36-hole finales.

What did "The Duel Between Champions" prove? Not much, except that there were indeed "scientific" reasons why both men were exceptional in their sports. And the process of taking the tests translated into some good teasing and laughs when the Haig and the Babe were out on the town.

The 1924 season saw a significant change in golf that didn't take place on a course. The U.S. Golf Association ruled that steel-shaft clubs could be used in tournament play. Shafts made of hickory were suddenly old-fashioned.

Many players mourned the passing of hickory-shafted clubs and the strict technical skill that went into making each one. However, the USGA's approval led to an explosion in golf club manufacturing in the middle of the Roaring Twenties and gave on-course competitors better tools.

For the first time, matched sets of golf clubs could be mass-produced, with each club having defined, standard specifications that machines could meet over and over again by the thousands. Soon, as a consequence, because it was more convenient for manufacturers, clubs were referred to by number rather than name—a brassie became a 2-wood, a spoon became a 3-wood, cleek became a 4-wood, baffy a 5-wood, mashie a 5-iron, and niblick a 9-iron.

For many reasons, one being the better durability of steel, this change was advantageous to players, from professional down to hacker. Initially this wasn't necessarily good news to the typical club pro who earned part of his income by making and repairing clubs by hand in the back of the shop. Eventually, they adapted to repairing golf clubs, selling them retail, and advising on which sets and individual clubs would work best for each customer.

In the interim, some players weren't quick to make the switch. For example, Bobby Jones was still using hickory-shafted clubs when he completed his "grand slam" in 1930. Billy Burke has the distinction of being the first player using steel-shafted clubs to win the U.S. Open, at Inverness in 1931.

The second British Open victory and the continuing exhibition forays that summer brought more attention than ever to the man who more frequently was being referred to as Sir Walter. Supporting such a title was Hagen's appearance and lifestyle, which couldn't help but attract notice.

"On and off the golf course, the ex-caddie and sandlot hurler comported himself in such a manner as imperial as a king or a Hollywood star," wrote Herbert Warren Wind in an essay titled "Sir Walter," written as a reminiscence about Hagen in the '20s. "He loved the high life . . . Walter broke eleven of the Ten Commandments and kept on going. He knew how to take care of himself. He had the right words and the right tie for every occasion. Loving clothes as he did, whenever he had the time he changed into a new outfit between his morning and afternoon rounds."

Despite the distractions of being a celebrity, Hagen kept winning. No doubt he did so because of a hunger to win and to maintain his stature as the world's top professional. But he also understood, and Harlow kept reminding him, that continuing to win, especially high-profile events, meant getting top dollar from exhibition tours and endorsement deals.

Hagen's price would go through the roof if he could capture his third National Championship. It had been five years since Brae Burn, the same amount of time between his first and second U.S. Open triumphs (though, in that instance, a war had intervened). Jones would defend. One might think that Hagen had an edge over Jones and the rest of the field because the Open in June 1924 was being held at the par-72 Oakland Hills, but the course had not been completed when Hagen left as head pro there.

He started out decently with a 75, but not well enough. Bill Mehlhorn posted a 72, a stroke back were Eddie Loos and Dave Robertson, and then shooting 74s were Jones, Cyril Walker, Gene Sarazen, and Herbert Lagerblade. In the second round Jones drew even with Mehlhorn at 147, and alone in second place a stroke back was Walker, a 118-pound English-born U.S. citizen who had predicted before the event that the winner would be "a big fellow with the physical strength to stand the strain" and that "I'll crack on the second day." Hagen was consistent, shooting another 75, leaving him only three off the lead.

In the third round, it wasn't so much that Hagen made his move—he turned in a 76—but that no one took control of the tournament. Walker shot a 74 to tie for the lead with Jones after a 75. Mehlhorn scored a 76, as did Bobby Cruickshank. Four shots behind as the final 18 holes began, the Haig assumed, as did most of the press and spectators, that Jones was the only one to worry about.

But Hagen shot himself out of the Open with a bloated 77, both his driving and putting deserting him. Mehlhorn, Cruickshank, and Jones did even worse, carding 78s. Limping to the finish line was Walker with a 75 for a 297 and the championship.

Mourning the missed opportunity to defeat a journeyman for the National Championship (Walker would not win another tournament), Hagen, with Kirkwood in tow, hit the road again, passing up the Western Open so they could complete exhibition tours in Canada, New England, and the Midwest.

The next big official event was the PGA Championship. Hagen's win in 1921 already seemed like a long time ago, and there had been turmoil and defeat in between. In September the PGA Championship was played in French Lick Springs, Indiana. Sarazen was going for his third straight. Hagen could become the first player to win the British Open and the PGA Championship in the same year, which would rival Sarazen's feat of the U.S. Open and PGA in '22. Everyone else wanted to prove that they deserved to be on the same course with Hagen and Sarazen.

The only one who came close to proving that was Jim Barnes. Sarazen was sent home early, losing a shocker in the first round to the unheralded Larry Nabholtz from Ohio. Hagen worked his way to the final by winning four matches, against Tom Harmon, Al Watrous, Johnny Farrell, and Ray Derr, and winning them without much trouble.

In the 36-hole championship match, it was Barnes and Hagen, who appeared quite dapper wearing a silk bow tie. Barnes had defeated Nabholtz in the semifinal, and no doubt wanted to avenge his defeat at Hagen's hands in the '21 PGA. But the Haig was 4-up after the first 18 holes and Barnes seemed finished.

Long Jim may have been revived by the break for lunch, because his drives became straighter and his putts started dropping. He did the first nine in 34 strokes, and with Hagen on cruise control, Barnes was only 1 hole down as they teed off at the 12th. Hagen won that hole to go 2-up, lost the 13th, and he and Barnes halved the 14th. It was a gutsy comeback that allowed Barnes to be only 1 down with 4 holes remaining.

Hagen outdrove Barnes on the 15th and reached the green with his second shot. He two-putted for par. Barnes lost his traction and the hole with short, wayward shots. They halved the par-3 16th. When Barnes took the 17th he had again pulled to within 1 going to the last hole. "There was still a hope for the lanky Cornishman, but it vanished when he pulled his drive behind a big oak tree and then in attempting to play a mashie niblick shanked the shot off to the rough below the green," reported the *New York Times* in its September 21 issue. Barnes got on the green with his third shot to find Hagen already there in 2 and his ball much closer to the hole.

Attempting to forestall the inevitable, especially with the Haig's putting prowess (on the day, Hagen had 7 one-putt greens) that Barnes had been witnessing firsthand for a decade, the game Long Jim tried for a 4 but missed by only inches. Hagen carefully left his putt close enough to the hole to tap in his fourth shot, and the two longtime competitors shook hands. Hagen won 2-up.

"Barnes failed in crises; Hagen generally rose to the occasion," was how the *Times* wrapped up the final match.

Sir Walter now had two U.S. Opens, two British Opens, and two PGA Championships as well as two Western Opens, and thus had drawn farther ahead of other professional players. No wonder that as 1924 drew to a close, Hagen thought what a difference a year makes. He surveyed the golf landscape and saw that he had vanquished all his rivals. There was even partial revenge for the trouncing he and Sarazen had suffered in San Francisco at the hands of two amateurs, Jones and Sweetser, when in late October, in another charity event, he and the Squire beat Sweetser and Francis Ouimet on Long Island.

More than ever, Florida was the place for a successful professional golfer to be in mid-decade. The Sunshine State was brimming with lucrative golf events and, even better, golf courses that would pay big bucks for representation by the best professionals. In the anything-goes boomtown atmosphere, Hagen found himself in great demand.

At first, it appeared that the opportunity consisted of more—and more lucrative—exhibition matches for the moneyed Northeast and Midwest industrialists and stock-market entrepreneurs who were building estates (some with private courses) in the state. In this regard, Bob Harlow was a very busy man, arranging exhibitions for Hagen with other wintering pros and private outings with wealthy players willing to pay the most for the best.

But the opportunity available was quite a bit wider. Courses were being built at an unprecedented rate and the best-backed, most ambitious ones wanted the top pros to represent them. The pros' presence would attract tourists, boost membership, and plant the seeds of a long-term reputation.

Barnes, Sarazen, Armour, Hutchison, and other first-rank players were much sought after by the golf-course developers because of what they would mean for the golf in their little Florida fiefdoms and to the residential communities being built around them. The pros would help persuade people to buy second homes or to move down permanently. But no one headed south with more positive copy and allure than Hagen.

The early part of 1925—with Mrs. Hagen enjoying what for her was a whole new experience of southern exposure—Walter spent in Florida as golf royalty, and apparently enjoyed every minute of it. "The Florida boom fitted in perfectly with my design for living: sunshine, beautiful scenery, people with time on their hands for fun, and of course money," Hagen recalled.

He was offered contracts to represent emerging clubs and all he had to do was play exhibition matches there—or elsewhere in Florida, representing the club—and just by his presence be a magnet for moneyed people from the Northeast and Midwest looking for warm-weather havens.

Then things got quite serious. Hagen was the prize in a bidding war between two Florida golf course entrepreneurs, and he was nabbed by Jack Taylor, who was developing what was first called the Bear Creek Country Club and then the Pasadena on the Gulf Course. The contract Hagen signed was $30,000 a year for two years and an acre lot for a new home. It was because he got the contract off to a good start that he decided not to make the time-consuming trip to defend in the British Open.

"Hagen Signs Contract," announced the *New York Times* in its April 21, 1925, issue. It also reported that the Haig would have the title of president of the Pasadena Golf and Country Club. Bob Harlow was also aboard, as the coordinator of exhibitions and other special events.

The course was completed, as was a new house for the Hagens. "Mrs. Hagen and I occupied a beautiful Spanish villa in the estates proper and were host to many wonderful parties for the people building homes in the Pasadena development," Hagen reported.

During the time when spring training was under way, Hagen was able to combine his love of baseball with golf—he had carte blanche to attend any exhibition game he wanted, and in return he invited golf-loving ballplayers to his course. Grantland Rice and H. B. Martin joined him in playing with Mickey Cochrane, Jimmy Foxx, and Rube Marquard.

And of course there was the Babe. He had to sneak over to play with Hagen because Miller Huggins, manager of the Yankees, had banned golf as too much of a distraction to getting ready for the 1925 baseball season. Ruth managed to sneak away, however.

"Babe and I played many rounds together," Hagen remembered. Then, seeming to confirm the results of the Columbia University tests, he added, "One thing I noticed peculiar to Babe's game, and to that of most ballplayers, was that for the length of time an average ball-game consumes Babe was a fine golfer. He could concentrate. But after the hour and fifty minutes' duration, or about the eleventh hole as golf is played, the Babe began to slop his shots away."

Being president of the club didn't mean that Hagen had to pay attention to administrative details. He was given an office that contained vases of flowers and a young, blond secretary. Among her talents was playing the ukulele, and with little else to do she composed a song called "Pasadena, Beautiful Pasadena." This actually came in handy because whenever a prospective club member was brought around, Hagen and his secretary would greet him with a lively rendition of the song.

The only problem was making sure one could find the Haig in his office. His schedule: "I went in about noon, stayed perhaps forty minutes, then checked out for lunch with some special pals. Business in the minutes at my desk consisted chiefly in lining up the afternoon golf and perhaps a few telephone calls to plan some doings for the evening."

Hagen also helped form what is considered the first professional "golf league," in 1925. Harlow even touted it as the Professional Golfers League of Florida. Up to this point, exhibitions between individual golfers or two-on-two professionals were loosely coordinated, sometimes impromptu affairs. As more golf clubs were developed in Florida, however, it made sense that each could be like a ball club, its players challenging other players for bragging rights and betting opportunities. As far as the pros were concerned, this was simply more fun and more money in the sun.

Hagen, representing the Pasadena club, grabbed Joe Kirkwood as his partner. Jim Barnes and Fred McLeod represented the Temple Terrace Club in Tampa. Gene Sarazen and Leo Diegel repped a club in Hollywood on Florida's east coast. Cyril Walker, Johnny Farrell, Tommy Armour, and others were also involved. In a way, it was like the feudal lords of booming Florida choosing their knights to represent and defend them in the jousting of golf.

The league lasted only the 1925 season. The Sarazen-Diegel team won the league title, and the players enjoyed receiving 60 percent of the gate receipts at two dollars a spectator per event. What happened to the league? Nothing, really. It just didn't start up again the following year because no one stepped forward to coordinate it. Another factor was the developing "southern swing" that included the Los Angeles Open and the Texas Open, and many of the pros wanted to participate in these tourneys and related exhibition matches in Texas and Southern California rather than play exclusively in Florida until the British Open was held.

Florida, despite its monetary and other virtues, in 1925 and especially beyond was not the only place to call home during the "off-season." Even an entire state couldn't hold Hagen. Nor could his marriage. During that year Edna frequently found herself left behind as her husband— with Kirkie, Armour, Barnes, Farrell, or whoever else was available—set off on exhibition trips. She often accompanied him when he participated in official tournaments, such as the Open at Worcester, and they were together during the Florida stay, but during the spring, summer, and fall exhibition swings Hagen went off with his pals.

Indeed, he had become such an experienced traveler and bon vivant that he had identified favorite places to party when he was on the road. "I was host many times to the languorous beauties of New Orleans, either at the Roosevelt Hotel or at one of the numerous famed French restaurants," he recalled.

"Seymour Weiss managed the Roosevelt at the time and Huey 'the Kingfish' Long lorded it over his home state. Although we never had any trouble rounding up plenty of the New Orleans belles to provide the necessary pulchritude, my policy of open house parties at my hotel suite had to be abandoned for the Senator's bodyguard insisted on screening the credentials of every guest when he was present."

Another favorite place to play, off the course, was Minneapolis. A party there "usually followed a duck hunting trip and I always served my own game, succulently roasted, garnished with wild rice and prepared by the chef of the hotel. Those second- and third-generation Norwegian, Swedish, and Danish girls were among the most beautiful and the healthiest I've ever met. Nicollet Avenue and the Flame Room of the Radisson glowed with their fresh blond beauty. Nothing gave me more pleasure than catering to those healthy appetites."

One legendary summer party took place north of the border. Hagen had just come in second in a tournament in Kansas City, but because Chick Evans had won, Hagen was given the $800 first-place check. He headed up to Winnipeg where he picked up $1,000 doing three exhibitions, then embarked on a tour of Canada.

Exhibitions were played in Moose Jaw, Saskatoon, Edmonton, Medicine Hat, Victoria, Vancouver, and Calgary. The total take was another $2,000. Hagen then headed back to Winnipeg, wiring ahead to the Royal Alexandria Hotel to reserve the best suite. The hotel manager was also instructed to stock the suite with food and drink and to round up local golf officials and players and their lady friends for a party.

When Hagen arrived he found about thirty people in attendance, and that not being enough, he invited the hotel's employees in too, made a few more calls, and eventually there were a hundred guests. The bathtub had been filled with ice, scotch, ale, and champagne. The phonograph was cranked up and the party, which would last through dawn of the next day, got under way.

During the party Hagen met a young woman, and the two slipped out of the hotel. They went to a popular nightclub to see the show. Hagen was recognized there and things got more festive. Before leaving to return to the hotel, Hagen picked up the check for the large group that had gathered at his table.

Presented with the hotel bill the next day, Hagen had to ante up. "I went back across the border with less money in my slacks than when I started," he remembered ruefully. "But I felt I'd helped cement the good-neighbor policy with our Canadian friends."

And it was a regular practice to spot and make the acquaintance of women on the golf course, even during the middle of play: "I was playing on a course at the Lake Placid Club in New York when I hooked a tee shot sharply and it struck the thigh of an unusually pretty girl just off the fairway. I walked over immediately and apologized, but as I told her, it's rather difficult to gauge the seriousness of an accident like that unless one checks personally."

He concluded about this episode, "We had cocktails later that day in the clubhouse. Romantic affairs had a pleasant habit of developing quickly in those days, and I usually managed to overcome any obstacles barring the way to my 'pursuit of happiness.'"

A few friends and fellow competitors wondered if Hagen's "pursuit of happiness" included drinking too much and whether, combined with all his other activities, he risked a flameout. Some were concerned for Hagen personally; some were concerned that his absence from the scene would impair the growth of golf and with it bigger purses.

At the risk of tarnishing Hagen's reputation as a major partyer: While it was true that he could dance, drink, and debauch almost anyone under the table, he wasn't living quite as hard as many people thought. As mentioned earlier, he wasn't about to throw away his career and all the advantages that came with winning. During Hagen's peak years he knew *his* limits—as opposed to limits for a less robust and resilient person—and he adhered to them. Only those closest to him saw this ability to pull the plug on partying when it was necessary.

Fred Corcoran, who later became head of the PGA Tour, knew Hagen very well from the player's heyday through retirement. In 1965, *Unplayable Lies* by Corcoran was published, and the memoir spent a good amount of time on golf's most colorful subject. "Hagen was the corporal of the color guard, no question about it," Corcoran wrote. "He had that magnetism, the electric quality, that fired the imagination. He lived the life lesser men dream about as they plod back and forth every day between their offices and the subway."

However, Corcoran continued, "The strange part of it is, the legend has distorted the actual portrait. Hagen loved life and people. He hated to go to bed because sleeping seemed like such a waste of time. But the picture of Hagen flashing through life with champagne bubbling out of his ears is a false one. The Hagen of his golden years took excellent care of himself. He was the world's champion hider of drinks. Hagen always had a full glass in his hand. But after the ball was over, the sweeper would find a dozen drinks lined up behind the piano where Hagen had slyly stashed them."

The sportswriter Charles Price once reported that Hagen "had studiously built up a public persona, a façade of indifference in which every offhand gesture actually had been as studied as one of Barrymore's. For an exhibition at 10 o'clock in the morning, the Haig would get out of bed at his customary hour of 6:00 a.m., a habit he had picked up as a country boy, and then lounge around for maybe three hours."

Sometimes, depending on his audience, Hagen would have his valet (the one who most often accompanied him was Spec Hammond from Los Angeles) unpack a tuxedo and throw it against the wall a few times. Hagen put it on, and Spec drove him to the golf course, making sure they were at least a half hour late. Hagen staggered out of the car to the first tee—everyone, of course, believing he'd been out partying all night—and then after a deep breath to clear his head he hit a long drive down the fairway, astonishing everyone. Whatever else happened that day, the paying customers already had their money's worth.

"Back in the clubhouse," Price continued, "the Haig would order drinks for the house, at least a dozen of which would end up in his hands and most of which he would surreptitiously pour into a jardiniere or a toilet. The heavy drinking came later, after the eleven major titles had been safely stashed away."

Apparently, Hagen was a big-time partyer whose constitution allowed him to continue to compete until his early forties yet he stuck to self-imposed limits in order to stay on top professionally and put on a good show for fans. That's certainly the Hagen the Squire knew.

"He was the biggest fibber of all time," stated Sarazen. "He was always the first to bed before a big match. What he would do is get into a cab the next morning and en route change into a rumpled tux, put a splash of whiskey and perfume on his clothes, and arrive like a big deal."

Sarazen also revealed, "Walter's scotches and water were actually iced tea, and it was not uncommon, after conspicuously ordering round after round, to dump his own drinks into handy flowerpots. He reveled in his bad-boy image."

Hagen himself admitted in his autobiography, "I could make one highball last longer in my own glass than any Scotchman ever born" during especially important tournaments.

It was all part of being cool and calculating during his best years: "Given the opportunity I checked and double-checked everything from the undulations of a putting green to the figures on a check and the curves of a pleasing number. I took nothing for granted, for I could not afford that luxury. I was trying to make a living out of a game which had never in its history supplied more than the bare necessities to its professional players, much less allowed them to live in comparative ease. I never wanted to be a millionaire; I just wanted to live like one."

In order to continue to do so, he had to keep winning, especially the major tournaments. And he had to be up to the challenge of his next great rival.

It is impossible not to have enormous admiration for Robert Tyre Jones Jr., not only because of his many golf accomplishments but for the strength of his character. Testimonies to the latter can be easily found throughout golf literature and in the words of greats like Arnold Palmer, Jack Nicklaus, Ben Crenshaw, and others for whom Jones is an idol.

What was special about Jones was evident early on, when he was still a teenager participating in tournaments and Red Cross exhibitions during World War I. (In the press, even earlier—an issue of the *American Golfer* in 1910 reported on a tournament in Atlanta won by eight-year-old Jones.) The man with the movie-star looks was soft-spoken, polite, had a keen intelligence, was driven to do his best, and by remaining an amateur was obviously playing purely for the love of golf and competition. Incessant smoking turned out to be his only vice (though not necessarily recognized as one at the time), and his inability to deal with adulation helped to cut his career short.

He turned twenty-three in March 1925. He had won the U.S. Open in 1923, and had been runner-up at Oakland Hills in 1924. He had won the U.S. Amateur Championship in '24, though just as remarkable he had been runner-up in the event in 1919 when he was seventeen. While in the three seasons from 1923 to 1925 Walter Hagen won eight official tournaments, including what are now recorded as three majors, in 1925 some fans and members of the press saw Bobby Jones as the best in golf.

With Sarazen having trouble winning, Jones had emerged as the Haig's chief rival. "When Sarazen ran into a few lean years after his initial threat, Bobby Jones took his place as enemy No. 1 in the Hagen camp," H. B. Martin reported.

The British Open offered a major opportunity in 1925 for Hagen and Jones to compete in the same field. But it didn't come to pass. The Open was held, but Jim Barnes—who wound up winning by 1 stroke over Archie Compston and the incredible Ted Ray—and Macdonald Smith were the only prominent American players to travel to Prestwick, Scotland. Hagen cited his new contract, packed exhibition schedule, and wanting to better prepare for the U.S. Open as reasons not to defend, and Jones cited family and education commitments.

Hagen seemed to be in a good frame of mind in anticipation of the Open. In Atlanta in May, he was interviewed by O. B. Keeler for the *American Golfer.* He told Keeler that part of his ability to bounce back from disappointment was "never making the mistake of feeling sorry for myself, or disappointed, because I could not win all the time. I always remember that no one can do that. Anyway, no one ever has."

More than any other interview, in this one with Keeler he expressed concisely his philosophy on winning and doing so for over a decade: "The point is, if I use my game properly and keep getting all out of it there at each particular time, I will win a proportion of matches and tournaments and championships. The percentage is bound to be with the player who gets most out of his game, provided his game normally rates along with the front rank. As long as my game will stand up with the others, I can keep on winning my fair proportion of events and maybe—as some folks suggest—rather more than my proportion. The game has been good to me, and there's no trick to it."

Jones and Hagen were viewed as the favorites going into the U.S. Open that year, at the Worcester Country Club in Massachusetts. They played a practice round together, the reigning National Amateur champion and PGA champion, and they invited Joe Kirkwood and Tommy Armour to complete the quartet. A good-sized gallery followed this foursome, and according to accounts the relaxed players were doing a lot of laughing, kidding around, and putting on quite an exhibition for the crowd.

At the fifth hole Hagen comically tried to slash his ball out of the middle of the brook, and in doing so cut it almost in half. On the tee at the 180-yard 6th, he discovered he hadn't brought spare balls. With some teasing, Jones tossed him a ball from his bag. Hagen took out a hickory-shafted club and was in the process of straightening it out (the wooden shafts tended to bend standing in the bag) when it too cracked almost in half.

The crowd thought this was hysterical—the hapless Hagen stood at the tee with a borrowed ball and a dangling club—and now the teasing from Jones, Kirkie, and Armour was relentless. Hagen took out a 1-iron and, just wanting to get out of Dodge, he swung quickly. The ball disappeared over the hill that made 6 a "blind" hole.

There were shouts from the few people at the green, then as they approached the flag the foursome found the ball in the cup. In the history of the Worcester Country Club, the 6th hole had never been aced before. Sir Walter had the last laugh, though Jones grabbed some bragging rights by shooting a 66 in the practice round.

Even though the biggest flaw in Hagen's game was hitting from the tee, it is amazing given his overall success in golf and the thousands of rounds he played that he had only this single hole-in-one to his credit. Somewhat galling is that there were several times when he played with partners who scored an ace, some of them far from being pros. One time in Florida, Hagen was playing an exhibition match and his partner was the mystery/adventure writer Rex Beach; he and the author had become friends in Hollywood. One of their opponents had put his ball only 4 feet from the pin on a par-3 and Beach was almost afraid to tee off.

Hagen, unperturbed as usual, said to the writer, "Now is the time to show what you can do. Save this hole by dropping it in for an ace."

"You know I never made an ace in my life, but if you think I can do it, I'll try," Beach responded. His tee shot ended up in the bottom of the cup.

The '25 Open at Worcester was a hard-fought contest involving America's best, held in horridly hot conditions, a Northeast heat wave that would be blamed for killing more than two hundred people.

Closing in on the finishing hole there were eight players with a good chance to win: Johnny Farrell, Leo Diegel, Hagen, Jones, Francis Ouimet, Willie MacFarlane, Gene Sarazen, and the grizzled Mike Brady, putting on one more good show for the locals. Hagen really wanted this one because, according to Martin, he "was not having any success in our own national open and it was beginning to get on Walter's nerves."

He gave what he could, opening with a 72, then posting a 76, and shooting a strong 71. He was happy to be part of the pack heading into the home stretch.

One by one they dropped out because of one misadventure or another—first Brady, then Diegel, then Farrell, then Ouimet, then Sarazen, and then Hagen, leaving Jones and MacFarlane. Hagen had been told that if he birdied 18 he would tie for the lead, but with his usual disdain for anything other than outright victory he tried a high-risk shot to eagle the hole; it went in the bunker, and he wound up with a bogey and a seat in the locker room, 2 strokes short.

One of the memorable moments of golf occurred during this Open and it involved Jones, with an interesting consequence. He had set up to hit a shot from behind a small hill on the par-3 11th hole during the first round, then abruptly stepped away. He notified the USGA officials that he was calling a penalty stroke on himself. Apparently, the ball had moved after he addressed it. No one had seen it move except Jones. The officials even tried to talk him out of the penalty, but he wouldn't hear of it.

The interesting consequence is that one stroke made all the difference because Jones and the Scottish-born MacFarlane (now an American citizen) ended in a tie after 72 holes. The next day, they were still tied after an 18-hole play-off. The nonplussed USGA officials, never having faced this situation, told the players to go back out in the heat and do another 18 holes. Both players, still tied after the additional 17 holes, staggered to the last hole, and this time there was a winner: MacFarlane, by 1 stroke after Jones missed a 10-footer for par.

When asked by reporters about the unselfishness of the self-imposed penalty, Jones snapped, "There is only one way to play the game. You might as well praise a man for not robbing a bank."

After the Worcester Open, Jones was lionized as an example of the best in golf. When Hagen was asked about Jones's penalty, he replied that "knowing Bobby, he could have done nothing else."

Still, though he never criticized Jones, the crowd's growing adoration of the young amateur did rankle Hagen. He was the showman, he had won two U.S. Opens to Bobby's one and two British Opens to Bobby's none, and for quite a few years he had been providing the great copy for the press. In comments made to friends at the time and then years later in his autobiography, Hagen harbored some resentment that Jones, who was only just breaking through as a golf star, could be more popular than a man who had been at the top of the game since 1914.

But Hagen was too busy to dwell for long on the Jones phenomenon. There was one major left in 1925, and he had to have it.

In the late summer of 1925 he faced again, as he had in 1915 and 1920 (U.S. Opens), 1922 (PGA Championship), and 1923 and 1925 (British Opens), the prospect of defending a major championship. He had squandered those previous opportunities. While repeating as champion in the same event may not be as big an accomplishment as it is today when the talent of the PGA Tour is so deep, in the 1920s it still was a measurement of excellence to keep one's crown in a high-profile event. Most likely, an added incentive for Hagen was having observed—very much up close—friend and rival Jim Barnes earning back-to-back PGA Championships in '16 and '19 (interrupted by war) and then Sarazen in '22 and '23. He wanted to join that exclusive American club.

The Olympia Fields Country Club in Chicago was the site of the '25 PGA Championship. As defending champion, Hagen could skip sectional qualifying, but he still had to play his way into the tournament itself. His 151 total over 36 holes got him in, but he also finished 11 strokes behind Al Watrous in the qualifying round, not a good omen.

This did not appear to shake his confidence, though. The day before the tournament began, Hagen arrived on the practice range to hear Watrous, Mike Brady, Tommy Armour, and a few other players talking about him: "Let me take Hagen this year," said one. "No, this is my year," said another. And, "I'll get him—he's mine!"

Hagen grinned at them as he stepped up to the practice tee, then nonchalantly said, "I wonder which one of you is going to be second."

Fittingly, Watrous fell first. He and Hagen finished dead even after 36 holes—with Hagen having been behind the whole time until the 32nd hole—then the Haig took the marathon match on the 39th hole. (Only now can we fully appreciate what part this match played in the still-unrivaled PGA Championship record that Hagen owns.)

Next up was defeating Mike Brady, his 1919 U.S. Open play-off competitor, which Hagen did without much trouble. Then came his friend Leo Diegel, who ignored that friendship by being 5-up at the 18-hole break. But there was a strategy in play. Throughout the match Hagen had smilingly been conceding 6- and 8-foot putts, which had the effect of making Diegel, who had a reputation of being high-strung, increasingly nervous. Hagen calmly performed better as the afternoon lengthened, and by the 33rd tee he was down 3. He won three of the last four holes to tie, most dramatically with a long putt on 36.

The next three holes, each one sudden death, were halved. Then came the 40th hole. With the match once more on the line and Diegel having a putt to halve within the range that Hagen had previously conceded, the challenger glanced at his opponent, expecting another smile and nod. This time Hagen just stared at him, his face grim. The putt has to be tougher than it looks, Diegel thought. He examined it this way and that, glanced again at the stone-faced Hagen, and struck the ball. He missed. Hagen advanced.

Then it was another tough fight, this time with the up-and-coming Harry "Lighthorse" Cooper, with Hagen winning 3 and 1. The final match was against the emerging pro Bill Mehlhorn, who already had a Western Open win to his credit. To get to the final, Mehlhorn had defeated Emmett French, Al Espinosa, Tommy Kerrigan, and Olin Dutra by a crushing 8 and 6. And Mehlhorn played a very good final round.

Unfortunately for the youngster, Hagen had one of the best 36-hole rounds of his life, and even when he was in trouble, he pulled a rabbit out of his hat. An example was the third hole during the afternoon's round. The Haig's comfortable lead had been trimmed to 2 when Mehlhorn eagled the day's 20th hole. On the par-3 21st, Mehlhorn was on the green off the tee. Hagen's tee shot came to rest on the edge of a bunker, and his chip barely made the far end of the green. No problem: Hagen sank the 70-foot putt. A shaken Mehlhorn two-putted for par, remaining 2 down.

Hagen pulled away from there, winning the match 6 and 5 and the championship.

The *New York Times* gushed, "For all the things that combine to make a really great golfer—skill, power, endurance, nerve, will-to-win, sportsmanship in defeat or victory—the golf world has never produced a man like Walter Hagen." This comment had to be most satisfying to Hagen and Harlow, but it did tend to overlook the accomplishments and contributions of Vardon, Braid, and Taylor. The U.S. and British Opens remained the true tests of golf immortality, and the Haig's four victories in those events, while impressive, still left him short.

Hagen's win in the '25 PGA Championship is recognized as his seventh professional major, tying him at the time with Harry Vardon. "Walter Hagen has won more championships and open tournaments than any other American," the *Times* felt it necessary to point out in its September 27, 1925, issue.

One might assume that the aftermath of the PGA win in 1925 was partying until dawn for the champion, and Hagen did his best but ended up taking a detour, if his and other accounts are to be believed. Predictably, there had been a huge, floating party after the victory. Hagen had done his part socially, and at 3:00 a.m. weaved his way to a guest cottage he believed was his. However, when he opened the door and switched on the light, he found a frightened lady in her seventies clutching the covers to her chest.

Hagen hurriedly identified himself and explained that he wasn't at his best because of the exertions of the final match and partying since late the previous afternoon. The woman recognized him. "You poor boy," she said, and got out of bed.

She put two glasses on the table, filled them with milk, and put out a tray of cookies. The woman had attended the final match of the PGA Championship. "Let's sit here and talk about all the fine shots you played yesterday," she said. Hagen did as he was told, finally leaving at sunrise. (Let's keep in mind, though, that this was the story he and friends offered to Edna.)

What he didn't realize until later was that night he'd lost the championship trophy. When the Haig had gone out on the town, he was holding the trophy. Heading back to his cottage, he spotted some acquaintances just going into a nightclub. Hagen got out of the taxi, and gave the driver five dollars to bring the trophy on to the resort. That was the last he saw of it.

CHAPTER 12

THE IDEA OF A "WORLD CHAMPIONSHIP OF GOLF" was not a new one. That's what the exhibition match between Hagen and Sarazen in the fall of '22 had been dubbed. And there had been the contest with Cyril Walker in February 1925 at courses in Miami and Pasadena, Florida.

There had been hope for a good match, or more specifically, that Walker would make a stand of it. He had won the U.S. Open in 1924, defeating the defending champ, Bobby Jones, by three strokes. Hagen had the British Open and PGA Championship to his credit in '24. This get-together could be compared to today's Grand Slam of Golf in which the winners of the four majors duke it out in an unofficial event for very nice money.

The match turned out great for Hagen, badly for the promoters. Hagen, like Jack Dempsey, didn't know how to carry an opponent for a few rounds: After the first 36 holes in Miami, he led by 11. Two days later they started the second 36 at Pasadena, but Walker was out on his feet. Hagen won the "World Championship" by a score of 17 and 16. As a competitor, Walker never challenged in a high-profile event again, seemingly unable to recover from such a beating.

Jones had won the U.S. Amateur in 1925, his second in a row, at Oakmont and had come within a hair of taking the U.S. Open. Hagen had won his third PGA Championship, and second in a row, that summer. As 1925 drew to a close, the public thought it was time for the next "World Championship," and in mid-decade the battle had to be between Hagen and Jones.

Golfers too wanted the match to happen. Of course, they were divided in their support along the lines of amateur and professional, depending on their own status. The pros were especially supportive because they had been made to feel inferior for generations and here was a chance for their leader to demonstrate that the tide was turning. Also, those who knew both men were intrigued by a head-to-head clash of personalities as well as skills.

As was already described, the outcome of the unofficial "World Championship" in 1926 was lopsided. Hagen felt afterward much better about the Jones situation and comparisons between the two. Jones smarted from the sting of the 12-and-11 dusting, but he proved to be a champion who could pick himself up off the canvas. Less publicized was that Jones and Hagen faced off only a couple of weeks later, in March, in the Florida West Coast Open at the Haig's Pasadena course. Jones played better in this stroke-play event, winding up in second by 2 strokes, but once again Hagen came out on top.

Making good on a vow he had made to return the following year when announcing he would not defend at the '25 British Open, Hagen was back for the '26 event at Royal Lytham and St. Annes. Barnes was there to defend, Sarazen was hoping to turn around his recent bad luck in majors, and Jones had a statement to make after the recent humiliation at Hagen's hands and having just lost in the quarterfinal of the British Amateur, which was won by Jess Sweetser, the first native-born American to take it. (Jones's anger was taken out on poor Cyril Tolley, who was crushed in a pre-Open exhibition match 12 and 11.) Some estimates had the crowds being the largest ever for a British Open, and they were ready for a show.

They got one.

Hagen qualified easily with a 72 and 71, but Jones played like a racehorse let loose, with a 66 and 68. He faltered in the first round of the Open, however, with a 72, while Hagen jumped out of the gate with a 68 to grab the lead. With Jones's 72 in the second round, it appeared that consistency had its advantages, as Hagen shot a dismal 77 to be in second place.

Hagen's friend Al Watrous from Detroit was leading the Open after three rounds, with Jones 2 strokes back. Since they would be paired in the final round, Jones suggested that they go back to his hotel for a quiet lunch and a nap to avoid the crowd. Watrous agreed.

They lunched, chatted, stretched out and slept. Then they went back to the golf course. The guard wouldn't let Jones back in. He had left his player's badge on the dresser, and what the guard saw was a twenty-four-year-old just trying to sneak in. Worried about missing their tee time, Jones told Watrous to go ahead in, then he raced around to the main entrance and paid the seven shillings to get into the course.

Showing remarkable maturity, Jones played well, but Watrous maintained a 2-stroke lead through 13 holes of the final round. Jones birdied two of the next three holes to Watrous's pars, and as they teed off on 17 they were tied.

On the par-4 hole, Watrous was on the green in 2 while the Georgian was in a bunker 170 yards away. Using a mashie-niblick, Jones made perfect contact and the ball landed on the green inside his opponent's ball. A rattled Watrous three-putted for a bogey, Jones parred. On the last hole, the result was the same, and Jones finished with a 291 total, first by 2 strokes and tying for the lowest score ever in the Open, set by James Braid in 1908.

But Hagen was in hot pursuit. He had teed off ninety minutes behind Jones and Watrous, and for Sir Walter, the next best thing to having an insurmountable lead in the last round was being within striking distance and having a target total to shoot at. As he paused at the tee of the par-4 finishing hole, Hagen could see Jones standing and watching from the balcony of the clubhouse. Sir Walter needed an eagle to tie and force a play-off.

The tee shot was a good one, leaving him 150 yards to the green. To the crowd and other competitors it appeared that he fully intended to earn eagle. Hagen asked the official scorer to run up to the green and hold the flag. Confused, the official asked him to repeat the request. Hagen did, and this time spectators in addition to the official heard him.

As the official trotted toward the green, the news traveled faster: Walter Hagen wants the flag held as though he's attempting a long putt!

It certainly did look like the Haig was dead serious. When the official stopped to stand on a mound short of the green, Hagen strode down halfway the distance of remaining fairway and then shouted, "I want you to hold that flag!" Not only was he heard by all the spectators but by Jones and J. H. Taylor standing with him. Hagen returned to his ball.

He carefully examined the lie, selected a club, set himself, and swung. The ball flew into the air and directly at the incredulous and by now trembling official. The ball landed just inches to the side of the cup, and without backspin continued on, past the green. The eagle he'd hoped for had not landed. Hagen was so disinterested in the comeback shot that he missed it, and the one after it, ending up in a tie for third.

Still, the crowd cheered lustily at the fearless attempt. Later, as Hagen congratulated the champion, Jones said, "I turned my back on you, Walter, because a guy with that much confidence would be a fool lucky enough to make it."

Hagen looked forward to another crack at Jones that July at the Scioto Country Club in Columbus, Ohio. This U.S. Open was the first one to use telephones to transmit players' scores to a central scoring tent. The professional at Scioto was George Sargent, who had won the National Championship in 1909. He failed to qualify, though his seventeen-year-old son did (but did not make the cut).

Because of the large crowd and the number of entries, at the 1926 Open the USGA introduced a three-day format. On the first two days the players would do 18 holes each, then the top 50 would return on the third day for the 36-hole finale. Among other things, this allowed for more admission fees being collected, and the purse of $2,145 would be shared by the top twenty finishers.

The Open pattern continued for Hagen: Starting out decently, then a high score in the second round. His 73 and 77 put him in a hole. On the final, 36-hole day he bounced back with a 148 total and was one stroke behind Diegel, Sarazen, Johnny Farrell, and Mehlhorn. The problem was, the championship duel was between Jones and Joe Turnesa.

The latter had begun the final round with the lead. Then the combination of heat, pressure, and cheers for Jones caught up with him. He staggered in with a 77 and a 294 total. Jones didn't have one of his best rounds, but his 73—especially the birdie on 18—was enough to overcome the deficit and give him a 1-stroke win. Jones became the first player to hold British Open and U.S. Open championships simultaneously.

Uncharacteristically, Hagen had a tirade after the Open. Accounts of Hagen talking to fellow pros in an angry fashion are more rare than aces, but in the locker room, as Jones was outside accepting his trophy, an agitated Hagen, who had placed sixth, told the others present, "Whenever I fail to stop Jones, the rest of you curl up and die too. All that blooming amateur has to do is show up on the first tee and the best pros in the world throw in the towel." (If you're thinking Hagen must have used another word than "blooming," think again, because Hagen, unlike the more verbally salty Jones, confined his swearing to nothing stronger than an occasional "goddamn.")

There was some revenge to be had on the rest of the field and on Jones. The Western Open that year was held at the par-70 Highland Golf and Country Club in Indianapolis. For the first two rounds many of the better players were in proximity of each other on the leaderboard. Then Hagen reached for something extra. His brilliant 66 in the third round put him well ahead of the others, and he coasted with par on the final round for 9-stroke victory over Gene Sarazen and Harry "Lighthorse" Cooper.

His 279 total established a new record in the event by two strokes. Even better, he had now won three Western Opens, and they each happened to be five years apart—1916, 1921, and 1926. Showing again what a class act he was, the first to congratulate Hagen after the final putt of the Western Open was Jones, who was to team up with Hagen for a charity event the next day. "That's the sort of golf Walter played last winter when he defeated me," Jones told a reporter as they walked off the green together. "When he is right, he can lick anyone." Beaming, Hagen said, "The same to you, Bob."

The PGA of America was now crediting Hagen with twenty-six official victories, far more than any other professional. Another example of the roll Hagen was on was his demolition of the competition in the Eastern Open in Pennsylvania in July. On the final day he carded 7 birdies in a row, four at the end of the morning's 18 and 3 to start off the afternoon round (despite a rainstorm between the rounds), leaving the other players well behind. He also established a world record in stroke play (on courses 6,500 yards or longer) over the first day's 36 holes, with his 132 eclipsing Bobby Jones's 134 during a British Open qualifier. His 275 total (13 under par) allowed him to win the tournament by 9 strokes over Johnny Farrell and Bill Mehlhorn, and he was one stroke short of the 72-hole record of 274 set by Emmett French at the Ohio State Open in 1922.

At a relatively old thirty-three, Hagen was still the man to beat. But in 1926, things were changing around him. In golf, Barnes and Hutchison were no longer winners, with Barnes having semiretired after his career-capping victory in the '25 British Open. (He did compete sporadically into the mid-'30s.) Jones and Sarazen, both ten years younger, were now Hagen's rivals. In boxing, Jack Dempsey was finally dethroned by Gene Tunney in a driving rainstorm in Philadelphia that September. Bill Tilden's career in tennis was over. Those who had risen to prominence before the Golden Age of Sport began were finished or in their mature years, and only Hagen and Ruth still seemed in their primes.

For motivation, there was staying in the spotlight as well as the continuing challenge of Jones. But Bobby couldn't face him in the PGA Championship, being played a decade after the founding of the Professional Golfers Association of America. It was held at the Salisbury Golf Club on Long Island, New York. As wonderful a triumph as two consecutive PGA Championships was, Sarazen had already done it in '22 and '23. (The Squire was not only the youngest winner of this event, at twenty in '22, but ended up the oldest participant when he played in the 1972 PGA Championship at seventy.)

Once more defying the odds, Hagen won his first four matches, giving him fourteen straight in the last three PGA Championships. In the final he was up against Diegel, who keenly wanted to unseat the master and make up for the previous year's humiliation. The night before the championship was to be decided, Sir Walter was holding court in the hotel bar. Someone there cautioned Hagen that Diegel was already in bed. "Yes," said the Haig, using a familiar line, "but he's not asleep."

Rested or not, the two adversaries ended in a dead heat after the next morning's 18 holes, and Hagen invited his opponent to lunch. Diegel should have remembered that he was facing one of the original sports psychologists.

For lunch Sir Walter had the waiter bring him vichyssoise, roast duck, and champagne. Diegel had a simple sandwich, which he had trouble getting down as he watched Hagen drop food into his mouth, lick his fingers, drink with a smile, and then sit back to enjoy a cigarette. Feeling ill, Diegel jumped up and ran away from the table to find a bathroom, not realizing that between him and the one in the clubhouse was a glass door—Diegel ran right into it, but was more embarrassed than hurt by the splintering glass.

According to the *New York Times* account, Diegel, "his nervousness indicating plainly that he was unable to rid his mind of the knowledge that he was playing Hagen, was never in front . . ." By the end of the day, Hagen had broken Diegel, 5 and 3.

No American had won the same major three years in a row, and no one has since. Three consecutive PGA Championships, it would seem, were as much as a golfer could ever hope for.

What about the missing trophy? Hagen had been too embarrassed to tell anyone. At the '26 PGA Championship award ceremonies, he didn't have the trophy with him and claimed that was because he had no intention of losing it to anyone. Everyone had a big laugh, and apparently believed him. Hagen's PGA trophy was eventually found in the 1930s, packed in a dust-covered crate and forgotten in the back of a Detroit warehouse.

"Sam Ryder donated the trophy. The golf press on both sides of the Atlantic canvassed readers for donations to fund the early matches. But the inspiration and impetus which shaped the Ryder Cup's tradition of sportsmanship and friendship, even as the teams were locked in mortal combat, were provided by a local boy from Rochester. The Ryder Cup is truly Walter Hagen's baby." This was not written by an American sports reporter nor a friend of Hagen's, but the British golf writer Peter Dobereiner more than sixty years after the first Ryder Cup.

The first true Ryder Cup Match was played in Worcester, Massachusetts, in June 1927. Only an international player with the personality and track record of Hagen—who had by then won four national championships and a total of eight majors in the U.S. and Europe—could make the Ryder Cup work as a worthwhile competition between professionals in Great Britain and America. Sam Ryder's enthusiasm and desire were crucial, but there was no doubt that Hagen was in the center of the spotlight and that people came out to see him and his teammates take on worthy opponents.

Today, the Ryder Cup is *the* preeminent international event in golf. But like Hagen himself, this unique tournament had humble origins.

The first seed planted for what would be an event named after a seed merchant was in 1920. That year the *Glasgow Herald* in Scotland sponsored a tournament at the Gleneagles King's Course with the total purse equivalent to $1,250. When the same tournament was held for the second time, in 1921, there was a sudden influx of golfers from the United States because the British Open that year was being held at nearby St Andrews. The Gleneagles tourney was viewed by the visitors as an opportunity to tune up and perhaps collect a few pounds.

After the British Open was held and before the U.S. contingent boarded the boat for the trip home, an exhibition match was organized there between British and American players. This informal joust ended with the local lads defeating their guests 10½ to 4½ (some accounts claim the score was 9–3).

Another seed was planted more than 3,000 miles away. In 1921, Sylvanus Jermain, president of the Inverness Club in Toledo, Ohio, which had hosted the U.S. Open the year before, proposed to the USGA the concept of British and American teams of golfers going head-to-head. Another account is that James Hartnett of *Golf Illustrated* in Great Britain offered the idea in 1920 that later became the Ryder Cup. And PGA of America records show that the organization voted that same year to allocate a small amount of funds to explore the concept of a competition between British and American professionals.

In 1922, the Walker Cup was founded. This event pitted the best amateurs of Great Britain and the United States against each other in match-play formats. The cup was provided by George Herbert Walker. The first match was played at National Golf Links in Southampton, New York. The Walker Cup was contested at St Andrews in '23, Garden

City (New York) Golf Club in '24, then back to St Andrews in '25. Because of the travel required and the interruption of the amateurs' "day jobs," the event became biannual.

It seemed inevitable then that there would be a contest on a golf course that involved the better professional players in the United States and Great Britain. Presumably, the Americans would be pushing for this because by the mid-'20s, with players such as Hagen and Gene Sarazen (and Jones, though not a member of the professional ranks) beginning to dominate the major tournaments, they would want to find further ways to flex their muscles and show their English and Scottish uncles that they had come of age in golf. The prosperity and enhanced transportation options of the 1920s also made going head-to-head on either side of the Atlantic more feasible. Yet it was an older English gentleman who made the suggestion.

What became the Ryder Cup Matches really took root in 1926. Before the British Open at Royal Lytham and St. Annes, Hagen took on one of England's best-known players at the time, Abe Mitchell, who was also the personal coach of businessman Samuel Ryder. The winner-take-all prize for the duel was 500 pounds, then the most ever offered in that country for a golf exhibition match.

The marathon match covered 72 holes, requiring two days of play and concluding at the St. George's Hill course in Weybridge. Certainly many British fans had to be wondering why Hagen had a reputation as a money player, because after the first 36 holes he was down 4. The British spectators who showed up on the second day expected Mitchell to feast further on the hapless Hagen.

This was not the first and would not be the last time that Sir Walter, with his back to the wall, focused and rebounded. This meant for a thrilling finale in what was one of Hagen's most significant one-on-one matches. The four thousand observers "were kept in a state of explosive interest as the mercury rose and fell in the national barometers," reported Anthony Spalding in a cabled report to the New York Times.

Hagen played far from perfect golf, but the golf he did play was a perfect example of one of his more well-known sayings, "Three of them and one of those means par." Mitchell had to be somewhat astonished as the Haig compensated for errant shots, putted superbly, and gradually made the lead disappear. According to the Times account,

"Five times during the morning round Walter was in the far country, but proved a regular prodigal son, who came home to the green when the fatted calf was ready."

"He is the one great golfer who takes criminal shots and escapes punishment," wrote Spalding. "The British crowd enjoyed his cycle of experiences, both inspiring and depressing, but whatever his fate, Hagen played like a soldier of fortune, perfectly acquainted with the danger and meeting it without a touch of panic."

The symbolic hole of the match had to have been the 25th. Mitchell's ball was on the green. With his approach shot, Hagen's ball struck Mitchell's and sent it to 3 inches from the cup, in Hagen's line, a seemingly impossible stymie to overcome. "Nothing was impossible to Walter," reported Spalding, "who called for his niblick and hopped gayly over the blockading ball straight into the hole."

The final result was that after Mitchell conceded on the 71st hole, Hagen had won 2 and 1.

A consequence of this rather irritating loss to a Yank—one who had discourteously kept his opponent waiting on the first tee for twenty minutes, as the British press reported—was that the players from both sides of the ocean talked among themselves that an interesting and diverting way to practice for the Open would be to form teams and have a series of match-play contests. By virtue of his two British Open wins and probably his popularity in England, Hagen was the natural choice for unofficial captain of the visitors. However, he chose to take a backseat, and the Americans selected Emmett French as their captain.

There was a sense of "there's so much talent here, let's put on a show" and do it again, for the first time since the 1921 matches, as teams. Hagen was delighted—this was a new reason to compete and win, even if the only earnings would be brews at the nearest pub and bragging rights. The exhibition match was arranged at the golf course at Wentworth.

So much for the upstarts: The British routed the Americans 13½ to 1½. Mitchell led the way. He and George Duncan crushed Hagen and defending Open champion Jim Barnes 9 and 8, then in singles he pounded Barnes again, 8 and 7. The Yanks never got untracked.

Perhaps the outcome as much as the event itself inspired a particular spectator to want to take the exhibition match a step further. Samuel Ryder was quite delighted with the contest he had just witnessed. He joined British team members Duncan and Mitchell and American teammates Hagen and French for tea afterward. They analyzed the competition between the two squads and expressed sorrow that it might be a onetime event. They then headed for a pub, and after more discussion Ryder stated, "We must do this again."

What may have been a heartfelt remark turned into even more serious business when Ryder was asked to put his money where his mouth was. He agreed to pay 250 pounds for a gold cup, crafted by the Mappin & Webb Company, that would go to the winner of a tournament between British and U.S. teams.

By this time in his life, Ryder was very passionate about golf and was devoting more attention and energy to it than to his business. Having a competition named after him, even if it turned out to be a onetime event, was the next best thing to being a professional.

Ryder was a wealthy man who had literally made his fortune penny by penny. He had grown up in Manchester, England, the son of a corn merchant and one of five children. Like most young men of the time his main sports interest was cricket, but it was no more than a hobby to pursue while he completed his education, and then he would enter his father's business.

Then the proverbial lightbulb lit up over his head. Ryder had the bright idea that packaging seeds in packets costing a penny each would be popular. At the time seeds for flowers and other forms of flora were purchased in bulk amounts by large estates. Sam Ryder thought that working-class folks who wanted to have small gardens would buy seeds if they were made very affordable, a penny a packet. His father disagreed.

The son struck out on his own, moving with his wife and three daughters to St. Albans in 1895. The young Ryder turned out to be right. The penny packets—he and his wife produced and mailed their own catalogs and packaged the seeds for shipping themselves—proved to be hugely popular and Sam made a bundle.

Business for Ryder boomed. He also became very involved in his adopted hometown. He was elected to the city council, then ran for mayor of St. Albans and won in 1905. In addition, Ryder became known for philanthropy and being a collector of flowers from all over the world.

Golf replaced cricket as a pursuit when, upon his fiftieth birthday in 1908, Ryder began taking lessons as a way to get fresh air and exercise to recover from work-induced exhaustion. By the 1920s Ryder was paying a top British professional, Abe Mitchell, an annual salary of about 1,000 pounds to be his personal tutor. (It is the figure of Mitchell, not Ryder, who stands atop the Ryder Cup.)

Ryder's home course was Verulam, and he played golf assiduously six days a week. (A very religious man, he wouldn't play on Sundays.) He became captain of the Verulam Club in 1911, and again in 1926 and 1927. As he grew older his golf got better, his handicap shrinking to 6. He became active in organizing and staging a variety of tournaments. In 1926, Ryder was overjoyed at the prospect of coordinating an event with an international flavor.

The older British businessman with a private life of even-keeled rectitude and the American commoner who daily switched from putter to party and back made for an unlikely pair to create an international event that would endure (and eventually prosper) for at least the next eight decades. But Hagen thought Ryder's suggestion of making the competition an annual event was a capital idea. They shook hands on it and determined to have the two teams go at it in America the following year.

This time, Hagen would lead the U.S. players, and when the PGA of America approved of the first official Ryder Cup the title of captain was bestowed on him.

Putting up a cup was one thing, underwriting the entire enterprise was another. It was decided that the first Ryder Cup Match would be held in Worcester, Massachusetts. Then there was a glitch: The British Professional Golfers Association announced that it didn't have the funds to pay the transportation expenses.

A campaign by *Golf Illustrated* raised $2,500 of the $3,000 sought. At first, there weren't high hopes of coming up with the funds because an effort in 1922 to underwrite the travel of British amateurs to play in the first Walker Cup had fallen short. (Walker himself made up the difference.) However, this time the goal was almost reached, with contributions coming in from the United States, Canada, Australia, and throughout Great Britain.

Ryder made up the difference and steamship tickets were secured. But what about additional expenses, such as uniforms? Never doubting that proper clothing for the competitors was important, Hagen, using some of the winnings from exhibition matches, paid for the uniforms and just about everything else required.

Hagen skipped crossing the Atlantic for the 1927 British Open, even though it was an opportunity to take the crown from Jones and the event was being held at legendary St Andrews. Sir Walter said he'd rather help get the Worcester course ready, and no doubt he wanted to get some practice rounds in, something his British counterparts could not do. Whether or not Hagen would have been up to the task, Jones won his second British Open, starting off with a 68, ending with a brilliant 285 for a 6-stroke victory over Aubrey Boomer and Fred Robson, who had tied Jones's 291 winning score from 1926.

The British squad arrived in New York City for the Ryder Cup Match that was to take place June 3–4, 1927. There was a sense among the players and their supporters that there was more to be gained than just competing in this particular contest. The British wanted to not only apply another drubbing to the Americans like the one in 1926, but less than two weeks later participate in and do well in the U.S. Open at Oakmont in Pennsylvania. After the reverses in majors during the last fifteen years, several of them at Hagen's hands, this was an opportunity for the Colonies to be subjugated once again.

Samuel Ryder, a year away from turning 70, was accompanied by Aubrey Boomer, Archie Compston, George Duncan, George Gadd, Arthur Havers, Herbert Jolly, Ted Ray (the captain), Fred Robson, and Charles Whitcombe. Ironically, Mitchell, the original captain, was there in gold only—he could not participate in the first Ryder Cup Match because of appendicitis. Just as well he stayed home: Crossing the Atlantic on occasionally storm-tossed seas took six days, and the Brits were a bit woozy when they arrived. To their credit, the U.S. team offered to delay the Match, and Havers commented that the visitors were "submerged with hospitality and kindness," but the British team members declared themselves ready to go.

Perhaps they were too assertive because Hagen, ever the bon vivant and gracious host, thought it best to take the guests out on the town to celebrate the first official Ryder Cup. According to G. A. Philpot, the manager of the 1927 British team, after disembarking on the Manhattan docks and being greeted by "a great crowd that had assembled to give us welcome," including PGA officials, the team was taken by cars up to the Westchester–Biltmore Country Club for a cocktail party, dinner, vaudeville performance, and an impromptu competition. (Surprisingly, the $100 prize for best score was won by the bleary-eyed Brit Aubrey Boomer.)

The next day it was more fun and games. Members of the British team were brought to watch their first baseball game. What an introduction it was. They went to Yankee Stadium where the home team was playing the Washington Senators. "'Babe' Ruth, of course, was the chief 'star' of the New York team, and he was cheered wildly by the crowd whenever he came out to bat," Philpot reported.

Although Ruth was in the midst of his record-breaking homer season, the Yanks lost 3–2. Perhaps this boded well for another team trying to defeat the Yanks. After the game the visitors were introduced to the Bambino by Hagen, his occasional golfing and carousing partner. When the weary British players refused their offer to go out on the town, Hagen reluctantly parted with Ruth and escorted his guests to their hotel.

Captain Hagen, with complete freedom to choose, had assembled a strong American squad: Leo Diegel, Al Espinosa, Johnny Farrell, Johnny Golden, Bill Mehlhorn, Joe Turnesa, Al Watrous, and Gene Sarazen. The Squire, only twenty-five, had been in a bit of a slump since beating Hagen in the '23 PGA Championship, but the captain believed that his friend and rival was still one of the best.

The competitors took a train to Worcester. Then on June 3, despite their long journey and the entertainment provided (and attempted) by their hosts, the British took to the course for the first official Match.

Both captains participated in the first of four 36-hole foursomes, Hagen pairing with Golden and Ray with Robson. The contest was close throughout, but not necessarily because of sterling golf: Hagen's and Golden's iron shots occasionally found previously unvisited parts of the Worcester course, and the Brits' putting was a picture of frustration. Finally, Hagen's birdie putt on the 34th hole and a halve on 35 allowed for a 2-and-1 win.

(Ryder Cup scoring is based on match play. An individual player in a singles match and a duo in a best-ball or alternate-shot match seek to win each hole, or at least a halve for a tie. A match is over when the opponents finish tied or one has a lead of more holes won than there are left to play. For example, if Hagen goes up 2 and 1—two holes up with only one to play—he has won the match. With total scoring, a team needs to have earned, via matches won and halved, a majority of the points [matches] available. Today, there are 28 total points available, but in the first Ryder Cup only 12 matches were played.)

In the second match, the 3 and 2 final score would imply an easier win for Gene Sarazen and Al Watrous. The reality is the Americans didn't play very well, finishing 9 over par, but Arthur Havers and Herbert Jolly played worse. The third match looked very promising for the visitors, with veteran stalwarts George Duncan and Archie Compston going after the less-tested Johnny Farrell and Joe Turnesa. Apparently, no one told the Yanks they were supposed to be intimidated, as they cruised to an 8-and-6 triumph.

It appeared that the British team had come all this way to cement defeat on just the first day. Thankfully, Aubrey Boomer and Charles Whitcombe refused to act out the script Hagen seemed to have written. Their impressive 7-and-5 victory over Leo Diegel and Bill Mehlhorn gave Ted Ray some hope at the end of the day.

In a column written for the *Worcester Daily Telegram,* Ray blamed the first-day setbacks on superior American putting, then reported, "The loss of the points in yesterday's foursomes has not killed the spirit of our team. We shall do better today. We must win six of the eight matches today to retain possession of the Ryder Cup . . . It is a very big task, but if fortune falls our way I am confident our men are good enough to bring off the match."

Only in his dreams, it turned out. The 36-hole singles matches held few rays of sunlight. Other than Duncan beating Turnesa and Charles Whitcombe halving with Sarazen, the visitors didn't score a point. Hagen won his match over Arthur Havers, the man who had won over Sir Walter in the '23 British Open, 2 and 1, and that was one of the closer U.S. victories.

"Then came the singles, and the British rout was complete," reported *Golf Illustrated* in its June 10, 1927, issue. "Charles Whitcombe managed to hold his own against Sarazen, but try as he would he could not finish on top. The American, as a matter of fact, was five holes in arrears at one point in the game, but one by one he pulled the holes back and ultimately finished level. And there the British success ended." As Hagen himself had experienced, when the chips were down Sarazen was almost impossible to beat.

The 9½-to-2½ victory for the "locals" sent the visitors packing. Ryder had paid for the cup, but he sailed home across the Atlantic empty-handed.

"The 'Ryder' Cup has gone the way all good cups in golf seem to go—it has gone to America for a year," lamented *Golf Illustrated*. The American victory shared the front pages of newspapers published on June 5, 1927, with photographs of Charles Lindbergh, who had just left France for the return trip (by boat) after his record-breaking flight across the Atlantic.

Despite their loss, or perhaps because of it, the British were keen on doing it again and Ryder was more enthusiastic than ever. (No doubt he wanted the gold cup, which stood seventeen inches tall and weighed four pounds, back in England.) However, it would be too much of an intrusion on the players' careers and too expensive to be crossing the Atlantic every year. The British PGA and the PGA of America agreed to continue the competition but to hold the Ryder Cup Matches every other year and to alternate between Great Britain and America.

Fresh from the international triumph, Hagen and his teammates turned their attention to the U.S. Open. It was time to dethrone Bobby Jones.

CHAPTER 13

NO PROFESSIONAL DOMINATED GOLF like Hagen did during the last six years of the Roaring Twenties when, in addition to his numerous wins in "regular" tournaments, he collected six majors. Only the presence of Jones, who competed much less frequently yet had a big impact on the press and public when he did, prevented Hagen from claiming the title of the world's greatest golf champion.

One can argue that with the occupation of professional golfer still in its childhood, dominating the professional ranks could have been done by anyone who got hot. But Hagen was the one who did it, and this remarkable second act to his career was played out from when he was thirty-one to thirty-six, when others of his prewar generation were fading or had retired to head-pro positions, and also as Sir Walter continued to expend plenty of energy in moneymaking exhibition tours and off-the-course activities.

Another perspective is that Hagen's accomplishment may not be fully recognized today because it was spread out over six seasons and took place eighty years ago, before TV, cable, and the Internet made golf events available to millions and now billions. Hagen's feats were covered by the print media, who wrote for a much smaller golf audience. And it is a fact that however good his years were, he didn't have that magical one that galvanized the press like Bobby Jones did in 1930.

Hagen very much wanted to win the National Championship in 1927. Taking the title from Jones would be sweet, and it would end his eight-year U.S. Open drought. But another important consideration was money. Winning majors was what impressed the sports public the most and resulted in lucrative endorsement deals and exhibition tours; it was the best path to golf immortality. Hagen had dedicated himself to traveling that path, and as enjoyable as the PGA Championships and Ryder Cup victory of the last three years were, no major meant more in America than the U.S. Open (though holding title to three Western Opens did help).

Jones hoped to defend at the par-72 Oakmont, which measured over 6,900 yards, a very long course for the time (the 12th hole was 621 yards) that sported swift putting surfaces. The amateur didn't give a good account of himself. His 309 total left him tied for 11th, the only time in eleven Open appearances Jones finished out of the top ten.

Hagen reversed his Open pattern by shooting a poor 77 in the first round and rebounding with a 73 in the second. The leader after 36 holes was Bill Mehlhorn, with Joe Turnesa 2 strokes back. Hagen's 150 left him 7 shots behind, but with a strong final day and the pressure getting to the nonwinners atop the leaderboard, there was a chance.

But the final day was disastrous for the Haig. His 76 in the third round wasn't that bad because the long, tough Oakmont course was producing many scores in the mid- to high 70s. An 81 in the final round meant wait til next year for Hagen. His 307 total left him 6 shots short.

Tommy Armour played the last six holes in two under par to tie Harry "Lighthorse" Cooper at 301. He shot 76 in the next day's playoff, which in most U.S. Opens would not get the job done, but Cooper ballooned to a 79—on 16 he put his tee shot in a bunker and needed 3 shots to get out—and Armour was the winner.

Hagen had mixed feelings after the Open. He was pleased that one of his best friends had taken the championship and that he had bested Jones by 2 shots. Unfortunately, the title had gone to someone who was not a homebred, though Armour was a U.S. citizen and the wounded World War I veteran Silver Scot was a popular player in the States. Hagen had to be bitterly disappointed at how his game had gone down in flames in the final round. His 81 was higher than any other fourth round of the top thirty-five finishers.

According to H. B. Martin, "Walter Hagen was doing big things and keeping his game intact. He had become golf's greatest winner . . .

but he was not having any success in our own national open and it was beginning to get on Walter's nerves. Others were winning."

To add insult to injury, Johnny Farrell earned $1,000 from a clothing manufacturer ($300 more than the first-place check) for being the "best-dressed golfer." He was adorned with a silver-white coat and knickers, a black-and-white sweater, black socks, and white shoes.

Redemption could be had by successfully defending at the Western Open. It was being played at another tough course, the par-71, 6,500-yard Olympia Fields outside Chicago.

Despite a strong field that included Mike Brady, Chick Evans, Johnny Farrell, Al Watrous, Tommy Armour, Leo Diegel, and Gene Sarazen, Hagen dominated from the beginning. He carded 137 for the first 36 holes, and his 69 in the third round had him in the lead by 9 strokes. He half-dozed through the final round, shooting a 75. Only Al Espinosa mounted a challenge, but all his 67 meant was a tie for second with Bill Mehlhorn, 4 strokes behind Hagen. At this point in his career, the Haig was miles ahead of the other professionals.

There are some legends about Hagen that aren't backed by strong enough evidence to be presented as pure truth. But the one about the 1927 PGA Championship semifinal had plenty of witnesses, including one of golf's legends.

It had been a struggle for Hagen to make it to the semifinal match. After the first 18 holes in the first match of the tournament, he was four down to Johnny Farrell. It looked like the chances of a fourth straight championship were evaporating rapidly. The competitors had lunch—actually, Hagen did; Farrell was too nervous to eat—and went out to the next 18. Hagen earned five of the first nine holes and went on to win 3 and 2. Next day, he crushed Tony Manero 11 and 10. In the quarterfinal, he was down to Open champ Tommy Armour for most of the match, then put on one of his patented rushes to win 4 and 3. Hagen arrived at the semifinal match.

The PGA Championship that year was being held at the Cedar Crest Country Club in Dallas, and the event was irresistible to a fifteen-year-old golf lover who lived over an hour from the city. The teen was just one of the thousands in suddenly golf-mad Texas who attended the 1927 major, and he would later refer to what happened as "my first real thrill in golf." It's too much to say that without witnessing and being a sudden participant in what happened, Byron Nelson might have chosen another line of work, but the experience was one of the most memorable events in his life.

"I wanted to follow Walter Hagen, who was paired against Al Espinosa in the semifinals," Nelson recalled. "I stuck real close to him—in those days they didn't have gallery ropes, so I was right beside him the entire match."

It was late afternoon when the players were working on the back nine, and Hagen and Espinosa were facing the western sun. Hagen hadn't worn a hat in competition since the U.S. Open at Brae Burn, and on one hole he was seriously squinting, alternating with a hand over his eyes, to determine where to land his approach shot.

"Would you like to borrow my cap?" Nelson suddenly offered from the gallery.

"Sure, kid, thanks," Hagen replied. He took the high school baseball cap Nelson handed him and put it on.

Hagen sized up his shot one more time, then swung. The ball landed 8 feet from the cup. Entertaining the gallery, he made a ceremonious gesture of handing the cap back to the awestruck Nelson. Even better, Hagen sank the putt to tie Espinosa. He won the match on the extra hole.

Does the cap reside in the Golf Hall of Fame or at least occupy a treasured place in Byron Nelson's trophy case? "You'd think that I would have kept that cap all this time," the golf legend lamented. "But I haven't. I've never kept most of the clubs or balls I won tournaments with or anything like that. Just not sentimental that way, I guess."

On the last day of the tournament Hagen was up against Joe Turnesa. By the end of the morning's 18 holes, Sir Walter trailed Turnesa by 6 shots but was down only 2 holes. The match-play format was helping him here because no matter how poorly he played a hole it still counted as just one hole, and on other holes he played well enough to halve or win it.

During the afternoon Hagen toughened up and stopped giving away holes, and the young Turnesa had a couple of miscues that prevented him from pulling away. By late in the day, at the 35th hole,

Turnesa was only 1-up. Still, all he had to do was par the last hole to win.

After two shots, Turnesa's ball was 25 feet from the cup and Hagen's had gone just past the green. With great calm, Hagen knocked his ball on the green and then sank his putt for par. Apparently rattled by the pressure, Turnesa three-putted for bogey and the match was tied. On the 36th hole, Turnesa's putt to extend the match came to rest on the lip of the cup. Hagen won the hole and his fourth straight PGA Championship 1-up.

"Never before in the history of the game of golf has anyone succeeded in doing anything equal to what Hagen has done in this yearly grind at medal and match play," declared the *New York Times* in its November 6, 1927, report on the championship. "He has now won four years running and has set up a record that has not only made history but may never be equaled again. The Hagens in golf come few and far between."

Writing in *PGA Magazine* that November, Kerr Petrie declared, "Hagen still remains the Big Boy. His record of four straight is something to marvel at in these days of keen competitive rivalry when the young fellows bob up from the spinach and think nothing of bumping off the men with the records and reputations."

As if there wasn't enough going on in his life, Hagen decided to become a baseball team owner. Not just any team, but his hometown Rochester Tribe.

During the summer of 1927, he learned that the ballclub was for sale. It was in danger of folding if a willing buyer wasn't found right away. Hagen scraped together $10,000 and gave it to Bob Harlow with the instructions to head to Rochester on the double and at least gain an option on the ballclub. Once the PGA Championship was won, Hagen followed north and east from Dallas.

Upon arriving, Hagen found that his $10,000 had earned him the Tribe. "I found I'd purchased fifty-three players," he remembered, with one of them being the ex–Major Leaguer Rabbit Maranville. "I began to think of myself as a baseball magnate. I needed a new ballpark, so I decided to call on my old friend, George Eastman."

The prodigal son had returned to Rochester—not to play golf but to save professional baseball in the city. The $10,000 invested was just the tip of the iceberg. As the season came to an end—with the Tribe finishing a lowly sixth out of eight teams—there were many expenses. Then there was the money needed to prepare for the following year's season. And every step of the way revenue streamed out for administrative salaries and promotional materials and other expenses.

Eastman and Hagen had breakfast together and discussed joining forces on the Tribe and building a new stadium. Eastman promised to contemplate the venture during a hunting trip in India. Hagen then motored back to New York City, where he attended a conference of Major League and Minor League baseball owners at the Commodore Hotel. He was unanimously elected the sole owner of the Rochester Tribe and was personally welcomed into the baseball fraternity by the first commissioner of Major League Baseball, Judge Kenesaw Mountain Landis.

This was heady stuff for Hagen, who as a teenager had led his own baseball team to three city championships. Reaching back into his past, Hagen persuaded John Ganzel, who had been his manager after a stint as a player in the Major Leagues, to manage the Tribe.

The venture did not start off well. Every week, even though the season had ended, there were a payroll and other expenses to meet. When his investment reached $25,000, Hagen asked the league for more time to raise additional cash. But as the year drew to a close, what the Haig was really contemplating was how to get out of a draining situation.

The International League took care of that. Seeing that the team seemed to be in an irreversible dilemma and that its finances were in disarray, the league asked Hagen to step down as president. He was happy to do so.

"The retirement of Walter Hagen, professional golf champion, from a brief and probably costly venture into organized baseball was disclosed yesterday, simultaneously with an announcement of an extension of time granted to the Rochester club of the International League to straighten out its financial difficulties," the Associated Press reported on January 5, 1928.

Ironically, upon his return from India, Eastman did like the idea of building a fine stadium for the city, but with Hagen out of the picture the seventy-year-old manufacturer lost interest. The club was eventually purchased by the St. Louis Cardinals and renamed the Red Wings. Under new management and ownership, the team won four consecutive International League pennants beginning in 1928. Among those who played for the Red Wings over the years were Stan Musial, Boog Powell, Bob Gibson, Eddie Murray, Jim Palmer, and Cal Ripken Jr.

As a postscript, two years later Hagen sued the ballclub's former owners, contending that they misled him on the precarious financial condition of the Tribe. He did accept some of the blame, however—the lawsuit was for only $8,500 and turned out to be unsuccessful.

No one likes to lose money but Hagen could afford to. During the second half of the 1920s he may well have been the highest-paid sports star on a consistent basis. According to Bill Cunningham, in a profile written for the *Detroit News* in 1927, Hagen "averages over $15,000 a year in prize money, $45,000 a year from his exhibition matches, and his annual salary as the golf expert of the Pasadena Golf and Country Club is just $30,000 a year more."

The total of $90,000 was an annual average for much of the decade, and may well have been an underestimate given that Hagen played more exhibitions than were reported or recorded, the side bets he liked to make on exhibition matches, and the likelihood that some of what he took in never showed up on a balance sheet or even in a travel notebook because it was spent before it touched Harlow's hand. Still, $90,000 per could not be beaten in any other sport with the possible exception of boxing, and there, once Dempsey was dethroned, heavyweight champions came and went with no one keeping the lucrative title very long until Joe Louis grabbed it and held on in the late 1930s.

The article continued: "Babe Ruth, the kingpin of baseball, draws $70,000 a year for six days of hard work a week [albeit seasonal]. Hagen gets over $100,000 a year for playing golf an average of three times a week and practically all his expenses, tobacco, wearing apparel, golf supplies, automobiles and what not besides.

"In return he has refashioned himself into a colorful personage, like a grand opera tenor, or a movie top-liner. He seldom moves without three trunks of clothes. His valet is in constant attendance. He drives only the fastest and flashiest cars. He wears lemon yellow gloves and spats upon occasion. . . . Hagen has elevated a lowly profession to the heights of a lucrative and decorative art. He has crowned it with dignity, and enriched it with elegance. And for all the scenery he is perhaps the world's foremost competitor. He hasn't subsidized cold skill to anything.

"Further power to his slashing blades. May he stick around for many a year."

At this time it was not unusual for Hagen to be mentioned in the same sentence as Babe Ruth, because they were two of the most prominent sports stars of the decade. It's not known if he checked this with Hagen first, but Ruth in his salary negotiations in 1927 used Hagen's income as a barometer.

Ruth wanted more money to begin the 1927 season (and of course he would earn every penny of it with a record-breaking 60 homers). Contending correctly that he was the best player in baseball, Ruth wanted his salary raised to $70,000. Jake Ruppert, co-owner of the New York Yankees, was aghast. That would be twice what the manager, Miller Huggins, made, and three times the next-highest-paid player.

The Babe had a card to play. Look at Jack Dempsey, he pointed out, whose annual income was higher just for one bout and a few friendly exhibitions a year. And then there's Walter Hagen, raking in a six-figure bounty. All he does is bask in the sun and tap a little white ball around and, like him (Ruth emphasized), I draw the biggest crowds. The argument was successful. Ruppert capitulated, offering Ruth a three-year contract at $70,000 per.

There was no golfer more in demand than Hagen for exhibition matches. Bobby Jones, of course, would have been a big box-office draw, but there was little incentive for him to do exhibitions. He now had two children, he was pursuing a law degree, he wasn't fond of crowds, and as an amateur he couldn't accept money. For a course owner or promoter, getting the Haig was the best way to guarantee a big crowd.

Bob Harlow continued as Hagen's publicist and business manager. The publicist part consisted of planting items about Sir Walter in the press and ghostwriting articles. For example, the *American Golfer* published a piece called "Championship Stuff" by Walter Hagen, but actually Hagen saw the article no earlier than the subscribers did.

The business part was coordinating a steady flow of exhibition matches and special appearances that were the foundation of Hagen's income. When he was not overseas or participating in an official tournament in the States, the bookings came fast and furious. Harlow arranged that for an exhibition match in a large city, Hagen could be paid as much as $1,000 (not including side bets he made). There were the occasional hit-and-run gigs for $150, but in general Harlow and Hagen would earn $300 to $500 per event.

This wouldn't be bad at all playing just a couple of exhibitions a week in the 1920s, but Sir Walter thrived on the pace of traveling, playing, and performing. There were months when he notched forty-five exhibitions, working morning and afternoon and earning double for playing on Sundays.

Most of this activity was about money, but not all of it. Traveling here and there offered the opportunity to share courses with old acquaintances. On October 26, 1927, Hagen headed to Massachusetts for a two-day, 36-hole match with Francis Ouimet. After the first day, the two were even. On the second day, the hero of 1913 equaled a course record and defeated the Haig 7 and 5. According to a newspaper account, "About 1,500 spectators saw the match on as fine a day as golfers ever had."

Back in Florida the following February, Hagen and Sarazen hooked up again, this time in a 72-hole marathon. The Haig crushed his friend 8 and 7, with Sarazen waving the white towel on the 11th hole of the final 18. However, the players as well as the crowd were having such a good time joking and laughing under the bright sun that Hagen and Sarazen finished off the full 18 anyway.

Sarazen had his revenge two months later when the Squire won 2 and 1 at the Greenbrier Golf Club (which would become Sam Snead's home course) in White Sulphur Springs, West Virginia. And in one of their oddest contests, Hagen and Sarazen teamed up three weeks later in Massapequa, New York, to, as the *New York Times* put it, "Defeat Girl Rivals." More than six hundred spectators watched the two male pros beat Glenna Collett and Maureen Orcutt, though only by 2 and 1.

There were times when Harlow booked an exhibition at a course he knew nothing about, and some of these venues were little more than cow pastures or scrubland with forlornly flagged holes spaced out across them. Perhaps more than ever, it was at these barren and far-flung places that Hagen truly earned his stripes as a touring professional. Instead of taking one look at the shabby course and getting back into his car, he'd go ahead and entertain the crowd and leave them with a big wave and a smile (and, yes, empty pockets).

Part of the drama of a Hagen appearance was getting the crowd wondering if he would show at all. He was far from the most punctual, either because he and his driver got lost trying to find some venues or he just refused to be hurried and arrived at a place when he wanted to. One time when Hagen showed up late on the first tee the starter said, "Practicing a few shots, Walter?" The Haig replied cavalierly, "No, having a few."

The day came when Hagen found himself at one such "course" somewhere in Iowa. Again he smiled, played a round with some locals, and at the end of the match he told the crowd (with fingers crossed behind his back, no doubt) how much he liked their little course and hoped it would encourage children to take up the game.

The match had been arranged by James Cooney, a member of the club and a freshly minted attorney. He had been astonished at his good luck in getting Hagen to come to their little corner of Iowa. Though he was breaking the law, he offered Hagen a drink at day's end. The two men had a few and got on fine; Cooney was especially grateful that the great golfer had gone ahead and played and entertained as though he was at Inverness or Pinehurst. The two would remain lifelong friends.

As the years went by, Cooney became one of the premier lawyers in the Midwest, was appointed a judge, and eventually became the chief legal and financial officer of the Wilson Sporting Goods Company. When it bought L. A. Young's manufacturing operation, Wilson created the Walter Hagen Division, with Hagen (and later Walter Jr.) as president. Cooney drew up a contract between the company and Hagen that would pay the player, though by then retired, $110,000 annually. Wilson cut a check for this amount every year that Hagen was alive, and after his death sent it to Walter Jr.

Between going back and forth to Great Britain, the tournament schedule, earning the salary to represent the Pasadena Club in Florida, the rigors of exhibition matches here, there, and everywhere that would exhaust anyone else, and the socializing in New York, Chicago, and Los Angeles, how could there possibly be time for his marriage? Edna wondered the same thing. She knew the answer: She had fallen far down the priority list.

Edna had tried to accompany Walter on his trips, but bouncing along dusty back roads was not her cup of tea. She wasn't particularly intrigued by golf at all, though she liked the money it brought in and the celebrity her husband was—depending on where she and Walter were, she could find herself in the company of hackers like Babe Ruth, Al Jolson, Oliver Hardy, Jack Dempsey, or Charlie Chaplin. (Harold Lloyd had built a private nine-hole course behind his home in Beverly Hills, and during one visit Hagen played it twice and shot a 61 to establish, by far, the course record.)

Edna had tried to overlook the fact that her husband was chronically unfaithful. A story circulated that one night Edna was in a hotel room waiting for her husband, who was somewhere out on the town. Finally, he arrived when it was close to dawn. As he removed his clothes, Edna pointed out that he was not wearing underwear, and certainly had been when he dressed the day before.

"My God!" Hagen cried, clapping his hands to his buttocks. "I've been robbed!"

To give him some credit, Hagen was happy to include his wife in the high life of New York and a few other haunts of the rich and famous. His wallet was open to her, he encouraged her to travel with him, and he indulged Edna in a few other ways, sometimes to his detriment.

Edna had somehow convinced him that he was suffering from high blood pressure and that there would have to be a radical change in his diet. He agreed, reluctantly, to eat only lettuce. Soon, he lost weight, appeared drawn, and had little strength. Still, his wife insisted this was good for him and Hagen didn't want to disagree with her.

Back at the Country Club of Rochester with Jim Barnes to play an exhibition match, he was joined by old friend Henry Clune. In one of his memoirs, Clune wrote that he took one look at Hagen and exclaimed that he must be seriously ill. He thought Hagen's story about Edna and the lettuce leaves was ludicrous, and insisted that the Haig see a doctor who was a member of the club. The sensible doctor prescribed rare roast beef and plenty of potatoes.

In a week Hagen was his old self. And he never listened to "good health" advice again.

This marriage wasn't working. The separation from Edna became official in 1927. A parting shot was her telling the press, "Unless a woman is a golf addict herself, she should never marry a confirmed golfer. It can only go on the rocks. Walter lived golf, asleep and awake. Before dinner and after he was practicing strokes in the living room."

She may not have meant this kindly, but the comments do give a good indication of why at this point in his life, with so many distractions, Hagen was able to continue playing golf at a championship level. The game and winning and the money earned were still his top priorities, and then there was everything else.

That everything else included another flirtation with being a film star. Hagen had spent plenty of time in Hollywood during the 1920s, not only hobnobbing with the stars there but being approached to be in movies himself. A few years earlier he had been signed to a picture called *The Man Who Cheated* and had done some filming on it in Northern California before the financing dried up and production closed down.

But in early 1928 the real thing came along, a starring part in a movie called *Green Grass Widows*. This made perfect sense: Hagen was not just the finest and most visible professional golfer in America, but he was a showman who could entertain an audience anytime, anywhere. According to Gene Sarazen, the Haig "could thrill a gallery merely by squinting toward the pin as he lined up his next shot."

The director was Alfred Raboch, the script written by Viola Brothers Shore, and the cast included Gertrude Olmstead, John Harron, Lincoln Stedman, Hedda Hopper (later to be the famous gossip columnist), and Ray Hallor.

The plot: A college student, Del Roberts, whose father has gone bankrupt, enters a golf tournament because if he wins he'll be able to pay off his father's debts and complete his college studies. Hagen, playing himself, is the boy's chief competitor. During the tourney the

Haig befriends Roberts and learns about his predicament. He keeps the contest close until the last hole, then secretly allows Roberts to win, so he not only gets the money but can marry his college sweetheart, Betty Worthing. The couple eventually realize what the great golfer did, and when they have twins boys they name them Haig and Hagen.

"I don't recall too much about the story, but I know I didn't get the girl," Hagen recollected. "I went back to my golf game." When the film was released later that year, it didn't come close to setting box office records.

Other than a third National Championship, for Hagen there wasn't much left to conquer in the U.S. golf arena. He had won nine professional majors, more than anyone in the world, four prestigious Western Opens, and four straight PGA Championships. Aside from having to reveal that he had lost the trophy, making it five in a row wasn't a goal he felt especially dedicated to.

He wanted a third claret jug. Though he had told the press that "the better man won," coming up just short and watching Jones take the 1926 British Open had been very disappointing. And the Ryder Cup experiences in '26 and '27 convinced Hagen that what he had left to prove as a professional was on an international stage. Another consideration had to be that Jones had successfully defended in '27, winning at St Andrews, thus tying Hagen as the only American with two wins in the world's oldest Open.

He may have also wanted to mend some fences. Other than the ridicule following his poor debut in 1920 and the front-page story in the *Daily Mail,* Hagen had been treated well by the British fans and press. However, before leaving England in '26, Hagen had offered that the reason why British golfers were not winning their own National Championship is because they were "lazy," lacking a sufficient competitive edge, more interested in being good sports than winners.

The British press chastised Hagen for his comments, but not with much vigor because they knew that Sir Walter had a point: Great Britain was not keeping up with the States in competitive play or depth of talent. America was producing more players who, at the highest level, had an opportunity to play strong golf in the expanding professional tour, while British golfers had to make do with the less intense competitions of exhibition matches, contests between the private clubs they worked for, and a handful of European tournaments. Hagen had been asked the question and he had responded candidly.

When the *Aquitania* docked on July 2, 1926, in New York, the focus was supposed to be on Jones, but many of the reporters pushed past the Open winner to question Hagen about the stir he had caused. "It was absolutely without intent to be critical," he said about his comments, and that seemed to settle the matter, at least on this side of the Atlantic. Finally, it was Jones's turn to have the spotlight to himself. With Hagen and Al Watrous marching right behind him, Jones was treated to a ticker-tape parade along Broadway to City Hall.

By the spring of 1928, Hagen was ready for the English fans and press again. He sailed to England with fresh ambition. The Open in 1928 was being held at Royal St. George's in Kent, site of his first British crown six years ago. The upstart Yank returned as a thirty-five-year-old with a lot of mileage but renewed desire.

The fresh conquest of England got off to a very poor, and embarrassing, start. As soon as Hagen arrived, he was to play a challenge match with Archie Compston, one of the more popular British players and who had been runner-up to Barnes in the '25 Open. The pot had been set at 750 pounds, at the time the most ever devoted to an exhibition golf match in England.

Hagen's ship arrived in Southampton on April 26. This left him only one day before the match began, at Moor Park Golf Club, thirty minutes from London, which for Sir Walter was a hundred miles away from port. Harlow hired a Scotland Yard detective to shadow Hagen to make sure the English amenities and sociability didn't lure Hagen away from Moor Park.

There were to be 36 holes on Friday followed by 36 on Saturday. Hagen arrived in time for the match, which turned out to be his only achievement. By the end of the second day, Compston had obliterated the visitor 18 and 17.

"He gave me the worst beating of my career, and I had only one statement to make to the British press: 'When you are laid out good and flat, you must not squawk,'" Hagen recalled about his biggest professional humiliation.

To the reporters in London he said simply, "I was beaten by a man who played better golf. That's all there is to it."

He had a much different statement for a shaken Harlow. On the way back to the hotel the manager was huddled in the back corner of the car, silent, unable to look at Hagen. "What's the matter with you?" the Haig asked. More silence. Then Hagen laughed and said, "You're not worried about that [the thrashing by Compston], are you? Hell, I can beat Compston anytime he wants to play."

The *New York Times* somewhat sheepishly reported, "With a broad smile on his face and a handshake for the victor, Walter Hagen admitted defeat today in his 72-hole match at Moor Park against Archie Compston by 18 up and 17 to play. Hagen had never been beaten before by such a wide margin, but he didn't seem to worry any . . . It may be that the 6,000-mile trip from Los Angeles overtaxed him, for he was playing like a tired man, although with his bronzed face he looked the picture of health."

The British newspapers, with the 1926 comments in mind, had a field day with Compston's triumph. Among the headlines the following day were "Conquering Compston!" "The Rout of Walter Hagen!" "American Gets His Own Medicine!" and "The Eclipse of Hagen!" The *London Daily Mail* published a cartoon showing the detective hired by Harlow following Hagen around the course, holding signs that broadcast the widening lead Compston had, and Hagen's face and posture further sagging. Certainly gripping another claret jug looked like a fantasy.

Hagen ruefully remarked, "Someone told me that the great castle at Moor Park, used as a clubhouse, had once been a favorite rendezvous of Henry VIII and Anne Boleyn. If so, their memories of it must have been far pleasanter than mine."

As his defiant statement to Harlow implies, being crushed by Compston might have been the best thing that could happen because it sure got Hagen's competitive juices flowing.

"That defeat by Compston had been a terrific blow to my pride," Sir Walter would recall. "I'd had the smile wiped off my face . . . and I had only one week to get some badly needed practice. I really went to work."

He checked into a hotel just outside Sandwich, on the Dover coast. He played "endless rounds of golf, existed on a rigid diet, spent numerous sessions in a Turkish bath . . . I locked my little black book in my trunk and even refused the tempting telephone calls," including one from his new friend Douglas Fairbanks Jr., who had a pretty young lady eager to meet the famous Yank. Hagen was a man on a mission.

While he was content to play a round of golf by himself on the windswept coast, Hagen was also open to locals with course knowledge who wanted to play along and might impart a few tips. During one such round, Hagen was studying the line of a putt when a stray dog suddenly appeared, grabbed Hagen's ball in his mouth, and trotted away. The spot was marked, the dog pursued by Hagen and his guest, and the ball was eventually retrieved and replaced.

Hagen holed the putt. His relieved guest said, "I was afraid you'd be upset by that dashed cur making off with your ball." Hagen responded, "Why should I be upset? It was still the same putt, wasn't it?"

The focus, dedication, and discipline didn't seem to pay off in the first round of the British Open. Hagen shot a 75 and was tied for third with, of all people, Compston, both 4 strokes back. Bill Mehlhorn was in first, with Gene Sarazen a shot behind.

The second round was encouraging. Mehlhorn fell back, and Hagen, with a 73, and Sarazen (despite a 7 on the 14th hole) were tied right behind the Argentine Jose Jurado, with Compston in third. The top of the leaderboard remained tight after the third round, with Hagen's 72 putting him one shot ahead of Sarazen and the somewhat deflated Compston 2 strokes behind. Jurado became a non-factor in the tournament by shooting 76 and 80 on the final day.

The last round that afternoon, with high winds buffeting the players, sent scores soaring. With the Prince of Wales, Captain of Royal St. George's, following him, Hagen stumbled, arriving at the 7th hole 2 over par on the round. But the 7th and 8th proved the pivotal holes. It took just 2 strokes to finish the par-3, then he birdied the par-5 hole. He parred the 9th and was ready for the back nine.

He couldn't be broken. On the 13th hole his second shot landed in very thick rough, but his next shot put the ball a foot from the flag-stick. On the 15th hole his second shot went into a bunker, but he dug it out of there and sank an 8-foot par putt. The 17th saw Hagen's best shot of the day, a long second shot to leave the ball 5 feet from the hole. But he missed, for a par, and had to recover on the 18th. His second shot was short but his next one placed the ball close to the cup, and this time there was no missing it.

Hagen had shot a defiant par 72 for a 292 total. He had finished first, but in the late afternoon the wind diminished, giving Compston and the Squire a better chance. Compston didn't take full advantage of it, finishing at 295. It was up to Sarazen. But instead of seizing the moment, Sarazen shot the back nine in 37 and finished 2 strokes behind.

The presentation of the claret jug to Hagen was special for three reasons. One was having won it, doing what he set out to do and grasping it again after four years. The second was continuing his streak of majors won to five consecutive years. And it was especially satisfying to be presented the claret jug by the Prince of Wales (who later became King Edward VIII and resigned the crown for the American Wallis Simpson). By the end of the '28 Open the two had become friends, and that friendship led to the breakdown of the last barriers in Great Britain to golf professionals.

Urged by many of the players and the prince to make a speech, Hagen climbed atop a platform and said, "I'm glad to have shown you that I am not through."

"Hagen's Third Open Victory Marks Seventh Time in Eight Years U.S. Has Taken Crown," went one account. "Prince Presents the Cup. . . . It is a humiliating record for British golf, but today's result was not unexpected; in fact, it was thought that the final honor must go to Hagen or Gene Sarazen."

The British press also reported that "His Royal Highness, dressed in a brown plus four suit, mingled with the crowd as an ordinary spectator and had a cheery word for all who rubbed shoulders with him. He applauded good shots and groaned with the rest of the gallery when a ball was found in the bunkers or went astray otherwise. He chatted with Hagen and Sarazen and the smiles on their faces showed he wasn't depressing them."

Far from being depressed, Hagen was quite taken with the prince, who in turn looked up to the Yank as the best golf had to offer. The ten-cent caddie from Rochester was now a three-time British Open champion and being invited to social occasions by his new friend, the heir to the British throne.

Despite coming from economic and social backgrounds that couldn't be more different, it's easy to see why by 1928 Edward and Hagen appealed to each other. The prince was passionate about golf, liked a drink and a smoke and a good story, enjoyed the company of women, basked in the outdoors, liked to travel, and was a sharp dresser. That Hagen was a flamboyant and successful golfer added much to Edward's regard. For Sir Walter, of course, being befriended by a man who was a heartbeat away from the British throne had to seem like his lifelong, lofty aspirations had been validated.

As usual, there are differing accounts of how Hagen and the Prince of Wales combined to break down the barrier to professionals in Great Britain. What is clear is that the Haig's friendship with the prince, which was to last for forty years, was a significant factor.

During the British Open in 1926, Hagen, Jones, and Sarazen had entered the clubhouse looking to have lunch. They weren't served, although Jones as an amateur could have stayed within and eaten. He wouldn't do so without his friends, and Hagen, unwilling to have a confrontation, got up and left with the other two accompanying him.

It was a different story after the '28 Open. Hagen decided to remain in Great Britain a little longer at the request of the Prince of Wales, who hoped the champion would help him with his golf game and share in off-course good times. After playing a round at the Royal St. George's Club, the Prince and Hagen entered the clubhouse for lunch.

After a few minutes without service, the prince sent for the club's secretary, who explained that a golf professional was not allowed into a British clubhouse, let alone to dine there. Hagen offered to leave so as not to cause his friend embarrassment.

"You stay right where you are," the future king said. He turned to the club secretary and told him, "You must stop this, here and elsewhere. If this man is not welcome here, I shall see that the name 'Royal' is removed from your club."

They enjoyed a fine lunch. Soon afterward, Hagen and the prince enjoyed another one at St Andrews. From that point on, professional golfers were not barred from British clubhouses. Word got around the nation fast, and back to America. A cartoon in the *New York World-Telegram and Sun* showed Hagen dressed as a knight holding a long sword, and hanging on its tip was an empty garment labeled the "Cloak of Snobbery." Sir Walter had slayed the dragon of golf professionals being treated like servants.

The British press was generous in its praise of Hagen's triumph, but not happy about the winner not being British. "Except for Bobby Jones, Hagen must be reckoned the world's greatest tournament golfer, especially in view of his comeback after the Compston defeat," said the *Daily Express*. "But this paper echoes British opinion again in asking 'What's the matter with British golf?' wondering why British golfers fail automatically at every supreme test of their skill."

Before heading home, and to further make up for his relatively monastic life to prepare for the British Open, Hagen headed for Germany. "Berlin Welcomes Hagen" announced a May 17 headline. He was to play a match there with Percy Alliss, then another one a few days later in Vienna.

Once again, as Hagen entered the Port of New York, this time on the *Mauretania,* clutching the claret jug, there was a rousing welcome for the returning conquering hero. A four-column photo in the *New York Times* of June 9, 1928, shows Hagen linking arms with Johnny Farrell, Gene Sarazen, and Mayor Jimmy Walker outside City Hall. There was music by the Street Cleaners Band and a police escort from the dock. "Welcome Walter Hagen" signs were carried by dozens in the crowd.

Hagen had an opportunity to duplicate Bobby Jones's feat: win the British Open and U.S. Open back to back. The 1928 edition of the Open was at a familiar site, Olympia Fields. It turned out to be one of the tightest contests in Open history.

After the first round the leaders were unheralded Henry Ciuci and Frank Ball. Bobby Jones, with a 73, was 3 strokes back, and Hagen was 2 strokes behind him. He made a move in the second round, carding a 72, which left him tied for third. The leader was Jones, who shot a 71.

In the third round, both shot 73, and the lead remained the same. Then the dramatics began. Johnny Farrell began the last eighteen 5 strokes behind Jones, then he went out and shot a 72. But Jones, playing with Gene Sarazen, fell into a funk and finished with a 77 and in a tie at 294 with Farrell. Hagen's last round was better than the year before, 81, but a 76 wasn't enough—he finished 2 strokes back.

For the first time, the USGA ordered a 36-hole play-off the following day. Farrell jumped out to a 3-stroke lead after the morning's 18. But Jones charged back and they were tied by the 15th hole. On 16, Jones missed a 3-foot putt and Farrell was up 1. On 17, Jones sank a 20-foot putt but Farrell made his too. On the last hole, Jones nearly chipped in for eagle and settled for birdie. Farrell notched a birdie too for a 143 total and the championship by 1 stroke.

Coming up short was another National Championship disappointment for Hagen, but at least he had the PGA Championship on the horizon. The event that year was played in Baltimore and Hagen, who had been on another exhibition tour, arrived in town just barely in time. Still, he won his first two matches to reach the quarterfinals.

Let's put in perspective the magnitude of Hagen's PGA achievement. By this point he had won twenty-two *36-hole* matches in a row. Every match since the first one in 1924 had been sudden death— meaning a loss in any one match and Hagen was out—and some of the matches went into real sudden death, with a loss on one hole resulting in instant defeat.

If the PGA Championship had been stroke play, as it is now, each year Hagen could have had a poor round, say shot a 79, yet compensate for it in the other three rounds and still win the championship. But in match play, a single poor round at any time in the tournament means you're out. True, Bobby Jones could not participate, but the best American professionals were in the PGA Championship, and Walter Hagen had beaten them twenty-two times in a row from 1924 to 1928. A comparable achievement occurred during the 1990s when Tiger Woods won three consecutive U.S. Junior Amateur Championships and three straight U.S. Amateur Championships, which are match-play tournaments.

In the 1928 quarterfinal Hagen faced Diegel, and his good friend, who had won the Canadian Open that year, was desperate to break through at a major. He had already defeated Tony Manero and Hagen's old friend George Christ. Diegel rose to the occasion and defeated Hagen 2 and 1. Diegel went on to win the PGA Championship by downing Gene Sarazen.

Hagen would never again be PGA champion, but his record of five victories in this major has been tied only by Jack Nicklaus. Writing in the *American Golfer* after the 1927 PGA, W. D. Richardson called the four-in-a-row achievement "the greatest record in golf," although a good argument could have been made at the time for Harry Vardon's six British Open wins.

"Having watched Walter Hagen snap his fingers in the face of fate and make new golf history by winning the P.G.A. title for the fourth successive time, one cannot help but feel that absolutely nothing remains to be seen," Richardson gushed, pointing out that if it hadn't been for Gene Sarazen's thrilling win over Hagen in 1923, Sir Walter would be celebrating his fifth straight PGA and sixth in seven years.

"When you stop to think that here's a man who has matched his wits and skill against the wits and skill of the best golfers America can muster and won twenty [in his PGA victories] consecutive matches . . . the deeds of other golfers, present and past, seem small and insignificant."

It was more of the same for Hagen the rest of the year and the beginning of 1929: barnstorming exhibitions, visiting the Hollywood elite (while there in December he hosted a goat barbecue after shooting seven of them on Catalina Island), then Florida. He didn't like to fly, preferring to tour from place to place in his very comfortable car, but one time he tried it and lived to regret it.

On September 9, 1928, Hagen was expected at an event at Brae Burn, where he'd won the 1919 Open. The problem was, he was in Philadelphia. An acquaintance there, George R. Hutchinson, owned a Challenger biplane and offered that his pilot could have Hagen and Bob Harlow in Boston in an hour. They took off from William Penn Field.

The plane didn't make it. Because of a mechanical problem, it had to make an emergency landing, and the pilot chose a roadway outside Providence, Rhode Island. There were no injuries, but there was a considerable traffic jam. A shaky Hagen and Harlow accepted a lift from a couple heading home to Wellesley, Massachusetts, and from there they took a train to Boston.

When spring arrived and Hagen was making his way north, he was undecided about defending his British Open title. He did have to go across the Pond anyway with a Ryder Cup squad. However, the possibility of winning four British Opens was more than any American should expect, and at thirty-six perhaps he was supposed to think that he'd had his fill. In addition, he had never won an Open in Scotland, and the '29 event was to be held at Muirfield. The best course of action could be to do the Ryder Cup, enjoy the company of Prince Edward for a while, then cross over to Europe for some more good times and some quick cash from exhibitions.

But there were several other considerations. Bobby Jones at only twenty-seven had won two Opens and easily had time to win a third and tie the Haig's total. Hagen had yet to successfully defend a British Open, as Jones had done in Scotland in '27. And after winning the British Open, the rest of 1928 had been somewhat disappointing for Hagen—for the first time since he emerged by winning the 1914 U.S. Open, he had failed to win an official tournament in North America. He prepared to sail with the other members of the Ryder Cup team he had, again as captain, chosen.

The first Ryder Cup controversy interrupted the preparations. During a dinner in Los Angeles featuring members of the U.S. Ryder Cup team, Hagen suggested that the competition allow for foreign-born players who become American citizens to be on the team. The rule that remains in effect to the present day, despite efforts after Hagen to change it, is that only native-born players could be on their respective teams. No doubt Hagen was hoping to include friends like Jim Barnes, Tommy Armour, and Joe Kirkwood who had become U.S. citizens.

When the remarks were reported in Great Britain, golf officials there weren't happy at all. First of all, it was the *Ryder* Cup, not the *Hagen* Cup, so it was not up to the American captain to be trying to change the rules.

Second—and this made a lot of sense—was the concern that the rule change would produce much stronger American teams, given that many more good pros had gone from Great Britain to the States than the other way around. Conceivably, an American squad could consist of Hagen, Barnes, Armour, Kirkwood, Jock Hutchison, Harry "Lighthorse" Cooper, Willie MacFarlane, and Macdonald Smith along with Sarazen. No matter how plucky, the British teams would not overcome such talent and experience.

The PGAs on both sides of the Atlantic responded to the controversy by declaring they were not changing the rules. Actually, the Brits developed an especially rigid interpretation of the native-born rule, and in '35 one of Great Britain's best players, Henry Cotton, winner of the previous year's British Open, was not allowed on the team because during that time he was head pro at a club in Belgium.

The Americans set off across the Atlantic on the *Mauretania* in April. On board with Hagen were Leo Diegel, Ed Dudley, Al Espinosa, Johnny Farrell, Johnny Golden, Gene Sarazen, Horton Smith, Joe Turnesa, and Al Watrous. One evening during the voyage, after everyone else had retired and Hagen was in the dining room, he noticed that all the empty tables had beautiful flowers as centerpieces. He had the stewards deliver a bouquet to each team member with a note, "Compliments of Mr. Hagen and Mr. Sarazen." The flowers looked oddly familiar to the players, and Sarazen was startled when the next morning his teammates kept coming up to him offering jolly thanks.

The 1929 Match was to be played at the Moortown Golf Club in Leeds, in the northwest section of England. The seemingly ageless Ted Ray, at fifty-one, had finally faded as a player and was not on the British team. He was replaced as captain by George Duncan, and joining him on the links were Percy Alliss, Aubrey Boomer, Stewart Burns, Archie Compston, Henry Cotton (only twenty-two then, he would go on to win three British Opens in total, the last in 1948), Abe Mitchell, Fred Robson, and brothers Charles and Ernest Whitcombe.

Enthusiasm in England was high. Daily newspapers and the weekly *Golf Illustrated* wrote about the Match months in advance. "This was the real thing and there was a mighty crowd to see it," remarked Bernard Darwin.

Bob Harlow had accompanied Hagen and the American team, and the captain asked him to arrange an exhibition match in Scotland so that Hagen could get in some practice and make some money while he was at it. Harlow obliged by arranging a match with Sam McKinlay, a Scottish newspaperman who agreed to play a shilling a hole.

The Haig had to be licking his chops. A newspaperman? Hagen won the first two holes. This was too easy. Then McKinlay battled back—it turned out that he had played on five international teams for Scotland and knew this course like the back of his hand.

As the two men stood on the 18th tee, Hagen was one down. By this point the money had long ceased to matter, he just wanted to show who was the better golfer. Hagen decided to hit the strongest drive he could, possibly even reach the green and be set up for an eagle. So he took a mighty swat. The ball faded far right, and not only went out of bounds but was last seen bouncing down the road toward the next town over.

The two shillings Hagen paid McKinlay had to loom larger in his mind than any $100 dinner check.

On the first day of the '29 Ryder Cup, April 26, ten thousand spectators showed up despite the cold and raw weather—or maybe because of it, since such dreary conditions favored the home team (it had even snowed lightly a couple of days earlier)—to watch the 36-hole foursome matches. As Darwin observed, "It was horribly, piercingly cold and the American players put on more and more jerseys and woolly waistcoats and yet looked and doubtless were frozen. I remember thinking that Joe Turnesa, a slightly built player with a most beautiful swing, had the air of a poor little shivering Italian greyhound." Seems like as good a time as any for British golf to reassert itself.

Hagen's strong track record on British courses and in competitions continued. Paired with Johnny Golden as they had paired in '27 at Worcester, the duo defeated Ernest Whitcombe and Henry Cotton 2-up in their foursome match. Leo Diegel and Al Espinosa crushed Aubrey Boomer and George Duncan 7 and 5. Already, the day was approaching disaster for the home squad. However, Abe Mitchell, finally getting his chance, and Fred Robson brought the Brits back from the brink with a 2-and-1 win over Ed Dudley and Gene Sarazen.

The Farrell and Turnesa versus Whitcombe and Compston contest appeared to be particularly pivotal. According to E. M. Cockell, covering the match for *Golf Illustrated*, "It was cold and raw, and in the afternoon it rained steadily. Charles Whitcombe and Archie Compston had a ding-dong fight with Johnny Farrell and Joe Turnesa." A loss would put the British in a deep hole with the Americans enjoying a 3–1 advantage.

The foursome played neck-and-neck golf through 35 holes. On the last hole, with the British duo 1-up, Turnesa "'hoicked' the ball round between mid-on and square-leg, and after it had hit the out-of-bounds fence it came to rest behind a marquee," leaving his partner an impossible situation, according to Cockell.

"Farrell then played *the* spectacular shot of the whole contest," Cockell continued. "He had just enough room to swing, and taking a niblick he got it over the marquee to within about three yards of the pin, and enabled his side to win the hole and save the match."

Even with the steady rain during the afternoon action, the United States still prevailed. With the Americans being strong in singles and the home team already down 2½ to 1½, the outlook for the second day was a gloomy one, even gloomier when the weather turned drier and a bit warmer.

Yet again ten thousand people turned out for the 36-hole individual contests. Hagen was feeling especially confident, not only because of the score, the weather, and the fact that it was singles to be played, but also because he had Al Watrous and Horton Smith rested and ready to go. The latter, though only twenty-one, was already being called one of the top five U.S. pros in 1929.

But Charles Whitcombe bolted out of the gate and immediately dashed Hagen's hope of a runaway victory. The British veteran destroyed Farrell 8 and 6. Compston easily handled Sarazen 6 and 4. Boomer took care of Turnesa 4 and 3. Cotton downed the perhaps too-rested Watrous by the same score. Espinosa did what he could to stop the bleeding, halving with Ernest Whitcombe. Smith came through, defeating Robson. Diegel celebrated his birthday in grand style by dusting Mitchell 9 and 8.

Diegel's lopsided win combined with his eccentric ways allowed him to become a bit of a cult figure in Leeds. According to Darwin, "The most alarming player on the American side . . . was Leo Diegel. This was the first sight that most British spectators had had of him and he was in one of his inspired moods. Within a week hundreds of British golfers were assiduously conjugating the verb 'to diegel' and trying to attain what they believed to be his pose. His chin nearly touched the top of his putter shaft, his elbows were stuck out at the extreme angle physically possible, his wrists were stiff as pokers, and, apparently with his shoulders, he pushed the ball unerringly into the hole."

Hagen's match was the most startling of all. He had deliberately put himself up against the opposing captain, and in doing so had picked the wrong man at the wrong time.

The final-day singles pairings are arranged by chance. Each captain lists his players (one through eight at the time) and then they trade lists. The players listed first face off against each other, second for the two listed second, and so on. Duncan, however, wanted to spice things up a bit and suggested to Hagen that they list themselves at the same number so the two captains could have at it. The Haig agreed.

Back at the hotel that evening Hagen called a meeting of the American players. Grinning and rubbing his hands together, he told them of the arrangement and declared, "Well, boys, there's a point for our side." Then the next day, just before the match began, Hagen said to Cockell, "This guy has never beaten me in a serious match and he never will." Clearly, the man was not worried about the former British Open champion.

Playing superb golf, Duncan built a big lead and never looked back. His 10-and-8 demolition of the U.S. captain would be Hagen's only loss in five official Ryder Cups as a player—and true to form, if Sir Walter was going to do something, good or bad, he was going to do it big. His stunning loss had the ten thousand British fans cheering and the usually dour Duncan declaring that his win made for "the happiest day of my life."

The cup named after Samuel Ryder with its tiny replica of Mitchell was back where the British believed it belonged. The 7–5 victory was touted in huge headlines the next day. It was an especially sweet moment for Ryder when late Saturday afternoon he picked the cup up off a table draped with an American flag and handed it to George Duncan.

For Hagen, the losses as player and captain could well have been as painful as the duel with Sarazen for the PGA Championship six years earlier and his failures in the U.S. Open. Graciously, though, he thanked the British crowd and team for their courtesy and hospitality. Then it was time to think about at least taking home another claret jug.

"We won the match, and this was a much more serious match with the invaders out to do their best, though still, as I cannot help fancying, with a main eye on the more definite and glittering prize of the Championship," observed Darwin.

Perhaps it would have happened anyway, but one consequence of the British victory in 1929 was the effort to ensure that the Ryder Cup would continue indefinitely as a biannual golf event. The closeness of the final score implied that the competition between the teams could be keen, and especially for the British, the outcome indicated that despite how well the Americans had done in the British Open during the decade, there was not a big gap between the two countries. Players as well as fans wanted the event to continue.

Samuel Ryder thought of a way to help that happen. A good and careful businessman, Ryder arranged for the drawing up of a deed of trust, which set up the format and rules of play of the Matches. Thomas Anderson Davis, Ryder's nephew and a solicitor, drew up the document. It was agreed to by the Ryder family and the respective PGAs, and was signed on December 8, 1929. The Ryder Cup Matches were official, thanks to a gentlemanly seed merchant and a local boy from Rochester.

Hagen could not leave Great Britain without gaining revenge and restoring his prestige. He was just going to have to win the British Open one more time, and preferably do it in convincing fashion. As soon as the concluding ceremonies of the Ryder Cup ended in May Hagen headed north, to Scotland. His long career and desire to win had brought him to the ultimate challenge—trying to win in the home of golf.

Friendship with the Prince of Wales wouldn't help him on the links at Muirfield, nor would the curiosity and support of different factions of the Scottish crowd. Sir Walter was on his own, somewhat a stranger in a strange land, goaded by pride into trying to take the country's most coveted golf prize.

He proved to be up to the challenge. "This was a championship that showed Hagen at his best," according to Herbert Warren Wind. "His opening salute was a 75 that might have been an 82 in the hands of a less dauntless golfer. He had to play through a punishing rainstorm the early starters escaped. Again he showed his unapproached courage for staying with a bad round, fighting it out by will power alone until he had made it, from the standpoint of figures, a fairly decent round."

The next day, Sir Walter went out and broke the Muirfield course record—68, set by J. H. Taylor in 1904—by shooting a 67 (which included hitting the flapping flag on the home hole), putting him in second place, 2 strokes behind Diegel and 3 strokes ahead of Johnny Farrell.

"Hagen knows that if he is in a tournament, and the title is worth winning, he is going to time a bomb to explode just where it is likely to create the most havoc," reported George Girard in *Golf Illustrated*.

The British placed their hopes on Percy Alliss, who shot a wonderful 69 in the first round. But his 76 in the second was a setback, and a 155 total on the final day put him a distant fourth.

On the final day it was reported that "a furious storm blew over Muirfield. It sent Diegel and Sarazen reeling into the 80s, and none of the top five finishers broke 75."

The weather had done its part, now it was time for Sir Walter to do his. He had what could be considered the grittiest day of his life on a golf course. With the wind howling and in driving rain, Hagen shot a 75 in the morning round. Diegel fell apart with an 82. Farrell managed a 76. Abe Mitchell had a 78, as did Jim Barnes. It was an 81 for Sarazen and a 79 for Tommy Armour.

It was Hagen's Open to win if he could just play sturdy golf. He started the fourth round wearing clothing that seemed to defy the elements—brown knickers, gray socks, black-and-white shoes, a white shirt, black tie, and white, V-neck sweater. The caddie he was allotted was all of sixteen years old.

The others fell further behind, or could not gain ground. Farrell had a 75, Diegel a 77, Mitchell a 78, Sarazen a 76, Armour a 78. Hagen, grinning into the wind, kept grinding, making sensational saves the few times he got into trouble. And he improvised. On the ninth hole his second shot hit a boundary wall and the ball bounced back only a couple of inches. Swinging left-handed with a putter, he put the ball back into the fairway.

His lead widened. "Hagen pursued his way with the utmost confidence that the weather could not beat him," Henry Crouch cabled the *New York Times*. "He just played low shots all the time and did not give the wind much chance to blow the ball into many difficulties."

He was given a loud ovation on the 18th green. He parred, and the British Open was over. Hagen finished with another 75 and a 292 total, a winner by 6 strokes over Farrell and Diegel.

The British golf writer Henry Longhurst observed that Hagen "had switched to a deep-faced driver and hit no drive more than twenty feet off the ground. This was the fellow who nine years before had been blown to fifty-fifth at Deal."

The *Times* of London reported that Hagen "was not only the best golfer in the field, but, in a golfing sense, far the greatest man in the field. . . . He has never before in this country played as well as he has this time" in overcoming, mentally as well as physically, such brutal weather conditions. And with Johnny Farrell and Leo Diegel finishing two-three behind Hagen, the American domination of the decade in Britain was complete.

"When the final scores were all posted, a well-known golfer from Scotland remarked, 'The Americans have us licked. We are not in the same class. Tom Morris would have wept bitterly to see this,'" *Golf Illustrated* lamented.

Bernard Darwin wrote the next day, "His victories this year and last, after heavy defeats at the hands of Duncan and Compston in match play shortly before the Championship, were both of them signal instances of his extraordinary courage. No reverse, no matter how severe, can, it seems, ruffle his equanimity or shake his nerve."

Darwin later wrote about Sir Walter: "He was a strange mixture of two usually contrasted elements, on the one hand the casual and the happy-go-lucky, on the other the shrewd, long-headed, observant and intensely determined. His manner while playing was a reflection of his nature, for he could 'let up' between strokes and converse in a carefree manner with a spectator and then switch off this mood and switch on one of single-minded attention to the next stroke to be played.

"No doubt while he was talking with such apparent *insouciance* his mind was busy looking ahead, but he had an almost unique power of relaxing and never presented that aspect of stern and solemn pugnacity without which the less happily gifted cannot concentrate their minds."

Hagen again made a gracious speech after being handed the claret jug: "I am the proudest man in the world today, and perhaps the luckiest. I've been fortunate enough in winning this championship four times, but I would like to mention that some of the British veterans of the game have won it more times than I have, and I take my cap off to them. I am thinking of Jimmie Braid, Harry Vardon, and J. H. Taylor. There's a triumvirate this country should be proud of."

With Sir Walter holding the jug, the implication was that the Americans had their own great triumvirate to set new standards in international golf—Hagen, Jones, and Sarazen. The British spectators, if they understood this, weren't bothered. The seven thousand fans cheered and shouted, "Good old Walter!"

The three members of the British triumvirate were there, and when they shook the winner's hand they each said, "Well played, Walter."

CHAPTER 14

BY THE COUNT ACCEPTED TODAY, the 1929 British Open triumph was Hagen's eleventh major. With four British Opens to his credit, he was only two shy of the legendary Harry Vardon for whom the Open was his National Championship. Hagen's four Opens would be the record for an American in Great Britain until fifty-four years later when Tom Watson won his fifth in 1983. (The Australian Peter Thomson won five British Opens between 1954 and 1965.) With the PGA Championship and British Open, Hagen had also successfully defended two different professional majors, which had never been done before.

Hagen was in no hurry to make the trip back to the States. The day after winning the British Open, he shot a 139 in the 36-hole qualifying round for the Yorkshire Evening News Tournament, 5 strokes better than the next qualifier. "Owing to a high and bitterly cold wind" at Moortown, the *New York Times* reported, "it is considered that today's performance is even more meritorious than yesterday's."

Then there was spending time with his new friend, Prince Edward. The prince, who had been receiving personal instruction from Ted Ray, invited Hagen to team up with him for a match against Sir Philip Sassoon and Aubrey Boomer. (Boomer and Hagen had been snuck out of their hotel "through a side exit to a waiting automobile that dashed off at top speed and eluded most of its pursuers," according to the English press.) Edward and Walter won 1-up in what was a semiprivate match because there were no photographers and few spectators present for the contest at Swinley Forest Golf Club.

The photographers missed out on a visual treat. Under a warm sun and among blossoming trees, Prince Edward wore brown plus fours and a tan pullover while Hagen "looked like a breath of spring," according to one report, "in silver gray plus fours, dark green stockings with white stripes, and flashy brown-and-white shoes" and "his face was deeply tanned."

Talking to the press afterward, Hagen said about the prince, "Every shot he made he asked me what it was he did and how it could be bettered. I think he is determined to make himself a really first-class golfer." With typical candor he added, "Of course, he is small and light and cannot expect to smack the ball as hard or far as a big fellow like Compston can, but he is tremendously keen and eager—almost too anxious—to master the game."

Buoyed by the British Open win, Hagen made a tour of Europe, playing exhibitions and being feted by golf organizations on the Continent. They were very pleased to be hosting the American who was the most dominant professional in the world, and a very sociable fellow to boot.

Again spreading the golf gospel, Hagen traveled to France, Germany, Hungary, Austria, and even Sweden. Then it was back to England and Moor Park for a rematch with Archie Compston. A weary Hagen lost the first 18-hole contest, but he rebounded to win the second one.

It was finally time to head home. For the fourth time in eight trips west, there were plenty of festivities on the ship (appropriately, the USS *Manhattan*) carrying the claret jug and Hagen back to New York City. At the approach to New York Harbor the fog was so thick that the captain announced that the ship would anchor for the night near the Statue of Liberty. That meant time for one last party.

Hagen hired the ship's orchestra to play all night. In one room were the sons of Quentin Roosevelt and their friends and Walter Jr., and they were supplied with all the hot dogs and soda they wanted. In another room were the adults, Sir Walter presiding. There was a seemingly endless flow of champagne and finger foods. When the boat docked the next morning, Hagen had to borrow some of his son's deck hockey winnings to tip the porters.

The 1929 Open victory coupled with his friendship with the Prince of Wales resulted in another first for Hagen. That summer he received a letter from the Honorable Treasurer of the Moortown Golf Club in Leeds, England, confirming to Sir Walter that he had been awarded an honorary membership in the old and exclusive club. Would he send off an autographed photo of himself that would be prominently displayed in the clubhouse?

He sure would. Finally, an American professional being given such an honor, one more barrier dashed. Coincidentally, Hagen was being inducted along with George Duncan and Abe Mitchell, and this same professional threesome had parted the gates of La Boulie, site of the French Open in 1920.

"Needless to say I complied with the request for the photograph and thanked them for the honor accorded me," Hagen recalled. "From that date on, whenever I was in England I was welcomed to those exclusive clubs. And I took my pro friends, both British and American, right in with me."

After receiving the photograph and Hagen's letter of thanks, the Moortown treasurer, Norman Hurtley, responded: "Whenever you do come to England, we shall look forward to you making use of your membership and coming up to the Club." How things had changed.

Hagen received the letter from Moortown while in the midst of making hay—or as he liked to say, the "healthy green stuff"—from returning to the States with the coveted claret jug. With Horton Smith at his side, Hagen went on another cross-country exhibition tour, making as much as $1,000 an appearance, and somehow in the summer and early fall of 1929 the two managed to play eighty-two matches, according to Hagen's recollection.

During the exhibition tour, Hagen and Smith arrived at the Thorny Lea Golf Club in Brockton, Massachusetts. The instant school let out that day, at 1:15, an eleven-year-old Herbert Warren Wind hurried to the course to see the legend in action.

"It was easy to pick out Hagen as the players walked up the fairway [of the sixth hole] to their balls," Wind recalled in an essay published fifty-eight years later in the *New Yorker.* "His black hair shone in the sun, his face was tanned a mahogany brown, his nose was tilted up a bit, his eyes were fixed on the distant green, and he carried himself like a grandee. . . . His impact on the members of the gallery was much different from Smith's. They regarded Smith as a well-mannered young man with a splendid golf swing. Hagen came across as visiting royalty and a master golfer.

"Hagen was the first great golfer I had ever seen, and both his ability [he shot a 70 that day] and his presence surpassed anything I had expected. Not until Arnold Palmer came along, in the late nineteen-fifties, did another golfer establish a relationship with his galleries that was as strong and dramatic as Hagen's."

The glow of the '29 British Open win and possibly some dawning nostalgia for the aging champion prompted testimonials in print publications. "He's the most generous of mortals," Tommy Armour wrote in an essay about Hagen in the *American Golfer.* "You can have the shirt off his back, if you can unbutton it and slide it off while he's slinking back into an easy chair like a contented and grinning Buddha and sipping a beverage. Take his shirt. He has a trunkful in the next room."

H. B. Martin recalled another incident: "His tact, his generosity, his infallible courtesy and kindliness allow no awkward situations to arise in his presence. Take for instance the young man dining with his best girl in a Midwestern city nightclub who called out as the Haig neared his table, 'Hello, Walter, how are you?'

"Walter paused by the table, shook hands warmly, and asked, 'And have you corrected that slice yet?'

"He told friends later he had not known the young fellow but, 'I've been in a similar spot when I wanted to impress my girl. And you never let a nice young fellow down.'"

Rather than slowing down, Hagen enjoyed strong results in the '29 season. In tournament play, he captured the inaugural Great Lakes Open, Long Beach Open, Miami Four-Ball (paired with Leo Diegel), and the Virginia Beach Open. His wallet was helped too by Smith's win at the Oregon Open in November, because Hagen's deal with his partner was to split all winnings. Though about to turn thirty-seven, and with a lot of wear and tear on him, it didn't seem that the Haig was ready to be put out to pasture.

But a clear indication that he could not keep pace with the younger generation of golfers was his diminishing results in the U.S. Open.

The 1929 event was held in late June at the Winged Foot Golf Club, in New York's Westchester County. The par-72, 6,786-yard course presented a challenge to an older player.

Two unfortunate things happened: Bobby Jones got off to a good start, and Hagen got off to an awful one. Jones had a 69 in the first round, then a mediocre 75 in the second. Hagen, however, was never in contention with scores of 76 and 81. Even though Jones faltered in the fourth round and was caught by Al Espinosa to force a play-off, Hagen's 152 total on the final day didn't draw him anywhere near the top ten. He finished tied for nineteenth with Joe Kirkwood. Jones blew Espinosa away the next day, winning the 36-hole play-off by an eye-popping 23 strokes.

As the season came to a close and Hagen found himself in California, he headed back to Hollywood and took a suite in the Roosevelt Hotel, which in the late '20s billed itself as the "Home of the Stars." It was time to party with friends in the movie business, court starlets, hook back up with his old pal Al Jolson, and get more face time in front of a camera.

He played a few rounds too, but just for fun and small side bets. Among his playing partners in Los Angeles were a Who's Who of Hollywood in 1929–30: Douglas Fairbanks Sr., Richard Arlen, Harold Lloyd, Hoot Gibson, Wallace Beery, Johnny Weissmuller, Humphrey Bogart, Pat O'Brien, Randolph Scott, Fred Astaire, and Bing Crosby.

According to Charles Price, "Between the First World War and the Second, the Haig was the best-known golfer in the world, not excluding Bobby Jones, who seldom socialized with anybody other than his Atlanta cronies and who otherwise preferred the company of straight-arrow businessmen. The Haig hobnobbed with everybody: Babe Ruth, Al Jolson, Grantland Rice, A. D. Lasker, Oliver Hardy, Clarence Budington Kelland, Marshall Field, Jack Dempsey, Harold Lloyd, Ring Lardner, Charlie Chaplin, Warren Harding, Eugene Grace, the Prince of Wales. He didn't so much prefer their company as they did his."

There is a photograph of Hagen in front of the Wilshire Country Club with his foot on the running board of his Cadillac, which looks to be half a block long. With his dashing brown-and-black outfit,

slicked-back black hair, and deep tan, he fit right in as one of the glamorous movie colony that was creating the "dream factory." (According
to Hagen, the car was a Madam X 16-cylinder, the first of its kind
manufactured; he got four miles to the gallon of gas, and because of all
his touring he put 75,000 miles on it.)

The famous comedy producer Mack Sennett, hearing Hagen was
back in town, visited him at the hotel and suggested making a short
golf comedy. Hagen agreed, as long as his friend Leo Diegel could be
in it too, and they would each get $3,600.

The film was made as part comedy, part instructional. Also in the
cast were Marjorie Beebe, Bud Jamison, and the cross-eyed comedian
Andy Clyde. The pro players earned their salaries by having to watch
the slapstick antics of Clyde and then demonstrating the correct way to
attempt various shots. The movie was released in 1930 to some favor-
able reviews but was not a hit (as few films were immediately following the fall of '29).

Hagen held court in the Blossom Room of the hotel in addition to
his suite. "As many as ten or twelve film beauties, either stars or on
their way up, might drop in for tea. Thelma Todd, the curvaceous
blonde, was often a guest. I knew Constance Collier, the Talmadge
sisters—Norma and Constance, Bebe Daniels, Bette Davis."

Hagen was the top player celebrity in the '29 PGA Championship at the Hillcrest Club in Los Angeles in early December (the
first time the event was held on the West Coast). In true Hollywood
fashion, each player was introduced at the first tee by a film star.
Hagen was assigned to the up-and-coming starlet Fay Wray (the love
interest in *King Kong* four years later), who knew nothing about golf,
especially the quite foreign British Open, and was rather nervous
and breathless at the crucial moment. Speaking into the microphone,
Wray told the audience that Hagen was the "Opium Champion of
Great Britain."

Hagen and defending champion Leo Diegel met up in one of the
two semifinal matches. The latter was 2-up after the morning round.
This time, however, Hagen couldn't mount an afternoon charge, and
Diegel gained the final 3 and 2. The next day he easily defeated Johnny
Farrell for the title, 6 and 4, helped by Farrell knocking Diegel's ball in
the cup on two different holes while trying to overcome stymies.

There were two more tourneys to finish out the '29 season, the Catalina Open and the Pasadena Open. Hagen did not come close to the winner's circle in either one, his appearances more ceremonial than competitive.

Of course, during the fall of '29 the stock market crashed, which along with aging heroes sounded the toll for the Golden Age of Sport. Babe Ruth would never equal the success of 1927 and would decline rapidly within a few years. Jack Dempsey was three years removed from being champion. The gridiron beatings were wearing down Red Grange, and he would retire from the Bears after the '32 season. Tilden was retired. Man o'War was off grazing in a field and siring Boys and Girls o'War.

Hagen barely paid attention to the crash. Thanks to Harlow secretly salting away money and continuing endorsement deals, Hagen was pretty much immune to the economic downturn. He had achieved a level of fame that would allow him to keep swimming even as the water level plunged.

He took a close look at the situation, though, in 1930 and decided to do something other than make the expensive trip to Great Britain to defend his Open title (which, alas, meant no matchup with Jones). "I knew that exhibition tours in the United States would be at a low ebb due to the Wall Street market crash the previous October," he noted.

The bad news in America meant that Hagen was more receptive to overtures to go on tour overseas. He received offers of well over $20,000 to play exhibition matches in New Zealand, Australia, and Japan. The latter was especially enticing because the Japanese offered a bonus for every course record broken in that country. He ended up collecting a good piece of extra change: "Breaking Japanese records became somewhat of a habit, but I must admit the course records in that country were not too difficult to break."

Off he went, on February 1, accompanied by Joe Kirkwood, who had become his Sancho Panza. There was a farewell party the night before sailing in Los Angeles that "lasted long enough for our friends to see us off at noon."

The first stop was Hawaii, where the duo played several exhibition matches, then it was on to Pago Pago. Then they hit the Fiji Islands. There Kirkwood had a problem: The heat was intense and insects plentiful, and his preferred drink, milk, couldn't be trusted. Hagen had no problem with the government's flowing supply of scotch and soda.

When they arrived in Australia they had to remain with the rest of the ship in quarantine for almost two weeks because a passenger had contracted smallpox. When they finally disembarked, the situation that greeted them was a bit embarrassing for Kirkwood. He had come home a mature and successful golfer. Better, he'd brought home with him the most famous and successful pro player in the world. But the Australians did not reach into their pockets and rush to the exhibition matches in great numbers, apparently unmoved by the contests being mere exhibitions. The duo broke even, and there was no big demand that they extend their stay.

Then the tour picked up steam. The next stop was Thursday Island, then Manila, and finally in late May headlines in the Kobe newspapers proclaimed, "Hagen and Kirkwood Arrive in Japan! World's Greatest Golf Champions!" Among the highlights for the visitors was playing a private exhibition before Emperor Hirohito on June 8. Before the match that day, Hagen presented the Japanese leader with a set of golf clubs (Walter Hagen ones, of course), and according to press accounts, the emperor was delighted. He reciprocated by presenting Sir Walter with an engraved gold cigarette case.

In all other respects the exhibition tour there was a success, and it is not an exaggeration to say that the enormous enthusiasm in Japan today for golf was given a big boost by Hagen's first appearance there in 1930.

"It was some ten years ago that no sooner was a report about Mr. Walter Hagen's coming to Japan than I was really moved as if I was going to be able to meet a shooting star from the land of a dream," wrote Rokuzo Asami, a pro at the Hodogaya Country Club in Yokohama, in 1940. "Till then, I had seen him in pictures and had heard of him in conversation, but when I actually saw him here playing a real golf game, I was totally fascinated. By the visit of Mr. Hagen, an immortal footprint on the history of golf in Japan was left."

At last it was time to head home. The weary duo arrived in Seattle on June 16, the day that Bobby Jones won the British Open again, this time at Hoylake. There was a new Open champion, but on Hagen's list of priorities, the experiences and the income generated on the tour were at the top.

Rather embarrassing, though, was that with Kirkwood handling the take from the trip and the two separating right after docking—and having spent his own pocket money on board the ship and upon his arrival—Hagen found himself forced to stay hidden in his hotel room for three days because he didn't have enough cash to pay for his laundry. Finally, Kirkwood or Harlow wired some money and, wearing dapper and clean clothes, Sir Walter checked out.

Harlow had not accompanied Hagen on this international journey because the two had decided to end their partnership. From accounts of the time it was a friendly parting. The practical Kirkwood could handle exhibition arrangements, but more important, Harlow's success with Hagen and other promotional efforts to help establish a professional tour had made him a good candidate to become the PGA's tournament bureau manager. May 1930, when he signed aboard, was not the most auspicious time to help the PGA expand its tournaments—and indeed, a big challenge during the decade was to have a pro tour survive at all—but Harlow had handled Hagen and was up to any task.

What is remembered most about the 1930 U.S. Open at Interlachen Country Club in Minneapolis in mid-July is that it was the third leg in Bobby Jones's "grand slam." Jones was playing the best golf of his career and appeared unstoppable.

He was. Jones opened with a 71 and 73, then took command with a 68 in the 3rd round. Macdonald Smith, Horton Smith, and Harry Cooper gave chase, but their efforts were not enough. Even when Jones slowed to a 75 in the last round, his 287 was his lowest score in 11 Opens, and gave him a 2-shot victory over Mac Smith.

The Haig finished a pedestrian seventeenth. (He had, however, created a fashion stir by finally trading in his knickers for white trousers.) His 72–75 on the first two days wasn't too bad, but once more the National Championship slipped away from him when it counted. His 76–80 on the final day put him at a bloated 303, 16 shots behind Jones.

Hagen didn't have to look for promotional opportunities, they still came to him. Later that summer, promoters flocked to Hagen and Jones to pitch another "world championship" match between the two when the official season was over. At twenty-eight, Jones was in his prime, and Hagen was always up to a challenge, especially if a large check was connected to it. Quite likely, a match between the two in 1930 would have turned out a lot tighter than the one four years earlier.

But the return engagement was not to be. By the fall Jones had had his fill of golf. He had won the British and U.S. Amateur Championships and the British and U.S. Opens within a few months. Exhausted by the effort and not necessarily looking for another major event, Jones decided, instead, to retire. "I believe, had we been able to set up such a series, all attendance records would have been broken," Hagen commented.

The second Hagen versus Jones "world championship" match must exist only as fantasy golf, though something like it, taking place in South Carolina in 1931, was portrayed in the book and movie *The Legend of Bagger Vance,* in which both players lost out to a local hero.

Hagen returned to Hollywood for the 1930–31 winter, renting a house this time and employing Hawaiian servants.

However much he traveled and socialized, Hagen was fully committed to continuing the Ryder Cup Matches. As he had in the 1920s, in the '30s he would be in full control of the American squads.

Hagen refused to allow the Depression, which was also having an impact on Europe, to ruin the event. "During my years as captain of the Ryder Cup team I insisted that our fellows be fittingly uniformed," Hagen recalled. "I ordered, and paid for, beautifully tailored marine-blue jackets and pale gray trousers from the Alfred Nelson Company in New York. I obtained permission from the Army to use an official government eagle ensign embossed with crossed golf sticks and the insignia 'Ryder Golf Team' for the pockets. Although I consistently picked my teams for their game and not their beauty, I must admit we stacked up pretty well in the Beau Brummel department too."

Hagen reached into his own pocket again to pay some of the PGA's expenses for staging the event and to bring the British team over for the 1931 contest, held at the Scioto Country Club in Ohio in June. Among the fascinated spectators was the father of Jack Nicklaus.

Jack remembers his father's description: "On the morning of the second day of the match, when the eight singles were played, Hagen put on one of those unforgettable shows of his before teeing off with his opponent, Charles Whitcombe. As he stood on the tee with his coat thrown majestically over his shoulders, a waiter appeared from the clubhouse carrying a tray on which was poised a martini in a shining stem glass. Walter took a sip or two of the martini and nonchalantly swung his driver a couple of times with his free hand, his left.

"He took another sip or two, shifted the martini, and took a couple of swings with his right hand. When his name was announced, he drained the martini with a flourish, and after taking a few practice swings with both hands on the club, hit a beautiful drive right down the middle of the fairway." Hagen defeated Whitcombe 4 and 3 in that match.

Whitcombe, the captain, brought along Percy Alliss, Archie Compston, William Davies, George Duncan, Syd Easterbrook, Arthur Havers, Bert Hodson, Abe Mitchell, Fred Robson, and his brother Ernest. Hagen, in his third time as captain, countered with Billy Burke, Wilfred Cox, Leo Diegel, Al Espinosa, Johnny Farrell, Gene Sarazen, Denny Shute, Horton Smith, and Craig Wood.

The Haig led the way, teaming with Shute for a 10-and-9 destruction of Duncan and Havers the first day and the 4-and-3 dusting of the opposing captain in singles the second day. Sarazen and Burke also dominated, and the final was an easy 9–3 win for the home team, which was no doubt aided by the intense late-June heat in Ohio on the last day.

Aside from this triumph, the 1930 and '31 seasons were disappointing because for the first time since World War I, Hagen went two consecutive years without a win in a major. Especially disappointing was not coming close in the U.S. Open. From 1920 to '30, no one except Bobby Jones had had a better record in the National Championship than Hagen and yet he couldn't win it again.

He hadn't stopped winning other tournaments, though. Hagen captured the Michigan PGA Championship in '30 and rebounded in '31 by winning that tourney again along with the Coral Gables Open and the Canadian Open.

The latter victory was especially satisfying. It had been nineteen years since his first pro venture in this event. He had arrived as an obscure nineteen-year-old making his first trip outside the States. In 1931, especially with his British Open wins and exhibition tours, he was as popular in Canada as in America and Great Britain. And the Canadian Open win enabled Hagen to claim another national championship, his fifth worldwide.

The win didn't come easy, and it showed that Hagen still had stamina. On the 72nd hole, Percy Alliss sank a 30-foot putt to tie Hagen at 292. Canadian officials mandated a 36-hole play-off the next day. The two shot 73s during the morning round. After 4 holes of the second round, Alliss was up by 2 strokes. Consecutive birdies on 8 and 9 drew Hagen even. They stayed even for seven holes, then Hagen birdied 17. When he and Alliss parred the home hole, Hagen had his trophy. To recuperate, he went on a fishing trip as a guest on the yacht of J. C. Penney.

"A confounder of prophets is Walter Hagen, for at the very moment people were counting him out and saying what a grand golfer he was in his time, up he bobs and wins the Canadian Open, the only major title that has eluded him in the seventeen years he has been following the tournament trail," wrote W. D. Richardson in the *New York Times* that July. "With that victory his list is now complete, and he can rest forever on his laurels in the knowledge that he has won more major titles than any other man, living or dead."

It was encouraging too that he had finished as the runner-up in the Western Open. And in the U.S. Open at Inverness in Ohio the first week in July, among the spectators was William Hagen, at seventy seeing his only son play in a tournament for the first time.

In his autobiography, Hagen does no more than imply that he was proud to have his father watch him play golf. We don't know whose idea it was for William to be there and why that particular event was chosen after so many years, given that Ohio is not close to Rochester. It appears that his father's presence did motivate Hagen as he played the first three rounds 74–74–73, his best start in an Open in almost a decade.

But others posted lower scores: Sarazen, Billy Burke, George Von Elm, Leo Diegel, Bill Mehlhorn. When Hagen could manage only a 76—perhaps withering in the Ohio heat, as could be expected—he dropped further back, finishing with a good 297 total. Burke and Von Elm had finished at 292, and Burke won the 36-hole play-off by a single stroke for the championship.

Hagen's experience in the 1931 PGA Championship at the Wannamoisett Country Club in Providence, Rhode Island, was a shocker. He was bounced in the first match by unknown Peter O'Hara.

With the Roaring Twenties over and with the victories more spaced out, the Haig seemingly became a bit more relaxed than before. He had usually been gracious and friendly on the golf course, but the competitive fire always burned bright. Now it began to dim a bit, and Hagen was completely comfortable in his celebrity and his noblesse oblige ability to do kindnesses for others.

James Henderson was a fifteen-year-old in Waterloo, Iowa, in 1930 when Walter Hagen hit town during one of his exhibition tours; this event was at the Sunnyside Country Club. "It costs $1 to get in, a top charge in those days, but you were also given a ball with Walter Hagen on it, a big deal to us," Henderson remembers.

While Hagen was demonstrating different shots, and after admiring the Haig's huge Cadillac, Henderson and his friends tried a few shots of their own. When Henderson hit his Hagen ball, it split open. His friends urged him to show it to Hagen and get a replacement. The boy was pretty nervous but decided to try it.

"Mr. Hagen was demonstrating to the men how to drive the ball," Henderson recalls. "He drank about three fingers of straight bourbon and then hit a bunch of balls straight down the fairway. He was a big man and had on his knickers. When he was done, I had my chance to go up to him. I said, 'Mr. Hagen, look at this ball, I hit it just once with a mashie niblick.' He took the ball out of my hand, looked at it, and handed it back. With a big smile on his face he said, 'Sonny, no one can be that bad. The lawn mower must have run over it.'"

There was plenty of laughing, and Hagen made sure the youngster had a bucket of brand-new balls and an autograph.

He had ceded British Open victories to the younger Americans. Five PGA Championships were plenty; winning another one didn't get his engine going. He would like to win another Western Open, which he hadn't done since 1927. But the crowning achievement of his career would be to win the National Championship one last time, especially in a field of emerging stars like Paul Runyan who were in grade school when Hagen last won the U.S. Open.

Hagen had always been a realist about his golf game, and it was undeniable that his skills were fading. More of his drives were way-ward, he was less successful with recovery shots, and even his putting was less reliable because of a combination of alcohol-related trembling in his hands and not having the same drive to win. He was still one of the better players in the sport, but more often he played to the crowd than to win.

There is no indication in his autobiography or interviews at the time that in the early to mid-1930s his reduced abilities bothered Hagen (other than wanting that one more National Championship). He seemingly accepted the consequences of aging and his lifestyle. The '29 British Open victory had been such a triumph and an exclamation point to his career that anything after that was icing on the cake. He enjoyed traveling, making ceremonial appearances, the occasional drive for a tournament win, and having outlasted Jones. Among spectators he had regained his status as the game's most popular player even as it became increasingly rare that he contended.

Hagen's apparent willingness to rest on his British Open laurels turned out to be Sarazen's gain. As they traveled to England together, Hagen bequeathed to the Squire a British caddie named Daniels for the '32 Open. According to Sarazen's account, after telling his friend how badly he wanted to win the British Open, Hagen said, "Gene, you can never win the Open unless you have a caddie like the ones I've had."

After sipping on a scotch, Hagen continued: "I've won the British Open a few times, so winning it doesn't mean as much to me as it obviously means to you. Take my caddie." (Sarazen paid for the offer. "I shared a liquor bill with him on the Atlantic crossing," Sarazen recalled, "and was staggered when my half came to three hundred dollars.")

Though well on in years, Daniels knew the Open courses intimately and was happy to carry the bag for a close friend of Sir Walter, with whom he had won Opens beginning with the one in 1922. More than that, he vowed that he would win a British Open for Sarazen if it was the last thing he did.

It was. Daniels gave everything he had during the 1932 British Open at Prince's in Sandwich, including walking the course in a fifty-mile-per-hour gale at dawn of the final round. At the end of the day,

Sarazen had won his claret jug, and in addition to sharing his winnings he gave Daniels a polo coat. The caddie wore it every day until he died, which was only a few months later.

During the summer Hagen entered the International Four-Ball Matches and was paired with one of the emerging stars of the tour, Paul Runyan. Runyan recalls being excited to be a teammate of Hagen's, and liked him as well as admired him.

"Hagen was an extremely cordial man," the ninety-two-year-old remembered in 2000 when he was still a teaching pro in Pasadena, California. "He never walked past you without saying, 'Good morning,' shaking hands, and asking how your family was."

There was his chronic lateness, and it was becoming less of an act. The devoted golfer who had poured some drinks in potted plants and made sure—the majority of the time—he had rested before a big day was now finding it more difficult to find the cutoff switch to partying. Runyan experienced this firsthand.

He was on the tee waiting, waiting . . . and waiting. "Walter was nowhere on the premises. I was sure we would be disqualified, but just as they called us to the tee for the last time, Walter drove up in a taxi and got out wearing a tuxedo. He had partied all night and hadn't even gone to bed."

Hagen played poorly on the first five holes, and he and Runyan were 2-down. When his second (or third, or fourth) wind kicked in, Hagen's game improved. He and Runyan caught their opponents at the 36th hole, and they won three holes later.

Hagen vowed to his partner, "Tonight I'll get a good night's sleep, and we'll be better tomorrow."

Runyan remembers, "Hagen got a good night's sleep. The next day we lost 4 and 2. Truthfully, I wished he had arrived again in the taxi and the tuxedo."

Apparently, Hagen learned nothing about "good" behavior from that experience. Not long afterward, Hagen was driving a bit too fast across the newly constructed George Washington Bridge; he and Babe Ruth and two women had woken up in New Jersey, and after collecting themselves had to get the Babe to Yankee Stadium for a game that afternoon.

They were pulled over on the bridge by a cop, who of course was rather startled by at least two and probably all four of the car's occupants. The officer accepted autographs instead of giving out a ticket, and the car continued on its way.

Hagen wanted wins in the U.S. Open and Western Open, in that order. The possibility existed that should he earn back-to-back victories, being about to turn forty that December, he would strongly consider retirement. It was getting a bit lonely out on the tour too. Of those whom Hagen competed with before and during World War I, by the summer of '32 only Mac Smith, Jock Hutchison, and Jim Barnes were still out there, and they confined themselves to just two or three events a year.

Open first. It was in June at the Fresh Meadow Country Club in Flushing, New York. The course was fairly difficult, 6,815 yards and only a par 70. Sarazen was the favorite, not only because of his comeback win in Great Britain but because he had been the club pro at Fresh Meadow 1925–31. After a practice round with the visiting Bobby Jones, Sarazen declared himself ready.

Not quite. His 150 total after two rounds left him 5 strokes off the lead, and 2 strokes behind Hagen. But the third round bedeviled Sir Walter again. His 79 dropped him out of the top ten, while Sarazen shot a 70 and Bobby Cruickshank a 69. Hagen came back with a 71 during the final 18, but it was a two-man race.

Cruickshank, playing with Harry Cooper and right in front of Sarazen, carded a 68. However, as he had done in the 1922 Open, Sarazen saved his best for last. He shot a blistering 66 for 286 and the 3-shot win. Hagen finished alone in tenth place, 12 shots behind. The Squire's 66 was the lowest round yet in the Open, the 286 equaled Chick Evans's score in 1916, and his 136 on the last 36 holes established a record.

It had been five years since his last Western Open win, and Hagen, playing several exhibitions with Walter Jr. in tow, almost skipped the "major" in Cleveland. Then he reconsidered. With hopes of a National Championship dwindling, and with him no longer being able to advance far enough in the match-play PGA Championship, a fifth Western Open title would be the last feather in his cap.

So at the last minute Hagen and his son flew in from Detroit. Hagen had never seen the course before.

That didn't matter. As the Associated Press reported, "Back on his happy hunting ground of golf where he first rose to national fame, Walter Hagen fought the battle of his life today to ascend the Western Open throne for the fifth time. While a heavy gale raged and a large gallery stormed the fairways, the veteran of a thousand golfing wars came from behind with a dramatic rush of par-crashing golf in the final four holes."

He shot a final-round 70 and 287 total to beat Olin Dutra by one shot. The thirty-nine-year-old still had some lightning left in his bag.

Winning the Western Open for the fifth time in 1932 was very satisfying, but Hagen talked to friends about slowing down or even walking away from it all. A disappointing second-round loss to John Golden in the 1932 PGA Championship (on the seventh play-off hole) at the Keller Golf Course in St. Paul, Minnesota, made getting away from golf more appealing.

"Hagen Is Planning to Retire After Golf Campaign of 1933," announced the *New York Times* in its March 8 edition. "Maybe the lure of the storming, admiring crowds will make the famous showman of the fairways change his mind, but Walter Hagen plans to retire from all active competition after his 1933 golf engagements here and abroad."

The article attributed Hagen's decision to having had a poor winter season (which included a loss just the week before in a Florida tourney won by Paul Runyan), turning forty in December, and the need to spend more time on the golf-equipment business. "In the past few years, scores of tournament officials admitted the Haig's presence in competition, like that of Bobby Jones's in the amateur and open tournaments, swelled the gate receipts far over the danger line of red ink."

A few days after the article (with none of the information attributed to Hagen) appeared, Sir Walter underwrote his own tourney in Jacksonville, Florida, and invited the top pros to vie for a $1,000 purse. They were eager to sign on, but then it didn't seem sporting that with a 71 and 67 over 36 holes, the Haig had won his own tournament. He must have thought so too, because he refused the prize money and had it divided between the two runners-up.

• • •

Sir Walter sailed over to Great Britain in 1933 to captain the Ryder Cup team and play in the Open. One motivation was finally winning a Match in Great Britain, but he also wanted to support Sarazen in his defense of the title and to show off his son to the British Open crowd.

Walter Jr. was fifteen and, inevitably, had taken up golf. He seemed to have talent. He was shy, however, and apparently didn't inherit his father's eagerness to be the center of attention. For once, Hagen was willing to share the spotlight, but Walter Jr. preferred to stay offstage.

For the Match in 1933, Great Britain reached into its heavy artillery for a captain and selected five-time Open winner J. H. Taylor. He had his troops—this time Alliss, Davies, Easterbrook, Havers, Mitchell and Charles Whitcombe were joined by Alan Dailey, Arthur Lacey, Alf Padgham, and Alf Perry—up at 6:00 a.m. in the weeks leading up to the event to run the beach. Perhaps he was expecting Scioto-like heat at the Southport & Ainsdale Golf Club.

The Americans weren't taking the Match quite as seriously. A piece of evidence is that one evening in Southport, instead of resting up and discussing strategy, Hagen suggested going out on the town and having a dance contest. Players on both sides were invited.

At first, just the American squad showed up at the large public dance hall in Southport. The Haig gave some money to the band and the music began, Hagen leading the way with his favorite, the Charleston, joined by his teammates. Then other golfers started arriving. The Argentine Jose Jurado (there because of the British Open) demonstrated the tango. Several of the English players showed up and offered a waltz or the Lambert walk.

According to Bob Harlow, who had accompanied the American squad, "All had no difficulty finding attractive and expert partners from among the hostesses at the dance palace. It was a grand affair. Jose Jurado won the contest. There were a million laughs. Nobody mentioned golf that evening. The wine was good and the price reasonable."

Back to the other contest. The '33 Match came down to the wire. The American team was pretty much the same except for Ed Dudley, Olin Dutra, twenty-four-year-old Paul Runyan replacing Cox, and Espinosa and Farrell. "It was an experience, suddenly sailing for England to play for America, and Walter had picked *me,* which was quite an honor," recalled Runyan, who passed away in 2002. "I'd never been much of anywhere before, then Walter signed me up."

Hagen and Sarazen teamed on the first day but only halved their match with Alliss and Whitcombe. It was a seesaw battle. The Americans had a 2-up lead after Hagen buried a 25-foot putt on the 12th. After the 16th hole, the Brits were 2-up. Sarazen's putting was shaky, and the morning's 18 ended with Alliss and Whitcombe 3-up.

Sarazen's putting woes continued, and Hagen had several poor drives after lunch. But the Brits were having their own problems and allowed their opponents back into the match. The home duo rebounded and had the lead 1-up going into the 36th hole. This time both Hagen and Sarazen executed, the Brits didn't, and the match was halved.

Beginning the singles matches, Sarazen bolted out of the gate, defeating Padgham 6 and 4. Mitchell crushed Dutra 9 and 8, then Hagen grinded out a 2-and-1 victory over Lacy. The Ryder Cup came down to the last hole between Easterbrook and Shute, who were all square. Each left their par putts 30 feet from the 18th hole. Easterbrook missed, but his ball was in tap-in range. For Shute, a par or even a bogey meant the United States would keep the Ryder Cup and win it for the first time on British soil.

Hagen stood at the large front window of the clubhouse with the Prince of Wales, and he had a dilemma. He suspected that Shute didn't know how crucial this putt was, and from having observed others on the 18th green the captain had a pretty fair idea of how to strike the ball. However, "I knew it would be discourteous to walk out on the future King of England just to whisper in Denny's ear and tell him how to putt."

Hagen stayed put. Shute missed, and his ball rolled 4 feet past. He missed the comebacker; Easterbrook didn't. The American captain had to grind his teeth as a jubilant Prince Edward presented the cup to the British team after the 6½–5½ victory.

An article by Hagen (most likely written by Harlow) in the June 28 issue of the *New York Times* offered, "After it was all over I met the Prince again, in the clubhouse, and he suggested that we have a little something, which, according to recent voting in various States, may be legal again in America before long. 'I came here entirely impartial as to whom I would award the cup,' the Prince remarked, 'but I must say now that I am glad to be able to hand it to the British team.'"

A big consolation for Shute was that soon after this crushing loss he won the British Open at St Andrews in a play-off. This was the tenth American win in a row, but would be the last until Sam Snead won it in '46. A consolation for Hagen was that while he was in the neighborhood he accepted a challenge match with the young Henry Cotton for 100 pounds. He won, though according to the account in the *Times* of London, "The golf was never really thrilling until Hagen's final thrust—a truly typical knockout."

The 1933 Ryder Cup Match is also distinctive because it was the last one personally witnessed by Samuel Ryder—he was unable to make the crossing to attend the Match in America in 1935, and he died the following year.

Seizing the opportunity to trade on his longtime fame and the Open champ's sudden fame, Hagen and Shute went on an exhibition tour of Great Britain and Europe, with Walter Jr. along for the ride. And there were more fun times with the Prince of Wales. One of the most famous stories about Hagen is that while playing golf with the prince, Hagen had a long putt and he shouted, "Hey, Eddie, pull the pin, will you?"

The story rapidly went around the world that Sir Walter had treated the future King of England like a caddie. This did make for a great story, especially among Americans and the British colonies, but Hagen denied it to his dying day. He insisted that when lining up the putt he had called, "Pull the pin, caddie!" but the gracious prince, being closest to it, had simply grabbed the stick and moved it away.

(This was the second embarrassing incident involving the Prince of Wales. Back in the United States in the fall of 1929, Hagen had a set of brand-new clubs from a Scottish company sent to the prince with a note that praised him as "the best sportsman he had ever met." The Haig had some quick apologizing to do when the Scottish company included with the clubs a bill for $325 that was supposed to have gone to Hagen.)

There were plenty more parties aboard ship on the way back, with Hagen picking up the checks. However, his money ran out before the

Atlantic Ocean did, so Hagen's pockets were empty again when the boat docked in New York. Walter Jr. gave his father what was left of his spending money, and with that the two took a taxi to the Delmonico Hotel. With total bravado—and helped by being instantly recognized—Hagen registered for the best suite in the house and ordered that $500 in cash and a case of the best scotch should be sent up to it.

Before the week was out, Hagen had arranged for and played a few matches and earned enough to pay the hotel bill, then it was off on his next barnstorming tour.

During the rest of '33, at forty Hagen was no longer a consistent tournament contender. This may have bothered him a bit, but it seems that competitively he had indeed mellowed. He wanted to win, and he always enjoyed collecting the "healthy green stuff" in tourneys as well as exhibitions. But increasingly, the motivation for entering tournaments and maintaining a busy touring schedule was to be with his friends and colleagues and to receive the appreciation of the crowd. At this point in his career the Haig was a very old friend to golf fans, the only still somewhat successful member of a golf generation that had changed the sport forever and made America proud.

He was still much sought after for corporate outings, even during the Depression, though by this time he was nothing close to a hired gun but a convivial friend. Speaking of guns, one time while back in Detroit Hagen played a round with Edsel Ford. The Ford family, like any famous family, was occasionally subjected to threatening messages. The latest were letters implying that Edsel's two sons, Henry and Benson, would be kidnapped, and Edsel was taking no chances.

The youngsters accompanied their father to the Detroit club to meet Hagen, who offered Edsel the honor of teeing off first. The car magnate topped his drive, and had trouble with his next couple of shots. He finally made it to the green to join Hagen. As Edsel reached into his golf bag to get a glove, a .38 handgun fell out onto the green.

Hagen jumped back in alarm and said, "Edsel, if you want this hole so badly, I'll concede it . . . it's yours!" Soon after, in locker rooms around the country, the story circulated that the only way to beat Hagen was at gunpoint.

Becoming an elder statesman of the golf scene didn't dampen Hagen's enjoyment of interacting with the crowd and playing practical jokes. The latter was even more fun if he could tweak one of his long-time friends and rivals.

The U.S. Open in 1933 was held at the North Shore Country Club in Chicago. On the morning of the first round, Hagen was handed a clipping from that day's newspaper that reported Gene Sarazen as saying that the Haig was all washed up as a tournament player and would probably need a wheelchair to get around the course during the Open.

Hagen gave credence to Sarazen's comment by having three mediocre rounds. However, during the final 18, he scorched the course, recording an astonishing 66 (tying Sarazen's record from the previous year), with 25 putts. When he was in the locker room, he sent for the club manager and told him to find an easy chair with big arms on it, and then gave instructions on what to do with it.

Sarazen, the Open defending champion, was having a tough day. At 17, his ball came to rest on the green a dozen feet from the cup; a birdie here would be most helpful. As he was lining up, a member of the club staff appeared carrying the chair. He placed it behind the green and told Sarazen, "Compliments of Mr. Hagen." A note affixed to the chair read: "Sucker, a fish never gets hooked until he opens his mouth."

The Squire was so angry that he three-putted for bogey.

The Haig had been too far back for the 66 to make a difference. Still, his 292, his best total since 291 in the 1922 Open, had him tied for fourth with Tommy Armour. Johnny Goodman took the National Championship, to this day the last amateur to do so.

Hagen was forty-one when 1934 began, and there was no escaping that he wasn't a threat in tournaments. The partying had become more serious, and he had less resilience to bounce back the next day. He entered fewer events, and in the high-profile ones his appearances were more ceremonial than effective challenges.

Hagen skipped going to Great Britain for the Open there. He did try again for a U.S. Open crown, qualifying for the tourney held at Merion in Pennsylvania. As in '33, he didn't play that well the first two rounds, and was more a cheerleader for his friend Sarazen, who at 145 was just one stroke back in his quest for a third Open.

The Squire shot a 73 in the 3rd round to take the lead. But he couldn't hold it, and in one of the biggest disappointments in the Squire's career, he lost to Olin Dutra by 1 stroke.

Hagen had been around long enough that significant anniversaries of past triumphs were beginning to be recognized. In August 1934 he returned to Rochester for Walter Hagen Day, which included a big party at the Oak Hill Country Club, all to celebrate the twentieth anniversary of the Haig's first U.S. Open win at Midlothian.

There was a tournament held that was named for Hagen, and for the second time he could count his father among the spectators. His mother had not and never would see Hagen play, even in Florida. In the 1920s Walter had arranged for his retired parents to live year-round in Orlando, and he visited them in between the winter exhibitions there. However, they eventually grew too homesick and moved back to Rochester.

A win would have been grand for his father and for Rochester, but Leo Diegel took top honors and Hagen finished tenth, tying with his boyhood pal, George Christ.

The celebration was reason enough for the *Rochester Democrat and Chronicle* to put Hagen's career in perspective. With locations and final scores, it listed two U.S. Open wins, four in the British Open, one in the Canadian Open, five in the Western, four in the Metropolitan, three in the North and South Open, and five in the PGA Championship. There had been other victories, lesser triumphs like the Eastern Open and the Michigan Open, but it was quite clear from his hometown newspaper that over a twenty-year period no one had a better record of accomplishment.

The event at Oak Hill was a happy one in several ways, but perhaps most important was its value as a distraction—Hagen still hadn't recovered emotionally from one of the most distressing incidents of his life.

The previous month Hagen had been in Minnesota, competing in the St. Paul Open. He finished tied for fourth, then started off with a friend, Jack Truss, for a few days of fishing at White Bear Lake.

Leaving St. Paul that evening, Hagen was stopped behind a streetcar. It moved forward, then so did Hagen. Suddenly, a six-year-old boy, Lawrence Johnson, the son of a St. Paul druggist, ran out into the street. Unable to stop in time, Hagen's car struck the boy.

Immediately, Hagen jumped out of the car and ran to the boy. Bending down, he brushed the boy's hair and pleaded, "Don't tell me you're dead, sonny. C'mon, speak to me." Sadly, the boy was dead. Hagen was taken to police headquarters, questioned, and released. According to a newspaper account, he "wept as he told his story to the authorities."

The official determination was that the death was by accident, the driver could not have prevented hitting the Johnson boy. Though off a legal hook, Hagen never fully recovered from the experience. As time went on, he increasingly disliked driving at all, and even as a passenger insisted on the vehicle traveling well under the speed limit.

"He hated driving," reported Charles Price years later about the time when he worked for Hagen. "I'd drive for him, but if we ever went faster than forty-five, he'd have a fit. I never knew about the incident."

In the spring of 1935 Hagen would have liked to win the Masters— at forty-two, he would have liked to win any tournament. Winning the event created by Bobby Jones and Clifford Roberts in Augusta, Georgia, would have been something special. The tournament was still in its infancy. The first one, called the First Annual Invitation Tournament, had been the year before. Horton Smith won, with Jones and Hagen tied for thirteenth place; between them, the two "masters" had won twenty-four major titles. Jones, in fact, had been a 6–1 favorite to win the event despite having been retired for four years. His pedestrian showing convinced him not to attempt a comeback.

But Hagen was willing to take another shot because of Jones's involvement and the top-notch field attracted by the event, now being called the Masters, was like that of an Open. Gene Sarazen very much wanted to win it and, as it would turn out, become the first player to earn the modern career grand slam. His longtime friend Walter Hagen would have a hand in Sarazen's Masters title in 1935 and what is considered the greatest golf shot ever made, dubbed the "shot heard 'round the world."

In the final round, Craig Wood had a three-stroke lead over Sarazen as the Squire stood in the fairway of the par-5 15th hole. His ball was sitting down, a bad lie, and he had 220 yards to the pin. His caddie suggested a 3-wood; Sarazen was inclined toward a 4-wood. He kept vacillating, reaching for one club then another.

Finally, his playing partner, Hagen, had had enough, given that it was 5:30 on a chilly afternoon. In his high-pitched voice he yelled, "Hurry up, will ya? I've got a date tonight!" That did it. Sarazen went with his instincts and grabbed the 4-wood. He struck the ball, it soared toward the flag, and it went in for a double eagle, tying him with Wood. They ended the round even, and Sarazen won the next day's 36-hole play-off.

Was Hagen indeed too old to win a last National Championship? It turned out there were a few last sparks in the old boy. One was the Gasparilla Open.

It had been held in February in Tampa. After the third round the Haig trailed a player named Clarence Clark, described in the press as a "towering curly-haired pro from Bloomfield, New Jersey." Close on Hagen's heels were Ky Laffoon and Jug McSpaden. Hagen went out on the town that night and, as was becoming more common, was not in good shape the next morning, weaving and bleary-eyed on the first tee.

He spotted three of his baseball friends, Jimmy Foxx, Mickey Cochrane, and Cy Perkins, all down for spring training, and went over to greet them. Then he played the first nine holes on guts and memory. On the ninth green, as he lined up a putt, he saw the same trio in the gallery. Hagen had woken up by this point and he grinned, walked over, and greeted the three the same way he had two hours earlier: "Hiya, Jimmy. Hiya, Mike. Hiya, Cy. Haven't seen you in a helluva long time." The three burst into laughter and had to explain to Hagen why.

Clark finished at 281 as Hagen stepped to the tee of the par-3 17th. He had to birdie both final holes to take the title. "It looked as if the veteran's cause was lost," according to the *New York Times*. "It still appeared that way after he had smacked his drive, an arching shot that found the green all right but came to rest 45 feet from the pin."

Tournament over? The account continued: "Nonchalantly, the 42-year-old veteran strode up to his ball, hit it crisply, and it rolled straight into the cup. The gallery, standing breathlessly around the green, cheered."

He had at least a tie, if he didn't bogey the par-5 18th. A bogey was the farthest thing from his mind: "The final hole was even more dramatic. Hagen got off a fine tee shot, a drive that carried 230 yards. His second, however, bounced over a tree and rolled into a bunker. He chipped out beautifully, his ball stopping just three feet from the pin, and he promptly holed out."

This was a fine way to start the year. Next up, after the Masters, was the British Open, but Hagen passed on making the trip. The Ryder Cup would be in the United States in 1935, though not until September, beginning the tradition of holding the Matches in early fall.

He determinedly wanted to taste U.S. Open victory one last time. He believed that he had one more genuine shot at it left in his bag. Hagen went all out at the Oakmont Country Club in Pennsylvania in the '35 Open, "a championship I wanted to win more than any other, for it was my last serious competitive threat," he later wrote.

His 77 in the first round was inauspicious. In the second round a rainstorm began that grew worse and worse. Many of the younger players fled to the safety of the clubhouse. But the old warhorse had emerged at a time in golf when rain didn't prevent players from continuing. Perhaps he was also thinking of what had happened to Harry Vardon in the '20 Open at Inverness, and he wasn't going to falter like the great Brit.

He didn't. Play was halted after the first nine of the second round, and Hagen had gone out in 33, putting him in contention. A friend of Hagen's later told him that watching the faces of the diehard spectators who followed the Haig around, "You couldn't tell if those were raindrops or tears on their cheeks."

In "A Golfer To You But Father To Me," published in the *American Golfer* a few months later, Walter Jr. recalled, "As I stood on a knoll and heard the outlet of emotion of that small, surging mass of humanity, then, more than any other time, was I proud to say of that sartorially excellent figure whose heart is made of only the finest quality of grit, 'That's my Dad.'"

Hagen gave his all—and in doing so, no longer having the physical skills and stamina to back up his desire and ambition, he was battling against the odds. He completed the second round with a 76. His third-round 73 put him right in the thick of things as many of the other players, because of poor weather and a very difficult course, were turning in higher scores—Sarazen a 78, Shute a 76, Horton Smith and Paul Runyan 79s.

This could be it, finally, if he could put together a solid second 18 on the day. Bold to the very end, during the front nine of the last round he tried for a green on a par-4 with the idea of getting a birdie, but this time the old magic wasn't there. He overshot the green, wound up in a bunker, got out too far from the pin, and took a 6. Another hole required 7 strokes.

He tried a stretch run, shooting the back nine in 34, on a day when not one of the top twenty in the tournament could score lower than 75. Hagen was 6 strokes behind when he teed off at the 15th, and he played the last four holes at 3 under par. But he ran out of holes before he could close the gap, and Sir Walter had to accept the jarring fact that the 1935 U.S. Open winner, by 3 strokes, was a man named Sam Parks Jr.

Hagen would also have to accept that after the finest career of any professional golfer, it would not be the U.S. Open listed as his final victory. But at least he had lost Hagen-style. As Walter Jr. wrote in the essay in the *American Golfer*, "There's nothing he likes better than standing on the first tee and feeling the bitter lashes of the elements against him. When most players casually pick up and others have to be picked up, he draws himself up and stands alone against the wind and the rain. . . . That's when Dad really fights."

There wasn't much fight left after the U.S. Open disappointment. This doesn't mean that the Haig was ready to be put out to pasture like Man o'War. There was a new Ryder Cup challenge, and he had one more world tour left in him. This one would turn out to be the grandest ever. Hagen would spread the gospel of golf to parts of the world no American player had ever been to before—and, for a few hours, stop a war while he was at it.

CHAPTER 15

THE 1935 RYDER CUP WAS TO BE HELD the last week in September at the Ridgewood Golf Club in New Jersey. For the assistant pro who had begun the job at Ridgewood in April, that first encounter with the U.S. Ryder Cup squad was a turning point in his life.

"Seeing these great players, I made up my mind then and there that I wanted to be on a Ryder Cup team," said Byron Nelson, interviewed in 2001 at his ranch in Texas. "I was just a young whippersnapper then, and it was a lot to think I'd be good enough to make a Ryder Cup team, but I vowed I would."

The Match of 1935 at Ridgewood was not only the last one that featured the core of the first generation of American professional players, but it continues to be the only one ever held in the New York metropolitan area. It was also the last one held during Samuel Ryder's lifetime, and in a way it featured the great, retired amateur Robert Tyre Jones Jr.

Unlike today's mega-event, in 1935 the Ryder Cup remained close to its roots as a gentlemanly competition between teams of professionals from the United States and Great Britain and Ireland. (The rest of Europe would not join the contest for another forty-four years.) Still, the 1935 Match was viewed by both sides as pivotal. Each side had won twice on its home turf, but the Americans had come close at Southport in '33, losing only 6½ to 5½. However, the British team of 1935 felt keenly confident about winning in New Jersey because of an infusion of young and eager players led by the veteran trio of Charles, Reg, and Ernest Whitcombe.

"The British team is far from suffering from an inferiority complex," declared Commander R. T. C. Roe, the team's manager. The British PGA was so confident, in fact, that before its team set sail for the Colonies, it took out insurance for the Ryder Cup on its passage back across the Pond in addition to the trip to the States. "We'll win. I feel sure of it," said Charles Whitcombe as the Brits left on the *Empress of Australia* on September 14.

It would indeed be a strong team Great Britain was sending. The Whitcombe brothers had visited the winner's circle more than once, had Ryder Cup experience (Charles on every team since the first one), and would be a veteran, steadying influence on the talented rookies joining the squad: Dick Burton, Jack Busson, William Cox, and Ted Jarman. Rounding out the team were the experienced Percy Alliss (father of Peter, the broadcaster), who had been part of every Ryder Cup since '29, and Alf Perry and Alf Padgham.

The U.S. side, in contrast, was a bit of a question mark. Hagen was back as captain for the fifth consecutive time (no other American has been captain more than three times), but he was a high-mileage forty-two and three years removed from his last significant victory, in the Western Open. Gene Sarazen was only thirty-two and the reigning Masters champion but was beginning to spend more time on his farm in Connecticut than on the pro tour.

The squad looked at first glance like a collection of holdovers from previous glory years—Hagen, Sarazen, and Horton Smith—and players who could be one-hit wonders: Olin Dutra, the 1934 U.S. Open champ; Paul Runyan, winner of the '34 PGA Championship; Craig Wood, with two previous, undistinguished Ryder Cups; Ky Laffoon; Sam Parks; Henry Picard; and Johnny Revolta. (Indeed, it turned out that Parks and Dutra were at best briefly shining lights on the tour, but Paul "Little Poison" Runyan was the real deal.) Dropped from the last American team were Leo Diegel, Ed Dudley, Denny Shute, and Billy Burke.

Another reason for special pressure on the Yanks was that the head pro at Ridgewood, George Jacobus, also happened to be president of the PGA. There could be no worse venue to witness the Ryder Cup taken away.

The Ridgewood Country Club was initially a two-hole course laid out in 1890 in a meadow in Ho-Ho-Kus, New Jersey. Thanks to these humble beginnings, it is the oldest golf club in New Jersey and is listed as one of the hundred oldest clubs in the country. The course that greeted the Ryder Cup squads was a project undertaken by A. W. Tillinghast at a 220-acre site in Paramus. "Tillie," as he was sometimes called, was the designer of courses that have helped to define New York metro-area golf, including Baltusrol, Winged Foot, and four of the five courses at Bethpage State Park. Jacobus, a friend of both Hagen and Sarazen, was in the midst of being head pro at Ridgewood for fifty years, certainly one of the longest runs in PGA of America history, and he would serve seven years as PGA president.

At seventy-seven, Ryder could not accompany the British team when it left on the seven-day voyage to Quebec. He was, however, kept informed by telegrams from Commander Roe, who was also secretary of the British PGA. No doubt nothing would have been sweeter for the old gentleman than to experience, albeit vicariously, a victory on American soil in the event he co-created.

On September 22, the British arrived at Ridgewood. They were greeted warmly by club officials, then they set right to practicing. The following day, a surprise visitor arrived and asked to play a round with the visitors' captain. Whitcombe readily agreed to an exhibition with three-time British Open winner Bobby Jones. This pre-battle skirmish was a thrill for those who saw it, and turned out to be a good omen as Jones carded a 72 to Whitcombe's 75.

The Americans finally arrived on September 24. There were two days of relaxed practicing with players from both teams mingling, then the squads were honored by a crowd of four hundred at a PGA of America–sponsored dinner at the Hotel Biltmore on the twenty-fifth.

Like most fans of golf then, Byron Nelson was most interested in the Haig and he observed everything the legend did. (Well, *almost* everything—Nelson was a teetotaler while Hagen enjoyed more than one "long cold one" during his nightly carousing.) Nelson took a special interest in how well decked out the U.S. squad was, following Hagen's sartorial example. "I thought they looked mighty sharp," Nelson remembered.

Hagen and Sarazen realized that if the American team was going to prevail it would be because for one more time—and for what turned out to be the last time—they led the way on the course. They stayed together in rooms above the pro shop, practiced together, then embarked on a couple of pre-Match contests to show others that the veterans could still win.

Two days before the Ryder Cup began, Sarazen beat Dutra 5 and 4 in a practice match, and Hagen downed Open champion Parks 2 and 1. Declaring that the squad needed to work on their games, Hagen sent the rest out to practice all afternoon while he and Sarazen relaxed on the clubhouse veranda. The next day, to rub it in a bit as they rounded into fighting shape, the Haig and the Squire defeated upstarts Picard and Revolta 3 and 2.

It was a cloudy, cool Saturday morning when official play began. The Ryder Cup itself was being guarded by New Jersey state troopers. For the 36-hole foursomes, Whitcombe paired the veteran Alf Perry with the newcomer Jack Busson. No fooling around for Hagen: He and Sarazen would challenge in the first match. This could turn out to be a smart move or disastrous. If the high-profile U.S. pair won, that would be inspirational to the rest of the team. But if the flagship is sunk at the battle's beginning, the fleet is on its own.

Hagen, as always, had confidence in himself. He also knew that even though he could provoke Sarazen almost to the point of strangling him (as in the 1923 PGA Championship), that rivalry plus a sincere friendship equaled a formidable team. "We were tough on each other as competitors but good friends when we took on other boys," Hagen remembered in his autobiography, mirroring comments Sarazen made in his own tome.

In the first match of the '35 Ryder Cup, Perry and Busson had no chance, though initially the Haig and the Squire had to fight for holes. The Americans were up by only 1 hole after the morning's front nine. Then, playing smoothly together like a veteran double-play combination, Hagen and Sarazen surged to a 5-hole lead by lunchtime. They coasted the rest of the way, with Hagen's 20-foot birdie putt on the 20th hole putting his team 6-up, and his 4-iron tee shot on the par-3 12th giving Sarazen a tap-in birdie for what would be the winning margin, 7 and 6.

"Just like always, Hagen was impressive because he was a showman," Nelson remembered. "He would have a real tough shot, and he would walk up and just play it. But when he had a shot that looked fairly tough, though it was easy, why he'd move around and look at it a bit and make people think it was a real hard one. Of course, then he'd do the shot that folks thought was almost impossible, and the crowd loved it."

The partisan though respectful crowd loved the results of the first day too, with the home squad enjoying a 3–1 advantage by the end of it. The team of Henry Picard and the Johnny Revolta, the man with the B-movie moniker, had the "toughest" victory, only 6 and 5 over the experienced duo Alliss and Padgham. Runyan and Smith introduced Cox and Jarman to Ryder Cup play by dusting them 9 and 8. The Whitcombes had to save the day. Charles and Ernest barely did so, downing Dutra and Laffoon 1-up. Even then, the host team had a chance, but according to William Richardson, reporting for the *New York Times,* "Although Ernest Whitcombe failed to get down his putt for a 3, it made no difference for Dutra knocked the balls away and went over to shake hands with the two British players who had made a ding-dong fight of it all day long."

The visitors could certainly rebound in the eight singles matches the next day, when the *mano e mano* duels would show which team had the better depth and grit. The expectation was that the captains would square off again first thing Sunday morning.

But Whitcombe decided to go with younger and presumably fresher legs and took himself to the sidelines. Upon hearing this, Hagen determined that he too would serve as captain only. What we know now is that the match with Sarazen on September 28, 1935, was Sir Walter's last appearance as a Ryder Cup player. His 7–1–1 record remains the fourth-highest winning percentage in Ryder Cup history.

If he wasn't going to show the way in the 36-hole singles matches, Hagen decided that his toughest competitor would. Sarazen struggled against Busson, not squaring the match until the 19th hole, and he could never quite pull away, yet he gained a gritty 3-and-2 victory. Runyan came bolting out of the gate and defeated Burton 5 and 3. It was time for a Whitcombe again, and Reg matched up against Revolta, but that was not enough this time around as the young Yank earned a 2-and-1 win. It was technically over when even Dutra joined the victory party, scrubbing Padgham 4 and 2.

The best the British could do was halve two of the three remaining matches, and Picard beat Ernest Whitcombe in the third. Of special interest for the crowd was the last match, Parks versus Perry, which pitted the reigning U.S. and British Opens champions against each other in the final contest. It appeared the visitor had it won, then Parks nailed a 40-foot putt on the 36th hole for the shocking halve.

The 9–3 score meant there was no need for trip insurance for the cup. Bernard Darwin, who could be enormously eloquent, was terse in his disappointment. "Yet another American tragedy," he characterized the outcome in a cable to the *Times* of London.

The outcome at Ridgewood had to be a disappointment for Samuel Ryder back in England, though of course he telegrammed congratulations to Hagen and the PGA of America. He promised a win by Great Britain and Ireland back home in 1937, and to enjoy it. However, on January 2, 1936, while with family for the holidays in London, he suffered a stroke and died almost instantly.

His youngest daughter, Joan, represented him at the 1937 Ryder Cup and for every Match held in Great Britain through 1985 when, at eighty-one, at the Belfry, she saw the British (now part of the European team) win her father's trophy back for the first time in twenty-eight years and give birth to the evenly matched, more intense competition of the present Ryder Cup.

In addition to the normal infirmities of middle age affecting his ability to compete on the tour, Hagen, according to Herbert Warren Wind, had developed "whiskey fingers" after almost twenty years of moderate and then gradually heavier drinking. A man who would always be rated as one of the top putters of all time was making fewer and fewer putts thanks to his quivering hands.

The desire was no longer there either. Though in the midst of the Depression, Hagen had the golf equipment contract with L. A. Young, the occasional exhibition series when he felt like traveling, and there were still corporate outings, so making money was not an absolute necessity. Depending on who was counting, he had won anywhere from forty to seventy-five tourneys worldwide including eleven or sixteen majors, so his place in the golf pantheon was secure, and there was nothing left to prove.

Crowds still cheered him, sometimes even away from the golf course. At the Detroit Tigers home stadium of Navin Field on October 1, 1935, fresh from the Ryder Cup triumph, the Haig doffed his topcoat to join players on the Detroit and Chicago Cubs teams who were going through their final practice before contesting the World Series. With the help of Gabby Hartnett, Hagen "went through a spirited bunting drill," to the cheers of a few hundred spectators and baseball officials, according to one account.

"Hagen got plenty of exercise out of the session, but was notoriously short of baseball form," the account continued. "He posed for pictures, too, teeing off with a bat for a spoon, and Hartnett's gigantic mitt for a tee."

Two weeks later he thrilled the spectators and reporters in Oklahoma City, where the PGA Championship was being held. Though now a slightly portly forty-two—the man who played at a solid 180 pounds during the prime of his career would top out at 240 pounds by 1947—during the qualifying rounds Hagen shot a 67 in the morning and a 72 in the afternoon. The 139 total led the entire field by 3 strokes. Unfortunately, the great golf didn't carry over to the next day, and in the first round Hagen lost 1-up to Johnny Revolta.

It could not have been pleasant to lose to players who were not members of his great generation of golfers. The Masters was Sarazen's last major victory and by 1936 he was semiretired to literally live the life of a squire. Jones would never seriously consider a comeback after his first two showings at Augusta, and was now free to attend to his family and law practice and the golf club he was further developing with Clifford Roberts. Hagen knew that even though they weren't crowd pleasers as he had been, the new crop of pros were simply much better than him now week after week. The PGA money leader in 1934 was Paul Runyan, the following year it was Revolta, and in '36 it was Horton Smith.

The group that would really rule for the next two decades was led by the three men born within months of each other in 1912: Nelson, Sam Snead, and Ben Hogan. Nelson in particular was making bold moves. The kid who had given Hagen his hat in the '27 PGA Championship won his first tournament, the Galveston Open, in 1934, won the Metropolitan Open in '36, and busted out in '37 by winning the Masters.

Having only briefly spoken to him at Ridgewood, later in '35 Nelson had to reintroduce himself to Hagen when they were partnered in the final round of the General Brock Hotel Open in Canada, "my second big thrill in golf," said Nelson. But the twenty-three-year-old, who was leading the tournament by 5 strokes, wasn't too thrilled when his partner showed up over an hour late. Irritated as well as nervous, Nelson shot a 42 on the front nine and finished with a 77, losing the tournament to Tony Manero by 1 stroke.

No hard feelings, though. "It was worth it, and he was really a pleasure to play with," Lord Byron remembered. "He had quite a bit of a gallery, so between my fans and his, we had a good group. It was a great growing experience for me, to learn that a so-called celebrity like Hagen was really just a nice person, as most such folks are."

Hogan was a late bloomer, and would not be a factor until after World War II. Snead was starting to win with some regularity, and would join Nelson on the '37 Ryder Cup team. Runyan, from Arkansas, came close to winning the money titles again in '35 and '36, and Lighthorse Cooper won the inaugural Vardon Trophy for the year's lowest average score in 1937.

Hagen couldn't hope to compete with these new, ambitious players. Also, all of the other competitors he had played, partied, and traveled with were gone from the tour by 1937. When Hagen looked around, it sure wasn't the same.

Though Sarazen would remain competitive into his fifties and would end up winning a total of thirty-eight PGA Tour titles and a career Grand Slam—and incredibly, at seventy-one, participating in a ceremonial way in the British Open in Scotland at Troon for his fiftieth anniversary in the event, he scored a hole in one—he was also having to accept a new breed of player, one who didn't wear plus fours and ties. He had a run-in with Snead because partly out of curiosity, partly as a lark Snead played a few holes of a round in a tournament in his bare feet. Seeing this, Sarazen shouted at officials, "Let Snead win something with shoes on before he tries grandstand stunts!"

"Hey, Gene," Snead drawled, "I only wanted to see how good the grass felt."

"*Mr.* Sarazen to you!" snapped the Squire, who according to Snead gave him a look "like a flash of lightning through a gooseberry patch."

Critics sided with Sarazen, Snead said, because "they wondered if I was even housebroken."

Hagen qualified for the 1936 National Championship at Baltusrol in New Jersey. He played respectably, being 3 over par after 54 holes, but a final round 78 put him well behind. His 297 total was okay, just 1 shot behind Sarazen, but Tony Manero won easily at 282. Two Hagen contemporaries had one last strong showing in the National Championship, Mac Smith at 288 and Tommy Kerrigan at 292.

Still, completing the event allowed him to set a record that stands to this day—the most consecutive years competing in the U.S. Open, twenty-two, from 1913 to '36. Two players have tied the record, Sarazen and Gary Player, and falling one year short is Jack Nicklaus. Hagen had already established another U.S. Open record, the most top-ten finishes, with sixteen; only Nicklaus, with eighteen, would surpass him.

Two other notable National Championship achievements: Part of his win in 1919 was that to this day Mike Brady owns the dubious distinction of having lost the largest 54-hole lead, of 5 strokes, and there were ten times that Hagen was within 5 strokes of the leader entering the final round of the Open; he's tied with Arnold Palmer and Snead (who never won the Open), second to Hogan and Nicklaus at fourteen.

Hagen didn't qualify for the PGA Championship in 1936. And without the Ryder Cup as incentive, he passed on going across the Atlantic for the '36 British Open. When he entered a tournament at all, it was to observe the new talent, socialize, and experience the intoxicating sound of applause from the still starstruck galleries. Playing golf had become more formal—thanks to Bob Harlow and Fred Corcoran (who succeeded Harlow in 1936) the haphazard and disjointed "Tournament Circuit" had become the PGA Tour, with purses higher than ever, even during the Depression.

Hagen even won an event—the Inverness International Four Ball Championship in Toledo in '36, partnered with Ky Laffoon. It was his last win, but he had to share it with Laffoon, as his own play had been mediocre and several times Laffoon's recovery shots carried the team over a tough course. Hagen did offer to the press in 1937 that he was about to retire, though he didn't make it official with the PGA until two years later.

Nelson recalls being paired with Hagen in another four-ball event. Hagen hadn't played in a tournament in a while, and Sir Walter had been up late the night before. After finishing the front nine, Hagen was already bushed.

"He told me, 'Play hard, Byron,' and he disappeared into the club-house," Nelson remembers. "As I'm playing the 10th I can see him having a drink in the grill. So I play the 10th, 11th, and 12th and the 13th comes back by the clubhouse. There's Walter waiting for me, looking rested and relaxed. We finished the round fine."

The fans cheering him on finally diminished in number, switching allegiance to Nelson, Snead, or others or staying home to live on memories. More than anything else, this may have prompted Hagen's next decision—he might be old news in the States, but it could well be a different story in the rest of the world.

One last big exhibition tour sounded like a good idea. Plus, he wanted to get away from the publicity surrounding his divorce from Edna.

He and Edna had been apart for a decade. In January 1929 in Los Angeles, he had sued for divorce "alleging that his wife had deserted him," according to an unintentionally amusing newspaper account. Edna responded by suing Walter for not making any of the monthly payments he had agreed to when they separated. When the case was heard in Los Angeles, Hagen didn't show up or send an attorney, and the judge awarded Edna $9,300 in back payments.

They were far from through with each other. According to a local newspaper account, on December 26, 1936, a judge in St. Petersburg, Florida, "ordered Walter Hagen, professional golf star, to pay his es-tranged wife, Edna C. Hagen, a total of $7,385. The amount represents twenty-seven monthly payments of $250 each, due Mrs. Hagen under a modified separation agreement entered into more than three years ago, plus interest of $585."

Edna then turned the tables and sued for divorce, in Trenton, New Jersey, on January 27, 1937. The action was filed in New Jersey be-cause she claimed that sometime during their marriage she and Walter had lived in her house in West End. Most likely, she was looking for a more sympathetic venue than Los Angeles and Florida, and she apparently found it: On June 25, the court granted the divorce, and, "Under the final decree she will use the name Edna C. Hagen."

The grounds were abandonment, dating from 1926; Edna told the press that she was "the world's number-one golf widow." Hagen did not contest the divorce, and for the record stated "he would never again live with his wife, and that he was about to leave on a golfing tour around the world."

The sooner the better. He contacted "Kirkie." It was time for the most extensive and action-packed exhibition tour ever.

The tour was arranged so that Hagen could lead the United States one more time in the Ryder Cup. Though Sarazen had been angling to be chosen as player-captain of the U.S. team in 1937, once more the PGA of America tapped Hagen. The feeling in the organization he helped found about the event he cofounded was that Hagen could have the job as long as he wanted it. Hagen accepted, but made one concession: He would not take up a roster spot as a player and would serve only as captain. Sarazen would be the senior player.

Hagen's selections made for an especially potent squad, a mixture of veterans and brash newcomers. Sarazen's colleagues consisted of Johnny Revolta, Denny Shute, Horton Smith, Ralph Guldahl, Byron Nelson, Henry Picard, and Sam Snead. The younger ones were somewhat in awe of the captain and grateful for the opportunity to play for their country.

When Nelson learned that he had been chosen, "Boy howdy, was I excited!" he exclaimed sixty-two years later. "I'd never been outside the United States before. There's nothing as exciting in golf as playing for your country."

According to Snead, in his memoir *The Education of a Golfer,* "I almost didn't make it on the team in 1937. I was one of the last players named, because some people felt I might not be able to handle the pressure. . . . Well, I did handle the pressure in Ryder Cup play," and as a captain and player the Slammer participated in ten Ryder Cups.

A potential problem was Hagen's boldness in putting the squad of older and younger players together could backfire if the players didn't mix well. Probably more of a challenge was that the '37 Ryder Cup was being contested at the Southport & Ainsdale Golf Club in England, and thus far in five Matches the home team had won every time. Could Hagen, a rather frayed forty-four and unable as well as unwilling to lead by example, possibly hope to change the pattern?

Certainly the British didn't think so. They wanted to believe that the American domination of golf was over. Indeed, the last four British Opens had been won by Henry Cotton (finally breaking the U.S. streak), Alf Perry, Alf Padgham, and Cotton again. (It should be noted that Sarazen was the only top American player who still bothered to make the trip across the Atlantic.) A Ryder Cup win in 1937 on their own turf would be a nice bit of gravy.

Hagen and his squad arrived in Southport with time to spare for practicing, even earlier than the host team. He went to meet the train bearing the British players and their wives. He shook hands with each opponent and gave each wife a hug. Asked afterward how he could keep track of the wives' names to greet them, Hagen replied, "I managed not to offend any of them because I called each one 'Sugar.'"

In his reports, Bernard Darwin noted the fresh young players on the American team, and was rather worried: "These newcomers were reinforced by a solid body of those whom we knew before, Sarazen, Shute, and Dudley, and the whole array was most menacing."

In the foursomes on the first day, June 29, Nelson and Ed Dudley easily defeated Padgham and Cotton 4 and 2. According to Nelson, Hagen had come to him before the match and said, "Byron, you've got a lot of steam, a lot of get-up-and-go. And Dudley needs someone to push him, so I'm going to put you two together. You can get him fired up."

Sarazen and his partner halved, and with other Yanks pitching in it was 2½ to 1½ by day's end. That, as it played out, was the good news for the Brits.

In the second-day singles, Sarazen got things going, as he had in '35. And it turned out that against Percy Alliss, he had a bit of an advantage. On the 16th his shot flew through the green and was heading for a bunker when it hit a rise and caromed into the lap of a woman seated on the grass. She asked her husband what to do, and he urged her to get rid of it immediately. She flicked her skirt, the ball popped out, and rolled to within 20 feet of the pin. Sarazen, who had seen nothing of this, made the putt. Two holes later he won 1-up.

Wins by Sarazen, Snead, Picard, Guldahl, and Dudley led the way to a 5½-to-2½ trouncing the second day and an overall doubling of the British score, 8–4. (Nelson lost his match, but the Texan was well favored by the British press because of his first and last names.) Perhaps it was best that Samuel Ryder by six months had not lived to see his trophy lost on home soil.

The British publication *Golf Illustrated* in its July 10 issue headlined the Match as "The Southport Debacle." Especially galling about the home team's loss was that for the Americans "the only player who appeared capable of contending with the weather conditions," the magazine had predicted, "was Walter Hagen, their non-playing captain," yet the windy and damp conditions had actually bested the home boys.

However, Sir Walter had a hard enough time contending with the victory speech. After being handed the Ryder Cup, Hagen told the crowd, "I am proud and happy to be the captain of the first American team to win on home soil."

At first there was puzzled silence, then some good-natured heckling. With a laugh, Hagen added, "You will forgive me, I am sure, for feeling so at home over here." And it was true—seventeen years after his first visit to Great Britain, he was most welcome and felt like royalty. After this verbal recovery, the crowd cheered.

Aside from wanting to go on a wide-ranging tour to escape divorce woes, Hagen was intrigued to see Japan again. He and Kirkwood had been a big hit there seven years earlier, and many invitations to come back had been extended since.

In 1935, Hagen had played host to a contingent of Japanese golfers who came to America, and three dozen exhibition matches were played with several ad hoc U.S. teams. Hagen was particularly impressed by "Torchy" Toda, a Japanese pro who was only 5'2" and 110 pounds but "was by far the longest driver of any golfer we'd seen in years."

The Japanese contingent caused Hagen some embarrassment. One exhibition match was set for Augusta, Georgia. The Japanese ambassador to the United States traveled down from Washington, D.C., for the match. The visiting players, eager to compete and impress the ambassador, were assembled at the first tee greeting the ambassador a half hour before the start time. When Hagen and the American players arrived at the first tee at 12:30 p.m., the start time, some reporters saw this as another example of the Haig's habitual lateness.

"Walter Hagen Keeps Japanese Ambassador Waiting!" blared headlines the next day. Knowing the truth of the matter, the ambassador was also embarrassed, and hoped that in spite of the awkward situation Hagen would come back to visit Japan.

"Going back again into partnership with Hagen seemed like a homecoming," wrote Kirkwood in his autobiography *Links of Life*. "Together we had eternal youth."

Feeling youthful meant having plenty of curiosity and energy. The first leg of the tour took them through Europe. The Continent, with rumors of war, wasn't as carefree as during previous trips, and for reasons he never explained, Hagen avoided Germany. With that swing finished, when Kirkwood suggested they try Africa "the reaction was instantaneous. The Haig was all for it."

Of course, first Hagen had to spend two days and several thousand dollars buying the appropriate safari clothes and equipment. Kirkwood arranged passage on a boat that left Genoa on October 8, 1937, and steamed for Capetown, South Africa. Upon arrival, all their trunks and equipment were piled on the dock, way too much material for a car.

Acting on a tip, the two hurried to Port Elizabeth where a movie company had abandoned a long mobile trailer that contained beds, a small kitchen and bathroom, and a bar. Everything was packed aboard and away they went, heading north.

The tourists knew nothing of the roads in South Africa, and their unwieldy vehicle had a hard time dodging fallen trees, fording streams, maneuvering around boulders, and swaying and shuddering as the awkward vehicle rode on the rough, uneven roads. Finally, a flat tire forced them to stop. As they worked on it, rocks kept flying off the hill down at them.

Looking up, they caught sight of a group of two dozen or so baboons advancing on them. Hagen and Kirkwood grabbed their rifles and fired away, killing some of the baboons, but more kept appearing.

"I must admit we were both scared, it being our first encounter in the interior of Africa," Kirkwood reported.

Suddenly, the crowd of baboons "set up a terrific hollering, a sort of screeching and calling, and as if at some secret signal they took off." The duo rushed to fix the flat and got their lumbering vehicle going again.

A few days later Hagen and Kirkwood stopped in a town at the edge of the jungle, intending to sleep in real beds and eat a hot meal. As Kirkwood unpacked, Hagen headed to the town's saloon. When Kirkwood arrived he found a big crowd of locals because "word had gotten round that a titled Englishman had just arrived in town—'Sir Walter'—who was ensconced in the saloon spending money like a drunken sailor."

Hearing the commotion, the local preacher entered, and Hagen soon learned that the man had a rather lax congregation and he was barely able to support himself. Hagen buttonholed his new friends and insisted that they treat the preacher better. They responded by passing a hat that ended up containing 70 pounds, which Hagen matched. The overwhelmed preacher couldn't refuse Hagen's suggestion that he have a drink to celebrate this miracle.

One drink led to a second, then a third. The preacher cheerfully confided to Hagen that he'd never touched spirits before, which the golfer found astonishing and disturbing.

Eventually, and after Kirkwood had returned to the hotel, it was closing time. By this point the preacher could barely walk, so Hagen brought him home, thoroughly shocking the preacher's wife. As Hagen turned to go, the preacher realized Hagen did not know the way from his house to the hotel, so he accompanied Hagen there. After a goodnight sip from Hagen's flask, the preacher had trouble walking again, so Hagen brought him home. He arrived back at the hotel as the dawn was breaking.

Before leaving town Hagen and Kirkwood arranged a fund-raising match for the chapel against several locals at a nearby nine-hole course. Kirkwood went out to the course first, but an hour after the start time Hagen still hadn't shown up. Kirkwood, worried his friend had been eaten by lions, went in search.

"I had no sooner started back toward town when I found him, in a clearing off the dirt road, teaching a bunch of fifteen- and sixteen-year-old native girls to do the shimmy!" Kirkwood reported. "What a sight their brown bodies were, all youth and jiggle, alive with rhythm, and only their beads for cover."

After the match (which they easily won) and on their way out of town, they passed the sign that read "To the Golf Club." Remembering how the preacher had lamented that more locals were playing golf on Sunday morning then attending service, Hagen and Kirkwood stopped, got out, and changed the direction of the sign so that it was pointing toward the chapel.

The tour through South Africa by Hagen and Kirkwood left a strong impression on the country, which has produced many fine golfers, especially Ernie Els, Retief Goosen, and Hall of Famer Gary Player. As a child in the years following Hagen's visit, Player remembers that mentioning the Haig brought instant recognition.

"He was most certainly well known in South Africa, and regarded as quite a character," Player remembered.

Many years later, Player was participating in a tournament (possibly the 1960 PGA Championship) in Akron, Ohio, which was attended by Hagen in one of his rare public appearances. The Haig was delighted to hear about the positive impression he had made on South African golf in the 1930s. "He was pleasant and a real gentleman," Player said about meeting Hagen.

On the Haig and Kirkie went, up and over the snow-covered Mountains of the Moon, through Uganda, climbing to the Gishu Plateau, around the Mount Elgon volcano, through the Rift Valley of Kenya where they decided to stay and hunt. The two golf missionaries, sweaty and dusty, jumped out of their clothes and into a lake. The water was refreshing; unfortunately, at dusk when the time came to get out they discovered seven lions perched between the lake and their trailer.

"As a rule lions do their killing in the evening," according to Kirkwood. "It was obvious that they were waiting for us to get out of there, and yet I thought that we were better off staying in the water, hoping eventually they would get tired and leave."

That didn't happen. The stranded and apparently appetizing adventurers were getting rather cold and being eaten by insects as night advanced. Finally, they moved close enough to shore to break off two sturdy tree limbs.

"At an agreed signal we started making a terrible commotion in the water, slapping it with all our strength to make the loudest racket possible," Kirkwood recalled. "Incredibly, the male stood up and stretched his whole body out toward us. Hagen followed with some more wild splashing maneuvers, and I had some of the longest 'back swings' with the best 'follow throughs' of my career. Unbelievably, that did it. Suddenly, the whole family got up and retreated off the bank and went away. You've never seen two fellows get out of the tub faster."

They continued through Africa. Along the way, they heard rumors of a Zulu king who had 103 wives. Hagen was so fascinated that he insisted they make a detour deep into the jungle to find the man, and after several days they did. He did indeed have over a hundred wives, each one with a hut and family of her own.

"Upon our arrival the old fellow welcomed us and showed us about," Kirkwood reported. "Most important to Walter was he wanted to find out what this man ate in order for him to be able to keep all of those wives happy. He found out after discreet inquiry that the secret to the man's prowess was due to a diet of baboon meat and rhino horn. When Walter heard that, he said, 'That's for me!'"

Inspired, Hagen ate baboon meat for every meal. This diet may or may not have improved his libido, but something it definitely did do was, according to Kirkwood, give the Haig "some uncomfortable consequences. The only real effect he realized was a high degree of constipation," but he couldn't be persuaded to stop until, in such a bad way, Kirkwood drove to the nearest city and dragged his friend to a doctor who "prescribed the largest pills ever taken by man."

On they went through the continent, spreading the gospel of golf and meeting people and seeing sights only a very few people on the planet had ever experienced.

"I believe the most unusual caddie that appeared on my horizon was in the Belgian Congo in Africa," Hagen recorded in his autobiography. "A tall, full-chested native stripped to the waist, wearing only the loincloth peculiar to the tribe, toted Joe's heavy bag of trick clubs around a course studded with diamond dust greens. Strings of ivory ornaments hung around a short neck, rings four inches in diameter

pierced contorted ears, a tight narrow band with cascading ivory ornaments and animal teeth encircled a head of short crimply-curled hair,
and several rings banded fingers on both hands.

"The costume and decorative ornamentation was regulation in
that country, but the eye-opening jolt to me stemmed from the fact
that Joe's caddie was a lady! I'm still wondering how Joe could keep his
eye on the ball and choose the correct club for his trick shots."

They crossed over to Indonesia and the Philippines, then it was on
to India. One exhibition match played there was before a maharaja,
who was so amazed by the demonstration that he presented the Haig
and Kirkie with a baby elephant. Hagen was overjoyed and wanted to
keep it. According to Kirkwood, "I stopped him by pricing the freight-
age [back to the U.S.], which came to some $5,000, and Hagen settled
for a girl out of the harem instead."

Arriving in Calcutta, Hagen wanted to shoot a tiger. Off they went
with guides on the hunt. They encountered one particularly large and
crafty tiger who kept eluding Hagen, though he set up various traps to
lure the animal in. He never did bag it, but instead contracted black-fly
malaria, which laid him low for weeks with a temperature that reached
as high as 105 degrees.

Somewhere along the way Hagen and Kirkwood found themselves
heading to Ceylon. Kirkwood decided to fly there, but Hagen, wanting
to avoid flying, had the romantic idea of hopping a tramp steamer, and
a German one was just leaving. As a celebrity, Hagen was given the
first mate's cabin, of which, as it turned out, "cockroaches three inches
in length were in full possession. At night I could feel the roaches playing tag over and under me."

Above deck wasn't much easier. As members of Hitler's Navy, the
officers and crew were enthusiastic about praising and saluting Der
Fuhrer. Because of his German descent, Hagen was viewed as a sym-
pathizer to the Fatherland's cause, while in actuality as an American
he was much more sympathetic to Great Britain and otherwise not
interested in politics. Hagen feared he might suddenly get tossed
overboard, especially when he couldn't match the fervor of the crew's
"Heil Hitler!" When the steamer docked, he couldn't get down the
plank fast enough.

Safely on Ceylon, an exhibition was planned for a day that turned out to be blazingly hot, and the two were warned not to play without wearing hats.

Kirkwood was happy to comply. The Haig, however, had long resisted wearing hats, plus he was being paid good money to endorse a hair tonic and while playing golf his glistening black hair was a walking billboard. On the ninth green, their playing partner, from Ceylon, keeled over, fainting. Kirkie, rather then tempt the same fate, soon retired. Hardly noticing that he was playing alone, Hagen finished the round.

Gene Sarazen, on his own exhibition tour, found his two friends there. "I was startled to come across a poster proclaiming to all golf fans that Joe Kirkwood and Walter Hagen would be playing an exhibition the next day at the country club, admission 30 rupees," the Squire reported. "Before my eyes had caught that poster, I hadn't the slightest knowledge that Walter was any farther east than Detroit."

Sarazen found out where Hagen and Kirkwood were staying, and when he arrived at the hotel lobby he dispatched a bellboy to tell Hagen that there was a gentleman downstairs who wanted to purchase fifty tickets to the exhibition. Within minutes, the Haig was in the lobby; he spotted Sarazen immediately and gave him a big hug.

"I suppose I should be surprised, Gene," Hagen said. "But the moment that bellboy finished his spiel I said to Kirkie, 'There's only one person I know who would come up with a gag like this. I don't know where Sarazen was yesterday, but today he's in Ceylon.'"

In January, Hagen remembered his son's birthday . . . sort of. From Rangoon, Thailand, he sent Walter Jr. a cable twenty-six pages long made up of traditional advice and other clichés in honor of his twenty-first birthday, in addition to how proud he was of his son. The problem was, however, that Walter Jr. was turning twenty. It was the thought that counted. (Six years earlier for his birthday, Walter Jr. received an Austin roadster from his father, who thought his son was turning sixteen.)

The fascination in Asia with the Haig and Kirkie was so strong that the two actually stopped a war during their tour there. The Chinese and Japanese were at war in 1938, and when Hagen and Kirkwood got to a Shanghai course to put on an exhibition, it was discovered that the day before a bomb had destroyed the 18th green.

The visitors weren't going to risk their necks while playing golf. Hagen explained to Japanese officers that the exhibition would go on only if there was a halt to hostilities. Under a flag of truce, the Japanese approached the Chinese officers. Hearing that the show featured Hagen and Kirkwood, the Chinese agreed to a twenty-four-hour cease-fire if they were invited to attend. The Japanese agreed. Part of the agreement too was that the two sides would remove the dead bodies from the course.

So all that day a crowd of Japanese and Chinese officers and relieved local residents watched as the Haig and his partner played an exhibition and then performed hours of trick shots. At one point the Japanese had some soldiers don Chinese uniforms, run to the end of the 18th fairway, then charge as Hagen and Kirkwood playfully sent tee shots their way. A few comically fell over, the rest turned and ran for cover. Everyone thought this was amusing—what only the Japanese officers knew was that the "act" had been filmed, and Japan would use the newsreel for propaganda services as it purported to show that the Chinese were so cowardly they would even run from golf balls.

When the show was over, the Japanese and Chinese showered them with applause, and there was a convivial get-together that evening. The American and Australian left early the next morning, and hostilities resumed.

The seemingly endless tour went well into 1938 in Japan. The Haig and Kirkie put on several exhibitions. One was set up with Prince Fumitaka Konoe. Hagen showed up two hours late. When a functionary delicately informed him of what could be a serious breach of etiquette, the Haig responded, "Well, the prince wasn't going anywhere, was he?" The prince and Sir Walter went on to enjoy a friendly round together.

The celebrated duo was again invited to play a match before the emperor. Hagen, who had had too much sake the night before, was not his best. It didn't help that on one hole he hit his ball out of bounds and struck a beehive, and when he went to retrieve the ball the angry bees set after him and he had to find shelter in a course-side shack.

Finally, Hagen made it to the last hole, but his ball was 70 feet from the cup. He'd had it by this point and, despite Kirkwood's hissed pleas, he just wanted the show to be over. More than ready to head to the clubhouse, Hagen hit the ball with his putter backhanded.

The crowd of Japanese royalty and dignitaries gasped as the ball made its way toward the hole, closer and closer, and with its last turn dropped into the cup. The crowd went wild. Never having looked behind him, Hagen turned and bowed, then continued on to the clubhouse.

Back in the States finally, Hagen was exhausted by the tour. Having had his fill of golf for a while, clearly there was no need to continue as an active player. Money was not an issue after what he had reaped from the world tour and his equipment deal. He could pick up ready cash whenever he felt like doing stateside exhibitions.

The Depression not only had little impact on Hagen's wallet, it had no longstanding effect on golf. The total prize money for the PGA tour in 1936 hit $100,000 for the first time, and there were twenty-two sanctioned tournaments. The number of qualifiers for the U.S. Open at Baltusrol that year was an all-time high of 1,277. Thanks to Hagen and his peers, professional golf was well established in America and prospering.

While there were some ventures that had gone belly-up along the way, by the late 1930s there were more than six thousand golf courses in the United States—providing an expanding number of jobs to golf professionals—compared to two thousand in Great Britain and approximately one thousand elsewhere on the planet. The United States was by far the leading manufacturer of golf equipment. And as almost two decades of winners of the British and U.S. Opens had demonstrated, America was producing the best professional players.

There was one significant golf victim of the Depression: The *American Golfer* was about to fold in January 1936. The magazine's subscriptions had peaked in 1929 at seventy thousand, and that year it was purchased by Condé Nast Publications. But during the next seven years, with automotive and other top-dollar advertising revenue down and the subscription base eroding, ownership saw a product with no future, and wanted to pull the plug. There was a short reprieve. The *American Golfer* appeared as an insert in *Sports Illustrated,* and it contained a farewell letter to readers from Grantland Rice. Within a few months, the venerable publication was history.

There were still a few exhortations for Hagen to give the PGA Tour one last try, even at forty-six. The calls were sentimental rather than realistic ones, inspired by the need to hold on to heroes, especially by hometowns.

"They give Hagen away every year," wrote Jack Tucker in the Sunday magazine section of the *Rochester Democrat and Chronicle* of March 26, 1939. "The man can't go on forever, they say. Look at Tilden; he's through. The Bambino can no longer point significantly to the fence and bust it out of the lot. Dempsey quit the ring long ago. . . .

"But not Walter. Not the hectic, hilarious, hold-on-I'll-be-there-in-a-minute Hagen. Not on your life, my sentimental citizens. The merry Mahatma, Rochester's contribution to big-time golf, is in a class by himself. Let the winds blow and the leaves fall; let the years yap and the petals pale—our man Walter carelessly and happily ignores the calendar with the aplomb of a Shaw, the zest of a zany and the hardiness of a prickly pear."

However, Hagen wasn't listening, or if he did, he knew more than his fans: This show was about to close, after success on Broadway and many tours. The U.S. Open was at the Cherry Hills Club in Colorado that year, and Hagen failed to qualify by one stroke.

"I no longer had the urge to spend time practicing, it was too much strain on my social life," Hagen admitted. "I was having greater difficulty dropping my ball in the hole, my putting touch was decidedly off. I tried out different stances—I tried standing with my feet close together, I tried standing with my feet wide apart. I tried bending over a bit more, and I tried standing straight." Nothing seemed to work, then he candidly added: "Actually, my main trouble was just a whiskey jerk."

Time to call it quits. Alerting the PGA of America, Walter Hagen officially retired from competitive golf in 1939. Explaining his decision to friends, he said, "I couldn't stand the thought of shooting an 80, so I quit."

No one in the world had a better total of tournaments won. The PGA at the time credited him with forty official victories, including his U.S. Open and PGA Championship majors. Today, that total is forty-four because in 2002 the PGA Tour policy board finally agreed to recognize a British Open victory as a win, and thus Hagen's total increased by four.

Though that was it for official tournament golf, Hagen could still have fun on the links, playing the occasional exhibition and visiting his favorite clubs to spend time with old friends and maybe pick up a buck or two. In the fall of '39 he was at Oakland Hills. According to the head pro there, the gathering at the bar went on til midnight, when Hagen offered a challenge that he could par the tough par-4 10th hole even in the middle of the night.

Even though this was the Haig, the bets against him came fast and furious. Hagen grabbed some clubs and went out of the clubhouse to the nearby 10th tee, a large and excited gathering following him, makeshift torches lighting the way. Hagen announced that he would put his drive in the fairway just short of a particular bunker.

He struck the ball. It disappeared into the night. Hagen led the crowd down the fairway, and sure enough the ball was found where he said he would put it. His second shot, he told them, would be on the green, ten feet from the pin. And that's where they found it. The Haig putted, just missing the birdie, then tapped in for par.

He collected his money and led everyone back to the clubhouse for one last round of drinks, his treat. Only after Hagen had left town did the head pro, Al Watrous, find out that earlier in the evening Hagen had paid a clubhouse boy to place the three balls out there.

The decision was made that the next Ryder Cup Match, in November 1939, would be played at the Ponte Vedra Country Club in Florida. When the event neared, Hagen was again anointed captain by the PGA of America. But because of World War II beginning that September with the German invasion of Poland, the Match didn't take place, and Hagen's Ryder Cup career was officially over.

However, just as in World War I, Hagen found a way to combine his passions with the nation's needs, and in the process enjoy one last bow in the spotlight.

CHAPTER 16

HAGEN'S RETIREMENT MAY HAVE appeared premature when at forty-six he qualified for the 1939 PGA Championship at the Paumanok Country Club on Long Island, New York. But he lost in the first round to Tony Manero. Hagen was winning after 11 holes but faltered, allowing Manero to gain a 1-up win.

During the match, an older woman went up to Hagen to remind him of the borrowed cap in the '27 Championship and revealed that she was Byron Nelson's mother. Nelson finished second in the event. Sarazen was also defeated in the first round, leaving the tournament completely to the next generation.

Dreams of winning another major had to remain just that. Hagen never again set foot in Great Britain. He entered the U.S. Open in 1940 then withdrew, and didn't enter again. He tried but failed to qualify for the '42 PGA Championship, and didn't try again. And given that he was drinking more steadily, even a regular tour tournament was out of reach because it required making a morning tee time three days in a row and having the stamina to play 36 holes on the third day.

Being officially retired apparently meant that Hagen was fair game to be honored for past achievements. The first major event along these lines took place in August at Midlothian in Chicago to commemorate the twenty-fifth anniversary of Hagen's first U.S. Open victory there. His original hometown newspaper, the *Rochester Democrat and Chronicle,* announced the event with the headline "Mahatma Hagen, Golf's Grand Old Man, Observes His Silver Anniversary."

Many of golf's luminaries, past and present, were there, including

Gene Sarazen, who made the trip from his farm; though only thirty-seven, his career as a winner had ended too. Also on hand were Bobby Jones, Horton Smith, O. B. Keeler, Tommy Armour, Paul Runyan, Chick Evans, and Byron Nelson, among others.

Anticipating the silver anniversary dinner, Jack Tucker of the *Democrat and Chronicle* wrote, "There will be speeches and wine, and flowers and tribute, and old Florid Face will rise up on his venerable haunches to thank the boys.

"Perhaps Walter will cry a little. It would be worth going a thousand miles just to see a tear trickle down the large and ripe nose, trickle across the humorous, big lips, trickle across the familiar jowls and down the Andy Gump chin." Tucker lamented that Rochester wasn't throwing a party too because, among other reasons, "his mother and father still live here, on Monroe Avenue, Brighton. His old friends are here."

Also writing about the dinner was Grantland Rice, who offered that Hagen's "vast army of friends and admirers are giving the veteran a big show over his first championship course. This will be a round robin best ball affair and it promises to be one of the golfing classics, given to one of the great names of golf for all time. It will be a tribute to Hagen, who has written more than his share of golf history since he dropped his last putt at Midlothian twenty-five years ago."

Rice used the dinner as an opportunity to look back at and sum up Sir Walter's career and life: "Hagen had everything it takes. He was a magnificent swinger with wood and iron—one of the great recovery masters and a brilliant putter. Hagen made well over a million in golf—and spent it all. Money has never meant anything to him, except something to get rid of quickly. How he ever took the beating that he gave himself is beyond anyone's imagination."

The night was full of tributes. "The honor being paid you certainly is no less than your due, and it is one in which every golfer in the country, if not in the world, would like to have a part," Jones said. Nelson offered, "Here's hoping to see you participate in many more tournaments and give hundreds of other ambitious youngsters the inspirations you did me." Harold "Jug" McSpaden declared, "You've done more for the promotion of golf and good sportsmanship than any other man in the game, and I'm proud to be listed among your friends."

Another honor arrived the following year. In 1940, the U.S. Golf Association asked for a set of clubs for its Hall of Fame that Hagen had used in one of his Open victories. He was able to offer the set used in the 1919 win, but it wasn't complete because the mashie iron was missing.

While at Oakland Hills during the unofficial Ryder Cup Match that year, he mentioned the missing stick to Midge Murray, a longtime friend and occasional assistant. He was quite surprised when Murray said that he had it and would bring it to him the next day.

"Sure enough, he turned up with it and carried it all over the course until he found me and presented it to me," Hagen recalled. "I took a couple of swings with it, and it was like meeting a treasured old number."

Murray had kept it as a souvenir with Hagen's permission, and he'd completely forgotten about it. It was with this club that Hagen had reached the green at 18 and eventually tied Mike Brady at Brae Burn, and then won in a playoff the next day. It is now at Golf House in Far Hills, New Jersey, the USGA headquarters.

There was hope that the Ryder Cup Match scheduled to be played in the States in 1939 could still be squeezed in. Hagen's selection as captain by the PGA of America once more upset Sarazen.

Having played on all six U.S. teams in the Matches since 1927 and with a 7–2–3 record, Sarazen felt again, more strongly than ever, that it was his turn for the honor. The PGA didn't necessarily disagree but maintained its position that it would keep Hagen as captain as long as he wanted it. While he was done as a player, Hagen did want one more turn as captain to defend the Cup at home. Sarazen grumbled, Hagen ignored him, the PGA stood fast, and Sarazen decided to stay home. (The Squire never did captain a Ryder Cup team in official action.)

For the 1939 Match at the Ponte Vedra Country Club in Florida in November, Hagen selected Vic Ghezzi, Ralph Guldhal (winner of that year's Masters), Jimmy Hines, Jug McSpaden, Dick Metz, Byron Nelson (U.S. Open winner), Henry Picard (PGA Champion), Paul Runyan, Horton Smith, and Sam Snead for the U.S. squad.

Throughout the year the British were putting together a team too. Henry Cotton, who had ended the American run in the British Open in 1934 and won it again in '37, was captain. On his squad were Jimmy

Adams, Dick Burton, Sam King, Alf Padgham, Dai Rees, Charles Whitcombe, and Reg Whitcombe.

But when Germany invaded Poland on September 1, hopes were dashed. There would be no official Ryder Cup Match until 1947, in Portland, Oregon. It certainly looked as though Hagen's days in the public eye were over.

Retirement from competitive golf and the related touring meant Hagen had more free time on his hands. This meant he could spend some of it with his son. That war loomed on the horizon, and Walter Jr. was of age for military service.

Hagen hadn't completely ignored the boy. There had been the trips back and forth to Great Britain, helped by the divorce agreement with Margaret Johnson that allowed Hagen to share custody once Junior, as he was called, turned fourteen—though Hagen's idea of sharing custody was whenever it suited him.

Junior seemed to think that his father tried to do what he could. "Golf is a business which compels a certain amount of travel," he wrote in "A Golfer To You But a Father To Me," in the *American Golfer.* "Thus I have always missed this companionship. So not being able to be a Dad (according to the Walter Hagen, Junior rules for a better Dad's Club), he decided to become the next best thing and that was a pal; and that is just what we are, two of the greatest pals on earth."

In 1939, Walter Jr. was twenty-one and it appeared he could take a shot at playing golf professionally. He was a good player who from time to time would play brilliantly for the golf team at Notre Dame University, where his major was radio journalism. However, if he was going to have a career in sports at all, his first love, like his father's, was baseball. In high school, he'd very much wanted to be the school's catcher.

"I was a pretty good catcher, had some heft and was a pull hitter," Junior told *Golf* magazine in an interview published in May 1980. "But they made me captain of the golf team because of the publicity it would bring the school. I never did get to play baseball."

The few times they were together over the years, Walter had given his son lessons, and physically they had a lot in common. A photograph from 1932 shows the fourteen-year-old and his father in the midst of their backswings, and except for wearing white knickers and being a few inches shorter, Walter Jr. is a carbon copy. It's interesting to note that while Walter Jr. correctly has his head down, his father, behind him, is looking intently at his son's form.

The occasional lessons and the experience at Notre Dame did forge a better player out of Junior. Before he gave up playing golf to go into the business end of the sport, he competed in two U.S. Amateur Championships and then, during his brief experience as a pro, shot a 68 in one round of the Canadian Open—where his father had made his pro debut.

"I learned to play pretty much out of self-defense," Walter Jr. told *Golf* magazine. "I felt a responsibility to my name—and to Dad. The trouble with being the son of a famous golfer is that you don't get any credit. When you make the shots, it's expected. But when you miss, you're a bum."

By several accounts, Walter Jr. was in awe of his father. According to a 1939 piece by Jack Tucker in the *Rochester Democrat and Chronicle,* "The little Mahatma . . . thinks the Lord tore up the pattern after making Walt Sr."

According to accounts by both Hagen and his son, the father was proud of Junior's golf accomplishments and was glad to offer advice and answer questions. However, Hagen did not try to push Walter Jr. into a golf career. This turned out well for both of them.

Golf plans and visits with Hagen were put on hold when Junior enlisted in the army after the attack on Pearl Harbor. They did get together for a sad event—the burial of William Hagen in July 1942, in the cemetery in Brighton.

It seems that something Walter Jr. didn't have in common with his father was skirt chasing. While the son was a reasonably handsome fellow and his name had to help him attract a fair share of female interest, Junior had a short bachelorhood. Not long after entering the army, he met Helen Marjorie Leonard of Watertown, east of Rochester, and before long they were engaged. She was a student at St. Lawrence College.

By the time of the wedding in December 1943, Walter Jr. was a lieutenant stationed at Fort Custer in Battle Creek, Michigan. He traveled east for the wedding, which took place in the Holy Family

Church in Watertown. Walter Sr. was the best man, which gave him an opportunity to see his former wife for the first time in some years. Junior's marriage would last until his death in 1982.

After the ceremony and a reception at the Hotel Woodruff, Walter Jr. and his bride headed west. They visited friends in Rochester, and the army man was a bit of a celebrity. A photograph that appeared in the December 14, 1943, issue of the *Rochester Times-Union* shows the smiling couple five days after the wedding, and an accompanying item is headlined "Golfer's Son Weds at Watertown." They continued west and moved into quarters at Junior's base.

Though for the rest of his life Junior performed a valuable service by handling his father's business affairs and running the Walter Hagen Division of the Wilson Sporting Goods Company, he never felt comfortable nor could he feel any confidence in the reflected light of the Haig. He told one interviewer: "When I was older and people told me that I was a nice golfer but couldn't play as well as my Dad, I answered, 'Who in hell could?'"

Because of the destructive impact of World War II in England, the British Open was canceled in 1940. It would not be played again until 1946.

In America, beginning in 1942 there was a sharp reduction in tournaments. Players were enlisting and being inducted into the military; the manufacturing of clubs and other golf equipment came to a virtual halt because the raw material was needed for the war effort; long-distance travel became almost impossible; and purses dried up. Baseball was able to continue, though at a diminished level of talent, but in golf the tournament schedule withered away.

The last Masters during the war years was held in 1942, and it went out with a bang with Byron Nelson beating Ben Hogan in a play-off. (Hogan would not win the first of his nine majors until 1946, when he was thirty-four.) The U.S. Open was canceled that year and didn't return until 1946. The PGA Championship missed only one year—Nelson won in 1940, Vic Ghezzi in '41, Sam Snead in '42 (after receiving permission to delay his navy induction by ten days), '43 was skipped, then Bob Hamilton in '44, and Nelson again in '45.

There was a one-shot effort to try to maintain some normalcy with the National Championship. The U.S. Golf Association, PGA of America, and Chicago District Golf Association teamed up to sponsor the Hale America National Open, a benefit for the Navy Relief Society and the USO, in 1942.

In announcing the event, the *New York Times* reported, "Another player who is sure to draw a big gallery is Walter Hagen, one of the game's greatest figures. The Haig has been placed in a threesome with Bing Crosby and Jock Hutchison, and their capers alone ought to be worth the price of admission."

More than 1,500 golfers, paying five dollars each, tried to qualify at twelve sites, and those who made the final field competed at the Ridgemoor Country Club in Chicago. Ben Hogan won, with Jimmy Demaret and Mike Turnesa both 3 strokes back.

Maybe more significant than the fact that the event raised $20,000 was that it was the last time Bobby Jones, who finished 19 strokes behind Hogan, played in a U.S. Open–type event. (He continued to compete in the Masters, though, until forced to stop playing because of illness in 1948.) Just a few days earlier, Jones had received a commission of captain in the Army Air Corps, and he would see battlefield action in Europe before the war ended.

Instead of confirming his career's demise, the World War II years gave Hagen the opportunity to remain in the spotlight, albeit a dimmer one, by helping the war effort. World War I had interrupted his career right when he was ready to make some early strides, which ended up having an impact on his overall career tournament victory total. It was fitting then that the second world conflict allowed him bonus time to stay in front of fans.

As during World War I, Hagen helped organize and participated in exhibition matches to benefit the Red Cross. Though far removed from his last tournament win, the Haig was still a famous sports figure, especially to that generation of folks at home who were available to come out and watch the exhibitions and support the Red Cross, so once again he played a significant role in raising a large sum of money.

Also helping to boost the fund-raising events were the celebrities who participated. The Bing Crosby Clambake had been started in California in 1937 by the famous crooner, which formalized a bit the golf outings of movie stars and the top players. Many of the stars knew Hagen and were happy to accept his invitations to play for a good cause.

Sports stars participated in fund-raising golf exhibitions too, and again Hagen helped to bring in the biggest names. In 1941 in Michigan, Hagen and a player who billed himself as "Mysterious Montague" took on a dynamic baseball duo, Ty Cobb and Babe Ruth. On a sweltering day the older Cobb and the overweight Ruth labored around the course, and Hagen and his teammate won easily. More important, a large paying crowd turned out and the match helped the coffers of the USO and American Red Cross.

Ruth and Cobb also played exhibition matches against each other, three at three different courses in 1941 for a British war-relief fund drive. Cobb, not the most charitable of people, at first turned down Ruth's request that he participate. Then Ruth sent him a telegram that read, "If you want to come here and get your brains knocked out, come ahead." Cobb showed up and won two of the three matches.

One of the more unusual odd-couple fund-raising partnerships that the war provided was Bobby Jones and Bob Hope, who played at the Ridgewood Country Club in New Jersey in June 1942. Ironically, Hope was more serious than Jones. Bobby was playing for fun and a good cause; Hope was funny except when trying to post a good score. This match was played a few days after Hope and reigning U.S. Open champion Craig Wood (thanks to his course-record 63) had defeated Corporal Vic Ghezzi (former PGA champion) and Babe Ruth, despite the latter's impressive 77, at the Forest Hill Field Club, also in New Jersey.

"With more than 2,000 spectators roaming pell-mell over the course, it was not surprising that someone was hit," reported the *New York Times*. "Ruth's tee shot clipped a man on the fourth and Wood's drive caught a woman on the third. Both went home nursing goose-eggs."

Fred Corcoran of the PGA Tour announced that same month the creation of the Walter Hagen Golf Award, which would be "open to anyone whose contribution to the game is deemed noteworthy." It was to be presented for the first time in December, on the Haig's fiftieth birthday.

However, this and most other sports awards were set aside because of the intensifying war, and it would be almost twenty years before Sir Walter could truly call an award his own. An honor that was offered and accepted was being part of the first class of the Golf Hall of Fame in 1944, along with Bobby Jones, Francis Ouimet, and Gene Sarazen.

Even with the war, interest in Hagen back in Great Britain remained high. Later in 1942, Corcoran went to England as a Red Cross volunteer. Hagen suggested he stay at the Savoy and drop Hagen's name to the hotel manager. This Corcoran did at the front desk, and the manager, Karl Hefflin, came out to greet Corcoran with a puzzled look.

But seeing Corcoran and the introduction, Hefflin laughed. "The bellboy must have misunderstood you," the manager said. "He thought you said you were Walter Hagen. We've had three bombing raids here in the past month, and as I was coming down to meet you I thought, 'How can I take these air raids and Walter Hagen too?'" Hearing that a good friend of Sir Walter's was in the hotel, the staff gathered to get details from Corcoran on how their old pal (and generous tipper) was doing.

Hagen and the PGA also had the idea of continuing the Ryder Cup Matches as exhibitions to help the war effort. This proved a popular concept, especially in Hagen's adopted home state of Michigan, and another important consequence is that the Matches kept the Ryder Cup alive during much of the decade when the United States and Great Britain couldn't officially go at it.

The PGA of America arranged that there would be an "official" Ryder Cup team and then challenge teams. Hagen once again was the Ryder Cup captain, and the first Match was at the Oakland Hills Country Club in 1940. He put on the course the same team he had chosen the year before.

Ironically, the challenge team was captained by Gene Sarazen. Why not help the war effort and get revenge at the same time? Among the Squire's selections were Ben Hogan, Jimmy Demaret, and Craig Wood. They were not enough: The forces led by Sir Walter won 7–5.

The best of these Ryder Cup challenge matches took place in August 1941, at the Detroit Golf Club. Hagen brought back the same team. Facing him this time, though, was his old nemesis Bobby Jones, who had championed exhibition golf as both a distraction from the war and as a good way to help underwrite the war effort.

Jones was thirty-nine and had been retired for eleven years, yet he was still a formidable player. In one of the singles matches he beat Henry Picard 2 and 1, and overall his team of challengers won, 8½ to 6½. Bad news for the Haig, but the best news was that just this one event raised $25,000.

The time had finally arrived for Hagen to step down as Ryder Cup captain. With American involvement in the war expanding during 1942, it was clear that the global conflict would not end in the near future and the resumption of the official Ryder Cup Matches was far off, if they ever resumed at all. Hagen turned over the event he had cofounded to the next generation.

There would be two more Matches during the war. Craig Wood was appointed captain, and in 1942 his team included Demaret, Ed Dudley, Ghezzi, Hogan, Lloyd Mangrum, McSpaden, Nelson, Horton Smith, and a newly welcomed Sarazen. Hagen apparently wasn't fully ready to exit, because he put together the challenge team. They went head-to-head at Oakland Hills that July, and the official U.S. team won 10–5.

The Haig was back with another challenge team in 1943, when the unofficial Match was held at the Plum Hollow Country Club in Detroit. By this time the player ranks were getting quite depleted because of military service, especially for the challenge team that had to make do with who was left over after Wood filled out his Ryder roster. Among the stars, Snead, Demaret, and Lawson Little were in the navy (the latter was allowed to play in the event, and beat Sarazen 6 and 4), and Hogan and Mangrum were in the army (the latter would be wounded twice in the Battle of the Bulge).

Hagen's team was ahead by one after the first day of foursomes, but the "official" team came back in the singles. His very last appearance in a Ryder Cup event, official or otherwise, ended with an 8½-to-3½ defeat for his squad, even though the captain's friend Bing Crosby had shown up to cheer on the challengers.

After this the Ryder-like Matches were dropped due to not enough players being available and war rationing cutting down on travel. In all of 1943, the PGA Tour consisted of three tournaments with a combined purse of $17,000 in war bonds.

There were still some exhibition matches, and opportunities for plenty of fun interspersed with the fund-raising. The war did not prevent Hagen and his old friend Edward from getting together. He was no longer the Prince of Wales, but the Duke of Windsor and married to Wallis Simpson. The Duke was serving as governor-general of the Bahamas, and his American friend was welcome to visit anytime.

Naturally, Hagen made sure to visit during the winters. He and Edward played golf for fun and sometimes organized fund-raising matches with special guests. The most lucrative one, not surprisingly, was one that Fred Corcoran helped organize, featuring the four American players to whom Edward had presented the claret jug—Hagen, Jones, Sarazen, and Tommy Armour.

The Red Cross benefit was played on Nassau. It was Armour and Jones against Hagen and Sarazen. According to the Haig, he and his old friend "took a beating," but the result had to have been far secondary to the show.

It was in this setting that one of Hagen's most famous sayings was heard, or reported. Edward was intrigued by Hagen's ability to be relaxed and friendly during competition, and to treat everyone from servants up to the Duke as equals. When Edward asked Fred Corcoran about this, he replied that the philosophy Hagen routinely expressed was, "Never hurry and don't worry. You're here for a short visit. So don't forget to stop and smell the flowers along the way." (The saying was used as the epigram for the final chapter in Hagen's autobiography.)

Edward was rather impressed with this. According to Corcoran, the Duke exclaimed, "Oh, I say, this is just priceless! Priceless! Let me write that down." He scribbled the philosophy on the back of an envelope, then jumped up.

"I've simply got to read this to the Duchess," Edward said. "I'll be right back." He told his wife, and in turn the philosophy was spread about to acquaintances.

•   •   •

During the final year of World War II there wasn't anything left for Hagen to do in golf. He was fifty-two in 1945 and fading in the public's memory. When reporters wrote about him at all, the emphasis was on remembering his carousing, drinking, and storytelling, and this served to diminish his real on-course accomplishments.

There was no longer much need for exhibition matches as the war wound down, in addition to there being few players to participate in them. Increasingly, Hagen remained in Michigan, going well north of Detroit for hunting and fishing and playing only the occasional round of golf.

A man who became friends with Hagen during the latter part of the war is Chuck Kocsis, regarded as the finest amateur golfer Michigan ever produced, and he had continued to play on almost a daily basis at eighty-eight when interviewed. He welcomed Hagen when he joined the Red Run Country Club just outside Detroit, and they arranged some local fund-raising matches.

According to Kocsis, the war years caused cutbacks in everything except Sir Walter's enjoyment of the nightlife.

One night, the billiards champ Willie Mosconi was in Detroit for a big pool-table matchup. Kocsis had met him before and went to see him win, which Mosconi did. The stick man and golfer hit a couple of bars to celebrate, then went to visit another partier in a hotel. At 2:30 in the morning they were in an elevator on the way down. When it stopped, Walter Hagen got in.

"He's just getting back from some outing," Kocsis recalled. "Walter and Willie get on right away, and of course Walter challenges him to a game of pool. Willie thought this was very funny, so off we went."

Hagen led them to the Detroit Athletic Club, but the game room was closed. So they had a couple of more drinks, went back, still closed, then went and found an all-night place and had breakfast. When they tried the club again at 6:30 a.m., it was open.

"The doorman knew Walter, of course, but didn't know Willie and me and didn't want to let us in," Kocsis remembered. "We finally were let in, went to the pool table, but by then Walter and Willie were too busy being tired and laughing to play pool. Too bad, I wanted to see it. You'd think Willie would give him a pasting, but with Walter you never knew what would happen."

In 1945, golf fans were focused on Byron Nelson. Though the ranks of players were depleted, it was still an amazing achievement to win eleven tournaments in a row, including the PGA Championship and Canadian Open, and a total of eighteen during the year.

A hemophiliac, Nelson had tried to enlist in the military twice and had been rejected by doctors both times. The same had happened to Jug McSpaden, in his case because of severe allergies and sinusitis. "So there we were, looking as healthy as could be, but not in uniform like the rest of the boys," Nelson recalled. "It was an uncomfortable feeling, believe me."

He and McSpaden did what they could, though, crisscrossing the country in 1943 and '44 to do a total of 110 exhibitions (including nineteen days in a row with Bing Crosby and Bob Hope) to raise money for the USO and Red Cross. During their fund-raising journeys, Nelson and McSpaden became known as the "Gold Dust Twins" because of their ability to defeat almost all of their challengers.

With the war winding down, Nelson's new motivation was that he wanted to buy a ranch, so he went about playing regular tournaments with intense focus in 1945. "Each win meant another cow, another ten acres, a bigger down payment," Nelson said, reflecting on his drive to win.

Lord Byron bought his ranch, 740 acres in Roanoke, Texas, and he retired from the tour.

Hagen followed Nelson's exploits from afar. Clearly, a page of golf history had been turned. Soon the war would officially end and the stars of the present generation would return to the links on both sides of the Atlantic. Hogan and Snead would be the dominant professional players in golf. The spotlight had shifted away.

Sir Walter accepted that his day was indeed, finally, done. He moved between the Detroit Athletic Club and lodges he rented in upstate Michigan, where he intended to fish off the dock in the summer and ice skate in the winter. The greatest career by an American professional golfer was over.

CHAPTER 17

HAGEN'S SELF-IMPOSED EXILE in the remainder of the 1940s and through the 1950s could be called "the lost years" because he faded from public view and then memory.

"There came a time when you turned around looking for Walter Hagen and expecting to find him because it seemed like he had *always* been there," said Paul Runyan, "but he wasn't there anymore. He just quit and walked away, and we sure missed him."

Not that he lived like a hermit. Thanks to investments, the contract with Wilson Sporting Goods, and Junior's supervision, Hagen was comfortable enough financially and could afford to host parties and long visits by old acquaintances. People collected at the Hagen camp in northern Michigan and drank, played a little golf, and reminisced about the glory days. Hagen presided like a wizened pasha, a cigarette in one hand and a drink in the other. Sometimes the party went on tour when Hagen led his companions to favorite lakes and tracts of woods for fishing and hunting.

Awards were offered but usually ignored or gently declined. But one award he was very happy to receive was given to him by the Michigan PGA in 1947. The testimonial read: "He scoffed at royalty, and put all professional sport on a democratic level. Starting as a caddie in Rochester, N.Y., he brushed aside a baseball career, and golf was the winner. Never one for regimentation, he couldn't confine himself to one club. He made the golf links of the world his home course, and laughs were just as important as titles. He drew the attention of the common man to golf, and wrote new pages in the record books of all lands. While folks of every race marveled at his game, they remember him best as a jolly good fellow."

He rarely attended a golf event, though he was routinely invited to them, especially to the U.S. Open and the PGA Championship. As World War II became a memory, the British would have been very happy to welcome Sir Walter again, but he didn't care to make the trip. He began to be viewed as a figure from golf's distant past by the present generation of players and officials.

There were exceptions. Sam Snead was to take a crack at the British Open when it resumed in 1946, at St Andrews. But the day before he was to set off for Scotland and after the last round of the Inverness Four-Ball Tournament, Snead told Fred Corcoran of the PGA of America that he wasn't going. "I'm just not putting well and there's no point in me going over there if I can't get the damn ball in the hole," the Slammer complained.

Snead was the best of the American players making the trip, and if he dropped out, the chances of a Yank winning the Open shrank considerably. Fortunately, Corcoran found a visiting Walter Hagen holding court in the clubhouse and explained the situation.

"Oh, what a shame!" Corcoran reported the Haig exclaiming. "And with his touch he'd putt those greens at St Andrews as if they belonged to him."

Hagen found Snead and brought him into the clubhouse for a lengthy putting lesson on the thin green carpet. After a while, Snead felt his touch coming back. With restored confidence, Snead stuck to his travel plans and won the British Open.

At the Red Run Golf Course, the members declared September 17, 1947, as Walter Hagen Day, which was intended to be an annual golf outing. The Haig was assigned a 2:30 p.m. tee time, and plenty of friends went to Michigan to honor the main attraction, including Gene Sarazen, Billy Burke, and Joe Kirkwood.

The only problem was Hagen didn't show up—until much later, as the sun was setting. "What's all the excitement?" he asked as he entered the clubhouse. The playing-golf part of the day was done, but the party was just beginning.

"Some of Walter Hagen's best friends are a bit worried about the old boy at present," wrote Bob Harlow in a 1950 essay titled "Hagen

Was No Saint," in *Golf World*. "They would like to see him go into training, take off a few pounds, get out and mingle with the golfers of the world, who would enjoy his company. He would be welcomed every place where golfers gather."

If he read this essay—which was unlikely—he didn't heed it. Hagen traveled in his own world and was not very interested in the role of retired sports celebrity who could trade on his long career of achievement. If he felt like showing up, he did; if he didn't, there was an empty seat at the dais.

Another exception was *Sport* magazine's second annual Awards Dinner in the Hotel Astor Ballroom in Manhattan in January 1950. Top sports officials and the best of the best athletes, past and present, were there, among them Jackie Robinson, Sugar Ray Robinson, Ty Cobb, Tris Speaker, Frankie Frisch, Otto Graham, and Willie Hoppe. Hagen sat on the dais between Eddie Shore, the four-time MVP of the National Hockey League, and Frank Hogan, Manhattan's district attorney.

One other exception occurred in October 1950 when Hagen was invited to be one of two guests of honor at the Rochester Club's Stag Night Dinner. Hagen made the trip east because he wanted to meet the other honored guest, Sam Urzetta. The young man had just won the U.S. Amateur Championship in Minneapolis and had, like Hagen, been born on Linden Road in Brighton.

Typically, the dinner almost didn't happen. Hagen received the invitation, decided he wanted to go, then threw it out. Receiving no response, the Rochester Club canceled the dinner. Then, the day before it was to be held, there was a telegram from Hagen that he was on his way. Urzetta was located in Pittsburgh and put on a plane. When Hagen arrived, he said, "I've been known to accept invitations then not show up. This time, I just wanted to be certain I would be here before accepting."

The sport he was most interested in, as he would be for the rest of his life, was baseball. He returned to his first love and became an enthusiastic supporter of the Detroit Tigers. When in the city he attended games, and for the rest of his life rooted for the Tigers to win a championship.

He did show up at the 1951 U.S. Open, and was the honored guest

because it was held at Oakland Hills. The course had been significantly redesigned by Robert Trent Jones to make it more difficult, and
indeed the players were cutting and slashing all over without approaching par.

According to Herbert Warren Wind, "One way or another, as Walter
Hagen remarked regally from his dais in the clubhouse, the boys were
not playing the course, they were letting the course play them." Ben
Hogan repeated as Open champion, but at 7 over par, and declared that
he had "tamed the monster."

Hagen seemed content to be a well-known figure just among the
"locals," the friends he had in Detroit with whom he partied when he
was in town—he stayed at either the Detroit Athletic Club or the Book
Cadillac Hotel—and the folks up in Traverse City with whom he
fished, played cards, casually chatted, and traveled. Though he wasn't
fond of driving, he would if he had to, at a slower-than-the-speed-
limit pace, but was happier when someone else drove. Either way, dating back to his days of almost nonstop touring, the Haig enjoyed
watching the American landscape pass by his window.

One of the more interesting travel adventures involved Joe Kirkwood. This was not an exhibition tour but a trip to pay their respects to
an old friend.

In 1951 Leo Diegel died in California of lung cancer. Kirkwood
read the obituary in the *Philadelphia Inquirer*, which told him that
Diegel would be buried in Detroit the following day. Bidding his wife
good-bye and cabling Hagen, Kirkwood aimed his car northwest.

When he reached the Detroit Athletic Club at 9:00 the next morning "The Haig was just coming in," Kirkwood recalled. "He had been
out all night on a binge and was feeling no pain or shame. I did my best
to bring him around, got him into a cold shower and some breakfast."

Hagen said he'd found out the church where the service for old
Leo would be held and had written it down. Kirkwood found the piece
of paper and drove to the church. The place was packed. Hagen and
Kirkwood had to sit on a bench at the back of the church. As the service went on, Hagen kept slumping over and snoring, and Kirkwood
kept shaking him awake.

Finally, Kirkwood realized that there wasn't one familiar face in the
entire church. Halfway through the service he approached an attendant,

who knew nothing about a Leo Diegel. When Kirkwood reported this, Hagen became fully awake and shouted, with the entire church hearing, "At the wrong funeral? What the hell!"

On their way out they encountered the undertaker, who knew of the right church. They raced to it, but when they arrived the mourners, some of whom were familiar (such as Sarazen), were filing out of the church. Too embarrassed to get out, the duo remained in the car and followed the procession to the cemetery, and they stayed on the fringe during the brief service there.

After everyone had left, Hagen asked, "Kirkie, are you in a hurry?"

Kirkwood said he wasn't, so Hagen hurried back to the car and returned with a six-pack of beer he had stashed in it. He opened three bottles, sat in the dirt, and draped an arm across the casket.

"Leo," Hagen said, "I couldn't leave you this way without wishing you a personal farewell. We've been together many years, been buddies all that time, played a lot of golf, and had a lot of laughs and beers together."

For the next twenty minutes Hagen recalled the tournaments and other times they had spent together, suddenly sober and his memory sharp even though he was draining the beers.

According to Kirkwood, "Suddenly it dawned on me that this was a tremendous attitude to take toward somebody who had passed away. Walter showed every emotion that a man could show. He had humor and kindness, some longing, but never any sadness, and his final comments were that he just wanted to share these beers for the long trip ahead."

"May you and your putter rust in peace," Hagen finished. He stood up, dusted himself off, put his arm around his other friend's shoulder, and said, "Come on, Kirkie, that's it."

An item in a newspaper in 1954 simply reported, "Hagen Hunts, Fishes: Walter Hagen, many times golf champ, lives on Long Lake, Michigan. Mostly he is hunting and fishing, but spends some afternoons driving golf balls into the lake."

There was still the occasional offer to make some "healthy green stuff" from his lingering celebrity, especially with the new hungry maw of television wanting to display sports greats. Boxers such as Jack Dempsey and Joe Louis and baseball players such as Joe DiMaggio made appearances on variety shows, as did Sam Snead and Gene Sarazen. Hagen received an invitation to appear on Ed Sullivan's *Toast of the Town* but declined because he "didn't have the courage to drive those Ping-Pong balls into the faces of theater audiences."

Some years later, Hagen was also invited to appear on *Shell's Wonderful World of Golf,* a program that pitted two competitors on the course in a relaxed and intimate round, and a cohost was Gene Sarazen, who after retiring had a solid career as a TV commentator. The Haig turned down the invitation. According to Sarazen, "I think he was worried he'd look too fat on TV."

Hagen's gallivanting bachelor days were long over, but he didn't lack for female companionship. After settling in Traverse City, he hired Doris Brandes as his housekeeper. Before long she was more than that, and would be his devoted companion for the rest of his life.

However, during these years the Hagen family had to pretend that Doris didn't exist. Margaret Johnson Hagen was still alive, and Walter Jr. was not at all happy about his father living with another woman, and one who had been a housekeeper at that. "Junior was a little prejudiced against Doris," says Joe Peck, an upstate friend of Hagen's.

Doris shared Hagen's enjoyment of car trips, didn't mind driving, and sat patiently when Hagen drove at a snail's pace. They went back and forth to Detroit for baseball games and to visit the Haig's friends there and to the few golf events that he agreed to attend, and at least one trip a year to New York for shopping. In the winter they drove to Florida and returned to Traverse City in the spring.

Because of the traveling, Walter and Doris became good friends of Shelby and Carlton Plyler, who lived just south of Cadillac, Michigan. Always a dog lover, Hagen had purchased a Brittany spaniel from them, and initially, when he and Doris went on the road, he would bring the dog back to stay with the Plylers. However, over time the visits to their home became purely social and frequent.

"You would not know from being with him that Walter was one of the greatest in his profession," remembers Shelby Plyler. "He didn't talk much about golf, and he didn't talk about his accomplishments. He was a good listener and wanted to know more about you and your life."

The Plylers also were the recipient of Hagen's generosity. They had three daughters, and the young family had no money to spare. When he and Doris returned from a trip, Hagen paid for the care of the dog and always put extra money in, for eyeglasses and visits to the dentist.

"He'd call too, just to see if we needed anything," Shelby says. "He was a real gentleman. My girls enjoyed when he visited, and then when he left he would always hug each one, then his parting words were, 'God bless you.'"

His favorite trip was to go visit Walter Jr. and Helen, which he had to make alone, not wanting to cause a fight by bringing Doris. His pride and joy was Walter III, who had been born in 1948. Hagen was wild about the boy, and like Walter Sr. and Jr., "Haigie," as he would be called, was the only male of his generation in the family and represented the continuation of the family name.

"For Christmas and birthdays and any other special event, Walter couldn't resist buying Haigie all sorts of presents," Shelby recalls. "He and Doris would spend an entire day just wrapping them up."

Beginning in the late 1940s, one of the Haig's closest friends was Joe Peck, who when interviewed at age eighty-eight still lived in the Traverse City area. Never having forgotten the 1934 accident, Hagen asked Peck to drive whenever they were going on a fishing trip or just into town.

"He always had me drive him wherever he wanted to go in the area," recalls Peck. "I was kind of his right-hand man. Looking back at it now, it's something that I don't think I ever saw him swing a golf club on a course. Walter just took it easy and drank his beer the way he liked, and that was about it."

So much for being "Sir Walter": His idea of a good time was to watch baseball on TV or at a local tavern, where he would spend as much time engaged in conversation with the person on the stool next to him—often at the Little Bohemia Bar—as on the game. To many of the folks in Traverse City, he was just a friendly older man who liked his beer (a doctor had persuaded him to give up hard liquor) and casual conversation.

"He loved to talk to people," Peck remembers. "Walter used to hit the local taverns, and he always liked to have a conversation with just about everybody. We thought he was a lot of fun. He never acted like a star of any kind, but of course when we'd go in someplace and he was recognized, suddenly there was a big crowd around him. But he never cared whether people knew who he was or not."

Given that he was a fine raconteur and still the most successful professional golfer in history, it was no surprise that he was approached to write his autobiography in the early 1950s. Apparently not known, or overlooked, was that the only writing Hagen enjoyed was signing his name on a bar tab and endorsing a check.

Months and then a couple of years passed, and still no story of his life for public consumption. He was too busy partying with friends and journalists who made the pilgrimage north, hunting and fishing, watching baseball, traveling with Doris, and growing old.

In December 1952 he turned sixty. The birthday wasn't observed with any fanfare. Because of the Haig's retreat from the spotlight, quite possibly some former acquaintances who knew were surprised that he was still alive, considering the normal toll of such a lifestyle.

At sixty Hagen was indeed much changed from the debonair and dynamic man who had ruled the fairways of the world for a quarter century. His hair was still slicked back but graying and covering only two-thirds of his head. The keen eyesight was a memory; now he wore black, horn-rimmed glasses. His jowls and neck had an extra layer of flesh. He still dressed with care, but the sizes of his clothes were larger and there were fewer new items. Most prominent was his nose, a red and bulbous fixture that inevitably became the focus of his face.

Sports reporters came and went—all were fun for a party, but none seemed right to help write an autobiography. Hagen claims that he asked Ernest Hemingway (the two supposedly had once gotten drunk together in Paris), but the writer, who had recently won the Nobel Prize for literature, responded that while the story would be fascinating, he knew absolutely nothing about golf and wasn't interested in learning.

The next request went to the biographer Gene Fowler, who had become friends with Hagen during stays in Hollywood. Fowler agreed to do it but wanted much more money than Hagen was willing to pay.

Then Hagen called Charles Price. In 1953 Price was twenty-seven and had written articles on golf and golfers for the *Saturday Evening Post* and other magazines, and his first job out of college had been helping Bob Harlow in the early days of *Golf World*. Hagen rarely read anything other than a racetrack tip sheet and *Outdoor Life* (and then only the photo captions), but Walter Jr., who was now managing his father's various business interests, had read and liked the pieces. That was good enough, and Price was invited to visit Sir Walter.

"The Haig spent years trying to write his autobiography with the help of newspapermen who thought they had known him," wrote Price in his memoir *Golfer-at-Large*. "All the newspapermen had long since left the scene with near-fatal hangovers."

The two first met at a house Hagen was renting for a short time in Lake Mohawk, New Jersey. Price noted how the once-famous golfer had gained ten inches around the waistline and that in appearance he was much older than the Hagen in photos from his heyday. And he no longer was a fashion trendsetter.

"In his day, the Haig had been considered the height of fashion," Price recalled. "But now his dress had become a hodgepodge of golf-shop clichés and remnants from Savile Row that had gone out with Edward VIII. He was wearing alligator loafers with tassles, orange gym socks, cuffed flannel slacks that left him with a lapful of pleats, a silk shirt with French cuffs to which were attached links the size of champagne corks, and a florid ascot around his neck that the Duke of Windsor might have hesitated wearing on the Riviera, let alone New Jersey."

Hagen had a local-brand beer in one hand and of course a cigarette in the other. "To this day it is impossible for me to visualize the Haig without a Chesterfield between his fingers," Price wrote. "In the fifteen years I was to get to know him, I never saw him without one, not even after his larynx had been removed because of them."

Hagen took a liking to the younger man, and they set to work on the autobiography. First they worked in New Jersey, then as summer neared Price accompanied Hagen to the house he had just purchased on Lake Cadillac, outside Traverse City. "Work" for the book's subject meant telling stories for a while, then going fishing or for a drive (with Price at the wheel), telling a few more stories, then it was cocktail hour, which may or may not be followed by dinner, which might be at a local restaurant or much later at home. After six months, they were only up to Walter in grade school.

With other writing offers and out of concern for his liver, Price dropped out of the project. The parting was amicable, and the two would remain friends until Hagen's death. The problem, though, was that by this time Hagen had accepted and spent the advance from his publisher, Simon & Schuster; the book was way overdue; there were threats of litigation; and there was hardly anything down on paper.

Hagen was put in touch with a local writer, Margaret Seaton Heck. Finally, there was progress on the project. As Price was to wryly remark, "Typically, for a man who might spend three-quarters of an hour shaving, the Haig spent more than six years of his retirement writing his autobiography, five of which were devoted to searching for just the right title. A dozen men, hard-bitten professional writers all, tried to help him before throwing up their hands in despair. Then a woman got him to spill the beans in three months."

In reality, it was well over two years from the time Hagen and Heck began working together to when the book, with the straightforward title of *The Walter Hagen Story,* was published in 1956. The book's dedication was: "For my son, Walter Hagen Jr.; my grandson, Walter Hagen III; and for my golf pals all over the world."

In her introduction, Heck (who knew very little about golf) wrote about spending time with Hagen: "A wonderful and hospitable host, the Haig likes to dine shortly before midnight on a thick steak and chef salad. And one sunny afternoon in the summer he cut a pretty fancy Charleston on the boardwalk near his boat dock. Football and baseball on television broke up many an afternoon of our collaboration. He is greatly interested in the promising young golfers coming up and always ready to give of his experience and skill to help them along."

Getting the book published and in stores was a long and frustrating path for Heck and the editor at Simon & Schuster, Peter Schwed. The contract was sent to Hagen at the Park Lane Hotel in Manhattan on May 3, 1954, with publication expected in a year, if not sooner. Yet in August Heck wrote to Schwed, "Hagen Jr. and his family will be in Traverse City the entire month of August, so I doubt we'll get much work done during that time. I am getting a bit anxious for there is still much to be gone over with Walter, but 'relaxation' ranks high on his order of business."

This was only the beginning:

- On September 28, Heck writes to Schwed, "I have relayed the contents of your recent letter to Walter and he is relaxed enough to go hunting for a few days."

- On November 2, she writes, "When we talked on the telephone a week ago last Friday, I told you the twenty-seven chapters would be forwarded to you the following Wednesday. However, I reckoned without Walter. He took off that same Friday with three of the chapters and is still up north."

- Two months later, Schwed writes to Hagen: "My calendar says it is January 10 and here I am without a complete manuscript," which he points out means a spring release is pretty much impossible.

- On June 1, 1955, the frustrated editor writes Hagen, "I have held off as long as I can waiting for those last chapters, but we are now having our Sales Conference for fall books. . . . I have removed your book from the fall schedule, and have rescheduled it for the spring of 1956."

- Then on August 24, to Heck: "Your letter of July 12 promised 'no matter what' that I would have the last three chapters by August 1. Here we are three weeks later than that absolute deadline and still no word. What's the matter? A couple of weeks more and we won't be able to make the Spring '56 date either."

And on it went. The book—pared down from the manuscript's original 210,000 words to 135,000—did barely get published before spring ended in 1956. The reviews were generally good, but after all the efforts and aggravations, the book was not a success. By this point, Hagen was not only many years past the last tournament he had played in but twenty-seven years beyond his last win in a major. An entire generation of golf stars had come and gone in the interim. It didn't help either that the book was subjected to some criticism for being full of inaccuracies, and that Hagen wasn't about to interrupt his comfortable lifestyle to go on the road to promote it.

He was willing to host a party for members of the press and radio and television commentators at the Detroit Athletic Club. After an hour of drinking the guests were feeling quite friendly, and Hagen stood on top of a table and told the group about his book. The audience cheered, then it was time for more drinks and food. No doubt the next day at least half the guests had forgotten what the party had been about.

A last, unpleasant chapter about the autobiography is that the publisher ended up suing Hagen over unpaid monies. The Haig and a couple of business cronies had devised a scheme to sell thousands of copies of the book directly to pro shops and targeted consumer groups. Simon & Schuster advanced the copies to Hagen, and by September 1957, when almost $18,000 due the publisher hadn't been paid, the lawsuit was filed in Detroit against the Hagenwise Company, a combination of Hagen and his main associate, Bob Wise, who lived in Miami. The dispute was eventually settled out of court.

After this, Hagen shrugged off the book's fate and continued to do what he wanted to do—dote on Walter III, watch baseball, be with Doris and take side trips together, occasionally pay attention to golf, hunt and fish, and be content with being a local celebrity in the Traverse City area, where nothing was pretentious or forced.

"You almost had to drag him away from his hunting and fishing to be so much as a spectator," remembered Charles Price. "In retirement, he lived in obscure villages where most of the neighbors, if they had heard of him at all, regarded him vaguely as some sort of athlete from a couple of wars ago. Here the Haig held court for those who took the trouble to find him."

When friends came to town, they were welcome to mingle with the local pals already in attendance. "Anyone who has ever met him knows him for life," Heck wrote after the "autobiography" was completed. "When these friends hit Detroit or Traverse City the first telephone they ring is Walter's. At noon he may get a call from a retired heavyweight champion and an hour later from a Chicago policeman he met years earlier who wants to go hunting or fishing with him."

As the 1950s ended, Hagen was occasionally sought out. While he was at his house on the lake, a woman arrived who asked if he would help her with her swing because she really wanted to win a local tournament she had entered. Hagen obligingly brought out a bucket of balls and had her hit them into the lake, then suggested some adjustments to her swing.

She returned a few days later, announcing that she had indeed won the tourney and in appreciation had baked Hagen a fresh loaf of bread. "I remembered the days in Florida when I received $200 for thirty minutes' golf instruction and decided I was pretty lucky," Hagen recalled, "for after forty years my instructions were still bringing in the dough!"

Old friend and traveling companion Horton Smith wrote a tribute to Sir Walter that was published in the *Detroit News* in 1954, and asked the Haig and Bobby Jones to write forewords to his book, *The Secret of Holing Putts.* Both complied. Hagen's contribution (whoever it was actually written by) was of course complimentary and gracious, remembering how he had first met Smith as a fifteen-year-old in Joplin, Missouri, and one of the sport's greatest putters concluded with, "If anyone can tell us a secret, it is Horton. As far as I am concerned, I would have appreciated it if he had told a little more a lot earlier."

Concerning Hagen's being missed by the public, sportswriter Lester Rice commented, "The Haig was great for reasons other than his ability to boil three shots into two. He had that certain something only the magnificently great possess. It was something that Ruth had and Dempsey. It was the distinctive quality known as personality. . . . Every year about this time when 'greatness' is bandied about with careless disregard of its true meaning and this writer is sometimes asked to name the greatest golfer ever to come within his focus, he always makes the same reply—Hagen."

And in a 1954 issue of *Esquire,* Jack O'Brian declared about golf, "The best that today's bunch can offer in the way of gallery-conning color, at a time when the tournament schedule begs for color, is Demaret's pink hats, yellowish green slacks, and lavender shoes. Walter Hagen could put more color than that into merely handing a club back to his caddie. Like the day he hit a $3,000 putt and, while the ball was still rolling, regally tossed the putter back to his caddie. Or the day he arrived at a golf course wearing last night's tuxedo and this morning's hangover—and shot a 67. Hagen's kind of color played a part in the winning of championships."

The Hagen-like color that pro golf needed was on its way, from a man who would become a big admirer and friend of the Haig, and like him would transform international golf.

The success of Arnold Palmer was certainly a major factor in the renewal of interest in Hagen as the 1960s got under way. Many veteran commentators compared the two champions because of their slashing and aggressive style of play, success in majors, adulation from the gallery, and lingering country-boy charm (Palmer was from western Pennsylvania). With these comparisons highlighted in print and on TV, which was expanding its coverage of golf thanks to the white-hot attraction of Palmer, longtime golf fans remembered Hagen and younger golf fans wanted to know more about him.

According to Herbert Warren Wind, Palmer was like Hagen in that he "had to count on his natural athletic talent to carry him a long ways, for his technique lacked the refinement of a great champion's." In addition, when Palmer "came tearing down the final holes—'charging' became the word favored by his fans—he made golf seem as exciting as any contact sport, and many sports buffs who had hitherto scoffed at the game became ardent converts after watching Palmer in action on television."

"What gave Arnold Palmer a bigger publicity splash than his tournament performance might warrant were his superior, decent manners," wrote Charles Price, comparing the emerging King to Hagen.

The Haig might not bother much with golf events—for example, he didn't show in June 1960 when the Country Club of Rochester had a special day to dedicate three new holes—but he bothered to keep an eye on Arnie and liked his style.

Right after Palmer won his second straight British Open (becoming the first American since Hagen, thirty-three years earlier, to successfully defend), at Troon in 1962, Hagen called him from Michigan, reaching the champion in the clubhouse. "That was certainly one of my greatest thrills," Palmer says about Hagen reaching out to him from 4,500 miles away.

According to Palmer, "That started a friendly relationship between the two of us." They exchanged phone calls over the years, and Palmer looked for opportunities to refer to Hagen and his accomplishments.

With the Hagen name somewhat prominent again, the Golf Writers Association of America had a fine idea: Let's initiate an award and name it after Sir Walter. That's what the group did, creating the Walter Hagen Award in 1961, to be given to someone who had made important contributions to international golf. Sensibly, the first recipient was the Haig. The announcement was made simultaneously in Rochester and in London.

The award presentation took place in July 1961 at the Olympia Fields Country Club in Illinois. This was one invitation Hagen couldn't ignore, an event he couldn't skip. He was actually glad to attend because in addition to the honor, the event represented a return to glory—at this course he had won the PGA Championship in 1925 and the Western Open two years later. Palmer, Gary Player, and most of the top pros, along with old pals Johnny Farrell and Gene Sarazen, were there because the course that year was hosting the 43rd PGA Championship.

It was an especially poignant moment when the award was next presented, on April 3, 1963, in Augusta, Georgia. According to one newspaper account, "Robert T. (Bobby) Jones Jr. received the 1962 Walter Hagen Award yesterday during a nostalgic interlude in the meeting of the Golf Writers Association of America."

The organization had come to Georgia to have the presentation coincide with the Masters (thus the time discrepancy) and because it was very difficult for Jones, though ten years younger than Hagen, to travel. He had last been able to play golf in 1948 because of syringomyelia, a degenerative disease of the spinal cord. He was now completely confined to a wheelchair. Those in attendance stood to applaud the great champion as he was wheeled into the room. Ever gracious, Jones said he was especially pleased to receive this particular award because of his friendship with Hagen and that "nobody is excited more over international golf than Walter."

Hagen had turned sixty-nine in December 1961, and his quip, "That's the easiest 69 I ever made," went out on the news wires around the globe. A year later, Oscar Fraley in a tribute titled "The Babe Ruth of Golf" in the *Albany Times–Union* wrote, "The time has finally arrived when 'The Haig' can no longer break 70."

There were other media salutes for this milestone birthday (a surprising one, considering his lifestyle), most of them using the occasion to repeat his most famous saying: "Don't hurry and don't worry. You're only here on a short visit, so be sure to smell the flowers."

In January 1962 the Metropolitan Golf Writers Association bestowed its Golden Tee Award on Hagen, and he traveled to New York City to accept it. He shared the stage with Paul Runyan, who was also honored. Newspaper accounts pointed out that because of a heart condition and the advice of doctors, Hagen "no longer swings a club" and that "his once coal-black hair is thinning at the temples and his waistline expanding proportionately."

He surprised people by attending the PGA Championship in 1961 in Los Angeles and the one in '62 in Florida. Some, though, weren't surprised because in addition to having won five PGA Championships, and despite a couple of disputes, Hagen had always remained loyal to and supportive of the PGA of America, just as the organization he had helped to establish stuck with him as Ryder Cup captain. In fact, soon after his death it was discovered that Hagen had been paying dues for fifty-three years, making him the PGA's longest dues-paying member. And in 1963, Sir Walter was on hand to honor Francis Ouimet when the U.S. Open was held at Brookline, the fiftieth anniversary of the amateur's watershed triumph.

The *Rochester Democrat and Chronicle* had a rather rude though truthful headline to its salute: "Recall Hagen? He's 70 Now."

But he hadn't been forgotten by the golf greats, nor by the emerging ones. About this time, Jack Nicklaus, who remains the only person to exceed Hagen's eleven professional majors, was introduced to Hagen at Oakland Hills in Michigan. "I never saw Walter strike a shot that day, nor did I have to," Nicklaus recalls. "As when any boy or young man meets one of golfing's greats, it was a special occasion."

Nicklaus, like many of the best players who ever strode a fairway, is knowledgeable and has great reverence for the game. What made the occasion of first meeting Hagen special—and even more so as the years passed—was noting some similarities. "Here is a man whose prime came well before I was born [in 1940], yet there are many parallels between his career and mine," Nicklaus says. "He turned professional at age twenty-one; he is closely associated with all the major

championships, not just the PGA Championship; and he even established his own equipment manufacturing company."

The Golden Bear also could have included an excellent record as a
Ryder Cup player, an ability to make his best shots when a tourney was
on the line, and being a tough but gracious competitor. Fittingly, The
Memorial, the annual PGA Tour tournament founded by Nicklaus in
Ohio, honored Hagen in 1977, and the course contains numerous
plaques dedicated to his accomplishments and famous sayings.

Getting old didn't seem to bother Hagen all that much. Life was
good—not perfect, but good. He had Doris to dote on him, was comfortable financially, enjoyed where he lived and the people there, with
just one exception he had a good relationship with his son, he could
still have beer or wine with dinner every night, and there were plenty
of fish in the lake. It was a good, quiet life.

That life was about to be shattered.

According to news accounts and Joe Peck, Walter Jr. and Helen
were not home when Walter III was shot, though the entire family was
with the fifteen-year-old when he died.

Haigie brought a friend home from school, and wanted to show
off the Luger pistol that his father kept under his pillow. The boys
went up to the bedroom and Walter III picked up the phone to ask his
father's permission. Before Walter Jr. could be found, though, the
friend took the gun out from under the pillow and, playing around,
held it up against Walter III's forehead. "Hey, Haigie, bang!" the boy
said and pulled the trigger.

The bullet entered and lodged in the teenager's brain. He was
rushed to Pontiac Hospital. "I was sitting across the table from Walter
when the phone rang," remembers Peck. "He picked it up, listened,
and I never saw such shock and grief and pain in a man's face. He was
never the same after that. He had six more years, and they were hard
ones."

The boy lingered in a coma for a couple of days before being pronounced dead. Because of the name, there was national media attention. Comments from Walter Sr. were sought, but he was so devastated
that he couldn't speak, and the same was true for Helen Hagen. Walter

Jr. was the family spokesman, providing the media with some details, clearly stunned and perhaps not yet fully accepting that his only child was dead.

"Original 'Haig' Shaken By Death of Grandson" was a headline in the May 3, 1963, issue of the *Rochester Democrat and Chronicle*, which made reference to the former Margaret Johnson only as "a local girl." Walter Jr. stated that his father was "taking it even harder," and then described how the accident happened, concluding, "Somehow the gun went off and the bullet went right through my boy's brain."

"When Doris called and wanted us to go up to Traverse City to be with them, we of course went," says Shelby Plyler. "We got to Walter, and he was just beside himself. Whatever else had happened in his life, this was the absolute worst, and it was heartbreaking."

"He didn't deserve what happened to him," Peck says. "First with his grandson—not only did he love that boy so much, but when he died that meant the end of the Hagen line. And then there was the cancer, but he never complained. Right to the end he was a tough, courageous man."

CHAPTER 18

IN THE AGONIZING AFTERMATH of Haigie's death, public appearances were out of the question, and Hagen had no interest in honors. Doris, ever loyal, was by his side and they still took some car trips, but the life-loving Sir Walter had seemingly faded away. He felt obligated to attend the U.S. Open at Congressional in 1964 outside Washington, D.C., because the USGA asked him to help commemorate the fiftieth anniversary of his first Open win, but he spent the entire week closeted in his hotel room.

Not long after the '64 Open, Hagen felt symptoms that went beyond the usual heavy smoker's irritation, coughing, and shortness of breath. However, it wasn't until the following spring, when the pain in his throat became unbearable, that he underwent tests. They confirmed that Hagen had cancer of the larynx. The forty-five-plus years of smoking and drinking had, at last, caught up with him at seventy-two.

Probably only having the "constitution of a rhinoceros" had allowed him by 1965 to outlive most of his golf peers. Diegel was gone, so was Harlow. Jones was gravely ill, Jim Barnes was in declining health and would die the next year, and soon it would be Tommy Armour's turn. Jock Hutchison, Tommy Kerrigan, and most of his other contemporaries were all gone.

Only surgery gave Hagen a shot at survival. He and Walter Jr. headed east, to New York City. (Before leaving, Hagen had given an interview to a local columnist in which he wryly referred to the impending surgery as "cutting my throat.") There they met Charles

Price. Wisely, Junior had requested that the writer help get his father to St. Vincent's.

Price recalled: "Getting him into the hospital was no easy chore. We must've gone to ten bars on the way to St. Vincent's. He was fairly loaded by the time we got him inside, but I'll be damned if he didn't make a pass at a nurse on the way."

More tests were conducted during the next few days. At one point, Hagen's breathing became so labored that a tracheotomy had to be performed. An operation was scheduled to remove his larynx. This was done on July 27, 1965.

Given his age and physical condition, it was iffy that Hagen would survive the surgery. The *New York Times* had done a quickie interview before the operation, and Hagen commented, "I guess I've seen and done everything," which certainly sounded like a deathbed summation.

Other newspapers around the country published tributes and reminiscences about the Haig, many of them highlighting the challenge match with Bobby Jones in 1926. Coincidentally, at the same time there was a lot of press leading up to the National Challenge Match, which was to be held in Washington, D.C., in a few days and featured Arnold Palmer, Jack Nicklaus, and Gary Player.

Price, living in New York then, was at the hospital day and night. "I had to have a perfect stranger forcibly removed because he had ghoulishly persisted in taking what he thought was this final opportunity to shake the master's hand," he reported.

But Hagen did survive, and he vowed to beat the cancer. Once more in his life he faced a difficult opponent.

"After the operation he had virtually no voice, but you still couldn't shut him up," Price reported. "He'd just get mad when you couldn't understand him."

In August, Junior brought his father back to Traverse City. Over the next few months, Hagen's strength returned and, with Doris hovering over him, he had a slightly more healthy lifestyle, though he just couldn't stop smoking. He fished and watched baseball and focused on overcoming his opponent.

Longtime Detroit sportswriter and columnist Joe Falls was a rookie at the *Detroit Free Press* in the fall of 1965, and he needed an assignment to impress his editor. A colleague suggested finding out if Walter Hagen was still alive, and Falls got his name from information.

Hagen picked up the phone, but couldn't speak. Falls heard a wheezing sound. Finally, Doris got on the phone, mentioned the cancer, and asked what he wanted.

"I was stunned, I didn't know what to say," remembers Falls. "I didn't know about the cancer. I mumbled something about coming up to visit Hagen and writing about him."

"That would be lovely," Doris replied.

Falls drove up the next day, after fortifying himself with past clips from the Hagen file in the newspaper's morgue. Once he found the home overlooking the lake, he was invited in by Doris. She led the reporter into the large main room that looked out at the water. Hagen stood smiling, "smoking a cigarette, and he had a white bib around his neck."

In just a few months Hagen had learned sign language, and with Doris filling in any gaps the interview was conducted. "It might have been the most marvelous two hours of my life," Falls recalls. "We chatted away about anything and everything."

When Falls got up to leave, Hagen "made some sounds," and Doris translated: "Mr. Hagen would like to know if you'd like to see him hit a golf ball?"

"Love to," the reporter replied.

Hagen plucked a club from a golf bag leaning against one wall. "He came back to the middle of the room and placed an imaginary ball on the carpet. He took his stance, drew the club back and swung through the invisible ball. He looked out the large picture window and let out a whoop."

Doris said, "Mr. Hagen made a perfect shot—right into the middle of the lake."

Over the years Joe Falls has interviewed and otherwise spent time with many sports heroes, but that afternoon is indelibly etched in his mind. "I was an absolute nobody to Walter Hagen, just a guy trying to keep his job," he said. "I went to visit a golf legend who could've treated me like dirt. He didn't. In fact, he couldn't have been more gracious and accommodating. I went back to Detroit with the material for a fine piece and as much respect for the man as the legend."

• • •

Hagen appeared to make a full recovery, and emotionally as well as physically was well enough to travel. In 1966, he attended the PGA Championship at Firestone in Ohio, the forty-fifth anniversary of his first of five wins in the event. To conserve his strength, though, he made just a couple of fleeting public appearances.

Back home, Hagen agreed to lend his name to the Walter Hagen Invitational, an annual tournament at the Traverse City Golf and Country Club that raised funds for cancer research. Over the years it would collect hundreds of thousands of dollars and became a local legacy of Hagen's, though at its founding he could do no more than be a figurehead and hobnob with some of the participants.

The cancer came back later in the year, requiring several procedures including radiation treatments to try to halt its spread. Then in January 1967, Hagen underwent another throat operation, this one at the Munson Medical Center in Traverse City. A bulletin sent out by the Associated Press reported that "the former golf star was in good condition and 'doing very well.'"

He wasn't, though. At seventy-four, it was something like a miracle that he had lasted this long. He would just not give up his well-lived life, which included some travel. That July, Hagen and Junior and Warren Orlick, president of the PGA of America, flew to Colorado for the PGA Championship. Walter Sr. couldn't answer reporters' gentle questions, but ahead of time he had prepared "cue cards" with answers to typical questions, and for any questions that were a bit more complex, Walter Jr. elaborated, with his father nodding and smiling in approval.

He was just not ready to die, but the cancer was winning this match. Even "three of those and one of them" wasn't enough to make par for the Haig. His friends in golf as well as those in the Traverse City area, where he spent all his time now, realized it was time to arrange a proper sendoff. American golf and its fans were facing the beginning of the end of its first champion generation.

It took a long time to get the dinner and various schedules arranged, and during these months Hagen bounced back yet again. Finally, on Monday night, August 14, 1967, the Traverse City Golf and Country Club was filled to bursting with three hundred friends and admirers.

There were drinks and food and stories and plenty of laughs, just as Hagen wanted it, though his own talking days were over. Then, unavoidably, it was time to get serious. One by one the testimonials were delivered by those in attendance or read on behalf of those who couldn't attend. Sir Walter was getting his full due fifty-five years after turning pro and playing in his first tournament, and he was having a hard time not melting into a puddle.

Ben Hogan: "Without you, golf would not be what it is today. I give you my deep thanks."

Byron Nelson: "There is absolutely no way that we golf professionals can properly thank you for your great contribution to our profession."

Former President Dwight Eisenhower: "Your achievements at home and in Great Britain have earned you both the PGA's Hall of Fame and an enduring place in the affections of all who esteem stout heart and great talent."

Bob Hope: "Walter's the fellow who said, 'After watching Bob's swing, you're not sure which restroom he uses.'"

Bobby Jones: "I always enjoyed the many rounds of golf we played together, even when you were giving me a good beating."

Old playmate Edward, Duke of Windsor: "I recall the great kick we all used to get out of watching you play and win on the great championship courses."

Gene Sarazen reiterated what he had said and written before: "All of the professionals who have a chance to go after the big money today should say a prayer to you, Walter. It was you who made professional golf what it is."

Cary Middlecoff was there, as were Chuck Kocsis, PGA president Max Elbin, old pals Johnny Farrell, Al Watrous, and Johnny Revolta; Joe Kirkwood was on his way until his plane was forced down by bad weather. The mayor offered a proclamation that made Hagen an honorary citizen of the city.

What excited all in attendance most, however, was a very special guest. That afternoon a plane had landed at the local airport, with the pilot being Arnold Palmer. While Nicklaus had fully emerged on the golf scene by 1967, no one in the sport was bigger than Palmer, thirty-seven then, and because of this, his schedule was full to the brim with tournaments, corporate exhibitions, endorsements, and other activities including being a husband and father.

But Palmer had punched a hole in his schedule and the bad weather and flown his own plane to be in Traverse City. That night, looking at the Haig, who was unable to say anything in response, Palmer spoke about how much it meant to him when Hagen had called him after Palmer's second British Open victory. Then he added, "If it were not for you, Walter, this dinner tonight would be downstairs in the pro shop, not in the ballroom."

The ovation that followed the King's speech was the last straw: Tears streamed down Hagen's face.

Appropriately, among the reports in the press about the dinner was one in the *New York Times* that referred to Hagen as "the father of modern professional golf."

Despite the illness, Hagen tried to keep to a normal routine. The car trips he and Doris took were shorter and further apart. There was no more staying up late, and his visits to the local taverns were less frequent. Still, he had baseball, he had fishing, there were the occasional bittersweet visits with Junior and Helen, and there were thousands of memories to dwell upon as he gazed out at the lake.

The last accolade that really meant something to Hagen was given in 1968, when he was made an honorary member of the Royal and Ancient Golf Club. He was only the fourth American in this ultra-exclusive club, joining Francis Ouimet, Bobby Jones, and Dwight Eisenhower. Sir Walter had, finally, done it—the kid from the wrong side of the Rochester tracks who had created the occupation of professional golfer had been accepted into the home of golf.

And that October, in an upset, the Detroit Tigers became the champions of baseball, defeating the defending champs. In the seventh and final game, sudden death, Mickey Lolich outpitched Bob Gibson of the St. Louis Cardinals. Detroit and Hagen were on top of the world.

A few months later, in early 1969, the cancer spread into his lungs. According to the Plylers and Ruth Matthews, Doris Brandes's cousin, Hagen's final year was a painful one, yet he didn't complain. He wanted to remain at home looking out at Cadillac Lake, and Doris was his round-the-clock nurse. He did not have the strength for visitors at home outside of Junior and Helen and a couple of close local friends like Peck.

During the last week of September he lost consciousness and was in a coma for about ten days. Walter Hagen died at his lakefront home on the night of October 5, 1969, two months shy of his seventy-seventh birthday.

The *New York Times* obituary, written by Alden Whitman, was over two thousand words. It offered a survey of his triumphs and included several of his most famous sayings. Most of all, it emphasized that Hagen had the sort of style and flamboyance no longer seen in professional golf: He had been an original.

"Mr. Hagen did a great deal to break down the caste barriers behind which golf professionals had been herded," Whitman wrote. "In many country clubs here and abroad the professionals had to use the servants' entrance, and they were not permitted in the dining room or the bar. His triumphs obliged the snobbish to seek him out, and for his friendship he insisted upon his social due. He got it, and so did the professionals that followed him."

Herbert Warren Wind wrote, "Great as he was as a golfer, Hagen was even greater as a personality—an artist with a sense of timing so infallible that he could make the tying of his shoelaces more dramatic than the other guy's hole in one."

Old friend Horton Smith was quoted in the *Detroit News*: "Though there were times when he endeavored to use psychology and strategy on his opponents, I never knew him to do an unsportsmanlike thing. He was a fine sportsman, a gracious competitor, a gracious person."

Francis Ouimet offered, "I never knew Walter to utter one unkind word about anyone, nor to make excuses of any kind."

"All golfers will mourn his passing," said Bobby Jones, courageously battling his own painful health problems. "Walter and I played a lot of fine golf together. I always enjoyed our association. He was a great personality and made a big contribution to the game."

"Such a colourful personality was he that Hagen the golfer has suffered eclipse from Hagen the man," offered the *Times* of London in an especially insightful obituary, which appeared in the October 7 issue.

"The stories that have been told about him, the epigrams that have been attributed to him, would fill a book. Not all of them would be true, but he was prepared to accept them even if they were not, and the legend of his gaiety, his nerve, and his approach to gamesmanship is now solidly entrenched in the history of the game."

Hagen's death was, predictably, big news in the Rochester area. Lottie still lived there, and three of his four sisters survived him. The news from Traverse City prompted longtime friends there to share stories with the press. George Collins, who had caddied for Hagen and then became the caddie master at the Country Club of Rochester, recalled how he had applied for a job at a course just opening in Florida.

After applying for the position, Collins went down there for an interview. It went well enough, and he was told that if Hagen would write a letter of recommendation, that would seal the deal. As luck would have it, Hagen was in Florida, staying about fifty miles away. Collins went to see him, but Hagen said he didn't know how to write a letter like that (nor any kind of letter, really), and when Bob Harlow arrived, Hagen would have him write it.

However, Harlow's plans changed and he couldn't go to Florida. Not wanting to cost Collins the job, Hagen forced himself behind the wheel and drove the fifty miles to the new course and personally delivered his recommendation, which certainly impressed the course owners.

Leo Fraser, who was president of the PGA of America in 1969, declared, "Walter Hagen was there when it all began in 1916 and, through the years, his loyalty and affection for his fellow professionals in the PGA of America never wavered or became diluted. From the beginning to the very end, the Haig considered himself no more nor less than a staunch member of our association committed to its principles, and sharing a common destiny with the youngest shop assistant in the game. That is what was so wonderful about the Haig: He was a professional's professional."

In a tribute in the *New York Times* published a month after Hagen's death, Arthur Daley wrote, "It could very well be that Walter Hagen was the most important single figure ever to swing a golf club. He transformed the sport and sent it rocketing toward the undreamed-of riches of today."

Hagen was buried at the Holy Sepulchre Cemetery in Southfield, Michigan, near Detroit, in a family plot. Among the pallbearers were Al Watrous and Arnold Palmer, who had again interrupted his busy schedule to fly in. The wide tombstone later placed there was engraved in the top middle with a cross and HAGEN below it. On the left side it simply lists "Walter 1892–1969" and "Walter III 1948–1963."

Charles Price recalled, "When the Haig died, Junior called me from Detroit to tell me there would be no funeral. Instead, a bunch of his cronies were going to throw a party at the Detroit Athletic Club. They thought the Haig would prefer that. I didn't go. Like Hamlet, golf's sweet prince, I thought, deserved a grander exit than that."

During the funeral service at Our Lady of Refuge Roman Catholic Church in Lake Orion, Reverend Edwin Schroeder said about Hagen, "His biggest game is over. He putted out."

Walter Jr. was added to the stone in 1982 when he died at the age of sixty-four, then Helen in 1998. The Helen Hagen estate continues to be involved in golf; in September 2000 it donated $200,000 to the PGA of America for youth programs.

During his father's final years, Walter Jr. had moved on because there wasn't much business to oversee. He too, with Helen, continued to live in Michigan, though they eventually bought a second home in Vero Beach, Florida, and spent more time there. He became an advertising sales representative for *Sports Afield* magazine, more for something to do than for the income, thanks to the Wilson checks that were now made out to him.

Out of grief for both his lost son and father, Junior began to drink heavily and couldn't escape his pain. According to several people interviewed for this book, when he died he had essentially committed suicide by giving up and destroying his health.

Doris Brandes hoped to remain in the house she and Walter had shared. Accepting the fact that death could occur any day, Walter and Doris had gone to the Grand Traverse County Clerk on July 19, 1969, and taken out a marriage license. He was seventy-six; she was fifty-eight. Both listed their occupations as "Retired." Both had previously been married twice. Her parents were listed as Hugo Brandes and Lillian Nemitz and his as William Hagen and "Louise (unknown)." They had even begun filling out the Certificate of Marriage, but in script written across the rest of it is "Not Used."

Unfortunately for Doris, the marriage did not take place during the three months before Hagen died. Though Hagen had given Doris the house and twenty acres on the lake in his will, not long after his death Walter Jr. contested the will. Because of mounting legal bills, Doris was forced to sell the house and property.

During the next twenty years Doris moved from one place to another in Michigan—in the Traverse City area, near the Plylers, near her cousin, and around the loop again. She lived on Social Security and the sale of the few artifacts Hagen had left her. She no longer had contact with the Hagen family.

"Doris was kind of isolated," remembers Joe Peck. "She kind of stayed to herself and nobody knew too much about her."

"It wasn't easy for Doris those years after Walter died," remembers Ruth Matthews. "Walter had been such a gentleman and treated Doris well, but that all came to an end. She was a bit lost, though she always tried to be upbeat, just like Walter had been."

After suffering a stroke that partly paralyzed her in January 1987, Doris was put in a nursing home. She was regularly visited there during the next two years by the Plylers and Matthews. On April 4, 1989, Doris died in Tustin, Michigan, at seventy-seven.

"Walter always had the guts of a burglar," the ninety-nine-year-old Henry Clune told *Sports Illustrated* in June 1989, the seventy-fifth anniversary of Hagen's Open win at Midlothian, with the Open that year being played at Oak Hill in Rochester. "For all of his truncated schooling and catch-as-catch-can upbringing, he was never a bumpkin."

In the same article, Gene Sarazen, then eighty-seven, said, "I think Walter Hagen contributed more to golf than any player today or ever. He took the game all over the world. He popularized it here and everywhere. Walter was at the head of the class. . . . It's a sad part about getting old, I suppose. Everybody you know is gone. But Walter should not be forgotten. What golf ought to do is build a monument to that man."

A poll was conducted in 1973 by the Golf Writers Association of America. It placed Hagen fifth, behind Nicklaus, Palmer, Hogan, and Jones. All were honored at a dinner in New York City that February— Jones as well as Hagen posthumously. The great amateur from Georgia had courageously endured the ravages to his body. He had died in December 1971, only a few days away from what would have been Hagen's seventy-ninth birthday.

The ultimate honor for an athlete is to be elected to his/her sport's hall of fame, and that too happened to Hagen in 1974. In fact, he was elected as part of the first group in the new American Golf Hall of Fame. Also inducted were the "Great Triumvirate," Harry Vardon, J. H. Taylor, and James Braid; Francis Ouimet; the great and enduring amateur Chick Evans; the three best of the generation after Hagen— Byron Nelson, Sam Snead, and Ben Hogan; the female champions Babe Zaharias and Joyce Wethered; the man who had restored British golf in the '30s, Henry Cotton; and three of Sir Walter's friends and competitors, Tommy Armour, Gene Sarazen, and Bobby Jones.

Where does Walter Hagen rank today among those who played on what became the PGA Tour? He has slipped a few pegs since the poll in 1950 that had him and Jones second and first. Still, in any survey more than a half century after the '50 poll Hagen is always ranked in the top ten of players in addition to being the first and only golfer during his lifetime to be named on the list of the "Ten Best Dressed Men."

Hagen, with 11, and Nicklaus, with 18, remain the only professional players with double-digit majors, though Tiger Woods will join the club. (Jones is credited with 13 majors when his Amateur Championships in the U.S. and Great Britain are included.) *Golf Digest,* in its April 2000 issue, provided an interesting comparison among players. It compiled a list of the players with the most top-ten finishes in major tournaments. Hagen with 32 over a twenty-three-year period ranked eighth, behind Nicklaus (73), Snead (46), Gary Player and Tom Watson (44), Hogan (39), Palmer (38), and Sarazen (36). Hagen, however, is the only one with no top-ten finishes in the Masters (he was forty-one when it was first held), plus no credit is given for his Western Open finishes, which include five wins, so the comparison isn't quite fair to him. Still, Hagen ranks higher than such other luminaries as Byron Nelson, Raymond

Floyd, Ben Crenshaw, Billy Casper, Nick Faldo, Harry Vardon, Greg
Norman, and Lee Trevino.

"Let's be fair about this," declared columnist James Achenbach in
a piece on Tiger Woods chasing Jack Nicklaus's record of winning
majors in the August 31, 2002, issue of *Golfweek*. "The Western Open,
which Hagen won five times, widely was considered a major. So figuring the Western Open in the major rotation until 1934, when the
Masters was first played, Hagen has 16 [majors]. No other player [but
Nicklaus] has reached double digits in the 75 years since Sir Walter's
last British Open win."

The millennium inspired *Golf* magazine to produce a "Best of the
Century" list. In its top ten, Hagen ranked ninth, one ahead of
Sarazen. Finishing in order ahead of him were Nicklaus, Jones,
Hogan, Snead, Palmer, Nelson, Vardon, and Player. A similar survey
done by *Golfweek* at the same time had Hagen at number eight, ahead
of Player and Watson but behind Nicklaus, Hogan, Jones, Palmer,
Nelson, Snead, and Sarazen.

In "The 18 Best Players Ever" in a 2003 issue of *Travel & Leisure
Golf*, Mike Lupica had Hagen as number four, behind only Nicklaus,
Hogan, and Jones, and one ahead of Woods. Among the reasons given
was that Hagen "legitimized the idea of Professional Golfer in this
country. And he won eleven majors, which gets dropped from the
conversation way too often. The Haig drank and smoked and laughed
a lot and liked girls even more. If he were around today he'd be more
colorful a figure than Tiger."

In its September 2000 issue, *Golf Journal*, published by the
USGA, compiled information on the majors played in to complete
the career grand slam. On top was Tiger, with only 21, and then
there was Nicklaus (27), Player (30), Hogan (33), and Sarazen (35).
All, of course, include the Masters among their majors. If, however,
the Western Open is substituted for the Masters, Hagen completed
the career grand slam with his British Open win in 1922, which
means that including the delay caused by World War I, the Haig
would fall between Player and Hogan.

"I think his greatest achievement was what he did for the game of
golf in bringing about a major advancement in the modernization of
the social aspects of the game," Palmer says.

"To win the British Open as he did four times in a decade was unbelievable, really an achievement that few people really appreciate sufficiently," says Gary Player. "He made a tremendous contribution to the professional game whichever way you look at it and rightly holds a high place in golf history."

"The records and the numbers alone speak volumes about Walter Hagen's career," Jack Nicklaus states. "But as I grew older, both personally and professionally Walter Hagen's place in history became very clear to me. Each time I was fortunate enough to carve out my own bit of history, my name was frequently linked to Hagen's, so I obviously became aware of the standards he set. To win five PGA Championships over an eighteen-year period in my career is something very special to me. For Hagen to have won as many but over a seven-year period [1921–27] is simply incredible."

"There's always in each era three or four players who are just outstanding," says Byron Nelson. "They push each other and raise the bar for the next era. When Ben Hogan and Sam Snead and myself were growing up, we looked to Walter Hagen, Bobby Jones, and Gene Sarazen, and I think Francis Ouimet too. They set the standard, and Hagen was out there first showing the way."

Putting the many golf accomplishments aside, perhaps Chuck Kocsis best summed up the view of Hagen held by the people who knew him: "Everybody loved the guy. He was a lot of fun."

Index

TOM CLAVIN has covered golf for the *New York Times, Golf Journal*, the *Met Golfer, Golf* magazine, *Distinction* magazine, and many other publications. He is the author or coauthor of six books, including *The Ryder Cup*.